Fundamentals of Organisation Development and Change Management

Second edition

Editors: Nico Martins and Dirk Geldenhuys

juta

Fundamentals of Organisation Development and Change Management

First published 2016
Second edition 2021

Juta and Company (Pty) Ltd
First floor, Sunclare building, 21 Dreyer street, Claremont 7708
PO Box 14373, Lansdowne 7779, Cape Town, South Africa
www.juta.co.za

© 2021 Juta and Company (Pty) Ltd

ISBN 978 1 48513 108 3 (Pdf)
ISBN 978 1 48513 109 0 (Web Pdf)

Production Specialist: Samantha Simmons
Editor: Wendy Priilaid
Proofreader: Simone Chiara van der Merwe
Cover designer: Drag and Drop
Typesetter: Lebone Publishing Services
Indexer: Lexinfo

Typeset in ITC Galliard Std 11 pt

Contents

Foreword

Organisation development (OD) had what we might call a 'short' history, which began in the 1950s and reached its peak in the 1960s with T-groups (training groups) and the hippy counter-culture, after which it lost its relevance and coherence, and fizzled out in the 1980s (see Bradford & Burke, 2004; Dawson, 1994; Thrift, 1995 in Chapter 1). In a similar vein, there has been a tendency in recent years to write of 'classical OD', based on Lewinian founding principles and approaches, which had its peak of success in the 1960s and has now been superseded by a 'new OD', which is based on newer perspectives on organisations, notably social constructionism (see Bushe, 2011; Marshak & Grant, 2008; Oswick, 2009 in Chapter 1).

In much the same way that OD became socialised in the US corporate environment during the early to mid-1960s through several high-profile and large-scale OD initiatives, the South African environment became aware of OD through major OD projects and initiatives in organisations such as Sasol, the South African army, Old Mutual and others. In the 1970s a number of South African universities began to introduce OD as part of their undergraduate and postgraduate courses.

One of the gaps in the OD market is the availability of academic books on OD for undergraduate students, focusing on the South African market with applicable and relevant southern African contents and context.

The focus of this book is to address this gap.

The book consists of 12 chapters, which cover most of the core concepts in OD. What follows is an overview of these chapters.

Chapter 1: Introduction to organisation development

This chapter introduces OD as a planned change discipline concerned with applying behavioural science knowledge and practice to help organisations adapt to change forces inside and outside their borders. It also emphasises the fact that OD as a profession has since its inception supported and promoted a set of humanistic values which can be distinguished from related concepts such as change management (CM), learning organisations and the capacity development environment or context within which individuals, organisations and societies, and not simply a single organisation, operate and interact.

Chapter 2: Organisation development and change management

This chapter starts by highlighting two different approaches to OD which OD scholars and practitioners often neglect to consider, namely the diagnostic and dialogic approaches. Each of these approaches, which are based on fundamentally different philosophical and conceptual assumptions about organisations and how to develop them, are explained and discussed. A short history of OD interventions is also discussed to explain the emergence of the two approached to OD. The chapter then concludes with a discussion of the differences and communalities between the practice of OD and CM. Whereas OD's most distinct and basic feature comes from the development part of its title, CM is about managing the people side of change.

Chapter 3: A practical approach to change management

In this chapter best practices in CM are discussed as well as the difference between individual and organisational CM. Five theories of individual change transition and five approaches to organisational CM are explained and discussed. The role of communication and stakeholders in CM as well as resistance to change then receives attention. This is followed by a discussion of the differences between CM and project management after which a new proposed practical structured CM process for managing organisational change is introduced. The chapter ends with guidance as to how to integrate CM with project management.

Chapter 4: The role of the organisation development consultant

In Chapter 4 the focus is on the role and task of the OD consultant, the professional values and ethics which apply to the OD consultant, as well as the competencies which are important for the OD consultant. Lastly, the systems-psychodynamic perspective on the role of the OD consultant is discussed.

Chapter 5: Facilitation skills

This chapter starts with an overview of the historic development of facilitation, explains the steps and phases of facilitation, and also sets out how to plan and conduct a facilitation session using a predetermined framework. The chapter also explains to facilitators how to apply listening and influencing micro-skills as well as problem-solving and decision-making techniques during a group facilitation session. The chapter ends with guidelines on how to defuse conflict in a group situation.

Chapter 6: Core theories and models

This chapter covers selected theories and models about organisations and change that are useful in the diagnostic phase of planned change efforts. Sources and forms of resistance to change are explored, and tactics to overcome resistance are discussed. Finally, the chapter reviews a number of conditions for successful, planned change efforts.

Chapter 7: The organisation development process

In this chapter a brief overview of the OD process is presented. Aspects such as basic marketing principles, preparation for a meeting with a prospective client, writing a proposal and a contract, as well as the development of a working relationship are covered. Ways to diagnose problems in a company and the selection of interventions are also explored. Lastly, the focus is on how to terminate a client relationship.

Chapter 8: Organisational diagnosis

In this chapter the focus is on organisational diagnosis, the justification thereof, the involvement of stakeholders, the development of a world-class diagnosis and the survey process. The chapter concludes with the analysis and interpretation of an organisational diagnosis, the feedback process and the often-neglected evaluation phase.

Chapter 9: Designing interventions

From this chapter onwards, the focus shifts from diagnosis to the next phase of the OD process, namely interventions, also known as the action thrust of OD. This chapter is about designing interventions. The focus is on the approaches to interventions, the principles of intervening, the structuring of interventions, the joint action planning (JAP) meeting, and the evaluation and monitoring of interventions.

Chapter 10: Interventions: From the individual to the team

The discussion in this chapter is based on the target of the intervention, namely individual, interpersonal and team interventions. Examples of interventions aimed at each target are discussed, such as the Myers–Briggs Type Indicator (MBTI) and assessment centres (as diagnostic interventions), and executive coaching and career planning and development with the individual as target. Regarding interpersonal or third-party interventions, two examples are discussed, namely the Johari window and an intervention new to the OD field, known as narrative mediation. The chapter concludes with a discussion of four examples aimed at teambuilding. These are the well-known process of consultation, formal teambuilding, the systems-psychodynamic group diagnostic intervention and the more recent appreciative inquiry (AI) intervention.

Chapter 11: Organisation-wide/large-scale intervention

In this chapter, the author explores the concept of large-scale organisational interventions, their classification and the role of culture in interventions. She also focuses on the tools and techniques for best practices, and discusses a knowledge economy and how it links to organisational interventions. Lastly, she discusses who needs to be involved in large-scale interventions.

Chapter 12: Major developments in organisation development

The last chapter explains the differences between the old and the new OD. It also assesses the effects of OD in the work environment, and explains the impact of technology on OD and how to practise OD in the virtual world. All these provide a future picture of OD. Lastly, with the international focus of many South African consultants in mind, the role of OD in international contexts is discussed.

About the authors

Benny Olivier is a retired associate professor in industrial and organisational psychology (IOP), having lectured at the Department of IOP at the University of South Africa (Unisa). He is an industrial psychologist and holds a BMil (BA) degree from Stellenbosch University, a BAdmin (Hons), an MAdmin and a DAdmin in IOP from Unisa. He is currently still supervising IOP doctoral and master's students at Unisa. His research interest is in organisation development (OD), change management (CM) and leadership. He also has 24 years' practical experience as a line manager, trainer, OD consultant and change manager. In this period he has trained hundreds of OD consultants, group facilitators and change managers and has facilitated work sessions on all organisational levels in both the private and public sectors.

Charles OK Allen-ILE earned a doctorate in human resource management from Nelson Mandela Metropolitan University, Port Elizabeth, South Africa. His other academic qualifications are BSc (Hons) in general and applied psychology, and an MSc in organisational psychology. He also holds an LLB in law, and is an enrolled/admitted advocate of the High Court of South Africa. Prof Allen-ILE is a registered master human resource practitioner with the South African Board for People Practices (SABPP) and is a member of other local and international professional/academic bodies. His teaching and research interests are in the areas of employment relations management, strategic human resource management, leadership, organisational behaviour and research methodology. He has contributed to various high-impact journal and book publications, and has supervised the research of numerous postgraduate students over his years of lecturing at various southern African universities. He was the assistant dean responsible for Research and Innovation in the Business and Management Sciences Faculty at the Cape Peninsula University of Technology (CPUT). He is currently a professor in the Department of Industrial Psychology at the Faculty of Economic and Management Sciences of the University of the Western Cape (UWC).

Dirk Geldenhuys holds a BA, a BD and a PGD from the University of Pretoria (UP), and a DAdmin in IOP from Unisa. He is registered as an industrial psychologist with the Health Professions Council of South Africa (HPCSA) and as a master practitioner with the SABPP.

Currently, Dirk is a full professor at Unisa, where he is teaching OD, CM and executive coaching. He chaired the Department of IOP from 2009 to 2014. He has published a number of scientific articles and presented papers at local and international conferences. He has supervised a number of master's and doctoral students, and is co-author of textbooks and published chapters in books on OD.

Dirk is also working as a freelance consultant and is mainly involved in leadership development, executive coaching, interpersonal relations and group dynamic interventions. As a science practitioner, his major fields of interest include applied neurosciences, systems psychodynamics, appreciative inquiry (AI), social constructionism and the use of relational practices as approaches to study and change. He is also interested in interdisciplinary studies in the applied fields of economic and management sciences such as risk management.

Dr Elsabé Keyser is a senior lecturer in the subject group of labour relations management at the School of Behavioural Sciences at the Vaal Triangle Campus of North-West University. She has been involved in various research projects related to employee relations (ER) and organisational behaviour over the past 24 years. She has co-authored a number of publications (books and articles) and presented papers at national and international conferences. Elsabé supervises mini-dissertations, dissertations and theses and also lectures at both the under- and postgraduate levels. She has advanced knowledge and expertise on issues related to group dynamics, labour relations management, skills development, collective bargaining and negotiations, research and contract types (contracts of employment, including permanent and atypical) as well as the psychological and social contract. She acts as referee for different national and international journals.

Frances de Klerk is a registered industrial psychologist, lecturer and entrepreneur. She achieved an MA degree in industrial psychology (North-West University), a BA (Hons) degree in industrial psychology (North-West University), a BA Communications (Hons) degree (North-West University) and a Higher Diploma in Higher Education and Training (CPUT). She is currently a lecturer in the Department of Human Resources Management at CPUT in subjects such as OD, management of training and labour law. She has also been a guest lecturer at other universities in forensic industrial psychology and counselling. Before accepting the position at CPUT, she served as a psychologist in the public and private sector for more than 20 years. She still manages a part-time private practice where she specialises in the fields of OD, psychometric assessment, counselling and skills development.

Leon Jackson (MBA, PhD) is registered with the HPCSA as an industrial psychologist and teaches CM at the North-West University School of Business and Governance. He has supervised 40 master's and three PhD students. He has published 16 articles in peer-reviewed scientific journals, 15 manuscripts in national and international conference proceedings accredited by the Department of Higher Education and Training (DHET), and two textbook chapters. He has also presented 19 national and 33 international conference papers, and reviewed 36 manuscripts submitted for publication in various national and international journals. He was a member of the organising committee of the first South African Burnout Conference in 2002, the first South African Wellness Conference in 2004 and the first South African Positive Psychology Conference, which incorporated the third South African Wellness Conference, in 2005. In 2012, he was the co-chairperson of the 21st Biannual Conference of the IACCP, hosted in Stellenbosch. He is also a member of the Society of Industrial and Organisational Psychology of South Africa (SIOPSA) and the IACCP. His research interests include topics such as diversity management, a multicultural workplace, and personal and situational antecedents of employees' attitudes and outcomes such as burnout, engagement, job satisfaction, subjective experiences of work success and organisational commitment.

Melinde Coetzee (DLitt et Phil) is currently fulfilling the role of professor in the Department of IOP at Unisa. Her research focuses primarily on careers, graduate employability capacities and the psychology of retention. She also lectures in organisational behaviour. Melinde is a professionally registered industrial psychologist with the HPCSA and a master human resource professional with the SABPP. She is a member of the International Association of Applied Psychology (IAAP) and SIOPSA. Melinde fulfilled the role of editor-in-chief of the *South African Journal of Industrial Psychology* (2013–2019) and is also the author, co-author and editor of a number of academic books on training and development, and career and personnel psychology. She has published in numerous accredited academic journals, and has presented numerous academic papers and posters at national and international conferences.

Nico Martins holds a PhD in industrial psychology and is registered as a psychologist with the HPCSA and as a chartered human resource practitioner with the SABPP. His MCom dissertation focused on organisational communication and his doctorate on organisational culture. His initial research in organisational culture formed the basis for research in related areas such as organisational climate, organisational trust, employee engagement and information security culture. Over and above his own research, a number of his master's and doctoral students have conducted further research in organisational culture, focusing on the assessment of subcultures, and the relationship between organisational culture and concepts such as organisational commitment, employee satisfaction, perceived leader emotional competency, personality type, occupational health and employee engagement. The collaborative research has led to the validation of assessment tools in organisational culture, organisational climate, organisational trust, employee engagement and employment equity.

He has attended several specialised programmes in the field at the National Training Laboratories (NTL) in the USA and is an international affiliate of the Society of Industrial and Organisational Psychology (SIOP) in the USA.

At present he is a research professor at the Department of Industrial and Organisational Psychology at Unisa (since 1995) and specialises in the field of organisational psychology. His fields of expertise are OD and change.
Prof Martins also supervises master's and doctoral students, currently 13 and 14 respectively. He moderates for the universities of KwaZulu-Natal, Stellenbosch and Johannesburg on a regular basis. He is acknowledged by the National Research Foundation (NRF) as a seasonal researcher (level C).

Articles which Prof Martins has published have dealt with organisational culture and climate, organisational diagnosis, organisational trust, employment equity and employee engagement. He has presented papers at more than 50 national and international conferences based on work done at various national and international companies. He has participated in about 500 reports on various aspects of organisational diagnosis, and has extensive knowledge in the fields of organisational assessment, (re)design and interventions. His research focuses on quantitative and qualitative research.

Acknowledgements

We would like to thank our publishers for their support and encouragement. We would also like to thank our team of authors for sharing their knowledge and practical experience in their valuable contributions, which required considerable time, effort and commitment. Their valuable insight into organisation development in the South African and international field contributed to a valuable book for practitioners, managers and students in the field.

Finally, we would like to thank our clients and students over the years, from whom we have learnt so much and whose participation has helped to shape this book.

The editors

Chapter 1

Introduction to organisation development

Leon Jackson

Learning outcomes

After reading this chapter, you should be able to:

- define the concept 'organisation development' (OD)
- explain what OD is not
- discuss the characteristics of OD
- discuss the internal and external forces that are currently impacting on your organisation
- list and discuss the specific values that guide the field of OD
- list the characteristics of successful OD practitioners
- briefly describe the history of OD
- distinguish between the related concepts of 'change management' (CM), 'the learning organisation' and 'capacity development'
- discuss the set of underlying values that inform practice within a learning organisation
- distinguish between the different perspectives on organisational learning
- discuss the assumptions about capacity development.

Introduction

Managers and leaders of organisations operate in environments that exert considerable pressure for change because of globalisation, improved communications and rapid technological innovation. In response to these challenges, managers and leaders drive changes to organisational structures and work practices essential for increasing efficiency and competitiveness. Strong leadership has been noted as central to successful change; therefore successful leadership behaviour appears to be dependent on the leader's own personal level of change adaptability, including his/her built-in coping mechanisms and the beliefs he/she holds about the drivers that make change successful.

Being able to manage change is regarded today as an indispensable skill in the repertoire of a manager. Preparing managers to cope with today's accelerating rate of change is the central theme of this chapter. The modern manager must not only be flexible and adaptive in a changing environment, but must also be able to diagnose problems and implement change (Brown, 2011). In order to do so, managers, especially in large organisations, use the services of consultants, more specifically organisation development (OD) consultants. This chapter introduces the practising manager, OD consultant and student to the field of OD. The purpose is twofold, namely:

1. to create awareness of the changing environmental forces confronting the modern manager
2. to provide a foundation of knowledge and skills for those wishing to continue advanced studies towards functioning as an OD practitioner.

There is a need for new ways to manage, because nowadays, changes are occurring so rapidly. OD is a discipline that applies behavioural sciences to help organisations adapt to these rapid changes. In this chapter, you will learn more about this exciting field and discipline by focusing on what OD is, why it has emerged, the forces of change, OD as a profession and field of specialisation and the development of OD. You will learn to distinguish OD from related concepts such as change management (CM), the learning organisation and capacity development.

What is organisation development?

OD is an emerging discipline aimed at improving the effectiveness of the organisation and its members by means of a systematic change programme. A truly effective organisation is one in which both the organisation and the individual member can grow and develop. This is exactly what OD is all about: making organisations healthier and more effective.

Defining organisation development

Over the years, OD has had many different definitions and conceptualisations (Jamieson & Worley, 2006), yet most share the same commonalities and only seem to differ on the scope of change targets and the ultimate intention of change. The most prominent definitions are presented in Table 1.1 on the next page.

Table 1.1 Prominent definitions of organisation development (Author)

Author	Definition
Wyatt Warner Burke (1982)	OD is a deliberate process of change in an organisation's culture through the use of behavioural science technology, research and theory.
Wendell French (1969: 23)	'Organization development refers to a long-range effort to improve an organization's problem-solving capabilities and its ability to cope with changes in its external environment with the help of external or internal behavioral-scientist consultants or change agents, as they are sometimes called.'
Richard Beckhard (1969: 9)	'Organization development is an effort (1) planned; (2) organization wide; (3) managed from the top; (4) to increase organization effectiveness and health, through (5) planned interventions in the organization's processes using behavioral sciences.'
Michael Beer (1980: 340)	'Organization development is a system-wide process of data collection, diagnosis, action-planning intervention, and evaluation aimed at (1) enhancing congruence among organizational structure, process, strategy, people and culture; (2) developing new and creative organizational solutions; and (3) developing the organization's self-renewing capacity. It occurs through the collaboration of organizational members working with a change agent using behavioral science theory, research and technology.'
Warren G Bennis (1969)	OD is a response to change, an educational strategy that is aimed at modifying the organisation's culture and structure, so that it may adjust more easily to the new technologies, to the new market challenges, as well as to the striking rate at which change takes place nowadays.
Richard A Schmuck and Matthew B Miles (1971)	OD may be defined as an intentional and sustained effort to utilise the behavioural sciences with the aim of improving the system, by using reflexive and auto-analysis methods.
Warren W Burke and David L Bradford (2005: 12)	'Based on (1) a set of values, largely humanistic; (2) application of the behavioral sciences; and (3) open-systems theory, organization development is a systems-wide process of planned change aimed toward improving overall organization effectiveness by way of enhanced congruence of such key organization dimensions as external environment, mission, strategy, leadership, culture, structure, information and reward systems, and work policies and procedures.'

It is clear that each definition in Table 1.1 has a slightly different emphasis. For example, some emphasise the process of OD work (Beckhard, 1969; Beer, 1980), whereas others attend to the object of the OD practice (Burke, 1982; French, 1969). Burke's (1982) definition focuses on culture as a target of change. In addition, Burke and Bradford's (2005) description broadens the range and interest of OD.

Worley and Feyerherm (2003) suggest that for a process to be called OD, (1) it must focus on or result in the change of some aspect of the organisational system; (2) there must be learning or the transfer of knowledge or skills to the organisation; and (3) there must be evidence of improvement in or an intention to improve the effectiveness of the organisation. Most OD definitions agree that it concerns system-wide planned change, uses behavioural science knowledge, targets human and social processes of organisations (specifically the belief systems of individuals, work groups or culture) and intends to build the capacity to adapt and renew organisations (Cummings & Worley, 2015).

The following definition is particularly useful in helping to develop an understanding of the context, content and processes involved in OD as a change and organisational performance intervention. French and Bell (1999: 25–26) define OD as:

> a long-term effort, led and supported by top management to improve an organization's visioning, empowerment, learning and problem-solving processes, through an ongoing, collaborative management of organization culture— with a special emphasis on the culture of intact work-teams and other team configurations, using consultant-facilitator role and the theory and technology of applied behavioral science, including action research.

This definition emphasises several features that differentiate OD from other approaches to organisational change and improvement, such as management consulting, project management (PM) and operations management. The definition also helps to distinguish OD from two related subjects (to be discussed later), namely CM and organisational change.

Another way of understanding OD is to explain what it is not, according to Brown (2011: 24–25):

- **OD is not a micro-approach to change.** Management development, for example, is aimed at changing individual behaviour, whereas OD is focused on the macro-goal of developing an organisation-wide improvement in managerial style.
- **OD is more than any single technique.** Whereas OD consultants use many different techniques, such as management training, quality circles or job enrichment, no single technique represents the OD discipline.
- **OD does not include random or ad hoc changes.** OD is based on a systematic appraisal and diagnosis of problems, leading to specific types of change efforts.
- **OD is not exclusively aimed at raising morale or attitudes.** OD is aimed at overall organisational health and effectiveness. This may include participant satisfaction as one aspect of the change effort, but also includes other effectiveness parameters.

The characteristics of organisation development

To build upon the definition of and expand our understanding of the discipline of OD, let us examine some of the basic characteristics and features of OD programmes (Table 1.2).

Table 1.2 Major characteristics of organisation development (Brown, 2011: 25)

Characteristic	Focal area
1. Change	Change is planned by managers to achieve goals.
2. Collaborative approach	It involves a collaborative approach and involvement.
3. Performance orientation	The emphasis is on ways to improve and enhance performance.
4. Humanistic orientation	The emphasis is on increased opportunity and use of human potential.
5. Systems approach	The focus is on the relationship among elements and excellence.
6. Scientific methods	Scientific approaches supplement practical experiences.

Based on the information contained in Table 1.2, it seems as if OD is a planned strategy, which includes the involvement and participation of those organisational members who will be affected by the change, using programmes that emphasise ways to improve performance, rely on humanistic values about people and organisations, use a systems approach and are based on scientific methods, techniques and procedures.

Cummings and Worley (2015: 3–4) emphasise the following features of OD:

- **OD applies to changes in strategy, structure and/or processes of the entire system**, such as an organisation, a single plant of a multi-plant firm, a department or work group, or an individual role or job.
- **OD is based on the application and transfer of behavioural science knowledge and practice**, including micro-concepts such as leadership, group dynamics and work design; and macro-approaches such as strategy, organisational design and culture change.
- **OD is concerned with managing planned change**, but not in the formal sense typically associated with management consulting or PM, which tends to comprise programmatic and expert-driven approaches to change.
- **OD involves the design, implementation and subsequent reinforcement of change**. It moves beyond the initial efforts to implement a change programme to a longer-term concern to make sure the new activities are sustained within the organisation.

- **OD is orientated to improving organisational effectiveness.** Effectiveness is best measured along three dimensions:
  1. OD affirms that an effective organisation is able to solve its own problems and to constantly improve itself.
  2. An effective organisation is characterised by high financial and technical performance, including sales growth, acceptable profits, quality products and services, and high productivity.
  3. An effective organisation has an engaged, satisfied and learning workforce as well as satisfied and loyal customers or other external stakeholders.

In a similar vein to Brown (2011), Rees and French (2013) and Cummings and Worley (2015: 3–4), Beckhard (1969) emphasised the long-term and planned nature, involving the whole organisation's top management commitment and aimed at improving performance, and action-orientation features of the OD approach to change.

The need for organisation development

Managers are often faced with a paradox. They are told to change their organisations or risk them perishing; at the same time, they are told that their organisations are at risk of perishing because of the disruptive impact of change (Abrahamson, 2000: 75). Many firms are involved in major organisational change, although many are deemed unsuccessful (Markus & Benjamin, 1997). Ghoshal and Bartlett (2000: 195) argue that for every successful corporate transformation, there is at least one equally prominent failure. Various publications (Burnes & Jackson, 2011; Leonard & Coltea, 2013) estimate that up to 70% of large-scale changes fail, with most companies involved not willing to openly discuss the failures publicly. This raises the question of why managers participate in change if it is such a risky activity. One position is based on the **economic perspective** on organisational change which assumes that in competitive economics, firm survival depends on satisfying stakeholders; therefore managers conduct change in order to produce better organisational performance. An alternative position is the **organisational learning perspective** that assumes that organisations and human systems of all sorts are complex and evolving, and therefore cannot be reduced to a single linear objective of maximising shareholders' value. In this view, a better understanding of the objective of OD is the need to increase an organisation's adaptive capacity, since how an organisation might achieve shareholders' value, and the knowledge needed to do so, are likely to change over time (Palmer, Dunford & Akin, 2009: 49–50).

Regardless of which position may be appropriate to explain why a specific organisation change occurs, there is a variety of pressures on managers to change. These pressures to change are frequently referred to as forces for change. According to Kreitner and Kinicki (1995), the forces for change that originate from within organisations are generally the result of human resource concerns and managerial decisions. The former originates from a mismatch between individual and organisational desires, whereas the latter encourages change as a result of inadequate organisational direction. Change forces are the factors that increase the need for change. Coetsee (2002: 192–193) agrees with the above-mentioned authors by making a distinction between external and internal forces of change.

Internal forces of change in organisations

According to Coetsee (2002: 192) and Palmer et al (2009: 65–69), examples of internal forces include:

- **the changing nature of the workforce:** for example changing values and lifestyles of employees, dissatisfaction with the status quo, more cultural diversity, as well as many new entrants with inadequate skills
- **new visions and goals:** for example the appointment of a new chief executive officer (CEO)
- **internal pressures to stay viable:** to be more effective, to survive and to increase performance
- **growth pressures:** change in the form of growth that occurs as companies age
- **integration and collaboration pressures:** to integrate companies or create economies of scale across different business units
- **identity pressures:** especially where different business units compete with each other or where there is a lack of a cultural identity
- **new-broom pressures:** when a new CEO or manager arrives
- **power and political pressures:** to alter traditional internal power relations to speed up decision making and to allow others to engage in it.

Activity

Which internal factors contributed to recent changes that you may have experienced in your organisation/institution of higher learning?

External forces for change in organisations

Cummings and Worley (2015) elaborate on some key external forces that will influence the future of organisational practices, including changes in the **economy**, the **workforce**, **technology** and **organisations**. The economy is trending toward more concentrated wealth, globalisation and ecological concern. The workforce is becoming more diverse, more educated and more temporary or 'at will'. Technology is driving productivity within organisations, e-commerce is affecting both the supply chain and sales, and organisations are becoming more networked and knowledge based.

Coetsee (2002: 192) concurs with Cummings and Worley (2015) and Palmer et al (2009: 50–60), highlighting various categories of external forces, namely:

- **political issues:** world, national or regional issues such as new world markets, new labour legislation, affirmative action and privatisation
- **competition:** for example global competitors, new mergers and acquisitions, and new opposition
- **new technologies:** for example information technologies, new organisational change and re-engineering methodologies
- **economic factors:** a wide range of important forces, for example the oil price, the rand/US$ exchange rate, interest rate fluctuations, etc
- **fashion pressures:** when organisations imitate the structures and practices of other organisations in their field of industry, usually ones they consider successful
- **mandated pressures:** normally following a court ruling to avoid fines and worker compensation cases, criminal conviction and payment of clean-up costs
- **geopolitical pressures:** normally in the form of immediate crises (eg September 11, 2001; the severe acute respiratory syndrome [SARS] outbreak in China and the Ebola outbreak in West Africa), which often lead to a drop in sales
- **market decline pressures:** for example a decline in the demand for a postal service as a result of the increase in e-mail usage, which forces postal service providers such as the SA Post Office to look for alternative products and markets
- **hyper-competition pressures:** the rise of e-commerce and the use of the internet, which confront organisations with global changes in preferences, industry boundaries, social values and demographics
- **reputation and credibility pressures:** the recall of defective products due to quality control problems, for example, which forces process and practice changes in manufacturing concerns as a damage control effort to save the reputation and credibility of firms.

Activity

Which external factors contributed to recent changes that you may have experienced in your organisation/institution of higher learning?

Despite the external and/or internal forces for change, all organisations and managers do not respond to pressures for change. Some resist them, some are slow to respond and some may simply not recognise them as real threats in the same way that other managers do.

Organisation development as a profession

OD remains in a seeming state of perpetual flux, with new influences impacting practice every day. Unlike other professional disciplines (eg law, medicine, psychology, finance) where the underlying knowledge base is secure and new knowledge is consistently incorporated and integrated, practitioners entering the field of OD often do so with very different backgrounds, personal attributes and skill sets, making a common definition of 'good practice' consistently difficult to articulate. While some associations (eg the Organization Development Institute and now the International Society for Organization Development) have put standards in place, and many formal academic programmes (largely at master's level) have been quite successful in consistently preparing newcomers to the field, there remains a considerable degree of variability in practice and belief systems today (Golay & Church, 2013).

Most OD professionals have had specific training in OD. That training can include relevant short courses, programmes and workshops such as one-day to two-week courses offered by reputable South African business schools such as the Gordon Institute of Business Science (GIBS) and Stellenbosch University (SU) as well as by lesser-known private training entities registered with the Department of Higher Education and Training (DHET). OD training can also be more formal and lengthy, including semester modules in undergraduate, honours, master's and doctoral programmes with the industrial psychology or human resource academic departments of South African universities such as the University of Pretoria (UP), the University of South Africa (Unisa), North-West University (NWU), the University of the Western Cape (UWC) and the University of Cape Town (UCT), to mention a few. Unisa offers a formal degree at honours level and a one-year programme.

Activity

Speak to staff in the human resource department (in particular those in the OD section) or lecturers in the human resource management, people management and/or industrial psychology department, and make a list of their OD educational attainments. Also determine where they obtained their qualifications and why they chose that particular institution of higher learning.

Career choices widen as people gain training and experience in OD. Those with bachelor's degrees tend to be internal consultants, often taking on OD roles as temporary assignments on their way to higher managerial or staff positions. Holders of master's degrees are generally split between internal and external consultants. Those with doctorates may join a university faculty and do consulting part time, join a consulting firm or seek a position as a relatively high-level internal consultant (Cummings & Worley, 2015).

Values have played an important role in OD since its inception. Founded around 1960 on a value base that derived from the human relations movement in general, and the sensitivity training (T-group, or training group) movement in particular, OD has always operated within a framework of humanistic and ethical concerns for people. Burke (1997) is of the view that, although not all practitioners would agree on the specific values that guide the field, most would concur that OD has tended to emphasise such concerns as the following:

- **Human development:** it is meaningful for people in organisations to have opportunities for personal learning and for growth toward a full realisation of their individual potentials.
- **Fairness:** it is important that people in organisations be treated equitably without discrimination and with dignity.
- **Openness:** it is imperative that communication in organisations be conducted with forthrightness, honesty and integrity.
- **Choice:** it is critical that people in organisations be free from coercion and the arbitrary use of authority.
- **Balance of autonomy and constraint:** it is important that people in organisations have the autonomy and freedom to perform their work responsibilities as they see fit.

With these values, OD has sought to help organisations build trust and collaboration among members, an open problem-solving climate, and member self-control (Cummings & Worley, 2015). In terms of the values of OD, data from 416 practitioners (Church, Burke & Van Eynde, 1994) indicated that practitioners perceive the field today to be focused more on business effectiveness and productivity issues than on the humanistic concerns and orientation of the past. In addition, it seems that OD practitioners have added to those humanistic values a concern for improving organisational effectiveness (ie increasing productivity and reducing turnover) and environmental sustainability (ie reducing the organisation's carbon imprint). They have shown an increased desire to promote human, economic and ecological values in practising OD (Church & Burke, 1995).

OD practitioners face challenges in practice in spite of wide support for the values of humanising organisations, improving their effectiveness and sustaining the environment in the OD profession. More practitioners experience situations in which there is conflict between employees' needs for greater meaning and the organisation's need for more effective and efficient use of its resources. In this regard, Cummings and Worley (2015: 61) noted that 'to its credit, the field of OD has always shown concern for ethical conduct of its practitioners'. There have been several articles and symposia about ethics in OD (Jamieson & Gellermann, 2005). In addition, various professional OD bodies and societies have published statements of ethics governing OD practices, such as the Association for Talent Development (ATD), formerly the American Society for Training & Development (ASTD) (https://www.td.org/), the International Society for Organization Development and Change (http://www.isodc.org), Organization Development International (http://www.theodinstitute.org) and Organization Development Network (https://www.odnetwork.org/), to mention but a few. OD practitioners who join these professional bodies also sign a pledge whereby they publicly commit themselves to act in accordance with their ethics, values and guidelines. If they contravene the guidelines, codes of ethics and values, they run the risk of losing their membership. Values and ethics will be elaborated on in Chapter 4.

Organisation development as a field of specialisation

OD as a field is now well established. Since its origins in 1959, there has been evolution, revolution, indifference and even outright resistance at times in various aspects of OD models, tools and applications when it comes to change from within. In that time, we have seen the introduction of new science, total systems interventions, appreciative inquiry (AI), and diversity and inclusion emerge as discrete areas of practice within the field. The tried and true frameworks of consulting skills, action research, survey feedback and individual development efforts to enhance self-awareness and growth have remained at the core all along (Shull, Church & Burke, 2013). However, multiple stakeholder methods based on dialogue and whole-systems approaches such as strategic scenario planning, whole-scale change and AI show that OD has expanded beyond individual and small-group dynamics (Van Nistelrooij & De Wilde, 2008). These new OD practices are taken to be applicable not only to interpersonal matters, but also to more strategic issues (Sminia & Van Nistelrooij, 2006).

On the other hand, the subject of change, CM and leadership – important and focal areas of OD – is at the top of CEOs' agendas. It is the central subject in business press and best-selling books, and the core of an increasing number of academic programmes. Moreover, large consulting organisations are spending a significant percentage of their investment capital, advertising funds and practice management budgets to develop their capabilities to lead and manage change for their clients (Worren, Ruddle &

Moore, 1999). We have seen solo consultants grow their practices in scale until they are acquired by big professional service firms and then start all over again with new ventures. We have also seen formal academic programmes in OD emerge and flourish while corporate OD groups have been downsized in the name of productivity (Shull et al, 2013).

Competencies of an effective organisation development practitioner

The literature about OD competencies reveals a mixture of personality traits, experiences, knowledge and skills presumed to lead to effective practice (Cummings & Worley, 2015). Research on the characteristics of successful change/OD practitioners yields the following list of attributes and abilities: diagnostic ability, basic knowledge of behavioural science techniques, empathy, knowledge of the theories and methods within the consultant's own discipline, goal-setting ability, problem-solving ability, ability to perform self-assessment, ability to see things objectively, imagination, flexibility, honesty, consistency and trust (Fordyce & Weil, 1979; Jamieson, 2006).

Two projects have sought to define, categorise and prioritise the skills and knowledge required of OD practitioners. In the first effort, a broad group of well-known practitioners and researchers were asked to review and update a list of professional competencies. This survey resulted in a list with 187 statements in nine areas of OD practice, including entry, start-up, assessment and feedback, action planning, intervention, evaluation, adoption, separation and general competencies (Sullivan & Quade, 1995). To understand the relative importance of this long list, Worley, Rothwell and Sullivan (2010) collected data from OD practitioners; the results suggested an underlying structure to this list. Twenty-three competencies were generated that reflected both the skills and knowledge necessary to conduct planned change and the individual characteristics necessary to be an effective OD practitioner (Cummings & Worley, 2015).

A second project (Worley & Varney, 1998) sought to develop a list of competencies to guide curriculum development in graduate OD programmes. More than 40 OD practitioners and researchers worked to develop two competency lists. The first list included foundation competencies, aimed at the descriptions of an existing system, and knowledge of organisation behaviour, psychology, group dynamics, and management and organisation theory. The second list focused on core competencies that are aimed at how systems change over time. This list includes knowledge on organisation design, organisation research, system dynamics, OD history, and theories and models of organisation change. They also involve the skills needed to manage the consulting process, to analyse and diagnose systems, to design and choose interventions, to facilitate processes, to develop clients' capability to manage their own change, and to evaluate organisation change (Cummings & Worley, 2015). The values, ethics and competencies of the OD consultant will be discussed in more detail in Chapter 4.

The development of organisation development

There appears to be a great deal of confusion as to when OD started, what it is, and whether or not it is still alive and kicking (Burke, 2011; Greiner & Cummings, 2004; Marshak & Grant, 2008; Oswick, 2009). According to Burnes and Cooke (2012: 1396), there are those for whom OD had what we might call a 'short' history, which began in the 1950s and reached its peak in the 1960s with T-groups (training groups) and the hippie counter-culture, after which OD lost its relevance and coherence, and fizzled out in the 1980s (Bradford & Burke, 2004; Dawson, 1994; Thrift, 2005). In a similar vein, there has been a tendency in recent years to write of a 'classical OD', based on Lewinian founding principles and approaches, which had its peak of success in the 1960s and has now been superseded by a 'new OD', which is based on newer perspectives on organisations, notably social constructionism (Bushe, 2011; Marshak & Grant, 2008; Oswick, 2009). Over the years, there has been no shortage of reviews of the history of OD (Beer & Walton, 1987; French, 1982; Weick & Quinn, 1999), textbooks (Cummings & Worley, 2015; French & Bell, 1999) and readers (Burke, Lake & Paine, 2008; Gallos, 2006).

As a social and organisation change movement, OD was closely associated with practice from its beginnings. For example, the action research methodology (Lewin, 1948) was associated with real-world problems and the application of group process knowledge to address contemporary issues. The earliest values, philosophy and methods of practice were influenced by findings from the behavioural sciences and leading management researchers. According to Jamieson (2006), OD change methodologies were clearly influenced by:

- early leadership work that brought legitimacy to participative and democratic methods (Follett, 1941; Lewin & Lippitt, 1938; Likert, 1961; Tannenbaum & Schmidt, 1973)
- early work on group dynamics and laboratory training, bringing attention to group behaviour, interpersonal relations and self-awareness (Bradford, Gibb & Benne, 1964; Bennis & Shepard, 1956; Cartwright & Zander, 1954; Schein & Bennis; 1965)

- early human relations work that highlighted the primacy of social factors, attitudes and feelings in organisation behaviour, influencing productivity and morale (Homans, 1950; Mayo, 1945; Roethlisberger & Dickson, 1939)
- changing views of the person, motivation and interpersonal communication (Argyris, 1965; Maslow, 1954; McGregor, 1960; Rogers, 1961)
- early work on environments, structures and systems, helping to bring design and process into the picture (Burns & Stalker, 1961; Katz & Kahn, 1966; Lawrence & Lorsch, 1967; Trist & Bamforth, 1951).

OD as a change intervention technique has developed over time, being influenced by a number of different trajectories. As such, there is no single underlying theory that unifies the field as a whole. Rather, it is influenced by a variety of differing perspectives, including theorists such as Herzberg, Maslow, Argyris and Lewin (Bazigos & Burke, 1997). Table 1.3 provides a brief overview of the evolution of OD.

Table 1.3 The evolution of organisation development (Author)

Period	Background	Developers	Focus
1940s/1950s+	National Training Laboratories (NTL) and T-groups	Kurt Lewin, Douglas McGregor, Robert Blake, Richard Beckhard	Interpersonal relations, leadership and group dynamics; the use of teambuilding to facilitate personal and task achievement
1940s/1950s+	Action research and survey feedback	Kurt Lewin, John Colier, William Whyte, Rensis Likert	Involvement of organisational members in researching themselves to help create new knowledge and guide change action
1950s/1960s+	Participative management	Rensis Likert	Assumption that a human relations approach, with its emphasis on participation, is the best way to manage organisations
1950s/1960s+	Productivity and quality of work life (QWL)	Eric Trist and the Tavistock Institute, WE Deming and Joseph Juran	Better integration of people and technology through joint participation of union and management; quality circles; the use of self-managing work groups; the creation of more challenging jobs; total quality management (TQM)
1970s/1980s+	Strategic change	Richard Beckhard, Christopher Worley	Need for change to be strategic, aligning the organisation with the technical, political, cultural and environmental influences upon it

For a recent extended review and update on the evolution and historical background of OD, refer to the article by Burnes and Cooke (2012) in the *Human Relations* journal.

In much the same way that OD became socialised in the US corporate environment during the early to mid-1960s through several high-profile and large-scale OD initiatives, the South African environment became aware of OD through major OD projects and initiatives. A few noteworthy examples are as follows (Serfontein & Van Tonder, 2008):

- In 1971, Barry Venter introduced Richard Beckhard's confrontation meeting design in collaboration with the then mine manager of Sasol Sigma Coal Mine, Paul Kruger (former chairperson of Sasol). This was aimed at tapping into the wisdom of the workforce and improving the productivity of the mine. This project proved to be a success and a historical event in more ways than one.

- Work was done under Dr Serfontein's guidance with the chief of the SA Army, which entailed the 1973 unfreezing activities structured around the Leadership Orientation Seminar, several diagnoses in 1974 and a series of team-based and large-group interventions (LGIs) in 1975, involving the chief of the army and his senior staff officers and commanding officers.

- In 1976, organisational diagnosis was applied companywide in Old Mutual by Leon Coetsee and Jack Blignaut, using a specially developed diagnostic instrument – called the Organisational Diagnostic Questionnaire (ODQ) – which was subsequently followed by a companywide survey-guided feedback and development intervention in which all employees were involved.

- Leon Coetsee introduced OD as part of undergraduate and postgraduate industrial psychology courses at Unisa during the period 1977–1979. Several other universities would follow suit, including the former University of Potchefstroom (now the North-West University) and the Rand Afrikaans University (now the University of Johannesburg).

- With the onset of the 1980s, OD flourished, with a great many projects launched in a number of organisations—typically large organisations such as Sanlam, Old Mutual, Armscor, Liberty Life and the South African Defence Force (SADF), to name but a few. In the SADF, the Directorate of Psychology (Director: Colonel Fred Oosthuizen) and the Military Psychological Institute (Officer Commanding: Colonel Piet Venter) performed key roles with the first trainees that graduated in 1982 from the Serfontein and Du Toit programmes. Currently, the SADF is actively practising OD, with the Organisation Psychology section undertaking 11 major diagnoses and a range of OD-based projects for clients across all arms of the SADF.

- The mid-1980s also saw P-E Corporate Service's (Gustav Pansegrouw) introduction and pioneering of the stakeholder approach to strategic management during a large-scale transformation of the Council for Scientific and Industrial Research (CSIR), based upon an adaptation of role theory and role clarification as utilised in OD. The CSIR assignment also led to the conceptualisation of a Situational Leadership® model for leading comprehensive organisational transformation, which was subsequently published in the seventh edition of the text by Hersey, Blanchard and Johnson, *Management of organisational behaviour*, in 1996.
- From 1997 onwards, Unisa also started training OD practitioners. Unisa's one-year Programme in Applied OD presented by the Unisa Centre for Lifelong Learning has produced 865 OD practitioners during the 22-year period 1997 to 2019. This course includes two practical workshops, during which participants are taught practical facilitation skills, how to apply the action research process in practice, and how to facilitate strategic planning and teambuilding as OD interventions. From 2016 onwards Unisa also started accommodating industrial and organisational psychology (IOP) interns from the Military Psychological Institute (MPI) and the private sector on the workshops as part of their practical IOP internship programme.

Organisation development and related concepts

Now that we know what OD is and what it is concerned with, it becomes important to distinguish it from related concepts such as CM, learning organisations and capacity development. Many use these terms interchangeably because they all are related to change, learning and the enhancement of skills and capacity, but they each refer to something different.

Change management

The general concept of 'change' is defined as a new state of things, different from the old state of things (French & Bell, 1999). Organisational change, on the other hand, is more difficult to define. For a better understanding, the easiest approach is not trying to define it, but rather comparing it to other types of change. The name itself, 'organisational change', already explains that we are talking about a change in organisational activities, but this statement alone does not say much about the type of activities that are subject to change. When comparing organisational change with operational change, it becomes clear that the former covers a much larger field – that is, all the operational processes of serving customers, of production, of logistics – whereas the latter refers exclusively to individuals, their roles and values (Salminen, 2000).

Besides these, organisational change also covers changes that appear in work processes, which may be understood as a set of work tasks fulfilled in order to reach a clear purpose (Davenport & Short, 2003), and in their subsystems.

Fincham and Rhodes (2005: 525) define CM as 'the leadership and direction of the process of organisational transformation, especially with regard to human aspects and overcoming resistance to change'. The Society for Human Resource Management (2015) defines CM as the systematic approach and application of knowledge, tools and resources in order to deal with change. CM means defining and adopting corporate strategies, structures, procedures and technologies to deal with changes in external conditions and the business environment.

Organisational change may also be defined as a state of movement between the current and a future state towards which the organisation is directed (Cummings & Huse, 1985). Although this definition is closer to that of change in general, a certain difference, though subtle, is indeed visible. The origins of this definition are found in the thinking of Lewin (1948), who formulated the concept of movement between two discrete and somewhat permanent 'states' related to organisational change, namely being in a state 'I' at a moment 'I', and in a state 'II' at a moment 'II'. The suggested movement is linear and static as well as, according to some authors (Kanter, Stein & Jick, 1992), unfit for the dynamic concept of organisational change, because it oversimplifies a highly complex process. However, it is for this very reason that it offers an extremely direct possibility of planning the change actions.

CM is a structured approach to ensure that changes are thoroughly and smoothly implemented and to achieve lasting benefits of change. The CM focus is on the wider impacts of change, particularly on people and how they, as individuals and teams, move from the current to the future state. The change could range from a simple process change to a major system change to achieve the organisation's potential.

OD can be distinguished from CM and organisational change. OD and CM both address the effective implementation of planned change. They are both concerned with the sequence of activities, processes and leadership issues that facilitate organisational improvement. They differ, however, in their underlying value orientation. OD supports values of human potential, participation and development in addition to performance and competitive advantage. CM focuses more narrowly on values of cost, quality and schedules. OD's distinguishing feature is, therefore, concern with the transfer of knowledge and skills so that the system is more able to manage change in the future. CM does not necessarily require the transfer of skills. In short, therefore, all ODs involve CM, but CM may not involve OD (Cummings & Worley, 2015).

Cummings and Worley (2015) furthermore suggest that organisational change is a broader concept than OD, because OD can be implied in organisational change. OD is primarily concerned with changing the organisation in such a fashion that skills are transferred and to build the organisation's capability to achieve goals and solve problems. It is therefore intended to change the organisation in a particular direction, towards improved problem solving, responsiveness, QWL and effectiveness. On the other hand, organisational change is more broadly focused and can apply to any change, including technical and managerial innovation, organisational decline or the evolution of the system over time. These changes may or may not be directed at making the organisation more developed in the sense implied by OD.

The learning organisation

The concept of the learning organisation has gone through many combinations and permutations over the last decade in terms of theoretical development and attempts at practical application. The keen interest in the learning organisation stems from what Senge (1990; 1994) calls the age of globalisation, where one source of competitive advantage is the ability and rate at which an organisation can learn and react more quickly than its competitors.

A learning organisation is 'an organization that is continually expanding its capacity to create its future' and for which 'adaptive learning must be joined by generative learning, learning that enhances our capacity to create' (Senge, 1990: 14). Senge described five different 'disciplines' as the cornerstones of learning organisations: (1) **systems thinking:** learning to understand better the interdependencies and integrated patterns of our world; (2) **personal mastery:** developing commitment to lifelong learning and continually challenging and clarifying personal visions; (3) **mental models:** developing reflection and inquiry skills to be aware of, surface and test the deeply rooted assumptions and generalisations that we hold about the world; (4) **building shared vision:** developing shared images of the future that we seek to create, and the principles and guiding practices by which to get there; and (5) **team learning:** group interaction that maximises the insights of individuals through dialogue and skilful discussion and through recognising interaction patterns in teams that undermine learning (Austin & Bartunek, 2006: 108).

A strong set of core values and behaviours is normally present in learning organisations, including, according to Roper and Pettit (2002), the following:

- Value different kinds of knowledge and learning styles.
- Encourage communication between people who have different perspectives and ideas.
- Develop creative thinking.
- Remain non-judgemental of others and their ideas.

- Break down traditional barriers within the organisation.
- Develop leadership throughout the organisation. Everyone is a leader.
- Reduce distinctions between organisational members (management versus non-management, line versus staff, doers versus thinkers, professional versus non-professional staff, and so on).
- Believe that every member of the organisation has untapped potential.

There are some **common characteristics that define a learning organisation**, though there is no set formula for how they are implemented. Constant readiness, best knowledge available, collaboration, continuous planning, improvised implementation and action learning are typical characteristics of the learning organisation (Garvin, Edmondson & Gino, 2008):

- **Constant readiness:** The organisation exists in constant readiness for change. The organisation is ready to take advantage of new opportunities by staying in tune with its environment and being willing to question its ways of doing business.
- **Best knowledge available:** The best knowledge, including real-time data, is available to implement change. The knowledge is widely gathered and widely disseminated. Knowledge is power, and in the learning organisation no one owns or monopolises knowledge.
- **Collaboration across the organisation:** Dissemination of knowledge through technology is common. Successful learning organisations foster opportunities for face-to-face collaboration. This occurs in meetings that cut across boundaries.
- **Continuous planning:** Instead of a few top managers formulating fixed plans, the learning organisation creates flexible plans that are fully known and accepted by the entire organisation. The plans are constantly re-examined and rewritten by those involved with their implementation.
- **Improvised implementation:** Instead of rigidly implementing plans, learning organisations encourage experimentation to stay on course when confronted with changing conditions, because the organisations of today experience conditions that change rapidly and without warning, and this requires people who are actively thinking and contributing.
- **Action learning:** Successes are identified and institutionalised within the organisation. Change is re-evaluated continually, not just at annual planning sessions. The learning organisation collects data to understand better what went wrong, what went right, and what could have gone better. It constantly takes action, reflects and makes adjustments.

Some writers have used the term 'learning organisation' interchangeably with 'organisational learning', while others have attempted to draw clear distinctions between the two (Stewart, 2001). Easterby-Smith (1997) makes a distinction between writers who focus on the learning organisation and those who focus on organisational learning, and then goes on to discuss several strains of thought within the latter category. He notes that the learning organisation is **pragmatic**, **normative** and **aspirational**. The literature is **pragmatic** in that it focuses on how organisations successfully acquire, share and use knowledge to achieve organisational goals. There is a strong emphasis on creating knowledge for action, not knowledge for its own sake (Argyris, 1993). Furthermore, it recognises that organisations are part of complex social systems over which they cannot exert full control. Rather than trying to isolate or protect itself from its environment, an organisation ought to be closely attuned to it, embrace the opportunities that changing circumstances can offer and, as more recent theorists have urged, 'ride the wave' (Duesterberg & London, 2001; Merron, 1997). Another aspect of the pragmatic orientation is that learning organisation theorists, unlike many of their academic counterparts, have also developed an array of techniques and tools to perform diagnostics, examining patterns of behaviour in organisations and engaging in 'transformative thinking' (Wycoff & Richardson, 1995).

According to Roper and Pettit (2002: 259), this approach is **normative** in the sense that there is a strong set of underlying values that inform practice within a learning organisation, which include a commitment to:

- **valuing different kinds of knowledge and learning styles and creating a 'learning environment'** so that each organisational member can realise his/her full potential
- **encouraging dialogue and the exploration** of different perspectives and experiences to generate creative thinking
- **working collectively and breaking down traditional barriers or blinders** within organisations so as to release creative potential
- **fostering leadership potential** throughout the organisation and reducing distinctions, such as those between management and staff, between strategists and implementers, between support and professional staff, etc.

The learning organisation literature is **aspirational** in the sense that the models are presented as 'ideal types' that no real organisation can realise in full. Individuals as well as the organisation are engaged in an ongoing quest for knowledge, their struggle to 'unlearn' dysfunctional behaviours is continuous, and because change is a constant, they must constantly change (Roper & Pettit, 2002: 259).

The organisational learning literature, according to Roper and Pettit (2002), is much more extensive and diverse. The following are a few of the streams in this literature:

- The **management science stream** focuses on the processes of knowledge acquisition and information management. It covers a variety of topics, from effective management information systems design to more challenging issues, such as the relationship between explicit and tacit knowledge.

- The **sociological perspective** focuses on organisations as social systems with structures and a culture that either improves or, more often, hinders learning. As social structures, organisations are characterised by internal politics, conflict and power differentials that have a huge impact on the capacity of individuals and organisations to learn and act on that learning.
- The third perspective focuses on how learning contributes to **increases in productive output, market share and/or profitability**. It sees organisations as embedded in competitive environments, and the effectiveness of their learning systems as based on the extent to which they keep their competitive edge. This stream scrutinises topics such as innovation and the adoption of new technologies and practices, the behaviour of organisations within a given sector and determinants of decisions to expand or diversify, and the efficacy of joint venturing.
- The fourth category in organisational learning literature includes **psychological and behavioural aspects** of individual learning and cross-cultural comparisons of organisational learning, mainly in the USA and Japan, but also in a few European countries. However, the latter have not been much developed in the mainstream literature.

Capacity development

In the field of development, the term 'capacity development' is relatively new, emerging in the 1980s. Despite its newness, capacity development became the central purpose of technical cooperation in the 1990s (UNDP, 1996). Capacity development is seen as complementary to other ideas that dominated development thinking (and still play an important role) over the past four decades. These concepts include institution building, institutional development, human resource development, development management/administration and institutional strengthening.

These and other concepts related to development work — OD, community development, integrated rural development and sustainable development — have been subsumed under the wider concept of capacity development, which can be seen as an umbrella concept (Morgan, 1989) that links previously isolated approaches to a coherent strategy with a long-term perspective and vision of social change. In part, the theme of capacity development has emerged in reaction to the lack of results produced by initiatives based on technical cooperation (Morgan & Baser, 1993; UNDP, 1993).

Capacity building is the ability of individuals, groups, institutions ganisations to identify and solve development problems over time , 1997). Capacity development is a concept that is broader than OD, ludes an emphasis on the overall system, environment or context within iduals, organisations and societies operate and interact, and not simply a single organisation (UNDP, 1998). Capacity development is any system, effort or process that includes, among its major objectives, strengthening the capability of elected CEOs, chief administrative officers, department and agency heads, and programme managers in general-purpose government to plan, implement, manage or evaluate policies, strategies or programmes designed to impact on **social conditions in the community** (Cohen, 1993).

Capacity development is seen as referring to the growth of formal organisational relationships and abilities—those changes in organisational behaviour, values, skills and relationships that improve the abilities of groups and organisations to carry out functions and achieve desired outcomes over time. Capacity development can therefore refer to **either process or outcomes**—those efforts to improve organisational performance and/or the results of those efforts in terms of capacities developed (Morgan, 1997).

Within the many definitions, there seems to be an emerging consensus that capacity development involves the long term, contributes to sustainable social and economic development, and is demand-driven (Alley & Negretto, 1999). Capacity development also suggests a shift towards the enhancement and strengthening of existing capacities. This is distinct from past approaches under the label of 'institution building', which entailed starting from scratch to build institutions based on supposedly universal models taken from industrialised countries of the West (Morgan, 1993).

Morgan (1997) sets out the governing assumptions about CD as follows:

- The scope of capacity development goes beyond the traditional focus on the internal functioning of individual formal organisations or the 'micro'-aspect. More and more, participants have to **look at the 'macro'-aspect or the behaviour and structure of larger work communities**.
- Capacity development is about complex learning, adaptation and attitudinal change at the individual, group, organisational and even societal levels. People at these levels have to assume new responsibilities and slowly devise new collective solutions to common problems.
- Participants need to think more in systems terms and see their contribution and those of others in much broader, interconnected ways. This in turn has implications for doing capacity assessments and designing indicators.
- Capacity development is also about power, control, risk and uncertainty. It depends upon the creation and harnessing of social energy, and the commitment and ownership of field participants and stakeholders.
- One of the challenges is to arrive at the right relationships among process, product and performance when designing capacity development initiatives. Products designed without sufficient attention to process can lead to outcomes and impacts with little sustainability. Both product and process must be directly focused on improving performance to be of interest to practitioners.

- There is a generic list of capabilities that projects could be designed to achieve. These have to do with learning and adapting, forming productive relationships both inside and outside the organisation, being able to recruit and develop the required staff, as well as setting and maintaining a clear direction.

Conclusion

This chapter introduced OD as a planned change discipline concerned with applying behavioural science knowledge and practice to help organisations adapt to change forces inside and outside their borders. It also emphasised the fact that OD as a profession has, since its inception, supported and promoted a set of humanistic values that include, but are not limited to, human development, fairness, openness, choice, balance of autonomy and constraint. This chapter also highlighted the fact that research on the characteristics of successful OD practitioners yields diagnostic ability, basic knowledge of behavioural science techniques, empathy, knowledge of the theories and methods within the consultant's own discipline, goal-setting ability, problem-solving ability, the ability to perform self-assessment, the ability to see things objectively, imagination, flexibility, honesty, consistency and trust as important attributes and abilities. The history of OD reveals its five roots, namely laboratory training, action research and survey feedback, participative management, productivity and QWL, and strategic change. The current practice of OD goes beyond its humanistic origins by incorporating concepts such as strategy and design to complement early emphasis on group processes.

OD can be distinguished from related concepts such as CM, learning organisations and capacity development. The CM focus is on the wider impacts of change, particularly on people and how they, as individuals and teams, move from the current to the future state. The keen interest in learning organisations stems from the age of globalisation, where one source of competitive advantage is the ability and rate at which an organisation can learn and react more quickly than its competitors. Capacity building is the ability of individuals, groups, institutions and organisations to identify and solve development problems over time. Capacity development is a concept that is broader than OD, as it includes an emphasis on the overall system, environment or context within which individuals, organisations and societies operate and interact, and not simply a single organisation.

Reflection questions

1. Define OD.
2. Explain what OD is not.
3. Discuss the characteristics of OD.
4. Discuss the internal and external forces that are currently impacting on organisations.
5. List and discuss the specific values that guide the field of OD.
6. List the characteristics of successful OD practitioners.
7. Briefly describe the history of OD.
8. Distinguish between the related concepts CM, 'the learning organisation' and 'capacity development'.
9. Discuss the set of underlying values that inform practice within a learning organisation.
10. Distinguish between the different perspectives on organisational learning.
11. Discuss the assumptions about capacity development.

Multiple-choice questions

1. Worley and Feyerherm (2003) suggested that, for a process to be called OD:
   a. it must focus on or result in the change of some aspect of the organisational system
   b. there must be learning or the transfer of knowledge or skills to the organisation
   c. there must be evidence of improvement in or an intention to improve the effectiveness of the organisation
   d. All of the above

2. The following is a category of internal forces causing change:
   a. Political issues
   b. Competition
   c. New technologies
   d. Growth pressures

3. _____ may also be defined as 'a state of transition between the current state and a future one, towards which the organisation is directed'.
   a. Capacity development
   b. OD
   c. Organisational change
   d. None of the above

4. _____ is a core behaviour normally present in learning organisations.
   a. Collaboration across the organisation
   b. The belief that very few members of the organisation have untapped human potential
   c. The development of leadership throughout the organisation
   d. a and c

5. _____ conducted a companywide application of organisational diagnosis in Old Mutual in 1976.
   a. Barry Venter
   b. Leon Coetsee
   c. Fred Oosthuizen
   d. Gustav Pansegrouw

References

Abrahamson, E. 2000. 'Change without pain'. *Harvard Business Review* 78(4): 75–81.

Alley, K & Negretto, G. 1999. *Literature review: definitions of capacity building and implications for monitoring and evaluation.* New York: UNICEF, Division of Evaluation, Policy and Planning.

Argyris, C. 1965. 'Explorations in interpersonal competence'. *Journal of Applied Behavioral Science* 1(1): 58–83.

Argyris, C. 1993. *Knowledge for action: guide to overcoming barriers to organizational change.* San Francisco, CA: Jossey-Bass.

Austin, JR & Bartunek, JM. 2006. 'Theories and practices of organization development', in *Organization change and development: a Jossey-Bass reader*, edited by JV Gallos. San Francisco, CA: Jossey-Bass: 89–128.

Bazigos, MN & Burke, WW. 1997. 'Theory orientations of organization development (OD) practitioners'. *Group & Organization Management* 22(3): 384–408.

Beckhard, R. 1969. *Organization development: strategies and models.* Reading, MA: Addison-Wesley.

Beer, M. 1980. *Organization change and development: a systems view.* Santa Monica, CA: Goodyear Publishing.

Beer, M & Walton, RE. 1987. 'Organizational change and development'. *Annual Review of Psychology* 38: 339–368.

Bennis, WG. 1969. *Organization development: its nature, origins, and prospects.* Reading, MA: Addison-Wesley.

Bennis, W & Shepard, H. 1956. 'A theory of group development'. *Human Relations* 9: 415–457.

Bradford, DL & Burke, WW. 2004. 'Introduction: is OD in crisis?' *Journal of Applied Behavioral Science* 40(4): 369–373.

Bradford, L, Gibb, J & Benne, K. 1964. *T-group theory and laboratory method: innovation in re-education.* New York: Wiley.

Brown, DR. 2011. *An experiential approach to organizational development.* 8th ed. Englewood Cliffs, NJ: Prentice Hall.

Burke, WW. 1982. *Organization development: principles and practice.* Boston, MA: Little Brown.

Burke, WW. 1997. 'The new agenda for organization development'. *Organizational Dynamics* 26(1): 7–20.

Burke, WW. 2011. 'A perspective on the field of organization development and change: the Zeigarnik Effect'. *Journal of Applied Behavioral Science* 47(2): 143–167.

Burke, WW & Bradford, DL. 2005. 'The crisis in OD', in *Reinventing organization development: new approaches to change in organizations,* edited by DL Bradford & WW Burke. San Francisco, CA: John Wiley & Sons: 7–14.

Burke, WW, Lake, D & Paine, J. 2008. *Organizational change: a comprehensive reader.* San Francisco, CA: Jossey-Bass.

Burnes, B & Cooke, B. 2012. 'Review article: the past, present and future of organization development: taking the long view'. *Human Relations* 65(11): 1395–1429.

Burnes, B & Jackson, P. 2011. 'Success and failure in organizational change: an exploration of the role of values'. *Journal of Change Management* 11(2): 133–162.

Burns, T & Stalker, G. 1961. *The management of innovation.* London: Tavistock.

Bushe, G. 2011. 'Appreciative inquiry: theory and critique', in *The Routledge companion to organizational change,* edited by D Boje, B Burnes & J Hassard. London: Routledge: 87–103.

Cartwright, D & Zander, A. 1954. *Group dynamics.* Evanston, IL: Row Peterson.

Church, AH & Burke, WW. 1995. 'Practitioner attitudes about the field of organization development'. *Research in Organizational Change and Development* 8: 1–46.

Church, AH, Burke, WW & Van Eynde, DF. 1994. 'Values, motives, and interventions of organization development practitioners'. *Group & Organization Management* 19(1): 5–50.

Coetsee, LD. 2002. *Peak performance and productivity: a practical guide for the creation of a motivating climate.* Potchefstroom: Ons Drukkers.

Cohen, JM. 1993. *Building sustainable public sector managerial, professional and technical capacity: a framework for analysis and intervention.* Cambridge, MA: Harvard Institute for International Development.

Cummings, TG & Huse, FE. 1985. *Organization development and change.* 3rd ed. St Paul, MN: West.

Cummings, TG & Worley, CG. 2015. *Organization development and change.* 10th ed. Stamford, CT: Cengage Learning.

Davenport, TH & Short, J. 2003. 'Information technology and business process redesign'. *Operations Management: Critical Perspectives on Business and Management* 1: 97.

Dawson, P. 1994. *Organizational change: a processual approach.* London: Paul Chapman.

Duesterberg, T & London, HI. 2001. *Riding the next wave: why this century will be a golden age for workers, the environment and developing countries.* Indianapolis, IN: Hudson Institute.

Easterby-Smith, M. 1997. 'Disciplines of organizational learning: contributions and critiques'. *Human Relations* 50(9): 1085–1113.

Fincham, R & Rhodes, P. 2005. *Principles of organizational behaviour.* Oxford: Oxford University Press.

Follett, MP. 1941. 'The meaning of responsibility in business management', in *Dynamic administration: the collective papers of Mary Parker Follett*, edited by HC Metcalf & L Urwick. London: Sir Isaac Pitman & Sons Ltd: 146–166.

Fordyce, JK & Weil, R. 1979. *Managing with people.* 2nd ed. Reading, MA: Addison-Wesley.

French, W. 1969. 'Organizational development: objectives, assumptions and strategies'. *California Management Review* 12(2): 23–34.

French, WL. 1982. 'The emergence and early history of organization development: with reference to influences on and interaction among some of the key actors'. *Group & Organization Studies* 7(3): 261–278.

French, WL & Bell, HC. 1999. *Organization development: behavioral science interventions for organizational improvement.* 6th ed. New York: Prentice Hall.

Gallos, JV. 2006. 'Introduction', in *Organization development: a Jossey-Bass reader*, edited by JV Gallos. San Francisco, CA: Jossey-Bass.

Garvin, DA, Edmondson, AC & Gino, F. 2008. 'Is yours a learning organization?' *Harvard Business Review* 86(3): 109.

Ghoshal, S & Bartlett, CA. 2000. 'Rebuilding behavioral context: a blueprint for corporate renewal', in *Breaking the code of change*, edited by M Beer & N Nohria. Boston, MA: Harvard Business School Press: 195–222.

Golay, LM & Church, AH. 2013. 'Mass customization: the bane of OD or the cure to what ails it?' *Leadership and Organization Development Journal* 34(7): 661–679.

Greiner, LE & Cummings, TG. 2004. 'Wanted: OD more alive than dead!' *Journal of Applied Behavioral Science* 40(4): 374–391.

Hersey, P, Blanchard, KH & Johnson, DE. 1996. *Management of organizational behavior: utilizing human resources.* 7th ed. Upper Saddle River, NJ: Prentice Hall.

Homans, G. 1950. *The human group.* New York: Harcourt Brace.

Jamieson, DW. 2006. What makes OD, OD? Unpublished manuscript. www.jhartleyconsulting.com (Accessed 17 February 2016).

Jamieson, DW & Gellermann, W. 2005. 'Values, ethics and OD practice', in *The NTL handbook of organization development and change*, edited by BB Brazzel & M Jones. San Francisco, CA: Pfeiffer/Jossey-Bass.

Jamieson, DW & Worley, C. 2006. 'The practice of OD', in *The handbook of organization development*, edited by T Cummings. Thousand Oaks, CA: SAGE.

Kanter, RM, Stein, BA & Jick, TD. 1992. *The challenge of organizational change: how companies experience it and leaders guide it.* New York: Free Press.

Katz, D & Kahn, R. 1966. *The social psychology of organizations.* New York: Wiley.

Kreitner, R & Kinicki, A. 1995. *Organizational behavior.* Chicago, IL: Irwin Inc.

Lawrence, P & Lorsch, J. 1967. *Organization and environment.* Cambridge, MA: Harvard Business School Press.

Leonard, D & Coltea, C. 2013. Most change initiatives fail, but they don't have to. *Business Journal.* http://www.gallop.com/businessjournal/162707/change-initiatives-fail-don.aspx (Accessed 15 August 2015).

Lewin, K. 1948. *Resolving social conflicts.* Washington, DC: American Psychological Association.

Lewin, K & Lippitt, R. 1938. 'An experimental approach to the study of autocracy and democracy: a preliminary note'. *Sociometry* 1: 292–300.

Likert, R. 1961. *New patterns of management.* New York: McGraw-Hill.

Markus, ML & Benjamin, RI. 1997. 'The magic bullet theory in IT-enabled transformation'. *Sloan Management Review* 38(2): 55–68.

Marshak, RJ & Grant, D. 2008. 'Organizational discourse and new organization development practices'. *British Journal of Management* 19(S7): S8–S19.

Maslow, A. 1954. *Motivation and personality.* New York: Harper.

Mayo, E. 1945. *The social problems of an industrial civilization.* Cambridge, MA: Harvard Business School Press.

McGregor, D. 1960. *The human side of enterprise.* New York: McGraw Hill.

Merron, K. 1997. *Riding the wave: designing your organization's architecture for enduring success.* New York: John Wiley.

Morgan, G. 1989. *Creative organization theory.* Newbury Park, CA: SAGE.

Morgan, P. 1993. *Capacity building: an overview.* Ottawa: CIDA.

Morgan, P. 1997. *The design and use of capacity development indicators.* Hull: Policy Branch, CIDA.

Morgan, P & Baser, H. 1993. *Making technical cooperation more effective: new approaches by the International Development Community.* Hull: CIDA.

Oswick, C. 2009. 'Revisioning or re-versioning?: A commentary on diagnostic and dialogic forms of organization development'. *Journal of Applied Behavioral Science* 45(3): 369–374.

Palmer, I, Dunford, R & Akin, G. 2009. *Managing organizational change: a multiple perspectives approach.* New York: McGraw-Hill Irwin.

Rees, G & French, R. 2013. *Leading, managing and developing people* (No 4). London: CIPD Publications.

Roethlisberger, F & Dickson, W. 1939. *Management and the worker.* New York: Wiley.

Rogers, C. 1961. *On becoming a person.* Boston, MA: Houghton Mifflin.

Roper, L & Pettit, J. 2002. 'Development and the learning organisation: an introduction'. *Development in Practice* 12: 3–4, 258–271.

Salminen, A. 2000. 'Implementing organizational and operational change— critical success factors of change management'. Helsinki University of Technology. Acta Polytechnica Skandinavica. *Industrial Management and Business Administration* Series No. 7.

Schein, E & Bennis, W. 1965. *Personal and organizational change through group methods: the laboratory approach.* New York: Wiley.

Schmuck, RA & Miles, MB. 1971. *Organization development in schools.* Palo Alto, CA: National Press Books.

Senge, PM. 1990. *The fifth discipline: the art and practice of the learning organisation.* New York: Currency Doubleday.

Senge, PM. 1994. 'Moving forward, thinking strategically about building learning organizations', in *The fifth discipline fieldbook*, edited by P Senge, A Kleiner, C Roberts, R Ross & B Smith. New York: Doubleday/Currency: 15–47.

Serfontein, S & Van Tonder, CL. 2008. 'A historical perspective on the theory and practice of OD', in *Organisation development: theory and practice*, edited by CL van Tonder & G Roodt. Pretoria: Van Schaik: 7–37.

Shull, AC, Church, AH & Burke, WW. 2013. 'Attitudes about the field of organization development 20 years later: the more things change, the more they stay the same'. *Research in Organizational Change and Development* 21: 1–28.

Sminia, H & Van Nistelrooij, ATM. 2006. 'Strategic management and organization development: planned change in a public sector organization'. *Journal of Change Management* 6(1): 99–113.

Society for Human Resource Management. 2015. 'Change management' in Glossary of HR terms. http://www.shrm.org/templatestools/glossaries/hrterms/pages/c.aspx (Accessed 23 May 2015).

Stewart, D. 2001. 'Reinterpreting the learning organization'. *The Learning Organization* 8(4): 141–152.

Sullivan, R & Quade, K. 1995. 'Essential competencies for internal and external OD consultants', in *Practicing organization development*, edited by W Rothwell, R Sullivan & G McLean. San Diego, CA: Pfeiffer.

Tannenbaum, R & Schmidt, W. 1973. 'How to choose a leadership pattern'. *Harvard Business Review* 51 (May–June): 162–180.

Thrift, N. 2005. *Knowing capitalism*. London: SAGE.

Trist, E & Bamforth, E. 1951. 'Social and psychological consequences of the longwall method of coal getting'. *Human Relations* 4 (February): 3–28.

UNDP (United Nations Development Programme). 1993. *Programme approach guiding principles*. New York: UNDP.

UNDP. 1996. *Building sustainable capacity: challenges for the public sector*. New York: UNDP.

UNDP. 1998. *Capacity assessment and development*. New York: UNDP.

Van Nistelrooij, ATM & De Wilde, R. 2008. *Voorbij verandermanagement; Whole Scale Change met de wind onder de vleugels* [Beyond change management; working with whole scale change]. Deventer: Kluwer.

Weick, KE & Quinn, RE. 1999. 'Organizational change and development'. *Annual Review of Psychology* 50: 361–386.

Worley, CG & Feyerherm, AE. 2003. 'Reflections on the future of organization development'. *The Journal of Applied Behavioral Science* 39(1): 97–115.

Worley, CG, Rothwell, WJ & Sullivan, RL. 2010. 'Competencies of OD practitioners', in *Practicing organization development: a guide for leading change*. 3rd ed, edited by WJ Rothwell, JM Stavros, RL Sullivan & A Sullivan. San Diego, CA: Pfeiffer: 107–135.

Worley, C & Varney, G. 1998. 'A search for a common body of knowledge for master's level organization development and change programs'. *Academy of Management ODC Newsletter*: 1–4.

Worren, N, Ruddle, K & Moore, K. 1999. 'From organizational development to change management: the emergence of a new profession'. *Journal of Applied Behavioral Science* 35(3): 273–286.

Wycoff, J & Richardson, T. 1995. *Transformation thinking: tools and techniques that open the door to powerful new thinking for every member of your organization*. Berkeley, CA: Berkeley Publishing Group.

Chapter 2

Organisation development and change management

Benny Olivier

Learning outcomes

After reading this chapter, you should be able to:

- explain the difference between the diagnostic and dialogic approaches to organisation development (OD)
- give examples of dialogic OD methods
- explain the similarities between diagnostic and dialogic OD approaches
- discuss the implications for OD and practitioners regarding the approaches to OD
- give a short history of OD interventions
- define change management (CM) and explain how it is used to facilitate the people side of change initiatives
- explain the commonalities and differences between OD and CM
- define and name typical change initiatives in organisations.

Introduction

This chapter highlights two different approaches to the practice of organisation development (OD) and also makes a clear distinction between OD and change management (CM).

The chapter starts by highlighting two different approaches to OD which OD scholars and practitioners often neglect to consider, namely the diagnostic and dialog approaches. Each of these approaches, which are based on fundamentally different philosophical and conceptual assumptions about organisations and how to develop them, will be explained and discussed. A short history of OD interventions will also be discussed to explain the emergence of the two approaches to OD.

The chapter will conclude with a discussion of the differences and communalities between the practice of OD and CM. Whereas OD's most distinct and basic feature comes from the development part of its title, CM is about managing the people side of change.

Definitions and the history of organisation development

In Chapter 1 of this textbook the most prominent definitions of OD are discussed and a summary of the history and development of OD is also provided. As such these two aspects regarding OD will not be given any further attention in this chapter.

Approaches to organisation development

A clear division in the practice of OD which has important implications for academia and practitioners was identified by Bushe and Marshak (2009). The authors argue that over the past 30 or so years a different OD practice has seen the light which is based on underlying assumptions that differ from classical OD, and that these philosophical and theoretical differences are not sufficiently emphasised in OD textbooks or well understood by OD practitioners. As such the majority of OD academics and practitioners tend to concentrate on only one, classical approach to OD. However, Bushe and Marshak (2009) make a distinction between classical or **diagnostic** OD and a new **dialogic** approach to OD. These two approaches to OD are based on fundamentally different philosophical and conceptual assumptions about organisations and how best to develop them. As such it is critical that OD scholars and practitioners are aware of and understand these two different approaches to OD and how these different approaches manifest themselves in different OD interventions.

The diagnostic approach to organisation development

Classical or diagnostic OD is based mainly on the change theories developed in the 1940s and 1950s by Kurt Lewin and Ron Lippit and their colleagues (Bushe & Marshak, 2014). Planned change is seen as 'unfreezing' the current situation, creating 'movement' to a new desirable state that then needs to be 'frozen' to sustain the change (Cummings, Worley & Donovan, 2020). A key aspects of this planned change is action research, a cyclical process which includes a diagnosis of the current situation to guide subsequent interventions to implement change and generate knowledge. It places a major emphasis on data gathering and diagnosis prior to implementation (Bushe & Marshak, 2014; Cummings et al, 2020). This diagnostic approach to OD, with its emphasis on action research, is based on the following underlying philosophical and conceptual assumptions (Bushe & Marshak, 2009):

- There exists an objective reality that can be investigated to produce valid data to influence change (positivism).

- A core task of an OD consultant is to gather valid data.
- This data gathering is called diagnosis – the organisation exists as an entity that needs examination prior to remedies being prescribed.
- Diagnosis is thus essential for informed and effective OD and change.
- The organisation is an open or living system.
- Organisations adapt to their external environments.
- In diagnostic OD we gather data to compare a given group or organisation against a prescriptive model or desired future state.
- Methodologies such as action research, survey feedback and SWOT (strengths, weaknesses, opportunities and threats) analysis are used to guide problem solving, decision making and action planning.

The dialogic approach to organisation development

Bushe and Marshak (2009) explain that newer OD practices have emerged which can be considered to be different to classical, diagnostic OD. They refer to these new practices as dialogic OD. According to Bushe and Marshak (2009) these practices did not always come from applying theory to practice, but were interventions that worked for achieving change without any real theory. These new OD practices are different to the practices of classical, diagnostic OD, which are based on positivism. These new dialogic OD practices base their change processes not on diagnosing the current situation (classical, diagnostic OD), but on developing narratives, stories or conversations that assist in establishing more effective patterns of organising (Bushe & Marshak, 2009). This dialogical approach to OD is based on the following underlying philosophical and conceptual assumptions (Bushe & Marshak, 2009):

- There is no inherent real form of social organising to be discovered (objectivism), but social organisations are open to infinite possibilities (constructivism).
- Rather than diagnosing, dialogic OD seeks to evoke new ideas that will compel self-organising change.
- Instead of objective facts, the data used are the narratives (stories) people hold about the best of something.

Examples of dialogic organisation development methods

Table 2.1 lists 10 examples of dialogic OD methods that deviate from classical, diagnostic OD interventions which are usually implemented only after a diagnosis of the current functioning of an organisation has been conducted.

Table 2.1 Examples of dialogical organisation development methods (adapted from Bushe & Marshak, 2014)

Examples of dialogic methods
Appreciative inquiry
Conference method
Dynamic facilitation
Future Search
Open-space technology
Organisational learning conversations
Real-time strategic change
Search conference
Visual explorer
World café

Contrasting diagnostic and dialogic organisation development

Bushe and Marshak (2009: 353) explain that one of the most important ways diagnostic and dialogic OD differ is that 'most of the newer OD practices emphasize a view of human systems as dialogic systems or meaning-making systems rather than biological or open systems'. This important distinction between the two OD approaches affects the type of interventions used to achieve successful change. Table 2.2 summarises the most important differences between the diagnostic and dialogic approaches to OD.

Table 2.2 Contrasting diagnostic and dialogic organisation development (adapted from Bushe & Marshak, 2009)

Diagnostic	Dialogic
Positivism, objectivism	Interpretive, constructivism
Organisations are living systems	Organisations are meaning-making systems
Reality is an objective fact	Reality is socially constructed
There is a single reality	There are multiple realities
Change can be created, planned and managed	Change can be encouraged but is mainly self-organising
Collecting and applying valid data using objective problem-solving methods – leads to change	Creating containers and processes to produce generative ideas – leads to change ➝

Diagnostic	Dialogic
Change is episodic, linear and goal-oriented	Change may be continuous and/or cyclical
Emphasis on changing behaviour and what people do	Emphasis on changing mindsets and what people think

Similarities between diagnostic and dialogic approaches

Although dialogical OD differs from diagnostic OD in fundamental ways, both approaches do embrace the humanistic and democratic values which are the bedrock of the classical (diagnostic) approach to OD. Table 2.3 sets out the main similarities between the two approaches.

Table 2.3 Similarities between diagnostic and dialogic organisation development (adapted from Bushe & Marshak, 2009)

Similarities
Humanistic and democratic values
Facilitation and encouragement of greater system awareness
Consultants focus on process – avoid content
Concern for capacity building and development of the system

Bushe and Marshak (2009) argue that these similarities between the two approaches to OD suggest that the diagnostic and dialogic approaches are different forms of OD rather than totally different types of consulting and change altogether. They base their argument on the fact that although dialogic OD involves different premises about the nature of social systems and how they change, it retains the core values and ideals of classical, diagnostic OD, such as free and informed consent, authenticity, integrity and collaboration.

Implications for organisation development and practitioners

OD scholars and practitioners currently tend to approach OD as consisting of a single entity based on common premises and beliefs (Bushe & Marshak, 2009). In fact, the majority of OD practitioners currently tend to (1) only use the diagnostic OD approach in practice; (2) use the action research model when conducting OD; (3) emphasise action research in that empirical research about the system should precede attempts to change it; and (4) insist on gathering data which are used to develop interventions to solve the identified problem(s). However, as has been discussed above, this single-entity OD approach is no longer valid, as it is clear that there are in fact two distinct approaches to OD based on different underlying philosophical and theoretical premises. If OD theory and practice are to advance, these two OD approaches will have to be embraced and applied.

Practitioners will also have to be able to understand the two OD approaches so as not to be confused and attempt to mix classical (diagnostic) and newer intervention patterns (dialogic). As stated by Bushe and Marshak (2009: 363), 'greater clarity and differentiation could also help avoid unknowing mixing and matching of diagnostic and dialogic practices that in combination may be inappropriate, out of alignment and even counterproductive'. Furthermore, Bushe and Marshak (2009) state that to implement dialogic OD practices practitioners will require a range of competencies and skills in addition to, and sometimes instead of, the classic list of OD consultant competencies.

A short history of organisation development interventions

As mentioned earlier, a summary of the history and development of OD is given in Chapter 1 of this textbook. However, in order to understand the emergence of the two approaches to OD (diagnostic versus dialogic), it is useful and insightful to reflect specifically on the history of OD interventions. In this respect Burke (2018) distinguishes between two specific periods under which the development of OD interventions can be discussed.

The period 1939–1969

Burke (2018) refers to this period as the 'special century' for OD, although the period only spanned 30 years. Although there were many OD events and actions during this period, Burke (2018) refers to the following events and actions as 'key' events:

1. **Lewin's contributions:** The first is Lewin's B = f(P,E), which identifies behaviour as a function of the person and the environment. Secondly there is Lewin's field theory and force-field analysis. Thirdly is the development of participative management at Harwood Manufacturing. Fourthly there is the T-group. Finally there are the three phases of organisational change and development – unfreezing, movement and refreezing.
2. **Intergroup conflict resolution:** Muzar Sherif, a social psychologist, concluded after practical studies that to resolve conflict between two groups there had to be a 'superordinate goal' that could only be achieved through the cooperative efforts of the two groups.
3. **Survey feedback:** In the 1950s Rensis Likert and Floyd Mann began to use surveys and interventions for organisational change by ensuring that those who answered the questionnaire received feedback and were then jointly involved in planning action steps for improvement.

4. **Large-group intervention (LGI):** This intervention attempted to assemble the entire system in the same room at the same time – to talk with one another about organisational problems and issues and to create ideas for positive change.

5. **The power lab:** This intervention was created by Barry Oshry in 1969 as an experiential learning process about human–system dynamics in a context of three conditions: the elites, the bottoms and the middles. The learning from such a power lab concerns social justice and how we cope with systems, which are mostly inequitable.

The period 1970–1987

Burke (2018: 194) contends, 'There was a dormant period in the 1970s for new and innovative OD practices and theory until appreciative inquiry (AI) emerged in the mid-1980s.' This emergence coincided with the positive psychology movement, as AI emphasised discourse and narrative as processes for organisation change focusing on strengths. AI deviated from the classical, diagnostic approach to OD and can thus be seen as one of the first OD interventions based on dialogic premises. AI was followed by various other dialogic OD interventions such as the conference method, Future Search, search conferences and the world café, to name but a few. See Table 2.1 for a more comprehensive list of dialogic OD interventions.

What is important is that Burke (2018) argues that with the exception of AI, no basic innovation has occurred in the field of OD since 1969, closing out what he referred to as the 'century' of OD interventions. This view is supported by Pasmore and Woodman (2017), who reviewed three decades of OD research and concluded that the larger world we work in is changing more and more rapidly, and OD must do the same to accommodate and remain relevant.

Comparing the definitions of organisation development and change management

Understanding the definition of organisation development

Most prominent definitions of OD share the same commonalities and usually only differ on the scope of change targets and the ultimate intention of change (see Chapter 1). The following definition by Cummings et al (2020: 2) is useful in understanding the difference between OD and CM: 'OD is a system-wide application and transfer of behavioural science knowledge to the planned development, improvement, and reinforcement of the strategies, structures, and processes that lead to organisation effectiveness.'

Elaborating on this definition, Cummings et al (2020) stated that OD is both a professional field of social action and an area of scientific enquiry, covering a wide spectrum of activities. An interesting approach is the one by Worley and Feyerherm (2003), who suggested that, for a process to be called OD, (1) it must focus on or result in the change of some aspect of the organisational system; (2) there must be learning or the transfer of knowledge or skills to the organisation; and (3) there must be evidence of improvement in – or an intention to improve the effectiveness of – the organisation.

From practical experience, this author has noted that OD practitioners usually follow the classical, diagnostic approach to OD in organisations and apply OD practically in one of the following two ways:

- The use of the action-research process in a system-wide application of OD as propagated by various researchers (Cummings et al, 2020; Worley & Feyerherm, 2003).
- The use of individual interventions to address specific challenges to improve an organisation's functioning, such as strategic planning, teambuilding, role clarification, conflict handling, leadership training and so on. In this approach, the organisation has already decided what the challenge is, so there is no need for a diagnosis. The organisation wants the OD practitioner to simply implement a specific intervention(s) to address the challenges without following the complete action-research approach. An OD practitioner must first try to convince the client to follow the complete action-research process in order to ensure that the correct interventions are implemented. However, should the client insist that only a specific intervention is required, the OD practitioner must decide whether he/she will do this or whether the work should be declined or referred to another consultant.

Defining change management

According to Schein (2002), there are three basic types of change that occur in all human groups and organisations:

1. **Natural evolutionary change:** This refers to all the learning processes that occur throughout any given organisation as its parts adapt to its environmental conditions. Each employee is learning all the time and is making changes to adjust to his/her local conditions. Some of these changes benefit the organisation and form part of the organisation's capacity to learn. However, some of the things that employees learn do not benefit the organisation, but merely make their lives easier at the expense of the organisation. These could even include sabotage and undermining management's intentions. Thus, evolution is not always progress from the organisation's point of view.

2. **Planned and managed change:** This is when the evolutionary processes are steered or when the direction of change and learning is actively controlled. Cummings and Cummings (2014) support this view and describe planned change as intentional and rational, a process that is formally initiated, designed and implemented to achieve expected results.
3. **Unplanned or revolutionary change:** As the name implies, this is change not foreseen or planned for, and it can have catastrophic consequences for an organisation. In these circumstances, leaders who can adapt to changing circumstances easily and who have the skills to manage unplanned change are required.

Although various definitions of CM exist, for the purposes of distinguishing between OD and CM the follow definition by Hiatt and Creasey (2003: 10) will be used: 'Change management is about helping people through change. It is the process, tools and techniques for proactively managing the people side of change in order to achieve the desired business results'.

Communalities and differences between organisation development and change management

According to Cummings and Cummings (2014: 143), 'the words development and change appear frequently in the OD literature, often used interchangeably or linked together as in "OD and change"'. The authors state that development has long been the distinguishing feature of OD, with its own values, concepts and methods. CM, in turn, has been used increasingly to suggest a harder, more business-oriented approach to change than the softer version associated with the name OD.

Cummings and Cummings (2014) state that OD and CM share the following common features:

- Both involve planned change aimed at helping organisations become more effective.
- They address similar change activities, such as creating readiness for change, overcoming resistance and sustaining momentum.
- They are concerned with the structures, processes and leadership that produce effective organisational change.

However, Cummings and Cummings (2014) argue that, in practice, OD and CM differ in fundamental ways. These differences have to do with their underlying value orientations and resultant purposes.

- OD's most distinct and basic feature comes from the **development** part of its name, which rests on certain assumptions about human beings and organisations. From the beginning, OD has drawn heavily on humanistic psychology and its underlying values that see people as inherently good and having a substantial capacity for self-determination, creativity and growth. This positive view of human beings is deeply embedded in OD's values and practices.

- CM, on the other hand, focuses on **helping organisations implement specific change**, such as a new structure, a new information and communication technology (ICT) system, a new work practice or something similar. CM's values and practices are highly pragmatic and aimed at making change processes more effective and efficient. Attention is directed towards how well change is implemented and at what cost and speed.

- Thus CM emphasises change implementation, with a relative neglect of development and its concern for employees' psychological maturity and transferring knowledge and skills to organisations. While OD addresses change implementation from a development perspective, CM's values and methods focus on implementing organisation change effectively and efficiently.

Another way of looking at OD and CM is to distinguish between first-order and second-order change. According to Bate (1994) and Newman (2000):

- **First-order change** involves adjustment to systems, processes or structures, but does not involve fundamental changes in strategy, core values or organisational identity. First-order changes maintain and develop the organisation. This is the type of change referred to as change initiatives (see the section on change initiatives below).

- **Second-order change** is transformational, radical and fundamentally alters the organisation at its core, and entails transforming the nature of the organisation. This is the type of change that would result from an OD approach to change.

In formulating a practical definition of CM, the approach of Cummings and Cummings (2014) as well as the approach of Hiatt and Creasey (2003) to CM can be combined as follows: CM is a structured process that uses tools and techniques to proactively manage the people side of any change initiative that is implemented in an organisation as effectively and efficiently as possible so that the desired business results can be achieved.

Change initiatives in organisations

In defining and discussing CM above, reference has been made to change initiatives in organisations. So what exactly are change initiatives? A **change**

initiative is generally defined as an action, a system, a procedure, a method of work or an intervention through which something becomes different, and the goal of this change initiative is ultimately to improve an organisation by altering how work is done. The facilitation of CM is thus the planning and implementation of a process to manage the people side of a change initiative to achieve organisational improvement. While OD addresses change implementation from a development perspective, CM focuses on implementing change initiatives in an organisation effectively and efficiently.

Conclusion

OD and CM have various commonalities. They both use planned change to help organisations become more effective and address similar change activities such as creating readiness for change, overcoming resistance and sustaining momentum. They are concerned with the structures, processes and leadership that produce effective organisational change. However, while OD follows a diagnostic action-research approach to organisational change, with an emphasis on the development of people and organisations, CM is a structured, step-by-step process concerned with implementing change initiatives.

Reflection questions

1. Contrast the diagnostic and dialogic approaches to OD.
2. Give five examples of dialogical OD interventions.
3. Discuss the similarities between diagnostic and dialogic OD.
4. Discuss the practical implications of the diagnostic and dialogic approaches to OD for OD practitioners.
5. Contrast OD and CM.
6. Define an organisational change initiative and give five examples of such initiatives.

Multiple-choice questions

1. The two approaches to OD are not very different from each other.
   a. True
   b. False

2. The diagnostic approach to OD is also referred to as the classical approach to OD.
   a. True
   b. False

3. Diagnostic OD is based mainly on the change theories developed by:
   a. Bushe and Marshak
   b. Cummings and Cummings
   c. Lewin and Lippit
   d. Lewin and Sherif

4. Dialogic OD is based on:
   a. objectivism and humanism
   b. constructivism and humanism
   c. single and multiple realities
   d. none of the above

5. OD and CM:
   a. both involve planned change
   b. both seek a quick-fix solution to change
   c. both seek to develop an organisation
   d. both seek to assist an organisation to successfully implement specific change initiatives

6. CM:
   a. gives attention to the people side of change
   b. does not give attention to resistance to change
   c. does not give attention to leadership
   d. is similar to project management

References

Bate, P. 1994. *Strategies for cultural change*. London: Universal Books.

Burke, WW. 2018. 'The rise and fall of the growth of organization development: what now?' *Consulting Psychology Journal: Practice and Research* 70(3): 186–206.

Bushe, GR & Marshak, RJ. 2009. 'Revisioning organizational development: diagnostic and dialogic premises and patterns of practice'. *Journal of Applied Behavioural Science* 45(3): 348–368.

Bushe, GR & Marshak, RJ. 2014. 'The dialogic mindset in organization development'. *Research in Organizational Change and Development* 22: 55–97.

Cummings, TG & Cummings, C. 2014. 'Appreciating organization development: a comparative essay on divergent perspectives'. *Human Resource Development* 25(2): 141–154.

Cummings, G, Worley, G & Donovan, P. 2020. *Organization development and change*. London: Cengage Learning.

Hiatt, JM & Creasey, TJ. 2003. *Change management: the people side of change.* Loveland, CO: Prosci Learning Center Publications.

Newman, KL. 2000. 'Organizational transformation during institutional upheaval' *Harvard Business Review* 25(3): 602–619.

Pasmore, WA & Woodman, RW. 2017. The future of research and practice in organizational change and development, in *Research in organizational change development*, volume 25, edited by AB Shani & DA Noumair. London: Emerald Group: 1–32.

Schein, EH. 2002. 'Models and tools for stability and change in human system'. *Reflections* 4(2): 34–46.

Worley, CG & Feyerherm, AE. 2003. `Reflections on the future of organization development'. *The Journal of Applied Behavioral Science* 39(1): 97–115.

Chapter 3

A practical approach to change management

Benny Olivier

Learning outcomes

After reading this chapter, you should be able to:

- understand best practices in change management (CM) based on research
- explain the individual and organisational dynamics involved with change
- understand the different approaches to organisational CM
- distinguish between CM and project management (PM)
- explain the Hugh Structured Change Management Process (HSCMP)
- integrate the HSCMP with a technical project plan.

Introduction

Personnel responsible for the implementation of a change initiative in an organisation are faced with various practical challenges, including (1) how to motivate people to accept the changes; (2) how to influence key stakeholders to support the changes; (3) how to plan the management of change; and (4) how to integrate the change management (CM) process with the phases of the technical project management (PM) plan. This chapter will enable all personnel involved in organisational change to focus on the structured, practical steps required to plan and implement specific change initiatives in an organisation successfully, without having to address the developmental issues propagated by a lengthy organisation development (OD) approach.

The chapter starts by looking at best practices in CM based on research conducted over the last 11 years by Professional Science (Prosci). This is followed by an explanation of the individual and organisational dynamics involved with change and four popular theories of individual CM and five approaches to organisational CM. After this the difference between CM and PM is explained and the chapter concludes with an explanation of a new proposed CM process called the Hugh Structured Change Management Process (HSCMP).

Best practices in change management based on research

Prosci has been conducting research for the past 12 years (1997–2019) to uncover lessons learned from practitioners and consultants, so that current CM teams can benefit from these experiences. Emphasis is placed on what is working and what is not, in all areas and roles of CM (Prosci, 2020). Consistently over the past 11 years the following seven aspects were rated as having the greatest impact on CM (Prosci, 2020):

- Active and visible executive sponsorship is the number 1 contributor to success.
- Apply a structured CM process, as CM effectiveness increases when a structured methodology is used.
- Communicate frequently and openly.
- Engage with front-line employees.
- Dedicate resources to CM.
- Integrate the CM process with the PM process.
- Engage with and support middle management.

The Prosci (2020) research thus shows that CM is indeed a success enabler and that there is a direct correlation between how well the people side of change is managed and how successful the effort is. More will be said about these CM success factors later in this chapter.

The difference between individual and organisational change

Before we proceed with any discussion of individual and organisational change, a distinction needs to be made between change and transition. According to Bridges (1991):

- **Change** is situational, something that happens to people, even if they don't agree with it. Change is external to an individual and can happen very quickly.
- **Transition** is the psychological process that people go through to come to terms with the new situation and is what happens in people's minds as they go through change. Transition is internal to an individual and usually occurs more slowly.

In CM it is thus important to make a clear distinction between what Bridges (1991) refers to as 'change' and what Hiatt and Creasey (2003: 10) refer to as 'organisational change', and what Bridges (1991) refers to as 'transition' and what Hiatt and Creasey (2003: 10) refer to as 'individual change' **Organisational CM** thus addresses the actual change initiative that is implemented, while **individual CM** addresses the transition that individuals go through when facing any change initiative.

Theories of individual change transition

Individual CM is the management of change from the perspective of the individual employees, and the focus is on the tools and techniques to help employees through the transition (Bridges, 1991; Hiatt & Creasey, 2003). The plain truth is that it is individuals who decide whether a change initiative will be successfully implemented or not. It is thus of critical importance for any person engaged in CM to firstly understand the phases that an individual goes through when faced with change, and secondly to assist individuals to navigate through these phases successfully. The effect of change on people has been studied for many years, resulting in various theories or models which explain what a person goes through during a change process, and four of the better-known models are discussed below.

The Kübler-Ross model

The Kübler-Ross change curve, which is also known as the five stages of grief, is a model consisting of the various levels or stages of emotions which are experienced by a person who is soon going to approach death or who is a survivor of an intimate death (Kübler-Ross, 1969). The five stages included in this model are denial, anger, bargaining, depression and acceptance.

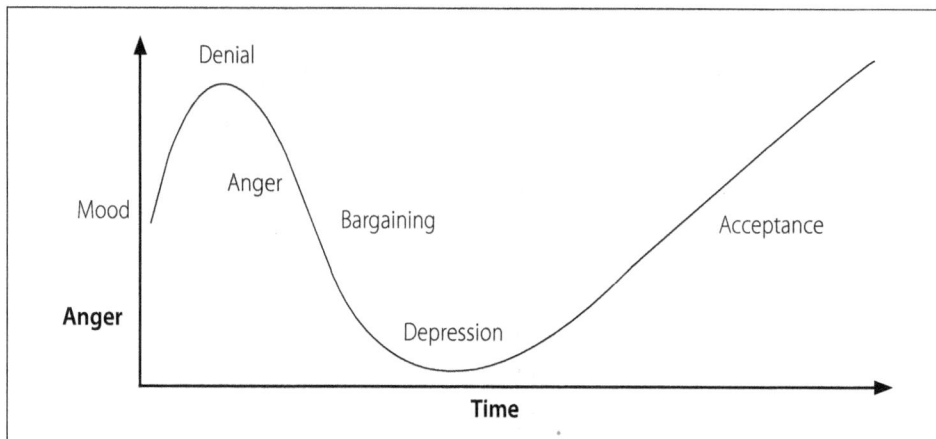

Figure 3.1 The Kübler-Ross change curve (adapted from Kübler-Ross, 1969: 26)

The change curve is a very trusted and reliable tool that can be used to understand the stage at which people are when they are going through a major or significant change in life. This insight can help managers and change practitioners in understanding the position in which employees are as far as adapting to change is concerned and can assist with creating tailor-made methods of communication and guidance for those on the path of change. The five stages are illustrated in Figure 3.1 and discussed below from a CM perspective.

Stage 1: Denial

This is the initial stage, at which employees may experience shock or denial, and they may not be able to digest the fact that they have to undergo change and adapt to something new. They don't want to believe that the change is happening. Often, they believe that if they pretend that the change is not happening, if they keep it at a distance, then maybe it will all go away. They may need time to adjust to the changes and, for a long time, they may deny that they need any help. Here, the role of a change agent or manager should be to help employees understand why the change is happening and how it can be helpful. This stage demands communication so that employees can have full knowledge and can have their questions answered. Employers must make it a point to avoid overwhelming the employees with a lot of information all at once, and of giving them the facts slowly and gradually.

Stage 2: Anger

When employees realise that the change is real and will affect them, their denial usually turns to anger, and they look to blame someone or something else for making this happen to them. This anger can be directed in many different directions and can also arise because they fear the unknown and what lies ahead. This stage has to be managed very sensibly by the organisation making use of change managers, change agents and management because some employees tend to vent their anger a little too harshly. This could create chaos and, to avoid it, careful planning must be done in advance. Clear communication and support should still be the focus for organisations at this level as well. To assist employees in advancing to the next stage, they can be provided with various options that are available to them.

Stage 3: Bargaining

When employees finally understand that the change is inevitable and that they will have to adapt to new situations and circumstances, they may try to find the best possible scenario or option for them to fit into and adapt to. They may try to bargain with management in order to put off the change or to find a way out of the situation.

Stage 4: Depression

When employees realise that bargaining is not going to work, the reality of the change sets in. At this point they become aware of the losses associated with the change and what they have to leave behind. This has the potential to move people towards a sad state, where they feel down and depressed with low energy. Employees may even reach a point of feeling demotivated and uncertain about their future.

Stage 5: Acceptance

As people realise that fighting the change is not going to make it go away, they move into a stage of acceptance. It may not be a happy space, but rather a resigned attitude towards the change, and a sense that they must get on with it. They start to embrace the change, accept the situation and start building new hopes and aspirations. This can be a creative phase, as it forces employees to explore and look for new possibilities.

Bridges' transition model

Bridges' transition model (Bridges, 1991), which is illustrated in Figure 3.2, explores human behaviours relating to change. It defines typical emotions individuals might exhibit during the change process and features three overarching stages of transition that people go through when they experience change. Bridges (1991) says that people will go through each stage at their own pace. For example, those who are comfortable with the change will likely move ahead to stage 3 quickly, while others will linger at stages 1 or 2.

Stage 1: Ending, losing and letting go

People enter this initial stage of transition when you first present them with change. This stage is often marked by resistance and emotional upheaval because people are being forced to let go of something that they are comfortable with. At this stage, people may experience the following emotions:

- Fear
- Denial
- Anger
- Sadness
- Disorientation
- Frustration
- Uncertainty
- A sense of loss.

People have to accept that something is ending before they can begin to accept the new idea, so if you don't acknowledge the emotions that they are going through, you'll likely encounter resistance throughout the entire change process.

Stage 2: The neutral zone

In this stage, people affected by the change are often confused, uncertain and impatient. Depending on how well you're managing the change, they may also experience a higher workload as they get used to new systems and new ways of working. This phase can be seen as the bridge between the old and the new; in some ways, people will still be attached to the old, while they are also trying to adapt to the new. During this stage people may experience the following:

- Resentment towards the change initiative
- Low morale and low productivity
- Anxiety about their role, status or identity
- Scepticism about the change initiative.

Stage 3: The new beginning

The last transition stage is a time of acceptance and energy, where people have begun to embrace the change initiative. They are building the skills they need to work successfully in the new way, and they are also starting to see early wins from their efforts. At this stage, people are likely to experience the following:

- High energy
- Openness to learning
- Renewed commitment to the group or their role.

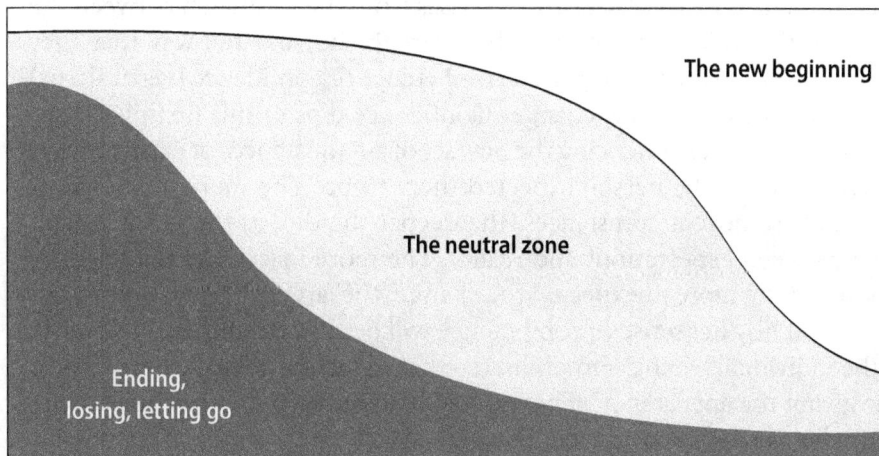

Figure 3.2 Bridges' transition model (adapted from Bridges, 1991: 70)

The transition curve

The transition curve developed by Adams, Hayes and Hopson (1976), depicts seven different stages which an individual experiences when he/she encounters significant change. These phases are illustrated in Figure 3.3 and discussed thereafter.

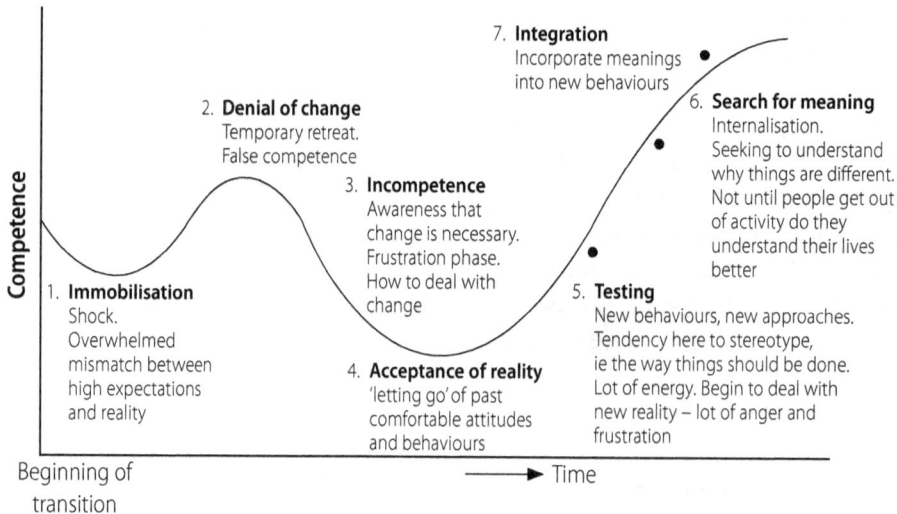

Figure 3.3 The transition curve (adapted from Adams, Hayes & Hopson, 1976: 152)

Phase 1: Shock

This first phase describes the reaction when the individual initially encounters the trigger for change. Shock or surprise arises from the mismatch between the way in which the individual believes things might be, and the way that they actually are. The individual's perceived competence or confidence (vertical axis) reduces in the face of the new change. Confidence dips in this first phase as a result of the impact of experiencing the new set of circumstances or expectations, which may not be as the person expected them to be. The more unknown or unexpected these new circumstances, the deeper the dip, as there is a greater mismatch between expectations and reality. The more inaccurate the person's perception and the more unexpected the change, the larger the negative impact experienced on his/her sense of competence will be. In extreme cases, this may lead to the individual feeling immobilised – that is, unable to make decisions or plans, or giving the appearance of being unable to manage the required action. Although this vertical axis reflects the individual's own sense of confidence and competence, it is an important indicator, as individuals' feelings of their effectiveness are strongly linked to their actual performance.

Phase 2: Denial

Following the shock stage comes a period of denial, during which the individual makes his/her own conclusions about the new situation in order to minimise the dissonance experienced in the first phase. This justification or reasoning prompts an increase in individuals' sense of competence – they gain a form of intellectual control over the situation. Whether this stage is a hill or more of a plateau, the only way to move forward from here is through individual choice. A number of individuals who are reluctant to make a change will be 'stuck' at this point in the transition; they are unable to accept a different view of themselves and of the need for the change to happen.

Phase 3: Awareness

While the previous phase corresponds with a perceived increase in competence while the individual ignores the reality of the situation, the third phase brings with it a greater awareness of his or her **real** level of competence in relation to the required level. This is an important phase, as the individual becomes emotionally engaged in the situation, and so this time is frequently marked by feelings of frustration or confusion about how to handle the change process. The areas which have now been defined as 'deficient' require attention and individuals may not know how to increase their level of skill or change their attitude.

Phase 4: Acceptance

The downward move in competence and confidence stops when the individual recognises and accepts the reality of the new situation. This is the lowest point on the figure. It requires letting go of attitudes and behaviours which have become comfortable or are appropriate or effective only for the old situation. Feelings of depression may occur as a result of not knowing what to put in place of the old behaviours and attitudes.

Phase 5: Testing

The identification of new behaviours is followed by the phase of starting to test them out. These new behaviours may be effective and achieve the desired outcome but, at other times, the individual may need to work harder to practise or 'polish' their new abilities. This phase of testing is characterised by success **and** failure at developing new skill areas. Hence it may not be a simple progression from left to right, as failure at trying out a new skill may push the individual back along the curve while the individual questions its relevance or searches for alternative behaviours.

Phase 6: Search for meaning

Learning from success and failure helps the individual start to search for meaning in the new situation. Rather than just trying new behaviours on for size, this stage also involves a questioning of why certain behaviours are effective, and why others, or indeed the same behaviours but on different occasions, may be ineffective. This knowledge enables the individual to take more control over his/her actions and to develop strategies for circumstances in advance.

Phase 7: Integration

The final stage is characterised by the individual taking ownership of recently acquired behaviours and thereby increasing his/her sense of confidence and competence to a level higher than before. The new ways of doing things become part of everyday activities and integrated into the individual's world view and natural reaction. There is little or no dissonance between the expectations of situations and the individual's perceived own ability to perform.

The ADKAR model

According to Hiatt (2006: 1), 'The ADKAR model… is a framework for understanding change at an individual level'. It has five elements or objectives, as shown in Table 3.1, and all five elements must be in place for a change to be realised.

Table 3.1 The ADKAR model (adapted from Hiatt, 2006: 2)

Element	Description
Awareness (A)	Awareness of the need for change
Desire (D)	Desire to support and participate in the change
Knowledge (K)	Knowledge of how to change
Ability (A)	Ability to implement the required skills and behaviour
Reinforcement (R)	Reinforcement to sustain the change

Awareness

Awareness represents a person's understanding of the nature of the change, why the change is being made and the risk of not changing. Awareness also includes information about the internal and external drivers that created the need for change, as well as 'what's in it for me'.

Desire

Desire represents the willingness to support and engage in a change. Desire is ultimately about personal choice; it is influenced by the nature of the change, by an individual's personal situation and by intrinsic motivators that are unique to each person.

Knowledge

Knowledge represents the information, training and education necessary to know how to change. Knowledge includes information about behaviours, processes, tools, systems, skills, job roles and techniques that are needed to implement a change.

Ability

Ability represents the realisation or execution of the change. Ability is turning knowledge into action. This is achieved when a person has the demonstrated capability to implement the change at the required performance levels.

Reinforcement

Reinforcement represents those internal and external factors that sustain a change. External reinforcements could include recognition, rewards and celebrations that are tied to the realisation of the change. Internal reinforcements could be a person's internal satisfaction with his/her achievement, or other benefits derived from the change on a personal level.

What is important is that the elements of the ADKAR model fall into the natural order of how one person experiences change. **Desire** cannot come before **awareness** because it is the awareness of the need for change that stimulates our desire or triggers our resistance to that change. **Knowledge** cannot come before **desire** because we do not seek to know how to do something that we do not want to do. **Ability** cannot come before **knowledge** because we cannot implement what we do not know. **Reinforcement** cannot come before **ability** because we can only recognise and appreciate what has been achieved. The life cycle for ADKAR begins after a change has been identified. From this starting point, the model provides a framework and sequence for managing the people side of change.

Conclusion regarding theories of individual change transition

Various models exist to explain the transition that individuals go through when faced with change. However, it is important to understand that these models of individual change must not be used in isolation but that they should rather be used 'within' an overall organisational change framework. This author supports the use of the ADKAR model (Hiatt, 2006) as the basis for individual CM–that is, to manage individual change transition in employees. The main reasons for this is that the ADKAR model:

- tells us **why** we need to implement a specific activity or undertake a specific action
- specifies **what** the desired outcome of the activity/action will be
- is **results-oriented**
- is **easy to apply** in different settings and circumstances.

Approaches to organisational change management

Background to organisational change management

Organisational change involves moving from an existing organisation state to a desired future state, which does not occur immediately, but requires a transition period during which the organisation learns how to implement the conditions needed to reach the desired future (Cummings, Worley and Donovan, 2020). This is illustrated in Figure 3.4. The transition state may be very different from the current state, which itself may be very different from the desired future state, and specific activities and structures may be required to get there. Cummings et al (2020) identify these activities and structures as (1) activity planning; (2) commitment planning; and (3) change management structures. Hiatt and Creasey (2003) refer to organisational change as a process consisting of different phases, which they refer to as (1) preparing for change; (2) managing change; and (3) reinforcing change. Schein (2002), in turn, states that any change process consists of three phases, namely (1) unfreezing; (2) changing or movement; and (3) refreezing. There are also other approaches to change which will be discussed in more detail below. What is important at this stage is that organisational change is not a single meeting, activity or announcement, but a process that must be managed continuously (Cummings et al, 2020; Hiatt & Creasey, 2003).

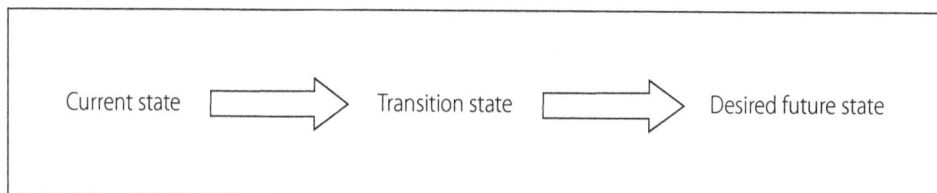

Figure 3.4 Organisation change as transition (adapted from Cummings et al, 2020: 173)

Organisational CM is the perspective of the organisation's management from the top looking down into the organisation. This is also managing change from the perspective of management and is the overall framework for managing change. A change agent or change consultant would also follow the steps in the organisational CM framework when implementing a change initiative in an organisation. There are various approaches to organisational CM, such as Lewin's three-step approach, the Prosci approach, Kotter's eight-step change model and others, as well as a new structured approach to organisational CM developed by the author, which will all be discussed in more detail below.

According to Palmer, Dunford and Akin (2006), common to all the approaches is that they provide multistep models of how to achieve successful change. Differences include the number of steps that need to be followed, whether all steps need to be followed, whether they need to be followed in sequence, and whether they need to be adapted to specific settings. In the following sections, we will briefly refer to five of the best-known approaches to planned organisational CM.

Lewin's approach to organisational change management

Schein (2002: 36), referring to the work of Kurt Lewin regarding the steady state of a system called a 'quasi-stationary equilibrium', states that any change process can be conceptualised as consisting of the following three stages or phases.

Stage 1: Unfreezing

The unfreezing stage entails creating the motivation to change. This is accomplished by changing the forces acting on the 'quasi-stationary equilibrium' system such that (1) the present state is disconfirmed; (2) some anxiety or guilt is aroused because some goals will not be met; and (3) enough psychological safety is provided for impacted individuals or groups.

Stage 2: Changing or movement

During this stage, new concepts, meanings and standards are learnt. This can take place through cognitive redefinition, imitation of role models or scanning for solutions and trial-and-error learning.

Stage 3: Refreezing

During this stage, new concepts, meanings and standards are incorporated into the self-concept of individuals or the culture of the group.

The professional science approach to organisational change management

Prosci propagates a research-based three-phase approach to planned organisational CM (Hiatt & Creasey, 2003).

Phase 1: Preparing for change

This phase includes activities to prepare the change manager and the change team for managing the change, to prepare business leaders to support the change and to create a high-level CM strategy.

Phase 2: Managing change

This phase includes the design of the CM plans and individual CM activities. The plans that are designed are a communication plan, coaching plans, training plans, a sponsor roadmap and resistance management plans. During this phase, use is also made of the ADKAR model (Awareness/Desire/Knowledge/Ability/Reinforcement) to manage individual change.

Phase 3: Reinforcing change

This phase includes an assessment of the CM activities and implementation of corrective action. This phase also includes celebrating early successes, conducting after-action reviews and transferring ownership of the change from the CM team to the organisation.

The accelerated implementation methodology approach to organisational change management

Implementation Management Associates (2010) propagate an accelerated implementation methodology (AIM) for organisational CM. They state that AIM is systemic (it must become part of the organisation's culture), is systematic (it is an integrated system of principles, tactics and tools), is practical (it is operationally focused on what to do), and is business driven (it is grounded in research, but translated into business-application language). The AIM consists of the following 10 steps:

- Step 1: Define the change.
- Step 2: Build agent capacity.
- Step 3: Assess the climate.
- Step 4: Generate sponsorship.
- Step 5: Determine the change approach.
- Step 6: Develop target readiness.
- Step 7: Build the communication plan.

- Step 8: Develop a reinforcement strategy.
- Step 9: Create cultural fit.
- Step 10: Prioritise action.

Kotter's approach to organisational change management

Kotter (1995) has an eight-step change model and he maintains that following the eight steps are important for achieving successful change:

- Step 1: Create urgency.
- Step 2: Form a powerful coalition.
- Step 3: Create a vision for change.
- Step 4: Communicate the vision.
- Step 5: Remove obstacles.
- Step 6: Create short-term wins.
- Step 7: Build on the change.
- Step 8: Anchor the changes in corporate culture.

The business change management approach to organisational change management

According to Jones and Recardo (2013), the business change management (BCM) methodology incorporates best practices and has been used to lead over 100 successful CM projects. The methodology is based on a systems approach and therefore takes into consideration how change will impact the technology, organisation, and process hierarchy. BCM methodology is comprised of the following four distinct phases of work:

- Phase 1: Create a change platform.
- Phase 2: Design change.
- Phase 3: Implement change.
- Phase 4: Institutionalise change.

Conclusions regarding organisational change management approaches

Although there are various approaches to planned organisational CM, many of the phases or steps propagated arc the same, and often just use different names to describe a phase or step. What distinguishes them from each other are the number of phases or steps involved, and the amount of detail provided under each step. The challenge for change practitioners is to apply these approaches in practice–that is, to determine what practical actions must take place under each phase or step. For this reason the author has developed a structured organisational CM process called the HSCMP, which contains the detailed steps that need to be following. The HSCMP will be discussed towards the end of this chapter.

The role of communication in change management

The communication process

According to Robbins et al (2016), before communication can take place it needs a purpose, as well as a message to be conveyed between a sender and a receiver. The sender encodes the message (converts it to a symbolic form) and passes it through a medium (channel) to the receiver, who decodes it. The result is transfer of meaning from one person to another. Figure 3.5 depicts this communication process. The key parts of this model are (1) the sender; (2) encoding; (3) the message; (4) the channel; (5) decoding; (6) the receiver; (7) noise; and (8) feedback.

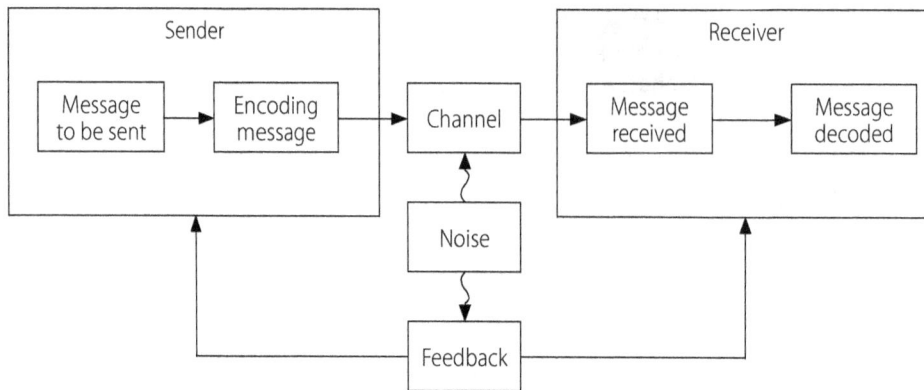

Figure 3.5 The communication process (adapted from Robbins et al, 2016: 409)

Robbins et al (2016) explain this communication process in the following way. The sender initiates a message by encoding a thought. The message is the actual physical product of the sender's encoding. When we speak, the speech is the message. When we write, the writing is the message. When we gesture, the movements of our arms and the expressions on our faces are the message. The channel is the medium through which the message travels. The sender selects it, determining whether to use a formal or informal channel. **Formal channels** are established by the organisation and they transmit messages related to the professional activities of members. They traditionally follow the authority chain within the organisation. Other forms of messages, such as personal or social, follow **informal channels**, which are spontaneous and emerge as a response to individual choices. The receiver is the person(s) to whom the message is directed and who must first translate the symbols into understandable form. This step is the decoding of the message. Noise represents communication barriers that distort the clarity of the message, such as perceptual problems, information overload, semantic difficulties or cultural differences. The final link in the communication process is *feedback*, the check on how successful we have been in transferring our message as originally intended. It determines whether or not understanding has been achieved.

Preferred senders in change management

According to Hiatt and Creasey (2003) and Creasey (2020), employees prefer two primary senders of change messages, namely immediate supervisors and executive leaders.

Immediate supervisors

Immediate supervisors are the preferred senders of messages related to personal impact. When it comes to personal issues, employees want to hear from someone they know and work with regularly, such as their supervisors, and such messages include the following:

- How does this impact me?
- How does this impact our group?
- How will this change my day-to-day responsibilities?

Executive leaders

Executive leaders such as chief executive officers (CEOs), managing directors (MDs), director-generals (DGs) and the like are the preferred senders of messages related to **business issues and opportunities**. When it comes to business issues and why the change is needed, employees want to hear from the person in charge, and such messages include the following:

- What are the external customer and competitor factors driving this change initiative?
- What are the current issues facing the business/organisation?
- Are there other marketplace drivers?
- What are the financial risks if we do not implement this change initiative?

Methods or channels of communicating

Channels of communication differ in their capacity to convey information (Robbins et al, 2016). Channel richness is the amount of information that can be transmitted during a communication episode. **Rich** channels can handle multiple cues simultaneously, facilitate rapid feedback and be very personal. **Lean** channels score low on these factors. Table 3.2 below gives examples of rich and lean communication channels.

Table 3.2 Examples of rich and lean communication channels (adapted from Robbins et al, 2016: 421)

High richness rating	Low richness (lean) rating
Face-to-face conversations	E-mail
Video conferences	Memorandums
Telephone conversations	Letters
Live speeches	Formal reports
Voicemail	Bulletins
Online discussion groups	

An important question for CM is: What is the most effective method of communicating? According to research conducted by Prosci (2020), participants in their study identified **face-to-face communication** as the most effective method. However, various alternative communication methods are also available which could be effective, depending on the audience and content of the message.

The role of different stakeholders in change management

According to Cummings and Worley (2015), key stakeholders in the organisation in which the change initiative is to be implemented must be identified. They define these stakeholders as **powerful individuals and groups with an interest in the change initiative**. Examples are senior and middle managers, supervisors, unions and different groupings of employees. These key stakeholders can hinder or support the implementation of a change initiative in an organisation, and it is important to gain their support to minimise the risk that one or a combination of these stakeholders will block the change initiative.

Identifying key stakeholders can start with the simple question, 'Who stands to gain or lose from the change initiative?' Once the key stakeholders have been identified, a map of their influence can be drawn. This map must show relationships among the stakeholders in terms of who influences whom and what the stake are for each party. This will provide the change manager with information about which individuals and groups need to be influenced to accept and support the change initiative.

The following five main stakeholders are important in any change initiative.

Change sponsors

According to Prosci (2020) and Implementation Management Associates (2010), the most important single factor to successful change implementation is active and visible **sponsorship**. Miller (2011) states that sponsors are accountable for the successful implementation of the change in their area of responsibility, and that these individuals must make sure that the benefits of the change initiative are fully realised. What makes an effective sponsor? According to research conducted by Prosci (2020), Miller (2011) and Implementation Management Associates (2010, effective sponsors):

- lead by 'doing', by setting an example, by walking the talk, and by participating actively throughout the change initiative
- demonstrate ownership of the change
- communicate effectively, consistently and congruently with employees about the change
- build a strong network with other sponsors, managers, supervisors and peers
- reinforce change.

In CM there are mainly two kinds of change sponsors: primary and secondary.

Primary sponsor

The primary sponsor, called an executive sponsor by Hiatt and Creasey (2003) and a key sponsor by Straker (2010), is the person who charters and authorises the change. There can be only one primary sponsor and this person has the power to sanction or legitimise change (Conner Partners, 2004). For large changes, this person is typically a senior manager, while for smaller changes, this person could be a department manager or supervisor. A primary sponsor should:

- participate actively in all project and CM activities
- support the project team
- acquire the needed resources
- obtain buy-in and support from all managers, supervisors and employees
- communicate constantly with managers, supervisors and employees.

Secondary sponsors (influencers)

Secondary sponsors, also called local sponsors by Miller (2011), are influencers who wield informal power. They cannot direct people to change, but they can influence people to do so, and they also have the ability to block change. As such, their support is needed to make any change initiative a success (Straker, 2010). If these influencers are excluded from the change initiative, they may take revenge by refusing to cooperate or otherwise blocking progress.

They thus require careful handling and usually need to be communicated with on a very regular basis. If you can't invite them to all meetings, then at least you can keep them up to date with progress and show how you are listening to them and taking their concerns into account.

Secondary sponsors include middle managers and supervisors (Miller, 2011). Unfortunately, in many organisations, these middle managers and supervisors are seen more as barriers than enablers, leaving them unskilled and unmotivated (Miller, 2011). Middle managers and supervisors play an important role in making a change initiative successful, as they must be able to coach and help their subordinates directly. According to Miller (2011), middle managers and supervisors must be made more effective by doing the following with them:

- Firstly, build their commitment to the change initiative. The primary sponsor must be used to build the commitment of middle managers and supervisors to make the change initiative successful. The primary sponsor must build their commitment first before building the commitment of the impacted employees.
- Secondly, give them the required change skills to enable them to coach and help their subordinates directly. Three types of training can be used to give them change skills, namely (1) giving them change leadership skills (how can they lead change effectively?); (2) giving them skills to assist their subordinates adapt to change (teach them how people adapt to change and give them tactics they can use in this regard); and (3) helping them with their own personal reactions to the change initiative.
- Thirdly, help them sponsor change. Help them to use role modelling and to provide hands-on support for their subordinates.

The change manager

It is important to appoint a change manager for every change initiative in an organisation, and this could be an internally appointed person or an external consultant. If the change initiative is relatively large and extends over a lengthy period of time, it is advisable to also appoint a CM team, which would consist of the change manager, change agents, the technical project manager (or a representative of the technical project team) and any other appropriate and relevant personnel. The change manager must manage this CM team (if such a team is appointed) and must ensure that the implementation of the change initiative in the organisation is integrated with the organisational technical project plan and that the change objectives are achieved on time and on budget.

The change manager, being concerned with the people side of change, must:

- apply and manage the organisational CM approach used to implement the change initiative
- integrate this approach with the steps of a technical project plan
- manage the individual change transition experienced by employees
- compile the CM plan.

The change manager must be an expert regarding the organisational change approach that will be used to implement the change initiative (whatever this approach may be) and must also have excellent knowledge of a particular approach to manage the people side of change (individual transition). The change manager is also responsible for compiling the CM plan and for supporting and training change sponsors and change agents.

Change agents

Change agents work under the change manager and must assist him/her to plan and execute all relevant CM tasks and activities. Change agents rarely have formal power and must rely on persuading and working with others to make change happen (Miller, 2011). What makes an effective change agent? According to Miller (2011):

- They have to have a basic level of credibility and trust within the organisation.
- They need to be able to challenge up, across or down the organisation.
- They must have or learn some influencing skills.

Unions

Labour organisations can wield considerable influence in organisations. If your change initiative takes place in an organisation which has a strong union (or unions), you will have to involve them in all CM activities. A union representative can even be invited to serve on the CM team.

Employees

At the end of the day it is employees who will determine whether the change initiative is successful or not. For this reason, you will have to identify all employee groups that will be impacted by the change initiative, either directly or indirectly. Then you will need to identify who is the leader of each impacted employee group, and this information will form part of your stakeholder analysis.

Resistance to change and how to manage it

Background on resistance to change

'Resistance is the behavioural consequence when someone feels that they have lost control of a situation' (Miller, 2011: 30). When you believe that you are losing control you will tend to 'slam on the brakes', as Miller (2011) calls it, as we all have a limit to the amount of change that we can handle at any given time. Usually, the greater the level of disruption that an individual must handle, the higher the level of resistance.

The natural and normal reaction to change is resistance, and every individual has a **threshold** for how much change they can absorb, based on their personal history, current events in their life, current changes at work and how much other change is going on (Hiatt & Creasey, 2003). If individuals have a limited capacity for change, and organisations are simply collections of individuals, then it is safe to say that organisations also have a limited capacity for change. This is especially true if organisations constantly embark on one change initiative after another, wearing down their employees (Miller, 2011). Although resistance is natural and is to be expected, ongoing resistance left unattended can become a threat to the entire change initiative, so resistance must be managed proactively. For these reasons do not react to resistance with surprise; rather expect it and plan for it (Hiatt & Creasey, 2003).

Symptoms of resistance to change

Resistance to change takes many forms. In this regard Hultman (1995) provides a valuable list of passive and active resistance to change which could assist in alerting us to the many ways that resistance can be manifested. These symptoms are given Table 3.3.

Table 3.3 Symptoms of resistance to change (adapted from Hultman, 1995: 16)

Passive resistance	Active resistance
Agreeing verbally but not following through (malicious compliance)	Being critical
Failing to implement change	Finding fault
Procrastinating or dragging one's feet	Appealing to fear
Pretending to be ignorant	Using facts selectively/distorting facts
Withholding information, suggestions, help or support	Blaming or accusing

Passive resistance	Active resistance
Standing by and allowing change to fail	Sabotaging
	Intimidating or threatening
	Manipulating
	Undermining
	Starting rumours
	Arguing

Why people resist change

Palmer et al (2006) provide the following explanations as to why people resist change:

- Dislike of change
- Discomfort with uncertainty
- Perceived negative effect on interests
- Attachment to the established culture/ways of doing things
- Perceived breach of psychological contract
- Lack of conviction that change is needed
- Lack of clarity as to what is expected
- Belief that the specific change being proposed is inappropriate
- Belief that the timing is wrong
- Excessive change
- Cumulative effect of other changes in one's life
- Perceived clash with ethics
- Reaction to the experience of previous changes
- Disagreement with the way the change is being managed.

Techniques to overcome resistance to change

Kotter and Schlesinger (1979) propose six techniques for managing resistance to change. Their approach is situational in that they argue that the choice of technique should be determined by situational factors. According to Kotter and Schlesinger (1979), a common mistake is using only one technique regardless of the situation. Their techniques are given in Table 3.4.

Table 3.4 Techniques to overcome resistance to change (adapted from Kotter & Schlesinger, 1979: 111)

Technique	Characteristic	When to use	Difficulties
Education and communication	Informing people as to the rationale for the change; providing information	Where resistance is due to lack of information or misinformation	May be time-consuming
Participation and involvement	Involving people in the change process as active participants	Where resistance is a reaction to a sense of exclusion from the process	May slow the process down and introduce an element of compro-mise in decisions
Facilitation and support	Providing resources – both technical and emotional	Where resistance is due to anxiety and uncertainty	Requires financial, time and interpersonal support
Negotiation and agreement	Offering incentives to actual or potential resistors	Where resistors are in a strong position to undermine the change if their concerns are not addressed	May lead to a 'watering down' of key elements of the change
Manipulation and co-optation	Selective use of information; 'buying' the support of certain individuals by giving them key roles in the change process	Where participation, facilitation or negotiation is too time-consuming or resource-demanding	May create a backlash
Explicit and implicit coercion	Threatening people with undesirable consequences (eg, firing) if they resist	Where the change recipients have little capacity to effectively resist; where survival of the organisation is at risk if change does not occur quickly	Support achieved in this manner is likely to be superficial; resentment may occur later

Change management and project management

The differences between change management and project management

While the skills required for change and project management are often similar, there are crucial differences between the two. CM provides a structured framework to transition individuals and organisations from one state to the next. PM is concerned with meeting a clearly defined outcome with a specific budget, scope and quality standards. Below are the five main characteristics which define the difference between CM and PM (Smith, 2014):

- **PM has a specific measurable goal.** One of the primary differences between PM and CM has to do with the nature of the desired outcomes. With PM there is a clearly definable and measurable goal. Whether this goal has or hasn't been achieved can be easily established and evaluated. CM typically involves less tangible and measurable ideas about what is being achieved.

- **PM necessitates a timeline.** An important part of PM is establishing and keeping to a timeline. A timeline will establish dates for when deliverables must be met. However, when it comes to CM there is no defined timeline, as it involves input from stakeholders in the business throughout the process. This means that as the idea is being developed it will be implemented over an undefined time period.

- **Milestones are integral to PM.** Milestones help to keep a project on track and provide a means to measure progress. Milestones for a project will established at the outset before the project begins. With CM there are not specific milestones that need to be achieved, as it is an open and consultative process. When done properly, CM will involve input and participation from employees, which can alter its progression.

- **PM has a limited scope while CM does not.** All good projects will have a definable and limited scope, and the scope defines what the project will achieve and what is outside of the project. Scope is critical, because without it, project creep can occur, where the project continues to expand without getting closer to its defined goals. With CM the scope can be very broad or not defined at all. For example, it would not be possible to define a change in company culture within a particular scope.

- **CM involves the input of multiple ideas.** CM is effective when it openly involves all stakeholders in the change. Therefore, it will typically involve a multiplicity of ideas and viewpoints to realise the vision for the change. In contrast, PM only requires a single idea from which it can be developed. So, for example, if an organisation wants to improve employee performance while operating an enterprise software, project managers might focus specifically on reducing errors, or picking up speed and efficiency is an effective solution in both regards, while change managers would focus on the bigger picture, from all angles.

In conclusion, CM techniques are an integral part of ensuring that a project is able to deliver on its desired outcomes. While CM is often incorporated into PM it is important to understand the differences in techniques and their implementation. Using both types of management correctly is critical to realising the final goal of the organisation.

The phases of a standard technical project

What is a project?

According to Lombardi (2018) and Mingus (2002), a project is a unique endeavour to produce a set of deliverables within clearly specified time, cost and quality constraints. Projects are different from standard business operational activities in the following ways:

- **Projects are unique in nature.** They do not involve repetitive processes. Every project undertaken is different from the last, whereas operational activities often involve undertaking repetitive (identical) processes.
- **There is a defined timescale.** Projects have a clearly specified start and end date within which the deliverables must be produced to meet a specified customer requirement.
- **There is an approved budget.** Projects are allocated a level of financial expenditure within which the deliverables must be produced to meet a specified customer requirement.
- **There are limited resources.** At the start of a project an agreed amount of labour, equipment and materials is allocated to the project.
- **Projects involve an element of risk.** Projects entail a level of uncertainty and therefore carry business risk.
- **They achieve beneficial change.** The purpose of a project, typically, is to improve an organisation through the implementation of business change.

What is project management?

As explained by the PMBOK Guide (PMI, 2017), PM is the skills, tools and management processes required to undertake a project successfully. PM comprises the following elements:

- **A set of skills:** Specialist knowledge, skills and experience are required to reduce the level of risk within a project and thereby enhance its likelihood of success.
- **A suite of tools:** Various types of tools are used by project managers to improve their chances of success. Examples include document templates, registers, planning software, modeling software, audit checklists and review forms.
- **A series of processes:** Various management techniques and processes are required to monitor and control time, cost, quality and scope on projects. Some examples include time management, cost management, quality management, change management, risk management and issue management.

The project management process

The PM process explained below and which is used to indicate how PM must be integrated with CM is a generic PM process based on the the work of Lombardi (2018), Mingus (2002), Prosci (2018) and the PMBOK Guide (PMI, 2017). The process followed by the technical PM team in a specific organisation may differ from the process explained below, but as a generic process it covers the main activities of any PM process. When managing change, the change manager must confirm with the organisation in which he/she is working what PM process the organisation is using to implement the specific change initiative. The steps of the CM process must then be integrated with the steps of the PM process that the organisation is using. In general, most projects consist of the following phases.

Phase 1: Project initiation

The initiation phase is the first phase in the project. During this phase a 'project charter' is completed, which outlines the objectives, scope, timelines and key milestones of the project. An initial project budget is compiled and the project team is selected, which could be internal personnel or external consultants. During this phase a project steering committee is also usually set up. Detailed stapes are the following:

- The need for a specific change initiative is identified.
- The identified need is presented to the organisation's management team for approval.
- The project steering committee is selected.
- Project objectives, scope, timelines and key milestones are identified.
- An initial project budget is compiled.
- The project manager and project team is selected (which could be internal personnel or external consultants).

Phase 2: Project Planning

The next phase entails the detailed project planning, which is usually presented to the project steering committee for approval. Data are then gathered about the current state and the desired future state. The solution to address the identified gap between the current state and the desired future state is then identified. Options are the costed and a specific option is chosen. The final option is then usually presented to the project steering committee for approval. At this point the project has been planned in detail and is ready to be executed. Detailed steps are the following:

- The project team prepares a draft project plan.
- The draft project plan is presented to the project steering committee for approval.

- Data are gathered about the organisation's current state and the desired future state.
- A solution to address the identified gap between the current state and the desired future state is identified.
- Solution options are then costed and a specific option is recommended.
- The recommended option is presented to the project steering committee for approval.
- The project plan is updated with all necessary detail and presented to the project steering committee for approval.

Phase 3: Project execution and monitoring

This phase involves the implementation of the approved solution in the organisation. The steps in the project plan are now implemented and monitored while modifications and adaptations are carried out where necessary. This includes the identification of changes, risks and issues; the review of deliverable quality; and the measurement of each deliverable being produced against the acceptance criteria. Once all of the deliverables have been produced and the customer has accepted the final solution, the project is ready for closure. Detailed steps are the following:

- Steps in the project plan are implemented and monitored.
- Measure progress and solution results/performance.
- Implement modifications and adaptations where necessary (this includes the identification of changes, risks and issues; the review of deliverable quality; and the measurement of each deliverable being produced against the acceptance criteria).
- Customer accepts the final solution once all deliverables have been produced.

Phase 4: Project closure

Project closure involves releasing the final deliverables to the customer, handing over project documentation, terminating supplier contracts, releasing project resources and communicating the closure of the project to all stakeholders. The last remaining step is to undertake a post-implementation review to quantify the overall success of the project and list any lessons learnt for future projects. Detailed steps are the following:

- The project team obtains permission from the project steering committee to terminate the project.
- Project termination is communicated to all applicable stakeholders.
- A post-implementation review is conducted.
- The project team is dissolved.
- The project steering committee is dissolved.

A new proposed practical structured change management process for managing organisational change

Having considered all the available approaches to organisational CM as well as incorporating years of experience in managing change, the author proposes a new, practical CM process which is referred to as the Hugh Structured Change Management Process (HSCMP). The HSCMP has been applied by the author with success in public and private organisations. This process consists of six main phases and various steps under each phase, which are given below.

Phase 1: Understanding the change initiative

Step 1.1:   Assess the scope of the change initiative.
Step 1.2:   Assess the current state of the organisation.
Step 1.3:   Summarised report: Your understanding of the change initiative.

Phase 2: Planning for the change initiative

Step 2.1:   Compile the CM team structure.
Step 2.2:   Assemble the CM team.
Step 2.3:   Conduct a sponsorship analysis.
Step 2.4:   Compile a communication plan.
Step 2.5:   Compile a resistance management plan.
Step 2.6:   Compile an integrated CM plan.
Step 2.7:   Integrate the CM plan with the PM plan.

Phase 3: Implementing the change management plans

Step 3.1:   Implement the communications plan.
Step 3.2:   Implement the resistance management plan.

Phase 4: Monitoring the implementation of the change management plans

Step 4.1:   Track progress of implementation against the CM plan.
Step 4.2:   Implement corrective measures where necessary.

Phase 5: Sustaining the change initiative

Step 5.1:   Gather feedback from stakeholders.
Step 5.2:   Implement corrective measures where necessary.
Step 5.3:   Celebrate and reward successes.
Step 5.4:   Evaluate the entire CM process.

Phase 6: Withdrawing from the change initiative

Step 6.1:   Transfer CM responsibilities.
Step 6.2:   Submit final CM report.
Step 6.3:   Dissolve the CM project team.

Integrating change management with project management

Of critical importance to the successful implementation of any change initiative is the ability of the change manager to integrate the activities of the CM process with the activities of the PM process. The earlier that CM can be started and involved in the PM process, the greater the chance of success of the entire CM process. This integration of the two processes will ensure that:

- activities can be sequenced
- the timing of activities can be aligned
- information can be exchanged between the PM team and the CM team.

Table 3.5 indicates how the CM process, in this case the HSCMP, can be integrated with the PM process, in this case a generic PM process.

Table 3.5 Integrating change management with project management (Author)

Technical project management phases and activities of a generic project management process	Change management phases and activities of the HSCMP
1. INITIATION PHASE	
1.1 The need for a specific change initiative is identified.	
1.2 Identified need is presented to the organisation's management team for approval.	
1.3 Project steering committee is selected.	
1.4 Project objectives, scope, timelines and key milestones are identified.	
	• Appoint change manager (Internal or external) • Step 1.1: Assess the scope of the change initiative • Step 1.2: Assess the current state of the organisation • Step 1.3: Compile summarised report: Your understanding of the change initiative ➝

Technical PM phases and activities	CM phases and activities
1.5 Initial project budget is compiled.	
1.6 The project manager and project team are selected (which could be internal personnel or external consultants).	
2. PLANNING PHASE	
2.1 Project team prepares draft project plan.	
2.2 Present draft project plan to project steering committee for approval.	
	• Step 2.1: Compile the CM team structure • Step 2.2: Assemble the CM team • Step 2.3: Conduct a sponsorship analysis • Step 2.4: Compile comm plan • Step 2.5: Compile resistance management (RM) plan • Step 2.6: Compile integrated CM plan
Technical PM phases and activities	**CM phases and activities**
2.3 Data gathered about the organisation's current state and the desired future state.	
2.4 Solution to address the identified gap between the current state and the desired future state is identified.	
2.5 Solution options are then costed and a specific option is recommended.	
2.6 Recommended option is presented to project steering committee for approval.	
2.7 Project plan is updated with all necessary detail and presented to project steering committee for approval.	
	• Step 2.7: Integrate CM plan with tech PM plan • Step 3.1: Implement comm plan for this step • Step 3.2: Implement RM plan for this step (if necessary)
3. EXECUTION AND MONITORING PHASE	
3.1 Steps in the technical project plan are now implemented and monitored.	• Step 3.1: Implement comm plan for this step • Step 3.2: Implement RM plan for this step (if necessary) ➤

Technical PM phases and activities	CM phases and activities
3.2 Measure progress and solution results/performance.	• Step 3.1: Implement comm plan for this step • Step 3.2: Implement RM plan for this step (if necessary)
	• Step 4.1: Track progress against CM plan • Step 4.2: Implement corrective measures where necessary
3.3 Implement modifications and adaptations where necessary (including the identification of changes, risks and issues; the review of deliverable quality; and the measurement of each deliverable being produced against the acceptance criteria).	• Step 3.1: Implement comm plan for this step • Step 3.2: Implement RM plan for this step (if necessary)
	• Step 5.1: Gather feedback from stakeholders • Step 5.2: Implement corrective measures where necessary • Step 5.3: Celebrate and reward successes
Technical PM phases and activities	**CM phases and activities**
3.4 Customer accepts final solution once all deliverables have been produced.	• Step 3.1: Implement comm plan for this step
4. CLOSING PHASE	
4.1 Project team obtains permission from project steering committee to terminate project.	
4.2 Project termination is communicated to all applicable stakeholders.	• Step 3.1: Implement comm plan for this step
4.3 Post-implementation review is conducted.	• Step 5.4: Evaluate entire CM process • Step 6.1: Transfer CM responsibilities • Step 6.2: Submit final CM report
4.4 Project team is dissolved.	
	• Step 6.3: Dissolve the CM project team
4.5 Project steering committee is dissolved.	

Conclusion

There are importance differences between individual and organisational change management which change managers must understand, as each one is managed differently. Although there are various available well-researched theories of individual change management, the change manager must choose and use the one most applicable to the current organisational change initiative being managed. There are also well-known theories of organisational change management available to provide a framework for managing organisational change. However, no matter what framework is used, the main challenge for the change manager is to integrate this framework with the steps of the technical project. Finally, a new proposed structured process called the Hugh Structured Change Management Process (HSCMP) is propagated for use by change managers to manage the implementation of any organisational change initiative. The HSCMP is structured, practical and consists of detailed steps that can be followed.

Reflection questions

1. Discuss the difference between change and transition.
2. Explain which theory of individual change transition you prefer and give reasons for your choice.
3. Discuss what the similarities are between the different approaches to organisational CM.
4. Explain rich versus lean channels of change communication.
5. Discuss the six techniques available to overcome resistance to change.
6. Explain why it is important to integrate CM with PM.

Multiple-choice questions

1. PM and CM follow different processes.
    a. True
    b. False

2. Individual and organisational change is the same, as both refer to change.
    a. True
    b. False

3. Research by Prosci has identified, amongst others, the following as having an impact on CM:
    a. Sponsorship, communication, dedicated resources and middle management

    b. Sponsorship, communication, enough resources and front-line employees

    c. Middle management, front-line employees, a structured CM methodology and a structured PM process

    d. Communication, dedicated resources, senior management and middle management

4. The ADKAR model includes:
   a. awareness, desire, theory, ability and reinforcement
   b. awareness, desire, knowledge, ability and reinforcement
   c. awareness, desire, theory, ability and sustainability
   d. None of the above

5. Kurt Lewin's approach to organisational change management entails:
   a. movement, unfreezing and refreezing
   b. preparation, movement and refreezing
   c. unfreezing, movement and refreezing
   d. All of the above

6. Regarding stakeholders in CM:
   a. A primary sponsor is the same as an executive sponsor
   b. A secondary sponsor is the same as an influencer
   c. Secondary sponsors include supervisors
   d. All of the above

References

Adams, JD, Hayes, J & Hopson, B. 1976. *Transition: understanding and managing personal change.* London: Martin Robertson.

Bridges, W. 1991. *Managing transitions: making the most of change.* Reading, MA: Addison-Wesley.

Conner Partners. 2004. *How to be an effective sponsor of major organizational change.* https://www ingeniumcommunications.com/wp-content/uploads/2018/10/How-to-Be-an-Effective-Sponsor-of-Major-Organizational-Change-.pdf.

Creasy, TJ. 2020. Understanding why some communications work and others don't. https://blog.prosci.com/understanding-why-some-communications-work-and-others-dont (Accessed 26 July 2021).

Cummings, G & Worley, G. 2015. *Organization development and change.* 10th ed. Stamford, CT: Cengage Learning.

Cummings, G, Worley, G & Donovan, P. 2020. *Organization development and change.* London: Cengage Learning.

Hiatt, JM. 2006. *ADKAR: a model for change in business, government and our community*. Loveland, CO: Prosci Learning Center Publications.

Hiatt, JM & Creasey, TJ. 2003. *Change management: the people side of change*. Loveland, CO: Proci Learning Center Publications.

Hultman, KE. 1995. 'Scaling the wall of resistance'. *Training and Development* 49(10): 15–18.

Implementation Management Associates. 2010. *10 tips for building readiness for change*. https://www.imaworldwide.com/hs-fs/hub/135807/file-21974536-pdf/documents/ebooks/10_tips_for_building_readiness_for_change_ebook.pdf.

Jones, DJ & Recardo, RJ. 2013. *Leading and implementing business change: making change stick in the contemporary organization*. New York: Routledge.

Kotter, JP. 1995. 'Leading change: why transformational efforts fail'. *Harvard Business Review* 73(2): 59–67.

Kotter, JP & Schlesinger, LA. 1979. 'Choosing strategies for change'. *Harvard Business Review* 57(2): 106–114.

Kübler-Ross, E. 1969. *On death and dying*. New York: Scribner.

Lombardi, J. 2018. *Method 123: empowering managers: project management guidebook*. https://edchivers.com/images/Method123%20PM%20Guide%20Book.pdf

Miller, D. 2011. *Successful change: how to implement change through people*. Haywards Heath: Changefirst.

Mingus, NB. 2002. *Alpha teach yourself project management in 24 hours*. Madison, WI: CWL Publishing.

Palmer, I, Dunford, R & Akin, G. 2006. *Managing organizational change: a multiple perspectives approach*. New York: McGraw-Hill.

PMI (Project Management Institute). 2017. *The project management body of knowledge (PMBOK guide)*. 6th ed. Newtown Square, PA: Project Management Institute.

Prosci. 2018. *5 dimensions of change management and project management integration*. https://www.prosci.com/resources/articles/change-management-and-project-management-dimensions (Accessed 28 July 2021).

Prosci. 2020. *Best practices in change management*. https://www.prosci.com/hubfs/2.downloads/research-executive-summaries/11th%20Edition-Best-Practices-Executive-Summary-11-2020.pdf?hsLang=en-ca (Accessed 28 July 2021).

Robbins, SP, Judge, TA, Odendaal, A, & Roodt, G. 2016. *Organisational behaviour: global and southern African perspectives*. 3rd ed. Cape Town: Pearson Education South Africa.

Schein, EH. 2002. 'Models and tools for stability and change in human system'. *Reflections* 4(2): 34–46.

Smith, C. 2014. The key differences between change management and project management. https://change.walkme.com/the-key-differences-between-change-management-and-project-management/ (Accessed 28 July 2021).

Straker, D. 2010. *Changing minds*. 2nd ed. Crowthorne: Syque Press.

Chapter 4

The role of the organisation development consultant

Charles OK Allen-ILE

Learning outcomes

After reading this chapter, you should be able to:

- describe who an organisation development (OD) consultant is
- differentiate between an internal and an external consultant
- identify some of the potential ethical dilemmas likely to confront an OD practitioner
- explain the attributes that a graduate OD consultant should possess.

Introduction

This chapter looks at what organisation development (OD) consultants do, their place in the people-management value chain and how they fulfil their roles in the organisation. The kind of professional mindset that OD consultants should possess and display is also elucidated in addition to the levels, and indeed depth, of knowledge someone should possess in order to make an effective OD consultant. This exposition is introductory and generic. Later, in Chapter 10 and onwards, the relevant varied tools and technologies in the OD consultant's arsenal of operation are dealt with in greater detail.

The OD consultant has become increasingly central to successful people management in organisations. This centrality relates not so much to the 'process' functions of people management, but rather to unravelling and maximising the innate, and sometimes latent, potential of individuals in the organisational context. It has been accepted that OD consultants can be regarded as 'change agents' (Argyris, 1992; 1997). They help their client organisations to identify and resolve potential or actual negative practices, thereby improving their overall performance. As such, OD consultants are expected to exhibit behaviours that are consistent with such a lofty role.

The themes pertaining to effective OD consultant behaviour include:

- the need for self-awareness and self-understanding
- the need for the consultant to have a cognitive map and an in-depth grasp of the theories that are needed for analysing what is going on and what is functional and dysfunctional in the client system.

Finally, it is also important for the OD consultant to appreciate and be able to articulate what the client is capable of learning from. This is in addition to understanding what could hurt the client, and indeed what could cause the client to become resistant to the system (French, Bell & Zawacki, 1994).

Some of these OD consultant behaviours can actually be regarded as almost intuitive as they balance, mediate or modify any of an array of countervailing forces in the organisation. These forces can be external or internal to the organisation and may include economic, technological or political to subcultural, inter- or intra-group and inter- or intra-personal dynamics in the organisation.

The complexity of the expected behaviours of the OD consultant makes it important to clarify and/or to explore the roles and tasks of the OD consultant.

The role and task of organisation development consultants

In the history and literature on OD, the term 'roles' is used interchangeably with 'behaviours'; thus in examining OD consultants' roles, the analyst is essentially focusing on the behaviours they should acquire and/or exhibit in their practice. This diffusion of meaning of the terms or concepts can be traced back to the earlier days of the T-group (training group) movement (French, 1982). The contributions of behavioural scientists and practitioners to the early origins of OD cannot be overemphasised, and have been well documented by French and Bell (1984).

In the life cycle of organisations, from time to time some may require help in improving their operations, help which may come from professionals who are not employees of such organisations. In other instances, some organisations may have the resources to employ an in-house professional. OD consultants may therefore be **external** or **internal**. The main role of such professionals is to assist organisations in identifying problem areas or the root causes of problems. They also help them to determine how to avoid the onset of problems. However, where problems have already arisen, OD consultants can implement measures for effectively resolving or coping with them.

In summary, the major generic roles of OD consultants are as follows:

- **Establishing or identifying the problem facing the organisation:** In this role, they set up or lay the groundwork or foundation for **naming,**

defining and **describing** the problem or problems being experienced by the organisation. Also in this role, they prove, demonstrate or show how the problem originated. This is achieved by employing specific diagnostic tools. This can be a very complex, elaborate and involved process because the problems are sometimes very intricate, with many strands or elements. Some of the diagnostic tools they employ to achieve this include specifically designed observations, employee interviews and questionnaires. The ease with which consultants are able to play this role may depend on whether they are internal or external consultants. Internal consultants are usually more familiar with the organisation and have easier access to the people and data. They also have a better understanding of the organisational culture and climate, and therefore how better to navigate the different barriers and nuances that constitute the organisation's experiences. On the other hand, the internal OD consultant is likely to be less objective and forthright in accessing and proffering solutions than an external one.

- **Designing an intervention programme for solving the problem:** This role is at the core of the role of OD consultants, because consultants have to secure the commitment of the client organisation's members, and especially the management. In this role, the consultant works with all the parties to formulate courses of action for addressing the identified problem(s). In doing this, it is acknowledged that the best solutions are usually those implemented with the active participation of all relevant stakeholders within the client organisation. Furthermore, where possible, such intervention should cause the least amount of disruption possible to the ongoing activities of the organisation and to the life of its members.

- **Impact evaluation and entrenchment:** In this role, the OD consultant endeavours to determine whether the intervention introduced is having the intended or desired impact on the client organisation and its people. Evidently, this ongoing evaluation of the intervention may be easier for an internal OD consultant to oversee than it would be for an external consultant. The time available to external consultants to implement and evaluate an intervention tends to be limited if they are to avoid overstaying their welcome. This challenge requires the external consultant to be more discerning and realistic in terms of the nature of the intervention that is designed or proposed if he/she is to realise the full dividends of the engagement.

- **Enabling the internalisation of the introduced intervention:** This is another major challenge in the role of the OD consultant, because an OD intervention would be considered fruitless if the consultant does not succeed in helping the client organisation's members to accept what was recommended. OD consultants are more likely to succeed in this role if they actively involve the organisation's members in all the phases of the intervention, from problem identification to impact evaluation. Some OD writers (eg Dayal, 1967) refer to this role as the **coping** role or phase in OD consulting. Also built into this role should be the ability of the OD consultant, and to some extent the client organisation, to reward or affirm the organisation's members who embraced the intervention, whilst exploring modalities for winning over those who may still be resistant.

The 'roles' highlighted in the foregoing section point to **what** OD consultants are expected to do and **how** they are expected to behave once they are engaged to intervene in an organisation. However, these derive from anecdotes and the general experiences of practitioners in the past. It has been argued (Bradford & Burke, 2014; Burnes & Cooke, 2012) that further research needs to be undertaken to empirically determine what the roles of OD consultants actually are. This is because Worley and Feyerherm (2003) argue that OD practice is presently in a 'fragmented state'. With the above in mind, we now turn to look at the position an OD consultant occupies in the organisation.

The position of the organisation development consultant

OD practitioners are usually individuals who have been given the responsibility of executing a planned change process within an organisation. They do this by challenging and changing the organisation's current practices (Mclean, 2009). An OD practitioner is therefore a person who carries out OD and who assists others (usually the organisation's employees) in implementing change interventions. The essential character of OD is that it is a helping profession that involves personal relationships between practitioners and organisation members. The OD consultant can therefore be seen as a person who specialises in OD as a profession. The practitioner may also be someone who has an OD-related 'content-oriented specialisation' such as organisation design or reward, or total quality management (TQM). Whilst such individuals may not have consciously set out to become OD consultants, their extensive experience in closely collaborating with OD practitioners would usually have gained them competency in OD. Furthermore, an OD professional can be any organisation manager or administrator (usually of a line unit or function) who, over time, applies OD competencies in his/her own work areas.

As has earlier been alluded to, there are generally two classes of OD consultants – external and internal – but in most cases, they are external. If they are employees of the organisation, they would need to distance themselves as much as possible from its internal dynamics; thus, it has been argued, the role of the OD consultant is a marginal one. The concept of **marginality** was earlier explored by Browne, Cotton and Golembiewski (1977: 494), who explained that 'the marginal person is someone who stands on the boundary between two or more groups that have differing value systems, goals, and behaviour patterns'. The OD consultant has to be someone who is unfettered by the internal dynamics of a particular organisation, and must be able to play roles that cross the boundaries of multiple parties of the organisation. More recently, Cummings and Worley (2015) further crystallised this concept.

The in-house or **internal OD consultant** is often perceived as a member of a particular unit within the organisation, usually the human resources or people-management function, or sometimes even a member of another professional service-provision unit, such as information technology (IT) or finance, that has a history of supporting internal customers with specific problems. These individuals have the specific responsibility of helping the organisation to implement and manage change programmes, and this state of being embedded in the organisation could compromise their effectiveness. This situation places a much greater burden on such consultants to raise their standards of objectivity and professionalism.

The **external consultant**, however, as the name implies, is a practitioner from outside who is completely independent of the organisation. It is becoming increasingly common for organisations to engage an external consultant to work with an internal practitioner as an **internal–external practitioner team**. This approach has been found to be effective in a number of circumstances. The external practitioner brings a particular level of expertise, objectivity and fresh insights, while the internal consultant brings in-depth knowledge about the organisation, ease of access to resources and organisational memory. This is probably the most effective approach to OD consulting.

Table 4.1 on page 83 compares and contrasts the differences between internal and external consultants, as well as the advantages and disadvantages. Regardless of whether the consultant is internal or external, Kenton, Moody and Taylor (2003) support the proposition of Cockman, Evans and Reynolds (1992) that, in any intervention, all OD consultants must work through the phases of the consultancy cycle with the client.

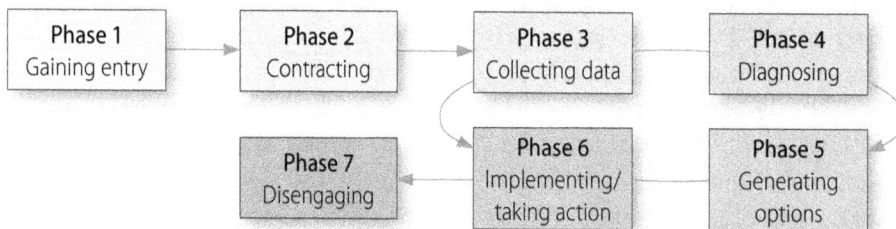

Figure 4.1 The consultancy cycle (Cockman, Evans & Reynolds, 1992, cited in Kenton, Moody & Taylor, 2003: 15)

Table 4.1 Comparison between internal and external consultants (adapted from Kenton, Moody & Taylor, 2003; Authenticity Consulting, nd)

Criteria	Internal	External
Primary concerns	Usually preoccupied with retaining their employment through maintaining long-lasting relationships with influential organisation members	Focus on the results to be achieved by the intervention. Also, relationships with organisation members tend to be short term
Perception of skills possessed	Being employees, their skill sets are usually well known to the organisation	Perceived as specialists coming in with strong expertise
Source of credibility with the client organisation	Record of previous performance and quality of relationships are known. Credibility through history of interactions within the business	Known by virtue of their reputation and expertise, which precedes them. Credibility through brand status
Possible biases that could affect them	Influenced by and part of the organisational culture. Also affected by the personalities and even internal politics	Influenced by personal and professional background
Knowledge base	Already know a lot about the organisation in addition to existing professional knowledge	Apart from acquired professional knowledge, they face the challenge of learning about the organisation from the onset
Client's perception of the consultant	Member of the organisation who might also be part of the problem. Perceived as organisational 'spy'	An independent outsider who is not part of the problem. Perceived as objective
Client's acceptance of the consultant	Is dependent on the support of top management and the strength of the internal relationships forged	Is dependent on top management and the skills they are coming with
Influence and range of influence of the consultant	Able to easily mobilise resources. Cannot readily opt out of the project	Works within the scope and terms of the contract with the client, which also allows him/her the option to leave the project
Stake in the success of the intervention	High investment in final success	Low investment in final success
Availability for consultations	Freely accessible and available	Charges time-on-task, rarely available and expensive to secure

Regardless of whether OD consultants are external or internal, the principle of marginality still requires them to exhibit certain characteristics in performing their roles. These include:

- maintaining high levels of **objectivity**
- remaining **neutral** in all situations
- exhibiting **open-mindedness** towards all issues
- being **flexible** and willing to accommodate alternative ideas and suggestions
- avoiding being **prejudiced**, bigoted, and intolerant or **dogmatic**.

Consultants who display these characteristics are better able to encourage cohesion and avoid extreme divergent or opposing viewpoints.

In general, an effective OD consultant should be someone who holds a 'position of trust' with both the internal stakeholders (owners, directors, managers and employees) and external stakeholders (customers, third-party service providers and the surrounding community) of the organisation. This position of trust is earned by the professionalism, expertise, skills and competencies of the OD consultant. These attributes will be discussed in a later section of this chapter.

Consulting on the boundary

This section of the chapter will briefly look at the place of (management) consulting as a human resource/people-management activity in organisations. An attempt will be made to reflect on the critique of people management's pretension of being able to strategically influence business organisations (Hammonds, 2005). As mentioned earlier, internal practitioners are people who have qualified as industrial-organisational (I-O) psychologists or graduates of human resource management and would most likely be located, as business partners, within the human resource department of the organisation. The questions then are: (1) How can such employees/operatives of the organisation be reasonably expected to provide effective and dispassionate OD consulting? and (2) What are the boundaries that they would have to navigate?

Studies on different management functions (Armstrong, 1986; Willmott, 1986) indicated that managerial professions have attempted to maintain positions of command of the organisation through specialism. However, until recently, human resource professionals have not been able to compete at group level for access to key positions of command. Attainment of such levels of recognition would enable OD consultants to attract the level of influence that would assure a significant impact for their interventions. Lawler and Mohrman (2003), Ulrich (1997) and Ulrich and Brockbank (2005) argue that internal OD consultants can only achieve significant impact if they are able to 'deliver value' to managers and shareholders by reconceptualising their role as 'strategic business partners'.

In an Australian study of 'internal consultants' conducted between 2004 and 2008, Wright (2008) attempted to construct a desired identity for human resource managers as 'business partners' and 'internal consultants'. The research found that the respondents (human resource internal consultants) believed that managers and executives were their 'clients', thus implying that they were able to demarcate the boundary of their consulting role as being able to 'positively influence' the organisation even as internal consultants. A prominent imagery reported by this research is that in which the internal consultants referred to themselves as 'trusted advisers' or partners to their clients, consistent with the terminology used by Ulrich and Brockbank (2005). The research goes on to assert that the imagery of the 'trusted advisers' implied the acceptance of 'internal consultants' as individuals with high levels of expertise in the organisation whose interventions are taken seriously. This situation extended the boundaries of their roles to those of being 'coaches', 'counsellors', 'sounding boards', 'confidantes' and even 'devil's advocates' to senior executives in their organisations. Wright's (2008) research also emphasised OD consultants' role as 'change agents' in terms of the superiority of their knowledge and their capacity to act as a bridge between their organisation and 'leading-edge methodologies' in their organisations.

A most significant outcome of this study is the fact that OD consultants reported that their roles and activities span several boundaries. These boundary-spanning activities reveal a structural ambiguity—that OD consultants, especially internal consultants, do not see any restrictions to their ability to move between organisational sub-units and functional and operational divisions. OD consultants thus see themselves as having a high status within the organisation, and as being self-sufficient and independent.

This boundary-spanning imagery of the roles of OD consultants implies that they see themselves not as mere administrators, but more as 'senior partners' and 'champions of change'. However, Wright (2008) cautions that despite this positive imagery, certain intra-organisational boundaries still exist. Ultimately, this author is in agreement with the suggestions of Harvey (1977), namely that the ideal consulting arrangement is a team composed of both internal and external consultants working together in 'draining organisational swamps', thereby cancelling out each other's weaknesses and building on each other's strengths.

In summary, the boundaries of the role of (internal) OD consultants would continue to shift and expand for as long as they remain professional, competent and objective, and display experience-based expertise.

Activity

Drawing on your knowledge of the disciplines and fields of psychology/I-O psychology and human resources management, identify **five core focus issues** in the scope or boundary of the role of the OD consultant that you consider to be unique to these disciplines or fields.

Compare your identified focus issues with those of two of your study colleagues, and analyse why two similarly identified focus issues are crucial for strengthening and/or expanding the boundary of OD consulting.

In concluding this discussion and consistent with the observations of Kitay and Wright (2007), Watson (2002) and Zabusky and Barley (1997), the caveat (refer to Varney, 1979) that arises in respect of the boundary of OD consulting is that it is not only the preserve of human resource management or I-O psychology, because appropriately experienced and skilled general management consultants are also able to provide OD consulting services to organisations. The main bulwark against the erosion of this preserve would be the continued professionalisation of OD consulting by practitioners.

Emotional resilience in organisation development consulting

The role of an OD consultant is often an emotionally demanding one. As the reader may be aware by now, most of the work OD consultants are required to do in any organisation involves bringing about change from an undesired state of affairs to a more constructive one. The process of change is stressful by nature.

Since the OD consultant is at the centre of this change process (Argyris, 1992), he/she would be expected to help the organisation and its members to address their experiences of anxiety and fear relating to the impending change. In doing this, the consultant also helps the organisation to manage the ambiguities and required recommitments from one set of values to another that would be expected. In all of these roller-coasters of activities, the emotional stability of the consultant would also be tested and challenged.

OD practitioners should thus be able to distinguish between their own emotional responses and the requirements of the intervention environment. This is necessary if they are to be able to appropriately model the emotional responses of all the parties involved in or affected by the intervention process. This emotional stability or resilience helps provide support to and reframe the perspectives of the client organisation. This level of emotional resilience increases with age, experience and training on the part of the consultant.

Emotional resilience, in the context of this section, refers to the ability to express, recognise and regulate emotions in oneself and others, and the ability to use emotions in decision making and thinking. As alluded to in the preceding section, by its very nature the OD field particularly calls for practitioners to perform with a high degree of self-awareness (Varney et al, 1999). According to Sullivan, Rothwell and Worley (2009), they are also expected to exhibit refined **human behaviour skills** (including interpersonal and communication skills, and the self-awareness referred to above). In the consulting role, emotional resilience helps the OD practitioner to recognise potentially emotional issues that may not be apparent in academic/theoretical models and diagnostic data.

In one of the seminal analyses of 'the depth of organisational intervention' that the OD consultant should be concerned with, Harrison (1994) identified the consultant as a 'group leader' whose role in the management of the emotions of members should include self-diagnosis and evaluation of the levels and/or direction of emotions at any given point in the intervention process. In this role, the OD consultant is expected to periodically disengage from the process in order to be able to effectively channel the emotions that may arise. In confirmation of this assertion, the study by Kaarst-Brown (1999) averred that emotional resilience enables OD consultants to become symbols of power redistribution and organisational empowerment in that it provides an opportunity for them to exercise the high level of specialised knowledge and expertise that they possess.

Professional values and ethics in organisation development consulting

Values

According to Worley and Feyerherm (2003), the field of OD was founded on humanistic values and ethical concerns. These humanistic values were articulated, a long time ago, by Tannenbaum and Davis (1969) to include the **belief in the inherent goodness of people** and to state that, with every possible opportunity, **people's humanity should always be affirmed**. OD consultants should thus have a democratic orientation and a sense of social justice. Furthermore, they should be concerned about the holistic development of the individual and should **display a sense of fairness, openness and choice, and the ability to balance independence and teamwork**. A study by Church, Burke and Van Eynde (1994) observed that OD practitioners had moved away considerably from these values and had become more oriented toward 'results' and the bottom line. They went on to argue that consultants were becoming more concerned with the expression of personal power and reaping the rewards of consulting relationships. Future OD practitioners need to return to the 'original values' to guide their behaviour and practice.

Having noted the foregoing, this author is not necessarily arguing against the school of thought that advocates that OD should 'serve business' (eg Worren, Ruddle & Moore, 1999; 2000), but is in agreement with Farias and Johnson (2000) and Hornstein (2001), who posit that OD should avoid creating a consultant–client relationship that fosters dependency, where the consultant becomes the omniscient expert who solves all the client's problems, which is in itself an untenable expectation. This position is also in support of the views of Block (1999) and Schein (1999), namely that OD practitioners should be 'a pair of hands' or 'experts' whose greatest value can be delivered when the consulting relationship is a collaborative one. The consultant guides the process with methods that encourage the client organisation to ultimately own the process and the result.

Ethics

The globalisation of organisations has heightened the need for OD to pay closer attention to the ethics of practitioners. Even though not much research has been done on the topic of ethics from an OD perspective, the field of OD cannot afford to overlook its importance. The questions that arise in this regard are: What ethical values are practitioners likely to transmit across cultures—within or across national/international boundaries? What conflicts in values are OD consultants likely to encounter in their practice?

On the question of cross-cultural ethics in OD consulting, a study by White and Rhodeback (1992) examined the nature and extent to which cultural differences have a bearing on perceptions of ethical OD consulting behaviours of US and Taiwanese samples. The result revealed significant cultural differences in perceptions of ethicality between the two groups. Whilst the US respondents were more aware of the possibility of encountering ethical dilemmas, the Taiwanese participants reported a higher likelihood of its actual occurrence. The study therefore recommends that the OD profession should incorporate ethics training and also adopt a code of ethics for practitioners.

The role episode model of **ethicality** (White & Wooten, 1986) proposes that change agents and client systems, upon their initial encounter, should bring their respective values, goals, needs, skills, abilities and resources to the OD effort. According to White and Rhodeback (1992), without the resolution of the issues surrounding these factors, the intervention or 'role episode' would be left vulnerable to role conflict and ambiguity. It is believed that this gap leaves room for the emergence of ethical dilemmas. Even though there may be numerous ways in which these ethical dilemmas may present themselves, White and Rhodeback (1992) synthesise and report five general categories:

1. **Misrepresentation/collusion:** On the part of the OD consultant, this dilemma occurs when there is a misrepresentation of the skill base that he/she possesses. It also occurs when an exaggerated claim is made of the intervention process or outcome. On the part of the client organisation, it exists when the client system misrepresents the organisation's interests, goals or needs (French & Bell, 1984; Maidment & Losito, 1980; Pfeiffer & Jones, 1977).

2. **Misuse of data:** This dilemma relates to situations where data that were originally collected to facilitate the OD process are then diverted and used punitively by members of the client system (Shay, 1965; Walton & Warwick, 1973; Zaltman & Duncan, 1976).

3. **Manipulation/coercion:** This is a broad group used to describe those situations where members of the client system are required, against their will, to participate in activities within the OD change process (Lippitt & Lippitt, 1978; Warwick & Kelman, 1973).

4. **Value and goal conflict:** This dilemma arises when the change goals are ambiguously defined or when the change agent or client system withholds needed services or resources, respectively (Warwick & Kelman, 1973; Zaltman & Duncan, 1976).

5. **Technical ineptness:** This ethical dilemma is evident where there is a lack of skill, knowledge or ability to effectively select or implement appropriate intervention strategies (French & Bell, 1984; Huse, 1980; Mosley, 1970).

A subtle insight emanating from the above discussion is the fallacy of the misplaced overemphasis, in historical OD ethics literature, on only the behaviour of the consultant. It is, however, becoming more apparent that there should be a shared responsibility for the resolution of ethical dilemmas between the change agent and the client organisation. If a code of ethics for OD consultants is implemented, it should also incorporate ways in which the change agent could effectively deal with the unethical behaviour of the client whilst being sensitive to the cultural nuances that exist in a cross-cultural intervention scenario.

Ethical dilemma scenario for OD consultants

Popular media in South Africa recently reported that the chief executives of certain state parastatals – among them the South African Broadcasting Corporation (SABC), South African Airways (SAA) and the Passenger Rail Agency of South Africa (PRASA) – had misrepresented the educational qualifications they possess. These revelations are beginning to negatively affect staff

➞

morale in these organisations. You are an **internal** OD consultant in one of these organisations who has been requested to look into the problem with a view to improving staff morale and organisational climate. Identify three ethical dilemmas, if any, that this assignment would present to you and how you would circumvent them.

The systems-psychodynamic perspective on the role of the organisation development consultant

According to Czander (1993), the systems-psychodynamic perspective has been traced back to the works of Sigmund Freud, even though there is no record of his actually commenting on its application to the world of work. Essentially, this view does not agree with the economistic view of work, but rather argues that the use of statistical analysis in an attempt to understand people at work is not, of itself, very useful. The psychodynamic perspective departs from the premise that work is an unpleasant experience for humans—that is, people only work because of the 'reward' that ultimately comes from it. The psychodynamic viewpoint further sees an organisation as a macrosystem (with sub-micro- and mesosystems) with its own conscious and unconscious life. According to this viewpoint, organisations, much like people, experience fears, anxieties, conflicts and other 'psychological states', which are sometimes repressed, projected or denied. Adherents of this viewpoint therefore believe that to get a deeper understanding of organisational dynamics, scholars and consultants need to study the unconscious behaviours of the organisation. For the purposes of this chapter, we will not delve in-depth into the tenets of this perspective. The interest in this perspective is thus only to appreciate how it helps in understanding the roles of OD consultants in organisational intervention. Apart from the brief mention made in this chapter, we will elaborate a little more on systems psychodynamics as an approach to interventions in Chapter 9.

Cilliers and Koortzen (2000) aptly articulate how this perspective can be employed in understanding the role of OD consultants in organisations. They identify two ways: (1) that OD practitioners can be consultants to the system and its parts; and (2) that OD consultants can serve as trainers of organisations' human resource personnel and other leaders or managers in order to better understand the psychodynamic way of thinking. They further agree with Czander (1993) by stating that consulting from this stance implies 'making sense of nonsense' by being able to explore the unconscious meaning of organisational events.

The competencies of the organisation development consultant and the role of 'graduateness'

Competencies

In the South African context, the South African Board for People Practices (SABPP) (2012) and Nel et al (2014) have proffered some 'standards' that should relate to OD practitioners, where competency is defined as managing oneself professionally to deliver a high standard of work. The SABPP's standards address those person- and job-specific requirements that organisations need to put in place in order to ensure that the organisation and its employees derive maximum mutual benefits from the workplace. Related to these lofty ideals are the 'competencies' that clearly express **what professionals in the field should be able to deliver**. These competencies, whilst specifically envisioned for the people-management profession as a whole, are also applicable to OD consultants.

Table 4.2 Summary of some of the most important competencies for the organisation development consultant (adapted from SABPP, 2012; Nel et al, 2014)

Competency	Description
1. Leadership and personal credibility	The leadership skill to drive the profession in the organisation and the personal credibility to secure acceptance and/or support for introduced initiatives
2. Organisational capability	A thorough understanding of and active participation in realising the strategic objectives of the organisation
3. Solution creation and implementation	The ability to design, introduce and implement interventions and practices that meet the immediate and long-term needs of the organisation
4. Interpersonal and communication skills	The practitioner's ability to successfully manage relationships and the ability to effectively transmit meaning
5. Citizenship for the future	The consultant's ability to identify, initiate and oversee innovative practices in relation to technology and organisational ecology in a manner that ensures the future sustainability of the organisation

'Graduateness'

Simply put, 'graduateness' has been described as 'the generic qualities that might be expected of any graduate' (British HEQC, 1995: 3); thus the focus of this section of the chapter is to examine the kinds of training, education and overall preparation that OD consultants should receive in preparation for effective and meaningful practice. As a starting point, it may be necessary to caution the reader that, since no universally agreed to standard of OD practice exists, the expected qualities that an aspiring OD practitioner should possess are also indeterminate. Having said that, it is still important to attempt to outline the qualities that should prepare someone for successful OD consulting. Therefore, what follows would by no means be definitive or absolute. However, before attempting this, there is a need to further explore the concept of 'graduateness'. Walsh and Kotzee (2010) attempted to reconcile 'graduateness' and work-based learning. They sought to explore the issues involved in drawing directly on experience in the workplace as material for higher-level learning. Their proposition may be of interest in the training of future OD practitioners by utilising a model that moves slightly away from too much focus on disciplinary content to one that draws from workplace experience. In the South African open distance learning (ODL) context, the concept of 'graduateness' has been extensively articulated by Coetzee (2011; 2012), among other scholars. For the purpose of this text, the concept is only highlighted in the context of presumed appropriate OD practitioner qualities.

Wheelahan (2002: 4) opines that 'graduateness' should be taken to mean 'the meta-thinking or learning skills that people acquire which are contextualised in the occupations or professions in which they work or are destined to work'. This idea was extended to include knowledge or **fitness for practice** which comes from one's sociocultural readiness (in terms of values, norms, morals, citizenship behaviour and emotional intelligence) to fulfil the demands and expectations of the workplace and society. Or, put differently, it is the 'excellence' in all spheres of endeavour which academic attainment prepares one for—including creative thinking ability, situational adaptability, intellectual integrity, flexibility and problem-solving ability.

Even though there are several university degrees and non-academic training programmes geared towards developing OD professionals, one question to which there has been no agreed answer is: What does it take to be a good OD professional? Over the years, it has been quite easy for people to proclaim themselves to be OD professionals. This situation has been enabled by a number of factors, including:

- the fact that OD grew out of multiple disciplines
- the fact that it is perceived as a 'soft' entry-point through which to claim 'professionalism'
- the fact that the field has resisted legal guidelines for defining what an OD professional does
- the absence of methods for measuring a practitioner's competency
- the difficulty of enforcing discipline with regard to errant practitioners.

Varney (1979), Bushe and Marshak (2009) and Marshak (2009) attempted to address these challenges by trying to answer the question: What is an OD professional? Variously, they suggest that the problem persists because there has been no systematic definition of what an OD professional is or does. Following a distillation of literature, the following model for the development of an OD professional has been proposed. The model's starting point is the definition of three major developmental areas for an OD practitioner:

1. **Self-awareness and personal impact awareness:** This developmental area emphasises the knowledge that an individual has of his/her own personal needs, values and abilities, including such factors as the need for control and power, the need to achieve, the need for affiliation, and so forth.

2. **Conceptual, analytical and research skills:** This second developmental area involves social research skills, the ability to link scientific and organisational information, the ability to research and diagnose problems within the organisation, and the ability to evaluate, with the client, the results of the change process.

3. **Organisational change and influence skills:** This third developmental area requires the development of such specific skills as the ability to design interventions to meet particular situations, and the ability to make conscious choices about the various change strategies to be recommended. It also involves following up and providing continuity of direction.

In summary, the model recommends that well-developed OD consultants would be those in whom all three areas of learning are **integrated**, in a developmental sequence, in their training and education whilst also drawing on experiences in other professional fields such as psychology, sociology and other social sciences.

Activity

The national carrier of South Africa, SAA, is often in the news because of one management problem or another. Its supervising minister, the Minister of Public Enterprises, has asked you to submit an intervention proposal. Based on your knowledge of your role as an OD consultant, describe how you would go about carrying out this exercise.

Conclusion

Commentators and scholars of OD are unanimous in agreeing that OD is essentially concerned with system-wide planned change. They also agree that it makes use of the knowledge gained from behavioural science to target the human and social processes that affect the mindsets and cultures of individuals and groups in organisations. This is because the primary role of OD is to help organisations to improve their effectiveness. To do this, the OD consultant's role would therefore be to establish helping relationships within the organisation with and between individuals and groups in order to achieve the goal of effectiveness. The consultant thus plays different roles in helping the organisation to achieve better health and greater effectiveness. In all of these roles, three aspects stand out, namely:

1. building relationships
2. demonstrating expertise in human dynamics and intervention processes
3. paying attention to continual self-development as an OD practitioner.

Reflection questions

1. Identify any three top additional issues that you think should be included in an OD code of ethical practice. Provide a brief rationale on each one, explaining why the issue is central to ethics in OD.
2. Drawing from practical though hypothetical examples, discuss each of the five categories of ethical dilemmas that OD consulting is confronted with.
3. Explain the concept of **marginality** and undertake a detailed analysis of the five core characteristics that OD consultants are expected to exhibit in performing their roles.
4. Drawing on your knowledge of the disciplines and fields of psychology/ I-O psychology and human resource management, identify five **core focus issues** in the scope or boundary of the OD consultant that you consider to be unique to the disciplines or fields.
5. Compare your identified focus issues with those of two of your study colleagues and analyse why two similarly identified focus issues are crucial for strengthening and/or expanding the boundary of OD consulting.
6. In this chapter, four main generic roles of the OD consultant were articulated. Identify, from current popular media reports, an organisation that you believe would require an OD intervention and discuss how you think these four roles can be played out in that scenario.

Multiple-choice questions

1. In playing their roles, OD consultants sometimes have to conduct research and collect data.
   a. True
   b. False

2. The internal OD practitioner is an individual who is exclusively trained in the field of I-O psychology, as is the external OD practitioner.
   a. True
   b. False

3. Someone who stands on the boundary between two or more groups that have differing value systems, goals and behaviour patterns is said to be:
   a. a change agent
   b. a practitioner or consultant
   c. a people manager
   d. a marginal person

4. The 'position of trust' which OD consultants occupy implies that:
   a. they can influence top management only
   b. they embody the organisation's best interest
   c. they must be likeable
   d. they have the final say in change implementation

5. The classes of OD consultants are:
   a. human resource and management consultants
   b. change management (CM) agents and human resource consultants
   c. external and internal OD consultants
   d. industrial psychologists and behavioural scientists

6. When OD consultants say their roles span several boundaries it implies that:
   a. they are able to navigate across sub-units and levels
   b. they operate only from outside the organisation
   c. they are the only champions of organisational change
   d. they can only be human resource management specialists or I-O psychologists

References

Argyris, C. 1992. *Organisational learning*. Malden, MA: Blackwell.

Argyris, C. 1997. Kurt Lewin Award Lecture, 1997. 'Field theory as a basis for scholarly consulting'. *Journal of Social Issues* 53: 811–827.

Armstrong, P. 1986. 'Management control strategies and inter-professional competition: the cases of accountancy and personal management', in *Managing the labour process*, edited by D Knights & H Willmott. London: Gower: 19–43.

Authenticity Consulting. nd. Comparison of internal and external consultants. http://www.authenticityconsulting.com (Accessed 2 October 2015).

Block, P. 1999. *Flawless consulting: a guide to getting your expertise used*. San Francisco, CA: Jossey-Bass/Pfeiffer.

Bradford, DL & Burke, WW. 2014. 'Is organization development in crisis?' *The Journal of Applied Behavioural Science* 39(1): 97–115.

British HEQC. 1995. Executive Summary to Interim Report (December): 3.

Browne, P, Cotton, CC & Golembiewski, RT. 1977. 'Marginality and the OD practitioner'. *Journal of Applied Behavioural Science* 13(4): 493–506.

Burnes, B & Cooke, B. 2012. 'The past, present and future of organization development: taking the long view'. *Human Relations* 65(11): 1395–1429.

Bushe, GR & Marshak, RJ. 2009. 'Revisioning organizational development: diagnostic and dialogic premises and patterns of practice'. *Journal of Applied Behavioural Science* 45(3): 348–368.

Church, A, Burke, W & Van Eynde, D. 1994. 'Values, motives and interventions of organisation development practitioners'. *Group & Organisation Management* 19(1): 5–50.

Cilliers, F & Koortzen, P. 2000. 'The psychodynamic view on organisational behaviour'. *The Industrial-Organisational Psychologist* 38(2): 59–67.

Cockman, P, Evans, B & Reynolds, P. 1992. *Client-centred consulting—a practical guide for internal advisers and trainers.* London: McGraw-Hill.

Coetzee, M. 2011. Exploring distance learning students' graduateness in relation to employability. Unpublished research report, Department of Industrial and Organisational Psychology, University of South Africa, Pretoria.

Coetzee, M. 2012. 'A framework for developing student graduateness and employability in the economic and management sciences at the University of South Africa', in *Developing student graduateness and employability: issues, provocations, theory and practical guidelines,* edited by M Coetzee, M Botha, N Eccles, N Holthausen & H Neinaber. Randburg: Knowres.

Cummings, G & Worley, G. 2015. *Organization development and change.* 10th ed. Los Angeles, CA. University of Southern California.

Czander, WM. 1993. *The psychodynamics of work and organisations.* New York: Guilford Press.

Dayal, I. 1967. 'Organisation of work', in *Readings in group dynamics for managers and trainers,* edited by H Baumgertel, W Bennis & NN De. Bombay: Asia Publishing House.

Farias, G & Johnson, H. 2000. 'Organisational development and change management: setting the record straight'. *Journal of Applied Behavioural Science* 36(3): 376–379.

French, WL. 1982. 'The emergence and early history of organization development: with reference to influences on and interaction among some of the key actors'. *Group and Organization Studies* 7(3): 261–278.

French, WL & Bell, CH Jr. 1984. *Organisation development: behavioural science interventions for organisation improvement.* 3rd ed. Englewood Cliffs, NJ: Prentice Hall.

French, WL, Bell, CH Jr & Zawacki, RA. 1994. *Organisation development and transformation: managing effective change.* 4th ed. Boston, MA: Irwin McGraw-Hill.

Hammonds, KH. 2005. 'Why we hate HR'. *Fast Company* 97: 40–47.

Harrison, R. 1994. 'Choosing the depth of organization intervention', in *Organization development and transformation: managing effective change*, edited by WL French, CH Bell Jr & RA Zawacki. 4th ed. Boston, MA: Irwin McGraw-Hill.

Harvey, JB. 1977. 'Organisations as phrog farms'. *Organisational Dynamics* 5(4): 15–23.

Hornstein, H. 2001. 'Organisation development and change management: don't throw the baby out with the bath water'. *The Journal of Applied Behavioural Science* 37(2): 223–226.

Huse, EF. 1980. *Organisation development and change*. 2nd ed. St Paul, MN: West.

Kaarst-Brown, LM. 1999. 'Five symbolic roles of the external consultant. Integrating change, power and symbolism'. *Journal of Organization Change and Management* 12(6): 540–561.

Kenton, B, Moody, D & Taylor, B. 2003. *The role of the internal consultant*. Horsham: Roffey Park Institute.

Kitay, J & Wright, C. 2007. 'From prophets to profits: the occupational rhetoric of management consultants'. *Human Relations* 60(11): 1613–1640.

Lawler, EE & Mohrman, SA. 2003. 'HR as a strategic partner. What does it take to make it happen?' *Human Resource Planning* 26(3): 15–29.

Lippitt, GL & Lippitt, R. 1978. *The consulting process in action*. LaJolla, CA: University Associates.

Maidment, R & Losito, W. 1980. 'Ethics and the consultant/trainer' (Selected Paper No. 11). Madison, WI: American Society for Training and Development.

Marshak, RJ. 2009. *Organizational change: views from the edge*. Bethel, ME: The Lewin Centre.

Mclean, GN. 2009. *Organisation development principles, processes & performance*. San Francisco, CA: Berrett-Koehler.

Mosley, DC. 1970. 'Professional ethics and competence in management consulting'. *California Management Review* 12: 44–48.

Nel, P, Werner, A, Poisat, P, Sono, T, Du Plessis, A, Ngalo, P, Van Hoek, L & Botha, C. 2014. *Human resources management*. 9th ed. Cape Town: Oxford University Press.

Pfeiffer, JW & Jones, JE. 1977. 'Ethical considerations in consulting', in *The 1977 Annual handbook for group facilitators*, edited by JE Jones & JW Pfeiffer. LaJolla, CA: University Associates.

SABPP (South African Board for People Practices). 2012. National Human Resources Standards for South Africa. HR competency model. http://www.sabpp.co.za/hr.competencies (Accessed 8 October 2015).

Schein, EH. 1999. *Process consultation revisited: building the helping relationship*. Reading, MA: Addison-Wesley/Longman.

Shay, PW. 1965. 'Ethics and professional practices in management'. *Advanced Management Journal* 30(1): 13–20.

Sullivan, R, Rothwell, B & Worley, C. 2009. 20th edition of the organisation change and development competency effort. http//www.odnetwork.org (Accessed 29 May 2015).

Tannenbaum, R & Davis, S. 1969. 'Values, man and organisations'. *Industrial Management Review* 10: 67–83.

Ulrich, D. 1997. *Human resource champions.* Cambridge, MA: Harvard University Press.

Ulrich, D & Brockbank, W. 2005. *The HR value proposition.* Cambridge, MA: Harvard Business School Publishing.

Varney, GH. 1979. 'Training organisation development practitioners: a need for clarity of direction'. *Journal of Management Education* (July): 3–7.

Varney, GH, Worley, C, Darrow, A, Neubert, M, Cady, S & Guner, O. 1999. Guidelines for entry level competencies to organisation development and change. http://www.division.aoonline.org/ (Accessed 17 May 2015).

Walsh, A & Kotzee, B. 2010. 'Reconciling "graduateness" and work-based learning'. *Learning and Teaching in Higher Education* 4(1): 36–50.

Walton, RE & Warwick, DP. 1973. 'The ethics of organisation development'. *Journal of Applied Behavioural Science* 9(6): 681–699.

Warwick, DP & Kelman, HC. 1973. 'Ethics in social intervention', in *Process and phenomenon of social change,* edited by G Zaltman. New York: Wiley: Interscience.

Watson, T. 2002. 'Speaking professionally: occupational anxiety and discursive ingenuity among human resource specialists', in *Managing professional identities: knowledge performativity and the new professional,* edited by M Dent & S Whitehead. London: Routledge: 99–115.

Wheelahan, L. 2002. *Recognition of prior learning and the problem of 'graduateness': the changing face of Vocational Education and Training (VET).* 6th Annual Conference of Australian VET Research Association (VETRA), Sydney.

White, LP & Rhodeback, MJ. 1992. 'Ethical dilemmas in organisation development: a cross-cultural analysis'. *Journal of Business Ethics* 11: 663–670.

White, LP & Wooten, KC. 1986. *Professional ethics and practice in organisation development.* New York: Praeger.

Willmott, H. 1986. 'Organizing the profession: A theoretical and historical examination of the development of the major accountancy bodies in the U.K.' *Accounting, Organizations and Society* 11(6): 555–580.

Worley, CG & Feyerherm, AE. 2003. 'Reflections on the future of organisation development'. *The Journal of Applied Behavioral Science* 39(1): 97–115.

Worren, NAM, Ruddle, K & Moore, K. 1999. 'From organisational development to change management: the emergence of a new profession'. *Journal of Applied Behavioural Science* 35(3): 273–286.

Worren, NAM, Ruddle, K & Moore, K. 2000. 'Response to Farias and Johnson's commentary'. *Journal of Applied Behavioural Science* 36(3): 380–381.

Wright, C. 2008. 'Reinventing human resource management: business partners, internal consultants and the limits to professionalization'. *Human Relations* 61(8): 1063–1086.

Zabusky, SE & Barley, SR. 1997. 'You can't be a stone if you're cement: re-evaluating the emic identities of scientists in organization'. *Research in Organisational Behavior* 19: 361–404.

Zaltman, G & Duncan, R. 1976. 'Ethics in social change', in *Strategies of planned change,* edited by G Zaltman & R Duncan. New York: Wiley & Sons.

Chapter 5

Facilitation skills

Benny Olivier

Learning outcomes

After reading this chapter, you should be able to:

- understand the historic development of group facilitation
- explain the process of facilitation
- plan and conduct a group facilitation session using a predetermined structure
- apply micro-skills during a group facilitation session
- apply problem-solving and decision-making techniques in a group facilitation session
- know how to manage conflict in a group situation.

Introduction

Background

Ever since Carl Rogers described a group leader as a 'facilitator' in the 1960s, there has been a continuous interest in the field of facilitation (Rogers, 1961). This coincides with the evolutionary movement, that started in the 1960s and continues today, towards greater personal involvement and growth in all spheres of life. However, there is also a division in the academic and applied worlds concerning what facilitation actually is and how it is to be applied in different situations (Cilliers, 1991; Schwarz, 2002; Weaver & Farrell, 1997).

This debate as to what facilitation really is and how it should be applied is highlighted by the different definitions of facilitation, the role that the facilitator is supposed to play and the results that should be achieved at the conclusion of a facilitation session (Cilliers, 1991; Rees, 1991; Schwarz, 2002; Weaver & Farrell, 1997). People often respond with a mystical viewpoint of the esoteric powers that a facilitator is supposed to have. With this power, the facilitator is expected to unlock mysteries in group functioning and enable group members to experience incredible personal insight and achieve their goals productively. Because of this aura that surrounds the facilitator, there are a number of misconceptions regarding this role. For this reason, this chapter will firstly review the history and origin of facilitation, differentiate between the types of groups, discuss the process of facilitation, then explain the micro-skills available to a group facilitator, discuss problem solving and decision making in groups and, finally, end with how to manage conflict in groups.

History and origin of facilitation

The history of facilitation basically evolved from two sources in a time period when changing values seemed to dominate. The main streams of development stem from group therapy in the 1940s and T-groups (training groups) in 1946 (Yalom, 2005). The fields of study behind these developments are, on the one hand, psychiatry, dealing with so-called 'abnormal patients', and on the other hand, those fields of study dealing with so-called 'normal persons', such as social psychology, education, organisational science and industrial management. From these two mainstreams, other groups such as the encounter group (1960s), sensitivity training and numerous self-help groups such as Alcoholics Anonymous, Compassionate Friends, Overeaters Anonymous, and so forth, developed.

The difference between T-groups, encounter groups, self-help groups and therapy groups

The difference between T-groups, encounter groups, self-help groups and therapy groups is well described in the literature (Camp, Blanchard & Huszczo, 1986; French & Bell, 1998; Lieberman, Yalom & Miles, 1973; McGregor, 1967; Riordan & Beggs, 1988; Schaffer & Galinsky, 1974; Yalom, 2005). The terminology used to describe the group leader of these different groups varied according to the type of group. The original T-group used the term **'staff members'**, and later **'trainers'**, as opposed to **'group therapist'** from the clinical environment. The ascribing of the group leader as a **facilitator** was later used by Rogers (1961).

Carl Rogers: Facilitation of learning

In his book *Freedom to learn*, Carl Rogers (1983) applied his knowledge and experience about group psychotherapy, encounter groups and experiential learning in the educational environment. He used the term **'teacher-facilitator'** to describe the group leader who facilitates learning.

Rogers (1983) theorised that no person can teach another in a continuously changing environment. The facilitation of learning rests upon certain attitudinal qualities that exist in the personal relationship between facilitator and the learner. The qualities he described are the same as those that need to exist between a therapist and patient, namely:

- realness
- respect
- empathy.

Facilitation in industry

Modern organisations are attempting to extend the involvement of employees to areas that were once the domain of individual leaders (Robbins et al, 2016). There is an awareness that employees' opinions and ideas may contribute to solving critical organisational problems. This has resulted in a movement toward greater employee participation, which in turn gives rise to the formation of various decision-making work groups. Employees are requested to perform tasks which they have not done before and their leaders are requested to try new ways of leadership (Daft, 2015; Rees, 1991; Robbins et al, 2016).

The greater emphasis on teams and employee participation requires various new leadership styles and skills. Employee participation requires leaders to be more facilitating and less controlling, to dictate less and to promote empowerment. Participating leaders must know how to involve others, build consensus and obtain unity from those being led. They must act like **facilitators** to help others solve problems and make decisions. Employee participation requires leaders who can utilise all employees' knowledge and experience to a greater degree than before. The participating approach requires knowledge of how to develop and lead a team, and how to use a group process to ensure effective group functioning (Cummings & Worley, 2015; Robbins et al, 2016; Weaver & Farrell, 1997).

Instead of leading people, a facilitator leads through people. Instead of directing and delegating, facilitators coach and enable others to act efficiently and productively. Facilitating can also be contrasted to (Cilliers, 1991):

- traditional classroom teaching, where the teacher/trainer accepts responsibility for the second person by structuring, deciding and acting for him/her
- conducting a meeting, where the chairperson acts within a structure or an agenda, rules and minutes
- being autocratic, deciding for another person and implying that every problem has a right answer
- instructing, prescribing, giving solutions or telling someone what to do, which creates dependency.

When one thinks of the traditional manager in the organisation or the group leader, one thinks of a decision maker, a delegator, a director and often a scheduler of the work of others (Daft, 2015). A facilitator, however, gets individuals to work closely together on defined tasks in defined time frames, to solve specific problems, or to reach specific objectives. This means the facilitator is not the most prominent figure in the group. The facilitator puts the power into everyone's hands, serving as a guide and a catalyst. In this way, everyone has a chance to be and feel powerful. The aim is not to gain power, but to complete the work assigned to the team. The aim is thus to work together to produce what could not be produced by individuals working alone (Rees, 1991; Schwarz, 2002; Weaver & Farrell, 1997).

Unstructured versus structured groups

The emphasis of this chapter is on groups in industry that are formal and structured. As the dynamics and processes manifested in structured and unstructured groups differ significantly, it is important to differentiate between the two types of groups. These differences can be explained by considering the main aspects on which they differ, which are shown in Table 5.1.

Table 5.1 The differences between structured and unstructured groups (Unisa, 2015)

Aspect of difference	Structured groups	Unstructured groups
Aim	<ul><li>Specific aim (eg to solve a problem)</li><li>A definite goal</li></ul>	<ul><li>Vague (eg growth, sensitivity)</li><li>Vaguely defined goals at best</li></ul>
Agenda	Decided beforehand, usually by leader	Members determine
Composition	<ul><li>Compulsory</li><li>Intelligence important</li></ul>	<ul><li>Voluntary</li><li>Personality has an influence</li></ul>
Climate	<ul><li>Cognitive climate</li><li>No real emotional risks involved</li></ul>	Provides a cultural island where group members build support and trust to open up and experiment with behaviour and take risks
Decisions taken	Must reach a decision	No need to reach a decision
Focus	'There-and-then' (past)	'Here-and-now' (present)
Feedback	Feedback given on content	Feedback given on behaviour and is more personal
Information	Mainly from leader	Generated from members
Leadership	Directive	Non-directed and leadership has little influence

The different types of groups discussed in the preceding sections can also be placed on a continuum ranging from unstructured to structured, as depicted in Figure 5.1.

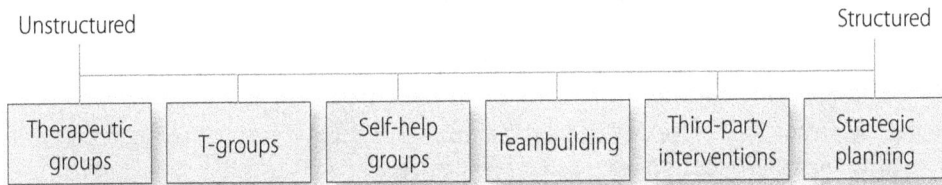

Unstructured   Structured

| Therapeutic groups | T-groups | Self-help groups | Teambuilding | Third-party interventions | Strategic planning |

Figure 5.1 Continuum of groups (Unisa, 2015)

Definitions of facilitation

In order to understand facilitation, it is necessary to look at a few definitions of the word. The word 'facilitate' comes from the Latin *facilis*, which means 'to make easy'. This is applied in the following definitions as follows:

- **Cilliers (1991):** Facilitating can be defined as creating a climate and providing opportunities for others to learn how to learn about themselves, and experience themselves to enhance their quality of life as manifested in psychological optimal functioning.
- **Rees (1991):** Facilitation is the act of leading others to participate in what was once the domain of management. It is the art of drawing fully on the expertise, knowledge and experience of individuals and teams. It is the ability to capitalise on synergy to improve the way work gets done. It knows how to use group processes to maximise participation, productivity and satisfaction in the workplace.
- **Hart (1992):** A facilitator is the person who leads a group or team of people. The facilitator holds the key role in a group so that it accomplishes its goals and tasks. Facilitation makes sure that things get done more easily. Thus, when facilitation is done properly, the facilitator eases a group through the process of solving a problem, making a decision, redefining its goals or restating expectations and responsibilities.
- **Bentley (1994):** Facilitation is the provision of opportunities, resources, encouragement and support for the group to succeed in achieving its objectives, and this is done through enabling the group members to take control and responsibility for the way they proceed.
- **Weaver and Farrell (1997):** Effective facilitation is about helping people get their work done, whether it is done in groups, with a few people or alone. It is also about helping people work together more effectively.
- **Schwarz (2002):** The facilitator's main task is to help the group increase effectiveness by improving its process and structure.

From these definitions, two directions of thought can be deduced. Firstly, there is the concern for the **task to be accomplished** and a more structured role for the facilitator, and secondly the **growth of the individual** concerned, with a more unstructured role for the facilitator.

Definition of 'facilitation'

For the purposes of this chapter, 'facilitation' is defined as making it easier for a group to function to reach its aim while a process of learning is made available to its members.

The group's **aim** will determine where the emphasis of facilitation ought to be. If the goal is a **task product** or **tangible** (eg a strategic planning document or a decision to be made), the emphasis will be on accompanying the group through a predetermined (often by applicable theories and models), structured process to reach this tangible product. Group growth will be of secondary importance, and will be reached more as a by-product of the task process. If the group's goal is the **growth** of the persons and group concerned (eg to achieve group cohesion, to improve interpersonal relationships or to reconstruct personality) the emphasis will be on the provision of a learning process so that group members may learn more about themselves and other group members and therefore grow as individuals and/or as a group. In this case, the structured process is merely a framework in which the group may reach its intangible goal.

The organisation development consultant as a facilitator

Organisation development (OD) consultants will often be approached by supervisors, managers and leaders in their organisation to act as facilitators for their work groups. The reasons for such a request could be all or some of the following:

- The supervisor, manager or leader does not possess the necessary facilitator skills and needs an OD consultant to fulfil this role.
- The supervisor, manager or leader wants to become actively involved in the group's discussion (content) and would like an independent person to act as facilitator in the process.
- The supervisor, manager or leader would like the members of his/her work group to participate fully, but feels that this would take place only if an independent person facilitated the group's functioning.
- The supervisor, manager or leader does not possess the necessary skills in order to utilise the full potential of all the group members to achieve a specific objective.

Facilitators can thus act as role models for formal supervisors, managers and leaders so that they can eventually acquire the skills needed in order to carry out the necessary task without further assistance from a facilitator. This will then ensure that supervisors, managers and leaders do not become too dependent on facilitators to fulfil a role which, with the necessary training, they would be able to do themselves.

OD consultants will need to act as facilitators in various situations, including:

- on being approached by a supervisor, manager or leader in an organisation and asked to act as facilitator for one of the reasons already discussed
- when doing OD consultancy with groups of people (entry/contracting)
- when gathering information about an organisation by means of small groups (diagnosis)
- when feeding back gathered data to groups of people (feedback sessions)
- when doing joint action planning (JAP) with groups of people (JAP sessions)
- when conducting various types of OD interventions with groups, such as teambuilding, third-party interventions, strategic planning sessions, etc
- when presenting any behavioural science training to groups of people
- whenever they work with groups as part of their task as OD consultants.

The facilitation process

When facing a group, facilitators are confronted with the question: 'What can I do that will assist the group in achieving its aim?' It is difficult to study facilitation without a frame of reference of the process that is going on. Figure 5.2 on page 106 can assist in understanding what the facilitator does as part of the facilitation process. This process was compiled and documented in 2000 by the author, using his theoretical knowledge and practical experiences of facilitation. The author postulated that five basic steps are involved in the process of group facilitation:

1. The facilitator needs to provide the group with structure to achieve its aim. See the **Evaluation sheet for a facilitation session**, which is attached on pages 126–127 as **Appendix A** to this chapter, for an example as to how a facilitation session can be structured.
2. The facilitator must **provide opportunities for all group members to participate** in the group's activities.
3. The facilitator must **observe** what is taking place on individual, interpersonal and group levels.
4. The facilitator must **analyse** what is happening in the group with some frame of reference in mind.
5. The facilitator does something (**intervenes**) to assist the group to achieve its aim. This intervention has an effect on the group, either good or bad.

The above-mentioned steps are then repeated until the group achieves its aim.

The intervention step is one of the most important steps in the facilitation process. The aim of any intervention should be to assist a group in achieving its aim. Any intervention which does not contribute to this should not be carried out. How, then, does a facilitator know what to focus on when trying to intervene? A useful guideline is to use the concepts of **content** and **process**, as developed by Edgar Schein (1987). According to Schein (1987), content is **what** we do, while process means **how** things are done.

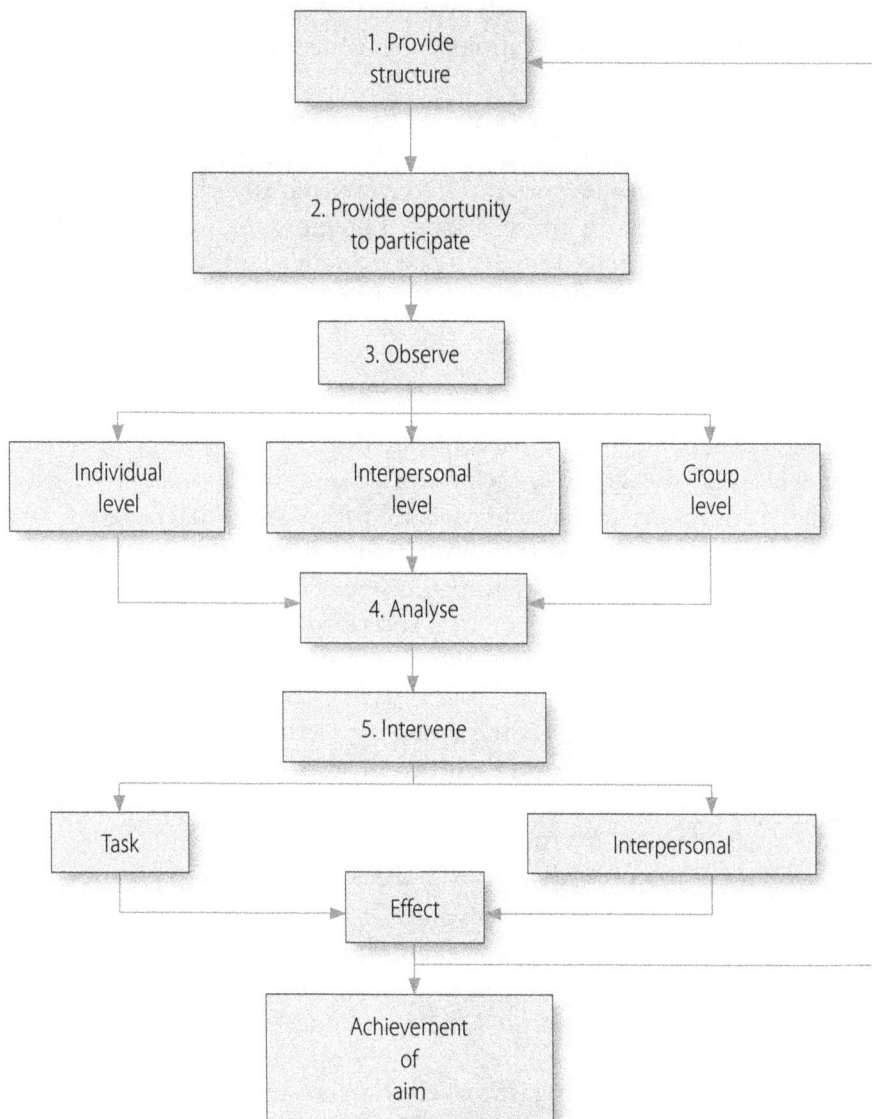

Figure 5.2 The facilitation process (Author)

Table 5.2 represents a simplified model of the possible types of interventions. The blocks in the table overlap and, in reality, the distinctions are not as clear-cut as the descriptions imply, but we need simplified models if we are to understand some of the complicated information that we normally come across. First, we have to separate a situation's **content** from its **process**. Second, we have to decide, for each of the two aspects of a situation, whether we are focusing on the **task** issues or the **interpersonal** issues.

Table 5.2 Types of interventions (Schein, 1987)

Types of intervention	Task	Interpersonal
Content	Cell 1 Formal agenda, aim	Cell 3 Who is doing what to whom
Process	Cell 2 How the task is done	Cell 4 How members relate to each other, communicate, etc

In summary

1. **Process** is always to be favoured as an intervention focus over content.
2. **Task process** is always to be favoured over interpersonal process.

Activity

Group interventions

In each cell, give two examples of group interventions that you have been exposed to during any previous group setting/session. Write out the examples verbatim in the applicable cell.

Types of intervention	Task	Interpersonal
Content	1. 2.	1. 2.
Process	1. 2.	1. 2.

Micro-skills

Micro-skills and facilitation

Micro-skills may be regarded as the interpersonal skills one uses in interaction with others (Ivey, Ivey & Zalaquette, 2014). These skills are very important to group facilitators, who must be ready to take effective interpersonal action in any group situation. Because of the specific position of facilitators, their personal action always has a great influence on group members and on the success of that with which they are involved.

The group facilitation micro-skills propagated in this chapter are based on and adapted from the individual micro-skills and micro-skills hierarchy developed by Ivey, Ivey & Simek-Downing (1987) and Ivey et al (2014). These micro-skills, which are used by Ivey et al (1987) and Ivey et al (2014) for counselling and psychotherapy, are regarded by this author as the most practical and effective methods available for successful group facilitation, having personally used and taught them for more than 15 years in the field of group facilitation.

The micro-skills hierarchy

The different micro-skills that are available to a group facilitator are represented by Ivey et al (1987) and Ivey et al (2014) as a hierarchy (see Figure 5.3). This hierarchy classifies the most important skills needed in terms of non-verbal and attending behaviour, listening skills, influencing skills, confrontation skills and the integration of all the previous skills.

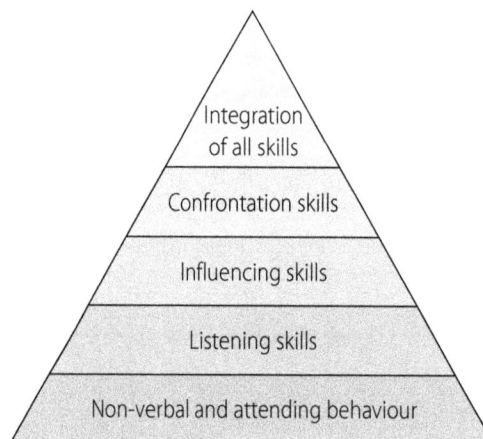

Figure 5.3 The micro-skills hierarchy (adapted from Ivey et al, 1987: 70; Ivey et al, 2014: 11)

Non-verbal and attending behaviour

Non-verbal and attending behaviour is to give physical attention to the other person, or in other words **to express with one's body that one is listening and is interested**. These elements are:

- a posture of openness, a relaxed attitude and involvement
- appropriate body movement
- good eye-contact
- a friendly and relaxed facial expression
- a tone of voice that varies and displays a measure of emotion.

Listening skills

The ability to be a good listener is probably one of the most fundamental skills a facilitator must have. Listening means not only hearing what someone says, but as far as possible understanding what it means. In the light of this, the listening process does not take place only between two people, but also within each individual. To understand others, it is also necessary to listen to and understand oneself.

The following listening skills are available to a facilitator:

- **Closed questions:** These are questions that usually give the group member only two options in the form of yes/no answers, for example: 'Do you like the person next to you?' Closed questions usually begin with words such as 'is', 'was' or 'did/do'. Although they may be used to gather information, to gain clarity or focus, one must guard against excessive use.
- **Open questions:** An example of an open question would be: 'How do you feel about the person sitting next to you?' Open-type questions usually begin with words such as 'why', 'can', 'how' or 'what', and tend to create opportunities to increase responses and to focus on the process rather than the content.
- **The encourager:** Encouragement or repetition is direct repetition of what a group member has said, or short remarks such as: 'Hmmm', 'Tell me more', 'Is that so?', etc. It is mainly used to create flow in a discussion and to encourage the group member to elaborate further.
- **Paraphrasing (reflection of content):** Paraphrasing is a central response to something a speaker has said. It summarises the essence of the other person's content in the listener's own words. This technique focuses on the content of what the speaker has said and takes only the essence from it—in other words, paraphrasing is a summary of the listener's understanding of the situation.
- **Reflection of feeling:** A clear understanding of the problem is not enough to help a group member with a problem, since it may also contain

emotional components. By means of reflection of feeling it can be determined where a group member stands emotionally in relation to the problem. Reflection of feeling deals with emotions—usually those associated with the same facts. By using this technique, the facilitator attempts to show that he/she is trying to see the world as the group member does by trying to understand his/her experiences.

- **Summary reflections:** A summary reflection is a repetition of the main ideas, facts, themes and/or feelings that a group member expressed during a discussion. This skill involves giving attention to the group member, experiencing the group member's feelings and thoughts, and arranging and organising the complex content of the discussion.

- **The use of attending silences:** Most people tend to talk too much and listen too little. Silence on the part of a listener gives speakers time to think about what they are going to say and enables them to look at themselves more deeply and continue at their own pace. During a silence, a facilitator has more time to give active attention to what the group member does and more time to think about it. Although silences can be uncomfortable at first for many inexperienced facilitators, this remains a very useful skill. Effective listeners are able to speak when they have to, but are equally at ease to remain quiet if applicable. During a silence, the focus must remain fixed on the group member.

The listening skills are summarised in Table 5.3.

Table 5.3 Listening skills summary (Author)

Skill	Description
Open questions	'What', 'how', 'why' and 'can' questions
Closed questions	Usually begins with words such as 'have' or 'is', and can usually be answered in a few words
Encourager	Repeating a few of the group member's key words
Paraphrasing	Repeating the essence of the group member's words and thoughts by using own phrases or words
Reflection of feeling	Paying selective attention to the emotional content of the discussion
Summary	Repeating the group member's facts and feelings (and reasons) to the group member in an organised way
Silences	Paying active attention to what the group member does and says

Influencing skills

Although group members will definitely benefit from the use of listening skills alone, growth will sometimes be very slow if facilitators do not give input from their side. If they become active participants in the discussion, they can influence and speed up the changing process. Because of specific knowledge and skills, personal experience and understanding of the circumstances and culture of the group members, facilitators can share knowledge for the benefit of the group members. Influencing skills are, however, complex and are often more effective when used sparingly.

- **Prescriptive skills:** Prescriptive skills are used especially to give certain instructions to the group. A facilitator would use these skills often at the beginning of a session to give structure to the group, for example: 'I would like us to follow the following steps during the session.'

- **Suggestions/advice/information:** This set of skills is useful but also potentially dangerous. It is a group of skills where the facilitator makes suggestions, can supply content information and may even say: 'If I were you, I would ...' At times it is necessary for facilitators to supply information because they possess important information that the group member needs. Advice and information must be used carefully, however, and should preferably be provided at the group member's request, otherwise the group member will react with a 'Yes, but ...' response. Should a group member do so, it would be preferable to change the style and use a listening skill such as questioning or paraphrasing, for example: 'You feel the suggestion won't help. What do you think will work better?'

- **Self-disclosure:** Self-disclosure takes place in two ways: firstly when the facilitator shares his/her feelings with the group member regarding how he/she experiences the group member, and secondly when the facilitator briefly shares a related personal experience with the group member. The facilitator then returns the focus immediately to the group member, by saying, for example, that he/she can identify with what the group member is experiencing because of personal experience. The facilitator follows this up with an open question.

- **Feedback:** Feedback can be given either to individual members or to the group as a whole, and can be positive or negative. Examples are: 'Thank you for that input, John', or 'Well done, group! You are progressing well.'

- **Logical consequences:** In terms of these skills, group members are led to realise the possible consequences of their actions, which could be either positive or negative. The use of the words 'if' and 'then' can help a facilitator in using this skill. Examples during a group session are: 'If group members continue interrupting each other like this, no one will be able to give good input' (negative consequence) or: 'If the group continues to progress so well, we will easily achieve our aim by the end of the day' (positive consequence).

- **Identifying or emphasising areas of agreement:** This skill is also used to motivate group members positively by pointing out areas of agreement. In this way a firm basis is formed with the group members, and their cooperation is obtained for reaching common objectives. An example is: 'I see that you all agree that this is indeed a cause of the problem.'
- **Influencing summary:** This skill is often used at the end of the group session when the facilitator summarises and reviews the whole session.

The different influencing skills are summarised in Table 5.4.

Table 5.4 Influencing skills summary (Author)

Skill	Description
Prescriptive	Telling the group member what to do—may be a suggestion or instruction
Suggestions/advice/ information	Providing suggestions, advice about how to act or think, information, ideas, etc
Self-disclosure	Sharing personal past experiences or reactions
Feedback	Providing the group members with specific data about how they are observed by yourself or others regarding their problem
Logical consequences	Explaining the logical consequences of group members' thoughts and behaviour: 'If ... then'
Areas of agreement	Motivating by identifying areas of agreement
Influencing summary	Often used towards the end of a session to summarise the session

Confrontation

Confrontation, also known as 'challenging', is used to increase the awareness of group members in certain areas. It is an action taken by facilitators based on the essence of how they understand the group members. The purpose of confrontation is to reduce the 'dual messages' and incongruence in the group members' experience, communication and behaviour by first helping them to replace their blind spots with new perspectives. Secondly, they must also be helped to become involved in problem-solving and opportunity-seeking behaviour. Confrontation is a skill that is based on the balancing and use of both attending and influencing skills. The most effective use of confrontation is usually found in the form of complex paraphrases or reflection of feeling. It is also possible to confront by means of influencing skills, but it does not allow for as much group member growth as paraphrase or reflection of feeling does. It is clear, therefore, that confrontation is a combination skill. In other words, it is a paraphrase, interpretation or any other skill, but a confrontation as well.

- **Facilitating confrontation:** Here facilitators use their experience to help group members examine and possibly extend their frame of reference. Two characteristics of this type of confrontation are that content is inclined to be closely related to the group members' existing frame of reference and that it is given in a relatively non-threatening manner.
- **'Hot-chair' confrontation:** 'Hot-chair' confrontations are very direct and strong challenges. Here facilitators show loudly and clearly that they are not prepared to listen to group members' excuses.
- **Didactic/interpretational confrontation:** Here the focus of the challenge is aimed at helping group members understand how they should handle their problems.

Integration of skills

The use of micro-skills usually follows a logical or natural course or structure. In this way, for example, there is a basic listening sequence (indicated on the hierarchy), where open and closed questions are asked first, followed by encouragers, paraphrasing, reflecting and reflecting summary. The objective of the hierarchy then is to indicate the natural sequence in the use of skills. Any discussion between a facilitator and group members thus also follows a logical course or structure, which means that, in certain phases of the discussion, certain skills are more applicable and should be used more often.

Although there is a specific course in the use of micro-skills (for example the basic listening sequence discussed above), it merely forms a general framework for the use of micro-skills. Depending on the specific situation facilitators are in, they must be able to adjust their approach to the situation. Different situations and different cultures thus very often require different patterns in the use of micro-skills. Furthermore, facilitators all have their own frame of reference (or theories) at their disposal, and their own specific style or way of doing things. It is therefore their responsibility to adapt their use of micro-skills to their own frame of reference and style, and to be able to apply them with ease. An important additional role of facilitators is always to strive to convey these skills to the group members with whom they are working.

Activity

Analysis of a transcript to identify micro-skills on an individual level

The following discussion occurred between a hotel manager and two of his subordinates. Supervisor A (Carl) is responsible for hotel cleaning and maintenance, and Supervisor B (Herman) is responsible for reception and admin.

Your task is to name the various micro-skills used by the manager. Each micro-skill has been numbered.

Manager	*Welcome to this meeting, chaps. (1) I would like us to iron out the problem that exists between your two sections. (2) I have often experienced these types of conflict myself in the past. (3) I want each of you to give me an overview of your understanding of the problem. I would like the other person to listen and try to understand the other's viewpoint. (4) Is that OK?*
Carl	That's fine with me, Bill.
Herman	Yes, I would like to see this thing settled once and for all.
Manager	*(5) I'm glad that you are both willing to solve this problem. (6) Let's start with you, Carl.*
Carl	Sure. I'm responsible for the cleaning and maintenance of the hotel but I am placed under a lot of unnecessary time pressure by Herman and his people ... (interrupted).
Herman	(Loudly) What do you mean unnecessary? If your people would stop wasting time by ... (interrupted).
Manager	*No, no, chaps, (7) if you continue with this quarrelling then we are not going to solve this problem. (8) I asked you in the beginning not to interrupt each other, Herman, and now you have interrupted Carl. (9) I want us to follow two rules for the rest of this meeting— one: no one interrupts the other; and two: no one speaks unless I give you the chance to do so. (10) Is that clear?*
Carl	Yes.
Herman	OK.
Manager	*Now (11) Carl, you sounded quite upset about something. (12) What is that exactly? (13) And can you tell me what it is without mudslinging, please?*
Carl	Well, as I was trying to say, Herman and his people put me under a lot of time pressure by booking in clients before the agreed time. This leaves me with clients complaining about rooms not being prepared properly and I get quite annoyed with this.
Manager	*(14) So you are having problems with clients arriving before 12:00 and that causes you to receive complaints against your department. (15) Is that the only problem?*
Carl	Yes. If I can get Herman to not check in clients before 12:00, my side will be clean.

Manager	(16) *When did you become aware of this problem, Carl?*
Carl	Well, let me see. Last week at our weekly meeting you reviewed the book with customer complaints and indicated that my share of complaints increased from 15 % to 35 %. At the same time the complaints increased from 19 for the month to 24. I interpreted this as you blaming me for all the increases.
Manager	(17) *Blaming you for all the increases?*
Carl	I reviewed each complaint and discovered that all the complaints against my department were customers complaining about rooms not being ready. Upon checking in more detail I discovered that most of these clients were early check-ins. Every time somebody was booked in before 12:00 I reprimanded the staff at reception. This ought to stop them from doing this and there should be no problem in future.
Manager	(18) *So the discussion on the increase of customer complaints triggered this whole thing, Carl. You think I am holding the increase in complaints against you. Your own investigation showed that other factors are causing this to be the case and that it is basically unfair to pin it on you. Now you are stopping reception from early book-ins by coming down on them. And all this is causing you to be annoyed at Herman.*
Carl	That's correct. We used to get on fine until this Customer Complaints book was introduced.
Manager	*Thanks Carl.* (19) *What is your side of the story, Herman?*
Herman	At last. I thought I would never get an equal chance. Carl is not the only one who is upset. I'm furious with him for reprimanding my staff. Who does he think he is?
Manager	(20) *Herman, I told you earlier to stop this unnecessary hammering, but you have done it again.* (21) *If you can tell me what Carl is doing that is causing the problem, then we can have this thing sorted out quickly.*
Herman	OK. I'm sorry. What Carl is doing that's upsetting me is coming down on my staff. He is not in charge of reception and I want him out of there.
Manager	(22) *What would you like him to do instead?*
Herman	I would like him to come and see me about problems with my staff and not to go to them directly.
Manager	(23) *I support Herman, Carl. This is normally the accepted norm of conduct between supervisors.* (24) *Why are you doing this?*
Carl	Well, I can see that it is not right. I wouldn't like him to approach my staff directly, but I was so upset about my complaints stats and they were right there when I went to check with reception, so I just let loose. →

Manager	OK. (25) *In future, I would like you to respect the lines of authority.* (26) *Can you do that?*
Carl	Alright, but then Herman must act upon my complaint immediately and help me solve the situation.
Herman	I'll make sure of that.
Manager	(27) *Thanks for your cooperation thus far. Now,* (28) *is this the only problem, Herman?*
Herman	Yes, Bill, but I would like to explain my staff's dilemma. Whenever a customer arrives early, what are we to do? Show them the door?
Manager	(29) *Definitely not.* (30) *So far we have determined that Carl is upset about the complaints against him and that he tries to remedy the situation by reprimanding Herman's staff. This causes Herman to be furious with Carl again.* (31) *I suggest that we put our heads together to see if we can come up with some solutions.*

Activity

Analysis of a transcript to identify micro-skills on a group level

The following group session took place with a facilitator (Benny) and a group of five participants, all supervisors in the human resources department of a retail company, who had to find a solution for smoking among staff in the department. Your task is to name the various micro-skills used by the facilitator where each number occurs.

Facilitator	*Good morning, group. I am Benny, your facilitator for this session and I am from the OD department. I have been asked to act as facilitator for this session so that you as a group can come up with solutions for a problem that is being experienced in the human resources department at present.* (1) *I would like to show you the following background to the problem.*
	Facilitator discusses the background, which indicates that too many people in the human resources department smoke.
Facilitator	(2) *My suggested aim of the session is: To determine how to get staff in the department to stop smoking.* (3) *Are you all comfortable with this aim?*
Facilitator	(4) *I would like us to follow the following structure to achieve our aim:* *Step 1: Determine why staff in the department smoke.* *Step 2: Generate solutions to stop staff in the department from smoking.* *Step 3: Prioritise solutions.* *Step 4: Evaluate the session.* (5) *Are you all comfortable with this structure for this session?* ➞

Facilitator	(6) *My role as facilitator during this session is to guide you through the framework in order to achieve the aim of the session. Your role as group members is to participate in all discussions and give the inputs needed to achieve the aim of the session.*
Facilitator	(7) *Let's compile some ground rules for this session.* (8) *Any suggestions?*
	The group gives five ground rules for the session, which the facilitator writes down on the flip chart.
Facilitator	(9) *Well done, group!* (10) *If we continue like this, we are going to have a very good group session.*
Facilitator	OK. (11) *Any questions from the group before we begin with the session?*
Facilitator	(12) *Let's list some causes for smoking in the human resources department.* (13) *Cebile, can you give me a cause?*
Cebile	I think that people experience many stresses in their lives and then they smoke, as they believe that this smoking habit of theirs will help to relieve their stress.
Facilitator	(14) *So what you are saying is that people smoke to relieve stress in their lives?*
Cebile	Yes, that is right.
Facilitator	(15) *Thanks for that input, Cebile. Let's note it on the flip chart.*
Jeremy	I think another reason is that people are just plain stupid! They think ... (interrupted by Tebogo)
Tebogo	I don't agree with that! How can you say ...?
Facilitator	(16) *Group, let's please give each person a chance to complete their inputs without being interrupted, as stated by our ground rule.* (17) *If we continue interrupting each other, we will not achieve our aim for this session.*
Facilitator	(18) *Now then, Jeremy. Please continue with your suggested cause.*
Jeremy	OK. I think people are stupid to damage their lungs by smoking.
Facilitator	(19) *How could you re-formulate that as a cause that we can note on the flip chart, Jeremy?*
Jeremy	Well, the cause could be that people are not fully aware of the health hazards of smoking, and thus cause damage to their health.
Facilitator	(20) *Does the group agree with this cause?*
	The group agrees and continues to compile a list of 10 causes.
Facilitator	(21) *You are doing well, group!* (22) *If we continue like this, we are going to have a very successful session.*
Facilitator	(Points to the structure flip chart.) (23) *Group, we have now completed steps 1 and 2. Now let's do step 3.*

Problem solving in groups

To be effective, a work group must be able to identify problems, examine alternatives and make decisions (Cummings & Worley, 2015). As such, problem solving and decision making are important group skills. Concerning problem solving, Buelens et al (2011) state that a problem exists when the actual state of affairs differs from the desired or ideal one. Therefore, we can view problem solving as the process of resolving unsettled matters and of finding an answer to a difficulty, and as a process that results in a solution to a problem and involves changing the actual state of affairs until it resembles the desired one.

There are four steps in this problem solving process, namely:
1. identifying the problem
2. generating alternative solutions
3. selecting a solution(s)
4. implementing and evaluating the solution(s).

Two styles of problem solving: Right- versus left-brain hemispheres

Two broad styles of problem solving can be isolated. The first style is a more rational approach, whereas the second is a more creative one. Many authors describe Western civilisation as dominated by the left hemisphere. By this they mean that most of our thoughts originate and are processed by the left side of the brain; thus most problems we are confronted with are addressed and solved by primarily left-hemispheric functioning. It is in this part of the brain where most logical and rational thinking takes place. It is also here that intellectual ideas are translated into words.

The right side of the brain is responsible for another type of thinking that is also crucial to problem solving. It is in this side of the brain where a number of different things are processed. These are emotional cues, which add significantly to our knowledge and understanding of a problem. The right side of the brain is primarily an intuitive domain, an area of irrational, illogical and spontaneous reactions.

Of great importance is not whether a person is functioning purely with the right or left brain but the amount and quality of interface between the two. The more a person uses the left brain, the more his/her reasoning would be scientifically logical and concrete, whereas right-brain dominance would be characterised by creative, intuitive and innovative thinking. In order to effectively solve a problem, both sides are needed, but the quality of the solution depends on the side most used and the amount of interface. It is also a question of 'horses for courses'. What is important for a group facilitator is that if a highly creative solution is sought, the right brain is crucial. When a typical rational and concrete solution is sought, the left brain is of more importance. A facilitator must thus know when to use the different available problem-solving techniques in order to assist a group to solve a problem.

Rational problem solving (the left hemispheric focus)

In solving problems of the real world, one deals with unpredictable variables such as norms, values, personalities, organisational structures and emotions. The more rational and scientific methods of problem solving have been criticised as artificially narrow and limiting in addressing the above-mentioned problems, yet the methods and techniques have proved to be very valuable if applied effectively at the appropriate time. Three of the most popular rational problem-solving techniques used by facilitators are: (1) the rational problem-solving technique; (2) the force field analysis technique; and (3) the nominal group technique, which are explained in detail in the literature dealing with problem solving.

Creative problem solving (the right hemispheric focus)

The techniques proposed under the right hemispheric focus do not represent a continuous or even complete problem-solving strategy, but rather a collection of intuitive and/or creative techniques that may be used at various points in the group problem-solving process after the problem has been identified. Three of the most popular creative problem-solving techniques used by facilitators are: (1) getting unstuck; (2) the brainstorming technique; and (3) the open chair technique. These techniques are explained in detail in the literature dealing with problem solving.

Framework for a group session

No matter which problem-solving technique a facilitator uses to assist a group to achieve its aim, it must be converted into a usable structure or framework for a group session. As an example, the framework for a rational problem-solving group session would be the following:

Opening (See Appendix A for an example of a complete opening phase.)
Step 1: Identify the causes of the problem.
Step 2: Generate solutions for the problem.
Step 3: Prioritise the solutions.
Step 4: Evaluate the session.
Closure

In this example, the nominal group technique would be used in Step 1, as this is a purely rational step. However, the brainstorming technique would be used during Step 2, as this is a creative step.

119

Decision making in groups

In today's world, groups are continually making decisions. The purpose of group decision making is to decide upon well-considered, well-understood and realistic action towards attaining goals which all members wish to attain. A decision implies that some agreement prevails among group members as to which of several courses of action is most desirable for achieving the group's goals. Making a decision is just one step in the broader process of problem solving (Buelens et al, 2011; Robbins et al, 2016).

Group versus individual decision making

There are a number of reasons why group decision making may be better than individual decision making (Buelens et al, 2011; Robbins et al, 2016):

- There is increased information exchange.
- New perspectives are provided.
- A more complete picture can be arrived at.
- Complete information is obtained.
- Complementary knowledge is exchanged and shared.
- Chance errors (over- or underestimations) can be corrected.
- New ideas in the group are stimulated.
- There is motivation to make a high-quality decision.
- More support and encouragement are given for contributing to high-quality decision making in groups.
- The group discussion can increase the level of understanding of the individual members.

Factors inhibiting effective decision making

There are a number of factors that inhibit effective decision making in a group. In order to be able to facilitate effective group sessions, a group facilitator should take careful note of the following factors, and actions should be taken to ensure that the decision-making process is not hampered by threats such as:

- a lack of group maturity
- conflicting goals among group members
- a failure to communicate information
- egocentrism among group members
- avoidance of disagreement
- dominance due to existing power structures.

Methods of decision making

The following are the most commonly used methods of decision making:

- **Decision by authority without group discussion:** The leader makes all the decisions without consulting the group members in any way.

- **Decision by expert:** The most expert member in the group makes the decision. The group does not discuss the issue, but rather lets the expert decide on his/her own.
- **Decision by averaging individuals' opinions:** The facilitator asks each group member separately for his/her opinion and finds the average result.
- **Decision by authority after discussion:** The group originates ideas and holds discussions, but the formal group leader makes the final decision.
- **Decision by majority vote:** At least 51% or more of the group decides, for example by voting.
- **Consensus:** A consensus is reached when all members of the group can say they either agree with the decision or have had their views heard. Not all group members may fully agree with the final decision, but everyone agrees to support the outcome (Buelens et al, 2011). This is the preferred method of decision making in groups, and a facilitator should always strive to get the group to agree to this method.

It is important that the facilitator asks the group at the start of the group session which method they want to use.

The relationship between time and decision making

Each and every method of decision making takes a different amount of time to execute. The general rule is that group decisions take longer than individual ones, but with a higher quality of decision (Buelens et al, 2011; Robbins et al, 2016). Facilitators should take into consideration the amount of time available and the quality of the decision they want the group to reach.

Dealing with conflict in groups

Conflict is a process that begins when one party perceives that another party has negatively affected, or is about to negatively affect, something that the first party cares about. This can include incompatibility of goals, differences over interpretations of facts, disagreements based on behavioural expectations, etc (Robbins et al, 2016). There is thus always a risk of potential conflict in a group situation consisting of members with different viewpoints and opinions. Preparation to handle such situations includes a thorough knowledge of conflict and group dynamics, micro-skills and conflict management as a process.

Effects of conflict

Conflict can have positive or negative effects, or both. For some people, conflict motivates and arouses enthusiasm, but for others it constitutes a major threat (Buelens et al, 2011; Cummings & Worley, 2015; Robbins et al, 2016).

Causes of conflict

Aspects which can lead to conflict in groups are the following (Buelens et al, 2011; Cummings & Worley, 2015; Robbins et al, 2016; Schwarz, 2002; Weaver & Farrell, 1997):

- **Conflicting interests:** The possibility of conflict is enhanced when group members have conflicting interests.
- **Communication obstacles:** The more obstacles that exist between group members and effective communication, the greater the possibility of conflict developing.
- **Need for consensus:** The potential for conflict increases as it becomes necessary for group members to reach a consensus.
- **Interpersonal skills:** Defective interpersonal skills (micro-skills) can be seen as a major deficiency in effective communication between individuals and/or group members. For this reason the facilitator must act as a role model for group members when using micro-skills to handle conflict.
- **Cultural origins of conflict:** In any group, various differences could be present, such as differences related to gender, race, language and religion, and such a complex group composition could easily lead to conflict. A facilitator must thus be sensitive and impartial regarding these differences, and use micro-skills and different techniques in order to assist the group to function effectively.

Management of conflict

Conflict in organisations and groups is a normal everyday occurrence that is almost always brought about by parties' differing opinions and insights or by one person pursuing his/her own concerns at another's expense. Positive conflict situations should be encouraged, while negative ones should ideally be prevented, or at least an attempt should be made to resolve them in a positive manner. Whilst maturing, we develop different ways of managing and solving conflict. That is why people, as a result of their experiences, develop a number of different approaches in handling conflict. They have learnt that with a certain approach a given conflict situation can be abated.

Handling conflict in a group

Conflict does occur in all group situations, but a facilitator can handle such situations by the use of appropriate micro-skills and techniques. These techniques include the following:

- Acknowledge that there is conflict in the group, eg: 'I notice that there is a difference of opinion in the group regarding …'
- Refer to the ground rules if they refer to conflict.

- Contract with the group at the start of the session about how they want to handle any conflict that may arise, and use this decision when needed.
- When conflict arises during the group session, acknowledge it and ask the group how they want to handle it at that stage, eg: 'Does the group want to discuss this issue now, or should we leave it for later?'
- Avoid competing, avoiding and accommodation conflict-handling styles, and strive for collaboration or compromising.
- Assist the group in resolving the conflict by using micro-skills.

Conclusion

In this chapter facilitation was defined as making it easier for a group to function to reach its aim while a process of learning is made available to group members. To achieve this a group facilitator, who is often an OD consultant, must manage the group process (how the group is functioning) and avoid becoming involved in the group content (what the group is discussing). The group facilitator must also make extensive use of interpersonal or micro-skills when facilitating. These micro-skills are in the form of a hierarchy, starting with non-verbal and attending behaviours and moving through listening, influencing and confrontation skills. The group facilitator must finally be able to apply all these skills in an integrative manner as and when they are required during the functioning of the group.

Reflection questions

1. Name the main differences between structured and unstructured groups.
2. Give your own definition of group facilitation.
3. What are the five main steps in the facilitation process?
4. What is favoured as an intervention focus in a group: content or process?
5. Give your own definition of micro-skills.
6. Which is better: left- or right-hemisphere problem solving?
7. What type of decision making should a facilitator always strive for?

Multiple-choice questions

1. The debate around facilitation is highlighted by:
   a. the different definitions of facilitation
   b. the role of the facilitator
   c. the results that a group should achieve
   d. a, b and c
   e. a and b

2. Structured and unstructured groups differ in terms of aspects such as:
   a. aim, agenda, feedback and composition
   b. aim, information and focus
   c. climate, decisions taken and leadership
   d. a and b
   e. a, b and c

3. A facilitator must be able to:
   a. use all the micro-skills
   b. use listening and influencing skills
   c. use integration skills
   d. a and b
   e. a, b and c

4. The steps in the facilitation process are:
   a. Provide structure, provide opportunity to participate and analyse.
   b. Provide aim, provide opportunity to participate, observe and intervene.
   c. Provide structure for participation, observe and analyse.
   d. All of the above
   e. None of the above

5. Which of the following is NOT seen as creative problem solving?
   a. Getting unstuck
   b. Brainstorming
   c. Force field analysis
   d. Open chair
   e. All of the above

References

Bentley, T. 1994. *Facilitation: providing opportunities for learning*. New York: McGraw-Hill.

Buelens, M, Sinding, K, Waldstrom, C, Kreitner, R & Kinicki, A. 2011. *Organisational behaviour*. 4th ed. Berkshire: McGraw-Hill.

Camp, RR, Blanchard, PN & Huszczo, GE. 1986. *Toward a more organizationally effective training strategy and practice*. Englewood Cliffs, NJ: Prentice Hall.

Cilliers, F. 1991. 'Facilitating: making a process available'. *Human Resource Management* 7(2): 37.

Cummings, TG & Worley, CG. 2015. *Organization development and change*. 10th ed. Mason, OH: South-Western Cengage Learning.

Daft, DL. 2015. *The leadership experience.* 6th ed. Stamford, CT: Cengage Learning.

French, WL & Bell, CH. 1998. *Organization development: behavioral science interventions for organization improvement.* 6th ed. Upper Saddle River, NJ: Prentice Hall.

Hart, LB. 1992. *Faultless facilitation: a resource guide for group and team leaders.* Amherst, MA: HRD Press.

Ivey, AE, Ivey, MB & Simek-Downing, L. 1987. *Counseling and psychotherapy: integrating skills, theory and practice.* 2nd ed. Englewood Cliffs, NJ: Prentice Hall.

Ivey, AE, Ivey, MB & Zalaquette, CP. 2014. *Intentional interviewing and counselling: Facilitating client development in a multicultural society.* 8th ed. Belmont, CA: Cengage Learning.

Lieberman, M, Yalom, I & Miles, M. 1973. *Encounter groups: first facts.* New York: Basic Books.

McGregor, D. 1967. *The professional manager.* New York: McGraw-Hill.

Rees, F. 1991. *How to lead work teams: facilitation skills.* San Diego, CA: Pfeiffer.

Riordan, RJ & Beggs, MS. 1988. 'Some critical differences between self-help and therapy groups'. *Journal of Specialists in Group Work* 13: 24–29.

Robbins, SP, Judge, TA, Odendaal, A & Roodt, G. 2016. *Organisational behaviour: global and southern African perspectives.* 3rd ed. Cape Town: Pearson Education.

Rogers, CR. 1961. *On becoming a person: a therapist's view of psychotherapy.* Boston, MA: Houghton Mifflin.

Rogers, CR. 1983. *Freedom to learn for the 80s.* Columbus, OH: Charles E. Merrill.

Schaffer, JBP & Galinsky, MD. 1974. *Models of group therapy and sensitivity training.* Englewood Cliffs, NJ: Prentice Hall.

Schein, EH. 1987. *Process consultation: lessons for managers and consultants.* Reading, MA: Addison-Wesley.

Schwarz, R. 2002. *The skilled facilitator: a comprehensive resource for consultants, facilitators, managers, trainers, and coaches.* 2nd ed. New York: John Wiley & Sons.

Unisa. 2015. *Dynamics of behaviour* (Study Guide 1 for APOD01-J). Pretoria: University of South Africa.

Weaver, RG & Farrell, JD. 1997. *Managers as facilitators: a practical guide to getting the work done in a changing workplace.* San Francisco, CA: Berrett-Koehler.

Yalom, ID. 2005. *The theory and practice of group psychotherapy.* 5th ed. New York: Basic Books.

Appendix A: Evaluation sheet for a facilitation session

Opening phase

No	Activity	Was it done?
1.	Greet members.	
2.	Introduce yourself.	
3.	Introduce co-facilitator (if applicable).	
4.	Finalise administration (if applicable).	
5.	Ice breaker (if applicable)	
6.	Contracting with the group	
	6.1 Give the background to the problem.	
	6.2 Discuss the suggested aim of session.	
	6.3 Show the framework (structure) to be followed.	
	6.4 How will time will be used (duration of session/breaks)?	
	6.5 Working methods (training aids, techniques, etc)	
	6.6 Will a scribe be used (or not)?	
	6.7 Explain your role as facilitator.	
	6.8 Explain the group members' roles.	
	6.9 Formulate ground rules (and how they will be used).	
	6.10 Determine decision-making rules.	
	6.11 How will conflict be managed in the group?	
	6.12 What would happen if time should expire?	
7.	Ask: 'Any questions before we start?'	

Use of micro-skills during the session

Listening skills	Times used	Influencing skills	Times used
Closed questions		Prescriptive	
Open questions		Suggestions/advice/etc	
The encourager		Self-disclosure	
Paraphrasing		Feedback	
Reflection of feeling		Logical consequences	
Summary		Areas of agreement	
Silences			

Actions during the session

No	Activity	Comment
1.	Is the writing on flipcharts clear, neat and large enough?	
2.	Are all flipcharts torn off and posted on the wall?	
3.	Are only black/blue/brown pens used, not red/orange/green?	
4.	Is everything that is written on a flipchart numbered?	
5.	Is balancing applied, giving everyone a chance to speak?	
6.	Are all techniques used explained on a flipchart?	
7.	Is the group seated in a U or semi-circle (if possible)?	
8.	Was time management done?	
9.	Do all flipcharts have a heading?	
10.	Are all flipcharts numbered in sequence?	

Chapter 6

Core theories and models

Melinde Coetzee

Learning outcomes

After reading this chapter, you should be able to:

- explain the basic principles of open systems theory and the properties of complex adaptive systems
- explain the criteria for and benefits of using theory and models in the organisation development (OD) diagnostic process
- discuss Lewin's and Kotter's models of planned change
- explain the elements of open systems models and how they apply to OD planned change efforts
- discuss examples of open systems models and how they can be applied in the OD planned change process
- explain the sources and forms of resistance to change, and discuss tactics to overcome resistance
- describe conditions for successful planned change efforts.

Introduction

Organisation development (OD) is about planned change interventions that seek to improve organisational effectiveness and employee wellbeing (Robbins et al, 2008). In the South African context, OD is seen as an important human resource practice concerned with planned systemic organisational change processes. These processes work toward the continual improvement of an organisation's effectiveness by utilising diagnostic data and designing and implementing appropriate solutions and interventions to measurably enable the organisation to optimise its purpose and strategy (SABPP, 2014) in a complex and changing business environment. Changes in organisational strategies, structure, technologies, products and services aimed at effectively responding to shifts in the environment can be planned. This book (and this chapter) is primarily concerned with planned change efforts as a core focus of OD (Weiss, 2001). Managers who conduct their businesses in the present and future marketplace must be flexible and adaptive in a constantly changing environment. They must be able to diagnose problems affecting the competitiveness and sustainability of the organisation, and be able to implement planned change programmes. Organisations and their managers are therefore using OD theories, principles and techniques to increase their effectiveness and their adaptability to changing conditions in the business environment (Brown, 2011). The planned change efforts of an OD programme involves the application and transfer of behavioural science knowledge and practice to organisational members by helping them to gain the knowledge, skills and attitudes necessary for the organisational system to adapt to and manage planned change in the future (Cummings & Worley, 2005).

Planned change involves organisational activities that are intentional and goal-directed. The goals revolve around improving the organisation's capability to adapt to changes in its environment. Changes in the external business environment act as forces for organisational change, requiring the organisation to adapt internally to enable its sustainability as a high-performing, competitive business in the marketplace (Robbins & Judge, 2011; Robbins et al, 2008). Chapter 1 outlined some of the key forces of change that the OD consultant needs to take note of when engaging in action research or planned change activities (also see Chapter 8). Change is often rapid and its implications are complex and often unpredictable. Technological advances can, for example, make old products, services or organisational processes redundant. Change directly impacts the nature and level of competition, and requires of individuals, groups or teams, and the organisation to respond rapidly in innovative ways (Brooks, 2009).

The forces of change discussed in this book (see Chapter 1) have various implications for OD. Innovative OD approaches and techniques are required to help organisations assess themselves and their environments, and revitalise and rebuild their strategies, structure and processes (Cummings & Worley, 2005). The traditional Newtonian organisation, symbolising predictability and stability, has become outdated in the knowledge economy, with OD practitioners seeking new and innovative means to design living system-organisations that will thrive into the future in this new environment (Veldsman, 2013; Wheatley, 2006).

Approaches to planned change

This chapter covers selected theories and models about organisations and change that are useful in the diagnostic phase of planned change efforts. All approaches to OD rely on some theory of planned change which is influenced by theories and models of organisational behaviour (Brooks, 2009; Cummings & Worley, 2005; Robbins et al, 2008). Theories and models of organisational behaviour and change have a significant bearing on current OD thought and practice in organisations. A sound knowledge and understanding of these theories and models will help to improve the OD consultant's ability to diagnose and resolve organisational problems which negatively impact the organisation's ability to effectively adjust to a fast-changing and complex business environment (Brooks, 2009).

Criteria for effective planned change models

Organisational change models differ in terms of their purpose, the level of analysis (individual, group or organisational), the components (phenomena) and the relationship between them. OD consultants therefore use a certain set of criteria to determine the effectiveness, appropriateness and usefulness of an organisational change model. The model and its structural components must be operationally well defined. It must also be explicit in terms of its description of the organisational phenomena (components) and the relationship between them. The model must have a sound theoretical base, and empirical evidence of its reliability, generalisability to other organisational contexts and face validity in OD practice must be clear (Olivier, 2011).

Benefits of using organisational change models in organisation development diagnostics

OD consultants generally use change models to explain an organisational diagnostic method by means of which organisational phenomena may be understood, and therefore managed, to improve overall organisational effectiveness and performance (Chawane, Van Vuuren & Roodt, 2003). Theories of planned change and the models provided by organisational behaviour theories are therefore useful OD tools in the organisational diagnostic process (see Chapter 8). Diagnosis is the process of understanding a system's current functioning. Change models provide a conceptual framework that describes the relationships between different features of the organisation, as well as its context and effectiveness (Cummings & Worley, 2005). Taking into consideration the complex nature of organisational phenomena, the taxonomy of key organisational dimensions described by the change models is useful to guide data collection and diagnosis in the action research process (Chawane et al, 2003; Martins & Coetzee, 2009). Models of planned change and organisational behaviour are not meant to be prescriptive; rather, they are meant to provide a convenient, shorthand method to diagnose, plan and manage change (Burke & Litwin, 1992; Martins & Coetzee, 2009).

Organisational change models are especially helpful at the planning stage to establish the parameters (boundaries) of the planned change effort and to monitor the facilitation of later stages. The conceptual framework provided by the change models can assist with data analysis and interpretation, and help maintain an orderly assessment of, and deepen insight into, the dynamics and complexities that the data may reflect. Change models also provide a useful framework for reporting the outcome of the planned change effort to management and other stakeholders in a meaningful manner (Olivier, 2011). In this chapter, we discuss five models (see Table 6.1 on page 132) relating to planned change, each with a unique focus and usefulness in OD initiatives.

The models (and their underpinning theories) outlined in Table 6.1 are relevant to contemporary change management (CM) efforts. Planned change efforts are typically informed by the **'what'** (ie the target elements of the planned change) and the **'how'** (ie the various steps that could be followed to help the organisational system and its members to adapt to the envisaged change). Open-system theories and models such as those of Burke and Litwin (1992), the organisational efficiency model of Veldsman (2013) and the organisational effectiveness measurement framework of Olivier (2015) could be applied as organisational diagnostic tools for planning and measuring change. The models provide a framework of well-researched organisational system elements that should be targeted (ie **what** to target for change) in order to ensure that the change effort addresses elements that will help the organisation to survive and thrive in fast-changing business environments.

Change programmes can be successful only if OD practitioners and managers understand **how** organisations and their members typically react to change, and **how** to manage and stabilise the change process. They therefore apply principles of planned change in the execution of a change programme. The classical model by Lewin (1951) outlines a three-stage model of planned change that explains how to initiate, manage and stabilise the change process. Managing the initiation, implementation and stabilisation of the change process has long been seen as one of the main challenges of organisational change (Sinding & Waldstrom, 2014). Lewin's model is a valuable OD tool that helps organisational members understand the factors that would support a change effort and what resistance might prevent the change from being adopted by organisational members who are affected by the change effort (Anderson, 2013).

Kotter's (1995) model helps OD practitioners and managers understand the factors (outlined as steps) that lead to the failure (if the steps are not addressed) or success (if the steps are followed) of change programmes. The model by Brown (2011) is a useful diagnostic tool for understanding how to assess the style or orientation of the organisation in adapting to change (ie **how** organisations adapt to change). Adaptation has become an important change-supportive trait of successful organisations and their members (Holt & Brockett, 2012). The notion of adaptation styles is therefore important to consider in the light of organisations having to adapt to rapid technological advances by promoting organisational innovation to survive in the more unpredictable and uncertain business environment of a globalised knowledge- and information-driven economy and society (Oldham & Da Silva, 2015).

Table 6.1 Models of planned change (Author)

HOW (steps in planned change and style in adapting to change)			WHAT (target elements of planned change)		
Steps in managing and leading change		Measuring organisational style/ orientation in adapting to change (how organisations adapt)	Open-system models applied as organisational diagnostic tools for planning and measuring change		
Lewin's three-step model of planned change	Kotter's eight-step plan for leading organisational change	Brown's model of adaptive orientation	Burke–Litwin model of organisational performance and change	Veldsman's organisational efficiency model	Olivier's framework for measuring organisational effectiveness

Lewin's three-step model of planned change

Lewin's model is not a diagnostic one. It rather explains **how** to initiate, manage and stabilise the change process (Kinicki & Fugate, 2012). Lewin argued that change is a dynamic process which takes the form of an ongoing struggle between a set of opposing forces: one pushing in the direction of change (called driving forces) and the other pulling in the opposite direction (called restraining forces). As shown in Figure 6.1 on page 134, the struggle between these two sets of forces is portrayed as a 'force field', where a stable situation consists of a state of equilibrium (balance) between these two forces (Rollinson, 2005). OD practitioners would typically help organisation members to identify these forces in the CM process.

An example of a simple force field of 'pushing' for change is the case where a group of employees who all have their own special tasks now have to become multi-skilled and learn how to collaborate in a virtual team environment across the globe to bring innovative thinking to their research and development.

Some of the forces driving the change are the prospects of more varied work, innovative thinking and creativity, greater value on the job market because of wider skills and intellectual capital, and greater social contact and networking with colleagues across the globe. Some of the restraining forces pushing for resisting the change and maintaining the status quo may be the employee's apprehensions about mastering a wider range of skills, collaborating in a virtual team environment, losing one's individuality and not gaining recognition for unique and novel contributions, being more easily replaceable and the effect on earnings.

Lewin further argued that the first step in initiating successful change is to destabilise the current state of equilibrium, which can be done in one or a combination of three basic steps (Kinicki & Fugate, 2012; Robbins & Judge, 2011; Rollinson, 2005):

1. **Unfreezing** (destabilising) the status quo situation can be achieved by a combination of either reducing the strength of the restraining forces and/ or increasing (strengthening) the pushing/driving forces. The direction of the forces can also be changed so that a restraint becomes a push factor. The focus of this stage is to create motivation for the change. Individuals are encouraged to replace old behaviours and attitudes with those desired by managers, and it is important that people become dissatisfied with the old ways of doing things.

2. **Moving to the new situation** (changing the current situation and moving toward the desired end state) can be achieved by, for example, having people see others around them doing the same thing, and applying the tactics to deal with resistance to change and other OD techniques described in this book. Research shows change has to happen quickly for it to be effective. Organisations that build up to change do less well than those that get to and through the movement stage quickly (Robbins & Judge, 2011).

3. **Refreezing** the new change to make it permanent can be achieved by, for example, rewarding new desired behaviour and discouraging regression to prior behaviour. Once change has been implemented, it must be refrozen so it can be sustained over time. Without refreezing the change, it will most likely be short-lived. The objective of refreezing is to stabilise the new situation by balancing the driving and restraining forces (Robbins & Judge, 2011).

The three stages outlined in Lewin's model constitute a valuable OD tool that helps organisational members understand the importance of the change effort (the 'why') and how to manage and stabilise the change effort.

Restraining forces resisting the change

MOVE
to new situation
(desired end state)

REFREEZE
the change

Desired end state

UNFREEZE
the status quo

Status quo

Time

Driving forces pushing the change

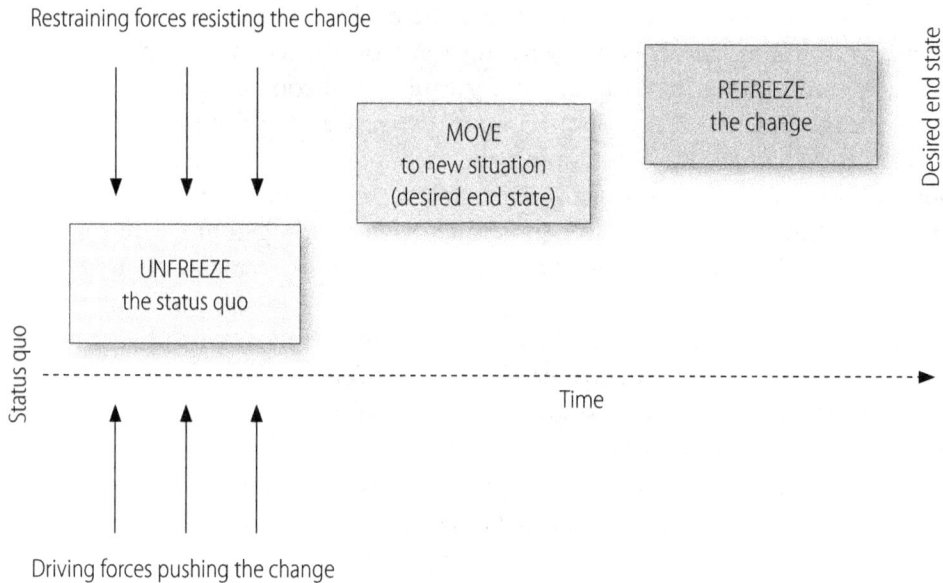

Figure 6.1 Compiled by the author based on Lewin's three-step model of planned change

Kotter's eight-step plan for leading organisational change

Kotter built on Lewin's model to create a more detailed approach for leading organisational change (Robbins & Judge, 2011). Similar to Lewin's model, Kotter's model of change prescribes **how** managers should sequence or lead the change process. It is not a diagnostic model; that is, it will not help managers and OD consultants to diagnose **what** needs to be changed (Kinicki & Fugate, 2012).

The eight-step process of Kotter's change model is based on his research on typical errors management makes when implementing change. The model therefore provides specific recommendations about behaviours that managers need to exhibit in order to successfully lead organisational change. The model subsumes Lewin's model of change. The eight steps are sequential and, if followed in this sequence, will help managers and OD consultants to overcome problems of resistance in leading change. The first four steps represent Lewin's 'unfreezing' stage. Steps 5, 6, and 7 represent the 'movement' (changing) phase, while step 8 corresponds with the 'refreezing' phase (Kinicki & Fugate, 2012; Robbins et al, 2008).

Unfreezing

Step 1: Unfreeze the organisation by establishing a sense of urgency. This is done by creating a compelling reason for why change is needed.

Step 2: Form a coalition with enough power to lead the change. This is done by creating a cross-functional, cross-level group of people with enough power to lead the change.

Step 3: Create a new vision to direct the change and strategies for achieving this vision. Developing a vision and strategy guides the change process.

Step 4: Communicate the vision throughout the organisation. This is done by developing and implementing a communication strategy that consistently communicates the new vision and strategic plan (Kinicki & Fugate, 2012; Robbins et al, 2008).

Changing

Step 5: Empower broad-based action. This is done by using target elements of change to transform the organisation, empowering other people to act on the vision, removing barriers to change and encouraging risk taking and creative problem solving.

Step 6: Plan for, create and reward short-term wins that move the organisation towards the new vision. Recognise and reward those who contribute to the wins.

Step 7: Consolidate gains and improvements, and produce more change. Reassess changes and make necessary adjustments in the new programmes. The guiding coalition uses credibility from short-term wins to create more change. Additional people are brought into the change process as change cascades throughout the organisation. Attempts are made to reinvigorate the change process (Kinicki & Fugate, 2012; Robbins et al, 2008).

Refreezing

Step 8: Anchor new approaches in the culture by reinforcing the changes. This is done by demonstrating the relationship between new behaviours and organisational success. Methods to ensure leadership development and succession must be developed (Kinicki & Fugate, 2012; Robbins et al, 2008).

Helping organisational members understand and move through the eight steps outlined in Kotter's (1995) model enables OD practitioners and managers to successfully manage and stabilise the change effort.

A model of adaptive orientation

The model of adaptive orientation is a useful diagnostic model to assess the style or orientation of the organisation in adapting to change. As shown in Figure 6.2 on page 137, Brown (2011) differentiates between four adaptation styles, namely: sluggish-thermostat management, satisficing management, reactive management and renewing/transformational management:

1. The **sluggish-thermostat management style** of adaptation describes organisations that resist change until cost trade-offs favour it. They are slow to adapt to change, which makes the term an appropriate metaphor because many organisations set their thermostats so low that they become insensitive to change (Brown, 2011). The sluggish management style is based on a stable environment, low risk, with formalised procedures and a high degree of structure and control. Organisations that use a sluggish adaptation style tend to have very stable goals, many layers of managerial hierarchy and a highly centralised structure. They may tend to value tradition and seniority more than performance and innovation (Brown, 2011).

2. The **satisficing management style** of adaptation relates to the term 'satisfactory' and describes management that is adequate, average and appropriate for a stable environment. Although the organisation functions in a stable environment, it is still high in its ability to adapt to change. The satisficing management style emphasises a centralised decision-making structure with problems referred to top management. Planning and decision making are usually concentrated at the top, with high clarity of procedures and roles. Change is accomplished at a rate adequate to keep up with industry (Brown, 2011).

3. The **reactive management style** refers to a low level of adaptation to change and a tendency to deal with problems in a hyperturbulent environment in the short term. Management reacts to a stimulus after conditions in the environment have changed. Reflecting a short-term, crisis type of adaptation, this often involves replacement of key people, hasty reorganisation and drastic cutting of staff and product lines (Brown, 2011).

4. The **renewing/transformational management** style refers to a high level of adaptation in a hyperturbulent environment. The organisation introduces change to deal with future conditions before these conditions actually occur. Organisations with a renewing/transformational management style tend to be champions of innovation—they are faster at developing new ideas, more responsive to competitive changes (that is, they have a more sensitive thermostat) and more participative in getting the commitment and involvement of organisation members in the renewal process (Brown, 2011).

Brown's model of adaptation styles is an important OD tool that helps managers and organisational members understand the fit between the organisational (management) adaptation style and the context in which the organisational system is functioning as a business. As stated, adaptation has become an important change-supportive trait of successful organisations and their members in today's more turbulent business environment (Holt & Brockett, 2012).

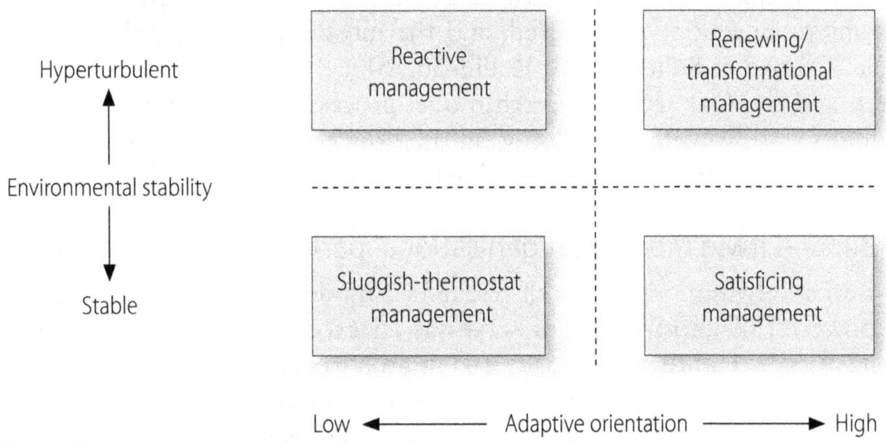

Figure 6.2 Model of organisational adaptive orientation styles (adapted from Brown, 2011: 56)

Systems models of change

Systems models of organisational change focus on the '**what**', or target elements, of planned change. Systems models (see Table 6.1 on page 132) offer managers and OD consultants a conceptual framework or model to use for diagnosing what to change and for determining how to evaluate the success of a change effort (Kinicki & Fugate, 2012). Systems models consider the organisation as an open system: 'open' suggesting that it interacts with other, broader systems outside the organisation (see Figure 6.3 on page 141 and Figure 6.4 on page 143). These external systems are seen as part of the organisational environment. As shown in Figure 6.3 and Figure 6.4, the organisation is viewed as an integrated and complex web of relationships between structures, technology, people, and all manner of technical and social processes that are regarded as the various components (elements) of the broader organisational system. These various organisational components are interrelated, implying that a change in one will result in change in the others (Brooks, 2009). OD planned change efforts therefore use a systemic approach in which an organisation is treated as a set of interacting phenomena relating to the various components of an organisational system. Taking an integrated and holistic perspective to change, OD assumes that all of these system components are likely to need change together. The systems perspective to change thus recognises the complexities of the interdependencies between organisational components, implying that if change is made to one of the components, this is almost bound to require some degree of modification in the others to restore the balance of compatibility with them. Major difficulties are often encountered in change programmes because these interconnections are ignored, and the most neglected variable is often people (Oxman & Smith, 2003; Rollinson, 2005). The models of Lewin and Kotter, and the OD action research model process (see Chapter 7), attempt to address this problem by focusing on the **how** of change, which centres on bringing about change in people's behaviour and attitudes (Rollinson, 2005).

The Burke–Litwin model of organisational performance and change

The Burke–Litwin model is a well-researched model used by OD consultants as a powerful diagnostic tool. It serves as an excellent example of an open systems model. Figure 6.3 on page 141 is an adapted version of the original Burke–Litwin model and illustrates how it is used in the OD context to report on the results of an organisational survey (OD diagnostic effort) which formed part of the diagnostic phase of an OD action research process (Martins & Coetzee, 2009). The Burke–Litwin model is described as one of the most comprehensive change models based on sound theory and research. The model has been found to enhance the efficacy of an organisational diagnosis and serves as a guide to planned change actions as a consequence of the diagnosis (French & Bell, 1999; Kraut, 1996; Martins & Coetzee, 2009).

The Burke–Litwin model of organisational performance and change differentiates between the **transactional** level of human behaviour, or the everyday interactions and exchanges that create the climate of the organisation, and the **transformational** processes that are required for genuine change in the culture of an organisation. Changes in the transformational components of the organisational system are usually caused by interaction with environmental forces for change (both internal and external) and therefore require entirely new behaviour sets on the part of organisational members (French & Bell, 1999; Jones & Brazzel, 2006; Martins & Coetzee, 2009). Changes in the transformational components (organisational mission and strategy, leadership and culture) affect the transactional components (organisational structure, systems, management practices and climate) (Burke & Litwin, 1992). The transformational and transactional components are mutually interdependent, and changes in the components of the two change focus areas eventually impact on individuals' and organisational performance (Chawane et al, 2003).

Transformational factors affecting organisational performance

- **External environment:** This system component refers to outside conditions or situations (eg forces for change) that influence the performance of the organisation. These conditions include things such as marketplaces, world financial conditions, political/governmental circumstances, competition and customers.

- **Vision, mission and strategy:** This system component refers to what employees believe is the central purpose of the organisation and how it intends to achieve that purpose over an extended period of time.
- **Leadership:** This system component refers to leadership behaviour that encourages others to take needed actions.
- **Organisational culture:** This system component refers to 'the way we do things around here'. Culture is the collection of overt and covert rules, values and principles that guide organisational behaviour and that have been strongly influenced by history, custom and practice.
- **Individual and organisational performance:** This system component refers to the outcomes or results, with indicators of effort and achievement. Such indicators might include productivity, customer or staff satisfaction, profit and service quality, salary and benefits, and recognition (Martins & Coetzee, 2009).

Transactional factors affecting organisational performance

- **Structure:** This system component refers to the arrangement of functions and people into specific areas and levels of responsibility, decision-making authority and relationships. Structure assures effective implementation of the organisation's mission and strategy.
- **Management practices:** This system component refers to what managers do in the normal course of events in using the human and material resources at their disposal to carry out the organisation's strategy. Aspects such as managerial behaviour, work etiquette, professionalism, planning, communication and control are included.
- **Systems (policies and procedures):** This system component refers to standardised policies and mechanisms that facilitate work. Systems primarily manifest themselves in the organisation's reward systems and in control systems such as goal and budget development and standard operating procedures (SOPs).
- **Departmental/work unit climate:** This system component refers to the collective current impressions, expectations and feelings of the employees in departments. These in turn affect members' relations with superiors, with one another and with other departments. A positive work climate may enhance retention rates, and a negative work climate may act as a 'push' factor, leading to a high labour turnover.
- **Task requirements and individual skills/abilities:** This system component refers to the behaviour required for task effectiveness, including specific skills and knowledge required for people to accomplish the work assigned and for which they feel directly responsible. This component deals

with concerns about the match between a person and the job, and thus reflects recruitment, selection, appointments and promotions.

- **Individual needs and values:** This system component refers to the specific psychological factors that provide desire and worth for individual actions or thoughts such as stress, wellbeing, recreational activities and living conditions.
- **Motivation:** This system component refers to behavioural tendencies to move toward goals, take the needed action and persist until satisfaction is attained. Motivation is the resultant net energy generated by the sum of achievement, power, affection, discovery and other important human motives (Martins & Coetzee, 2009).

Figure 6.3 on page 141 shows two additional system components which do not form part of the original Burke–Litwin model. These relate to the transactional aspects of the Burke–Litwin model and were identified by the diagnostic process that formed part of the organisational survey conducted by Martins and Coetzee (2009):

- **Equipment:** This system component refers to the tools to do the job and the quality of available technology.
- **Working environment:** This system component refers to facilities such as the buildings, offices, staff cafeteria and recreational facilities for staff.

Activity

Study Figure 6.3 on page 141 (applying the Burke–Litwin model as a diagnostic tool) and work through the following activities:

1. Review the forces of change in Chapter 1 and the model of adaptive orientation (Figure 6.2 on page 137).
2. Review the results of the diagnostic survey by Martins and Coetzee (2009) summarised in the adapted version of the Burke–Litwin model (Figure 6.3).
3. What type of organisational adaptive orientation style do the survey results reflect? Give reasons for your answer.
4. Identify the principles relevant to Lewin's and Kotter's models of planned change that could be applied to improve the adaptive orientation style of the organisation.

The Burke–Litwin model provides a systems perspective to change and helps organisations and their members recognise the complexities of the interdependencies between organisational components. Major difficulties are often encountered in change programmes because these interconnections are ignored. If change is made to one of the components, this is almost bound to require some degree of modification in the others to restore the balance of compatibility with them.

External environment
+ Good reputation/identity
+ Good business/profits
+ Good customer service
– Inconsistent service
– Competition

Mission & strategy
+ Clear objectives/targets
– Strategy planning does not consider all future scenarios
– Operational strategic planning is lacking
– No staff communication strategy

Leadership
+ Excellent Excom team
– Leadership skills are lacking/lack of adequate knowledge and experience
– Leadership makes false promises

Organisation culture
– Old management ideas
– Management is 20th century

Structure
– Staff shortage
– No training manager
– High staff turnover

Management practices
+ Supportive management
– Poor staff communication
– Lack of basic management skills

Systems, policies & procedures
– Too much red tape and paperwork
– Outdated human resource systems
– Staff not trained in SOPs

Task requirements & individual skills/ abilities
– Succession planning not done
– Recruitment: right people not selected
– Promotion: right people not promoted
– Lack of training and development

Departmental climate
+ Good team work in departments
+ Friendly staff
– Lack of cooperation and communication between departments

Individual needs & values
+ Interesting jobs
+ Job security
– Inadequate welfare system/recreation and staff facilities

Motivation
+ Job satisfaction
+ Yearly bonus
– Negative impact of salaries based on nationalities

Equipment
– More convenient uniforms
– Upgraded equipment
– IT systems not operational and software outdated

Working environment
– Old property, expensive to maintain
– Old furniture and facilities

Individual & organisational performance
+ Satisfied customers
+ Proud to work for company
– Poor benefits and lack of staff recognition

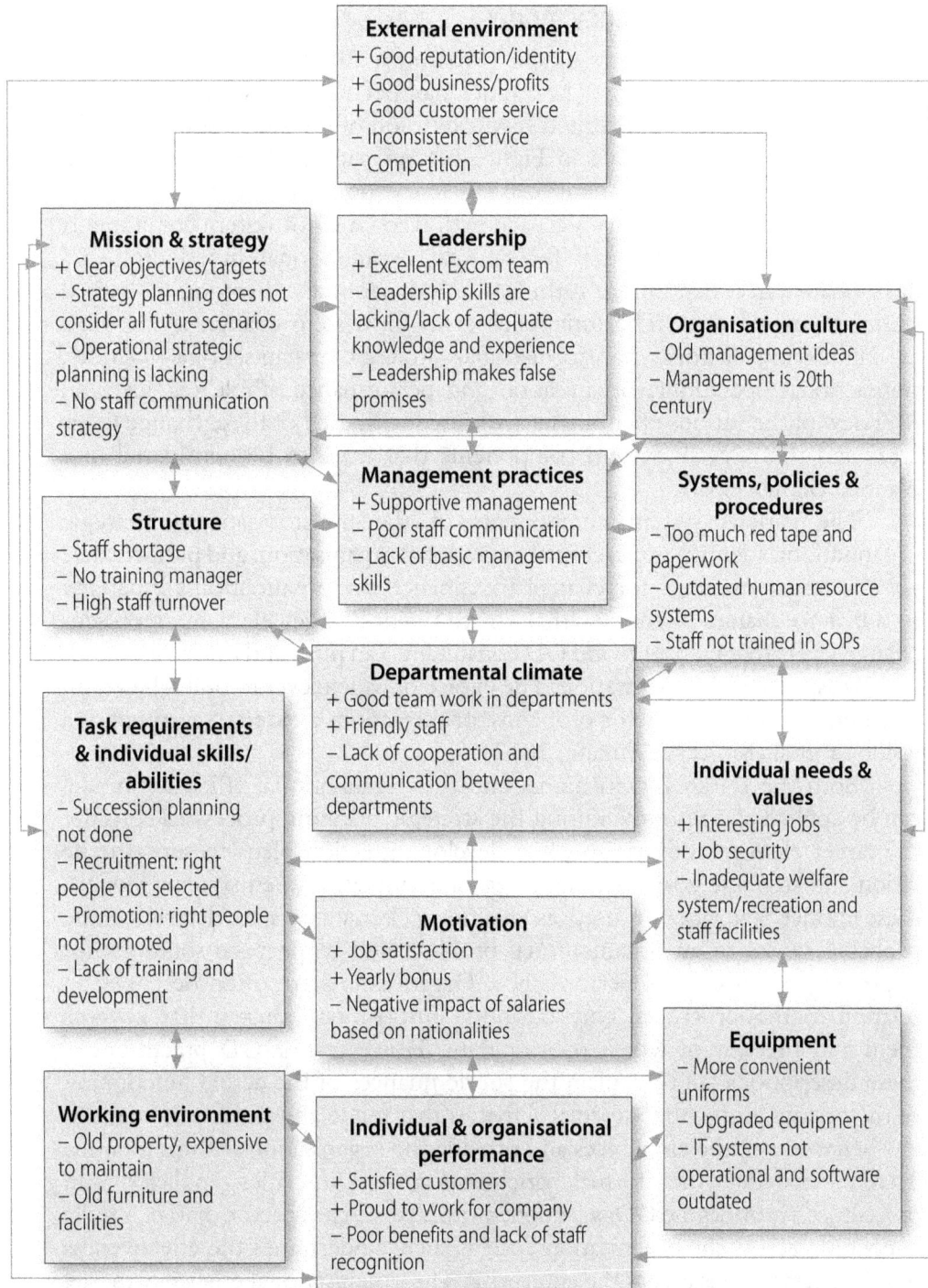

Figure 6.3 Applying the Burke–Litwin model as a diagnostic tool in OD (Martins & Coetzee, 2009: 153)

141

The organisational efficiency model

The organisational efficiency model (Veldsman, 2013) is another example of an open systems model. The model has been designed for the South African organisational context and is an extension of the Burke–Litwin model (Veldsman, 2013). As shown in Figure 6.4 on page 143 and in Table 6.2 on pages 144–146, the organisational efficiency model differentiates between four focus areas of system change, each with its own set of system components that are regarded as essential for optimal organisational functioning and performance in today's more turbulent and dynamically changing globalised business environment. The four focus areas for system change are labelled as influencing factors, transformational strategic organisational identity, transactional operational organisation and performance. Table 6.2 gives an overview of the various phenomena associated with each of these change focus areas and the relevant system components that need to be considered in a planned change effort.

The various system components of the transformational strategic organisational identity, transactional operational organisation, and performance are the target elements for change to enhance the organisation's capability to adapt to change in the external environment. Target elements represent change levers that managers and OD consultants can push and pull to influence various aspects of an organisation. The choice of which lever to pull is based on a diagnosis of the problem or problems, or the actions needed to accomplish a vision or goal (Kinicki & Fugate, 2012).

Both the Burke–Litwin model and the organisational efficiency model can be applied as a resource during the strategic planning process to consider the target elements of change when developing action plans to support the vision and strategic goals. Serving as good examples of open systems models, these models can also be used as diagnostic frameworks to determine the probable causes of an organisational problem and to propose solutions for improving organisational performance. Organisations are often described in relation to the structures, core business, purpose or industry that governs them and the way in which they operate. However, for OD practitioners, these descriptions fail to explain the subtle nuances of the actual functioning of the organisation—the informal activities that guide and govern the day-to-day behaviour of the employees and provide the organisation with its identity. Merely studying the formal organisation – the rules, policies and procedures – provides the OD practitioner with a skewed perspective of what is really happening across the organisation and, as such, undermines the effectiveness of OD interventions across the enterprise. The organisational efficiency model proposed by Veldsman (2013) aims to describe the organisation in relation to the formal and informal components that exist in an attempt to explain, understand and incorporate organisational culture as a guiding principle in all OD interventions that are planned for the organisation.

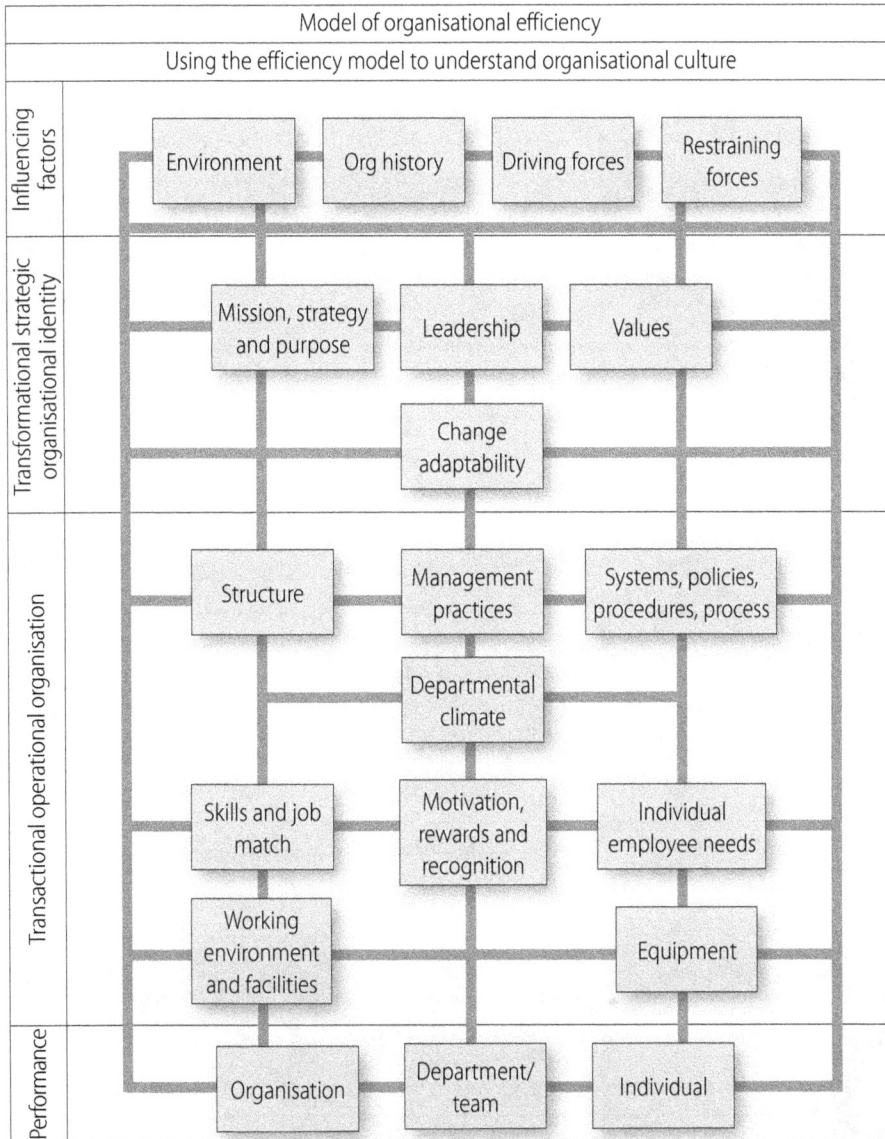

Model of organisational efficiency			
Using the efficiency model to understand organisational culture			

Influencing factors

- Environment
- Org history
- Driving forces
- Restraining forces

Transformational strategic organisational identity

- Mission, strategy and purpose
- Leadership
- Values
- Change adaptability

Transactional operational organisation

- Structure
- Management practices
- Systems, policies, procedures, process
- Departmental climate
- Skills and job match
- Motivation, rewards and recognition
- Individual employee needs
- Working environment and facilities
- Equipment

Performance

- Organisation
- Department/ team
- Individual

Figure 6.4 The organisational efficiency model (Veldsman, 2013)

Activity

Review the forces of change discussed in Chapter 1. Compare the system components described in the Burke–Litwin model and the organisational efficiency model. Which model would you recommend as a diagnostic tool to ensure that the forces of change are properly considered in the planned change effort? Give reasons for your answer.

Table 6.2 System components of the organisational efficiency model (Veldsman, 2013)

	System component	Description	Core factors/phenomena
Influencing factors	Environmental influence	Factors that will influence organisational performance and that are not under the direct control of the organisation	● Industry ● Competitors ● Market and global trends ● Legislative impact ● Resources
	Organisational history	Factors that have had an impact on the shaping and the forming of the organisation into what it is today	Organisation profile
	Driving forces	Forces that are key areas of strength and competitive advantage for the organisation and can be leveraged to optimise organisational performance	Organisational strengths
	Restraining forces	Forces that are inhibiting the organisation to achieve its maximum potential	Developmental/renewal opportunities
Transformational strategic organisational identity	Mission, strategy and purpose (value proposition)	The motives and intent of the organisation that will inform the task-level activities related to the organisation	● Strategic intent and market relevance ● Clarity ● Employee buy-in ● Goals and objectives
	Leadership	The influencing and empowering of organisational members to achieve the goals and direction of the organisation	● Authenticity and credibility ● Leadership style ● Direction and guidance ● Leading and deciding ➝

	System component	Description	Core factors/phenomena
	Change adaptability	The extent to which the organisation is adaptable to and embracing of change, and the current level of maturity as it relates to change practices	● Attitude towards change ● Change competence ● Resilience ● People energy, creativity and innovation
	Values	The integrated patterns of behaviour that shape and reinforce the behavioural frameworks within the organisation	● Behavioural norms ● Value awareness ● Informal organisational practices
Transactional operational organisation	Structure	The hierarchy and the reporting structure of the organisation	● Span of control ● Effectiveness of structure ● Governance
	Management practices	The daily operational management practices and relationship between employees and their direct supervisors	● Management style ● Span of control ● Support ● Feedback ● Communication
	Systems, policies, procedures and processes	The elements of the formal organisation that governs the daily operational components of how tasks get delivered	● Processes ● Policies ● Systems ● Expectations
	Departmental climate	The current impressions, expectations and feelings that employees have about their immediate working environment	● Stress levels ● Relationships ● Skill utilisation
	Skills and job match	The optimisation and fit for purpose of the human workforce of the organisation relevant to the strategy and performance output of the organisation	● Skill development ● Skill–job fit ● Reward and recognition structure
	Motivation, rewards and recognition	The drivers of individual and team achievement as well as the reinforcement of desirable behaviours	● Motivational mechanisms ● Employee wellbeing

	System component	Description	Core factors/phenomena
	Individual psychological needs	Factors pertaining to the wellbeing and congruence of employee–organisational fit	○ Engagement and empowerment ○ Organisational value fit ○ Organisational support
	Working environment facilities	The physical work environment and infrastructure that exist	○ Work practices ○ Technology ○ Infrastructure
	Equipment and technology	The physical equipment available to the members of the organisation to do their jobs	Facilities
Performance	Organisational performance	Factors related to the performance output of the organisation in relation to its strategy, mission and purpose	○ Achievement of strategic goals/outcomes ○ Return on investment and expectations ○ Financial performance ○ Retention of talent/ intellectual and social capital ○ Innovation and creativity ○ Adaptability
	Departmental/team performance	Factors related to the performance of the individual business units or teams within the organisation	○ Achievement of departmental goals ○ Financial performance ○ Innovation and creativity
	Individual performance	Factors pertaining to the individual performance of employees	○ Contribution to organisational success ○ Performance management ○ Innovation and creativity

The case study on pages 147–157 illustrates the usefulness of the principles of planned change and the organisational efficiency model in the OD action research process.

Case study

Study the forces of change and work through the case below. Evaluate the usefulness of the organisational efficiency model as a diagnostic tool for planning change. Review the principles of change explained by Lewin and by Kotter—identify the steps or phases of planned change relevant to these models as you work through the case study. Also study the action research process in Chapter 8 before working through this case study. Would you say that the OD planned change intervention assisted in changing the organisation's adaptive orientation style? How was it accomplished?

Improving the organisational efficiency of Etiket

Etiket, the focus of this case study, is a young entrepreneurial organisation that has grown significantly, both in number of staff and clients, over the past six years since its inception in 2006. The average age of the workforce is 24, with the executive leadership team ranging between the ages of 29 and 36. The business has experienced significant success through its ability to solve business problems in a creative and innovative manner, and building a culture of narrative belief within its own ranks. The essence of the organisation's success is its ability to understand its clients' story, conceptually understand the business problem from a marketing perspective, and apply creativity to drive and enable organisational outcomes.

However, the organisation had reached a tipping point, with formalisation threatening to disrupt the core of what defined Etiket's past and current successes. Constant growth and a bigger client portfolio demanded the formalisation of organisational practices and the clarification of reporting lines and structures that would enable responsiveness and dictate responsibility. As such, Etiket needed to re-evaluate its current business model according to certain design criteria, namely:

- formalising the organisation without losing the current culture and identity that defines it
- designing the organisation to create innovation as part of the delivery value chain
- keeping work practices flexible and allowing employees the freedom to innovate
- bearing employee age in mind; allowing junior employees to, at times, take on more responsibility to keep them challenged and engaged
- designing talent practices that would enable and motivate the GenY workforce, rather than inhibiting their freedom.

1. Diagnosis methodology

The project was initiated through a collaborative organisational analysis that utilised an emergent change approach aimed at involving the workforce in the future that they want to create. The diagnosis focused on evaluating the elements listed in Table 1 (on page 148) to understand the current organisational identity.

Table 1: Outcomes of the OD diagnosis (Veldsman, 2013)

System elements	Description	OD diagnostic findings
Environmental context	Evaluate industry and market trends that will inform the organisational strategy and value proposition.	It is a vibrant industry dictated by the rise of multifunctional agencies that can deliver end-to-end client solutions. The rise of digital solutions and the need to remain competitive are a critical source of success.
Business strengths	Inherent strengths that enable organisational success are evaluated and incorporated into design criteria in order to build on current areas of competitive advantage.	There is conceptual strength in relating business problems to plausible and executable solutions through flexibility and responsive client practices.
Purpose and identity	The reason for the existence of the organisation, as well as the difference that it makes to society and its clients, is evaluated.	Etiket exists to create and tell a compelling narrative that solves business problems.
Behavioural values	The behavioural framework that governs organisational activities is explored.	Etiket had a behavioural value system, but it was undefined and incongruent with the organisational identity.
Strategic goals	The strategy is evaluated in terms of the organisational goals.	Etiket had a one-dimensional, top-down strategy that was not facilitated or shared by all levels of the organisation. The strategy did not contain measurable objectives, goals or criteria.
Products/services	Products and services that the organisation provides as part of the core business are explored.	Etiket delivered creative marketing solutions that incorporated all elements of below-the-line marketing, as well as a recent merger to incorporate a digital marketing agency.

System elements	Description	OD diagnostic findings
Finance	The functional financial governance and controls are evaluated according to specific client requirements.	Limited financial controls existed, with no management information provided to make strategic decisions.
Processes/systems	Existing processes and systems are evaluated and incorporated into the organisational value chain. Inefficiencies and constraints are also explored.	Process inefficiencies were identified within the value chain, as well as limited understanding of system functionality and how processes and systems contribute towards organisational goals.
Stakeholders	Organisational stakeholders are defined, and avenues of interaction are evaluated.	Stakeholders were well known, but interaction with them was limited. Etiket was unable to answer the question of 'what a happy client looks like'.
People	Current people practices are explored and evaluated according to the needs of the organisation.	No people practices in terms of performance management, knowledge sharing or talent management existed.

Based upon the organisational diagnosis, the following transformation process was designed to facilitate the organisational design process according to positive psychology principles and large-scale change methodologies:

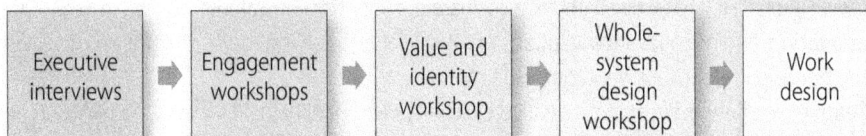

Executive interviews → Engagement workshops → Value and identity workshop → Whole-system design workshop → Work design

Figure 1: The intervention process

Executive interviews

Each of the five executive directors was interviewed according to a semi-structured interview design (based on Britten, Campbell & Pope, 2002) focused on exploring the original idea behind the business, the strengths of the organisation and the visionary dream for the future. Current practices relating to people were explored within the narrative design (Riley & Hawe, 2009), as well as the high-level organisational processes.

Core themes across all interviews were analysed and used as planning for the engagement workshops. The identified themes are shown in Figure 2 on page 150.

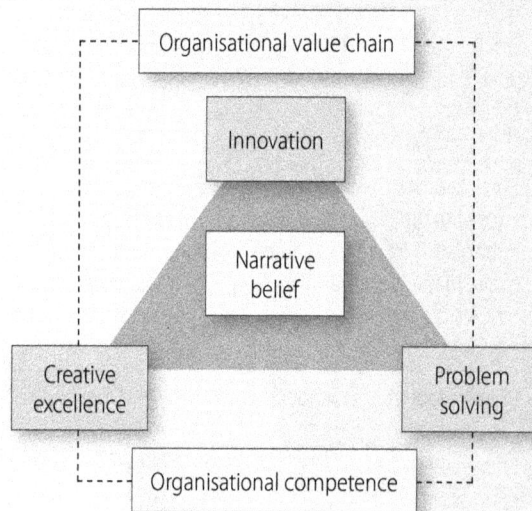

Figure 2: Themes derived from the organisational narrative

At the heart of the organisation was a theme called '**narrative belief**', which is a term that describes the core business of Etiket: telling the organisational story from both an internal and a client perspective. Narrative belief was achieved through three organisational themes of significance, namely:

1. **problem solving:** understanding the conceptual business problems of clients in light of the organisational story described in terms of character, identity and values
2. **innovation:** finding innovative solutions to assist clients in solving their problems in a manner that brings competitive advantage to the market
3. **creative excellence:** striving for creative excellence and quality in all aspects of delivery that would enable Etiket to exceed client expectations.

These themes were supported by two concepts: the high-level organisational value chain, which defined the high-level process of delivery and organisational competence; and the framework, which stipulated the required skills, tools and behaviours required to create narrative belief.

Engagement workshops

All staff members were involved in collaborative engagement workshops where their current experience of organisational practices and the envisaged future were explored. The workshop methodology used an interactive software design that allowed for the collection of both quantitative and qualitative data through the mixed methods research design. ➝

Core themes derived from the engagement workshops were the following:

- Theme 1: No clear definition of the organisational value system
- Theme 2: Unstructured lines of authority and responsibility
- Theme 3: No feedback on performance
- Theme 4: No clear definition of what is rewarded within the organisational value system
- Theme 5: Lack of trust on the part of leaders in the delivery capability of younger staff
- Theme 6: Limited opportunity for growth within the organisation.

Based upon feedback received from staff members, a subsequent value and identity workshop was initiated to prepare the design landscape and transition the workforce to the new way of working.

Value and identity workshop

An interactive value and identity workshop was conducted, focusing on co-creating the values that the organisation believed to be core to a code of conduct that the organisation wanted to adopt as part of the new organisational design. The workshop was based upon appreciative inquiry (AI) principles (Cooperrider & Whitney, 1999) and crafted a shared behavioural code to which the employees subscribed and held each other accountable for. The behavioural code was based upon various values, namely:

- **mutual respect:** always treating each other with respect and respecting the idea, regardless of by whom it was generated
- **open communication:** talking honestly and transparently with one another in an environment where sharing is regarded as essential to success
- **ownership and responsibility:** taking ownership of and being responsible for one's own contribution to creating magic for clients
- **trust:** trusting each other's skills and coming to work to be the best that one can be.

All employees co-created and committed to the behavioural code during the workshop.

Whole-system design workshop

The next step focused on a whole-system design workshop, where the entire organisation facilitated a workshop to define the potential future by using real-time strategic change principles as part of the workshop methodology. The session included a strategic presentation by the CEO, who conveyed the reality of the industry, the environment within which the organisation functions, as well as trends that inform the manner in which the organisation operates. As a secondary activity, the organisation collaboratively designed the high-level value chain that guides client delivery, as indicated in Figure 3 on page 152. The session was held with the behavioural code as basis, with all participants actively engaging and signing off the high-level value chain as an outcome of the workshop. The value chain was documented, and current business practices were transitioned into the new model as part of a pilot period, so that all organisational members could experience the new way of working before finally agreeing to the feasibility and viability of the model.

151

| New business generated | Business pitched internally | Internal team compilation | Pitching session | Feedback | Project awarded | Execution |

| Reward and recognition |

| Knowledge management |

| Performance management |

Figure 3: The high-level Etiket value chain

Each element of the value chain was evaluated in terms of its purpose, as well as the extent and characteristic of the change experienced in the new design.

Table 2: The Etiket value chain and change elements for the future

Process step	Description	What has changed in the new design?
New business generated	Etiket initiated new client briefs through its existing network of contacts.	A Business Partner model was implemented, which allowed for the broadening of scope in terms of new client briefs.
Business pitched internally	New briefs were then pitched internally to the agency for presentation, with a deadline for proposal feedback.	Pitches were no longer assigned to a certain creative, but briefed into the general system, with anyone within the organisation being able to collaborate in solving the client's business problem.
Internal team compilation	Organisational members were allowed to form their own teams according to skill sets required to solve the business problems.	Multidisciplinary teams were compiled across divisions, and these collaborated according to skill sets, availability and willingness to participate.
Pitching session	A pitching session was held before a panel consisting of executives, account managers and SMEs. All teams were allowed to present their ideas to the panel, and were evaluated according to a set of defined criteria.	This process allowed the idea to become the guiding principle for solving problems, and the number of possible solutions to clients' problems increased by almost 400%.

Feedback	Everyone who pitched an idea received panel feedback, and areas of strength and improvement were identified. Peer feedback was also encouraged after the pitching session.	All participants received feedback on their ideas, rather than only members who were successful, and immediate feedback was given to participants to encourage flow within the environment.
Project awarded	A project was awarded to the winning team, and for that project the creative was made the creative lead, with team members assigned according to skill sets and availability.	This allowed multidisciplinary teams to work together, and gave individuals more responsibility based on creative skills. It also allowed teams to work across different clients.
Execution	The execution phase was then planned with the resource planner to enable successful delivery. A creative lead coach, a role fulfilled by an executive, was also assigned to each creative lead to guide and support him/her through the project.	The creative leads on each project would be different, and one team member could be the creative lead on a particular project whilst still being a team member on another. This allowed junior members to take on additional responsibility within the business and grow their own skill sets.

The new business model, as well as the subsequent value system, was reinforced through the implementation of the practices discussed in the following sections.

Performance management, reward and recognition

A peer feedback system was implemented, which allowed all participants in any part of the value chain to give each other feedback based upon contribution according to criteria, namely:

- **creative excellence:** delivering quality solutions that meet the client's need
- **innovation:** providing a solution that is an innovative approach to the problem
- **problem solving:** adequately achieving the business objectives stated by the client
- **behavioural values:** exemplary interactions with each other during this process in terms of the defined Etiket behavioural code of conduct.

A subsequent reward and recognition system was implemented as part of a peer review process, with employees being rewarded and recognised according to the defined performance criteria outside of the normal performance cycle, with immediate feedback being expressed as a crucial motivating factor to foster flow in the work environment.

All feedback was incorporated into a performance portfolio, which was used as the basis for career growth and performance feedback sessions conducted by the line managers or technical leads, to enable individual guidance and career growth.

Knowledge management

Core to the business was the retention of knowledge and ideas, to be reused or reworked for future projects. A knowledge management process was incorporated within the value chain, which allowed all participants to share ideas after projects and share the learning that was experienced from that particular client and the execution of the idea. This was documented and owned by the Centre of Excellence that was created to manage the knowledge-sharing process. This allowed all employees to share in each other's lessons learnt, as opposed to being restricted to the scope of their own work.

Work design: business architecture and functional design

Subsequent to the defined value chain, a high-level business architecture and functional design session was held with the executive leadership team in order to conceptualise the business model based upon the stipulated criteria defined within the large-scale workshop. The following high-level architecture was implemented, based upon the defined value chain:

- **Leadership direction:** Leadership provides alignment between strategic and operational goals, which dictates all functions within Etiket.
- **New business:** New business is generated through the business partner programme, and is an executive responsibility.
- **Creative enablement:** This is responsible for creating feasible ideas to solve client problems.
- **Centre of Excellence:** This is responsible for driving knowledge management, people practices and stakeholder management.
- **Support services:** IT and financial services are provided by the support services function.

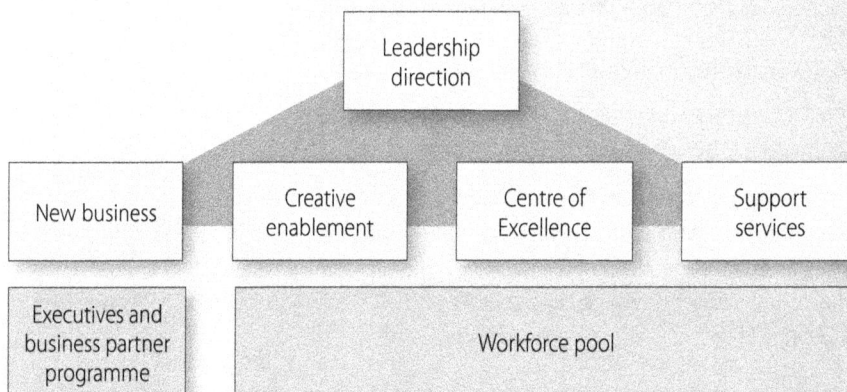

Figure 4: The functional design

Owing to the nature of the new business model, the workforce can function across divisions according to availability and skill sets; for example, an account executive that would traditionally be restricted to the Centre of Excellence can be appointed as the creative lead if his/her idea wins the project within the creative enablement area.

As a workshop outcome, individual work design sessions were held with each of the different roles within the organisation in order to facilitate a new work design based upon the newly defined high-level value chain. Work design was based upon a competency framework that supported the new organisational business model and incorporated the defined behavioural values as part of the measurement scale. The work design was then mapped back to the business model in order to provide a clear, functional design to support the value chain.

Throughout the project, change navigation and management were core to implementation success. The following section of the article describes the research findings regarding the implementation process studied in this case study.

2. Findings

Regarding the implementation and adoption of the new business model, the following findings are deemed to be significant:

Finding 1: The desire for a new type of leadership

The project proved the desire of the new GenY workforce to be engaged by a different type of leader: one who operates within the organisational system and collaborates throughout the thinking process, and allows employees to become part of the future they want to create. This implies a different type of leadership style, as authoritative and dictatorial leadership has proven to be ineffective and inefficient in the GenY entrepreneurial organisation.

Finding 2: The value of collaborative thinking

Owing to the enablement of a cross-functional model, the value of collaborating with individuals with different worldviews and skill sets became apparent, as the organisation not only increased the quality of their ideas to solve client problems, but also the avenues from which ideas could originate. This allowed an interactive organisation without hierarchical constraints, where the ideas were the priority, rather than the resulting output of the task (Smit & Carstens, 2003).

Finding 3: The design principles relating to the GenY workforce

Apparent from the case study were the different design criteria that dictated organisational success. Stability, predictability and traditional career pathing proved to be insufficient in enabling organisational goals. The GenY workforce wanted multifunctional experience, the opportunity to have more responsibility than their current position dictated, and the ability to influence and contribute towards the overall organisational purpose. Creating a line of sight between all work and the organisational purpose has never been more important in order to create strategic alignment and subsequent employee engagement.

155

Finding 4: Creating a shared behavioural value system to inform organisational practices

Within the GenY organisation, the creation of a shared behavioural value system determined the success of the subsequent interventions. By co-creating a common understanding of 'who and what the organisation is' and connecting employees to the core of the organisational identity, the values dictated the method and unwritten rules that would, in time, enable a culture of creative problem solving, collaboration, creative excellence and innovation as core competencies. From an interpersonal perspective, the behavioural values enabled the successful delivery of the programme through the common understanding of the behaviours that would be rewarded, acknowledged and accepted as part of the organisational delivery system.

Behavioural values were core to the design criteria, not necessarily influencing the functional lines of delivery, but dictating the design methodology in order to incorporate the entire organisation into the design process. This implies that change navigation should become an essential part of organisational design even earlier than current methodologies dictate in order to effectively transform the organisation. This implies a process of co-creation by all members of the organisation, with the leader yet again acting as catalyst for change.

Finding 5: Honouring the original idea and designing

Crucial to the design was the exploration of the original idea that led to the existence of the current organisational truth. Throughout the exercise, the question: 'Why do we exist?' was explored as part of the organisational value chain. In essence, all other design criteria were rooted in the fact that Etiket believed that it existed to tell stories that would solve business problems. This was seen as core to the Etiket identity and, as such, all new design criteria were subjected to the litmus test of answering the question: 'How will this help us to tell our organisational story?'

The following conclusions can be made as they relate to organisational behaviour and design within GenY entrepreneurial organisations in the South African context.

3. Conclusions

Based upon the literature and the case study findings, the following conclusions can be made:

- Collaborative leadership should become part of the new 'normal'.
- Often, the original entrepreneurial idea and strengths are lost as SMEs move to the next phase of the growth life cycle.
- Co-creation seems to be the basis theme of OD practices going forward.
- Organisational design needs to be based upon a solid behavioural framework.
- The GenY workforce is motivated by the opportunity to gain new experience, collaborate with others outside of their field, and take ownership of their own ideas.
- The GenY workforce seeks mentorship rather than management in their quest to take on more responsibility at an earlier age.
- Change navigation needs to start with preparing the organisational landscape before the start of the design process, to effectively and collaboratively transform the organisation.

- GenY wants immediate feedback on performance, and traditional performance management cycles are proving to be inadequate.

4. Future research

Future research from a longitudinal perspective is proposed in order to determine the impact of organisational design and methodology on organisational culture. The methodology applied in this case study should also be duplicated in another industry and context in order to test the validity and viability of the findings.

5. Limitations

Owing to the nature of the project, the scope was limited to an organisation within the creative industry in South Africa, and a possible limitation of the study exists with regard to whether the design can be duplicated with a workforce not necessarily motivated by creativity and innovation. The longitudinal component of the project also needs to be evaluated to establish the effectiveness of the business model over time.

Source: Veldsman (2013)

The organisational effectiveness measurement framework

The organisational effectiveness measurement framework (Olivier, 2015) is another example of a South African model designed to measure the effectiveness of service organisations as open systems. The premise is that healthy subsystems within the overall system (organisation) contribute to overall organisational effectiveness, the achievement of the goals stipulated in the company's vision and mission, and the enablement of effective and efficient service delivery resulting in customer satisfaction. As shown in Table 6.3 on page 158, measuring organisational effectiveness in a service delivery environment relates to three core factors: (1) the health of various subsystems within the organisation (diversity, training and development, rewards and recognition, management practices, internal functioning, work environment, internal relations and workforce equity); (2) goal achievement (vision and mission); and (3) service delivery (customer satisfaction) (Olivier, 2015).

Similar to the Burke–Litwin model and the organisational efficiency model, the organisational effectiveness measurement framework can be applied as a resource during the strategic planning process to consider the target elements of change when developing action plans to support the vision and strategic goals in service organisations. The model can also be used as a diagnostic framework to determine the probable causes of an organisational problem and to propose solutions for improving performance.

Table 6.3 Measurement components relating to organisational effectiveness in a service delivery system (adapted from Olivier, 2015)

System component	Subsystem component	Description
Healthy systems	Diversity	The preference given to people from designated groups (Africans, coloureds, Indians, women and people with disabilities) when recruiting in an organisation, and the degree to which an organisation accommodates the different ethnic cultures and beliefs of all employees in the workplace
	Training and development	The systematic effort by organisations to facilitate the learning of job-related knowledge and behaviours (eg skills, rules, concepts or attitudes) that result in improved performance
	Rewards and recognition	What is done to compensate employees for work delivered and to recognise superior performance by employees
	Management practices	What managers and leaders do in the normal course of events with the human and material resources at their disposal to carry out the organisation's strategy in order to achieve the set goals
	Internal functioning	The variety of processes taking place in an organisation, such as the treatment and involvement of employees, the flow of communications, the effectiveness of processes and procedures, and the implementation of changes for improvement
	Work environment	The availability of the required resources for employees to do their work as well as the physical aspects of the actual work space
	Interpersonal relations	How people relate to each other in the workplace, including aspects such as how people feel about each other, how they support each other, how they work together and cooperate, to what degree they trust each other and how conflict is handled
	Workforce equity	The lack of discrimination, racism and sexual harassment in an organisation ➡

Goal achievement	Vision and mission	The stated goals that have to be achieved at every level in an organisation
Service delivery	Customer satisfaction	The identification and satisfaction of the needs, expectations and perspectives of various relevant organisational constituencies

Chaos and complexity theory in organisation development

The open systems model approaches to organisational change need to be understood in the context of chaos and complexity theory. The planned organisational change approaches by Lewin and Kotter are generally underpinned by the belief that change is best accomplished through a predetermined sequence of steps, implying thus a universal formula for success. However, emergent approaches to planned change such as, for example, chaos and complexity theory, criticise the idea of a success formula for change and assume change to be an unfolding and continuously developing process in which the issues that arise cannot be predicted but have to be tackled as and when they occur (Rollinson, 2005).

Chaos and complexity theory is especially relevant to today's more turbulent and chaotic business environment, which is more complex than traditional stable environments. Whereas chaos theory is strikingly similar to complexity theory, chaos itself does not account for the coherence of self-organising complex systems. Complex systems reside on the edge of chaos, allowing the complex system to be spontaneous, adaptive, alive and self-organising. The complex adaptive system tends to fluctuate between stability and instability in the process of self-organisation (Okes, 2003). Complexity theory is used in organisations as a way to encourage innovative thinking and real-time responses to change, allowing the organisation to self-organise. However, in order to put complexity theory to work in OD, organisation leaders need to give up rigid control of the organisational system as a whole by stepping back from the day-to-day running of the organisation and watching for emergent properties and organisational patterns to emerge. Conditions and patterns that bring about the best solutions should be preserved whenever possible. Organisational strategy should evolve based on feedback and change as it occurs. By establishing a corporate strategy first, an organisation defines itself through conditions that were previously in place, and becomes non-adaptive to continuously evolving global market conditions (Hout, 1999; Okes, 2003; Sherman & Schultz, 1998).

A central theme of open systems theory is that non-linear relationships might exist between the organisational system components. Small changes in one component can cause huge changes in another, and large changes in a component might have only a nominal effect on another. The concept of non-linearity adds enormous complexity to the understanding of organisations and planned change efforts. Non-linearity makes it difficult or impossible to fully understand the relationship between the organisational system components (Walonick, 1993). However, with the advent of technological advances in computer technology, it has become easier to map chaotic organisational behaviour and find interesting underpinnings of order in the chaotic complexity of non-linear interactions between the organisational system components.

Chaos and complexity theory builds on the principles of the open systems theory of organisational change. The OD of a business system is seen as the management of the apparent chaos of a complex systems environment. As illustrated by the Burke–Litwin model (see Figure 6.3 on page 141) and the organisational efficiency model (see Figure 6.4 on page 143), complex adaptive systems consist of a number of components (or phenomena) that interact with each other according to a set of rules that require them to examine and respond to each other's behaviour in order to improve their behaviour and thus the behaviour of the system they comprise. Complexity results from the interactions and interdependencies between the components of a system (Waldrop, 1992). In complex environments, the real management task of planned change is that of coping with and even using instability, irregularity, disorder, unpredictability, clashing counter-cultures, dissension, contention, conflict and inconsistency to change the organisational system (Olsen et al, 2001).

Properties of complex adaptive systems

Complex adaptive systems have a number of properties of which the OD consultant should take note when planning organisational change. Some of these are described below (Okes, 2003; Olsen et al, 2001):

- **Patterns of order emerge.** In complex systems, some patterns of order emerge due to the patterns of relationships between subsystem components.
- **There is an ability to self-organise.** Complex systems have the ability to self-organise without any external control or design. The basic premise of complexity theory is that there is a hidden order to the behaviour (and evolution) of complex systems. Self-organisation occurs spontaneously as a result of the subsystem components (agents) constantly adapting to each other. Complex systems always adapt in ways that benefit them.
- **Relationships between the system components are short-range.** Information is normally received from near connections with other components. The richness of the connections means that communication will pass across the organisational system but will likely be modified on the way.

- **Relationships are non-linear.** This implies that there are rarely simple cause-and-effect relationships between the organisational system components. A small stimulus in one component may cause a large effect in another component or components, or have no effect at all.
- **Relationships contain feedback loops.** Both negative and positive feedback are key ingredients of complex systems. The effect of the actions of the system components – usually referred to an agent – is fed back to the agent, and this in turn affects how the agent behaves in the future.
- **Complex systems are open systems.** Energy and information are constantly being imported and exported across system boundaries. Complex systems are therefore usually far from equilibrium. Even though there is constant change, there is also the appearance of stability.
- **The parts cannot contain the whole.** System components cannot 'know' what is happening in the system as a whole. If they could, all the complexity would have to be present in that system component, which is impossible because complexity is created by the relationships between the system components. No component could therefore hope to control the system.
- **Complex systems have a history.** This cannot be ignored. Even a small change in circumstances can lead to large deviations in the future.
- **Complex adaptive systems are nested.** The system components (agents) are in themselves complex adaptive systems. An economy is made up of organisations, which are made up of people who have intellectual capital made up by their brains, which are made up of cells—all of which are complex adaptive systems.
- **Boundaries of a complex system are difficult to determine.** The decision is usually based on the observer's needs and prejudices (subjective views) rather than any intrinsic property of the system itself. The greater the proportion of connectivity between the various system components, the stronger the boundaries of the system are. If all connections are made between the organisational system components, the organisation forms a closed system.

OD planned change efforts that incorporate the principles of complexity theory will be more successful if leaders set fewer specifications by identifying what needs to be addressed and leaving others to decide how to proceed. Organisational leaders need to distribute their control by empowering others. They need to create a sense of urgency in meeting deadlines for change, and establish systems for monitoring and regulating the pace of change. Organisational leaders have to set the organisational direction by establishing the organisational value proposition, mission and values. They need to explore contradictions and encourage different viewpoints on solutions to problems that impede adaptive responses to the environmental forces of change. Leaders must be willing to accept a certain level of internal conflict and differences, and raise tough questions to stimulate creative problem solving. Diversity must be encouraged by inviting a broad range of ideas and opinions. Leaders need to scan the external environment for innovations and assess how these will affect the business. They must encourage feedback on progress and establish professional networks for successful change and adaptation. Networks must be assessed in terms of whether the flow of information is optimal, and whether the networks should be tightened or loosened. Organisational learning should be encouraged by inviting questions and solutions from others in the system (Olsen et al, 2001).

Organisational creativity theory

Organisational creativity theory builds on the principles of the complexity theory of adaptive systems and Kotter's eight-step plan for leading organisational change. This theory has increased in importance in the light of organisations realising the importance of encouraging creative leadership in an increasingly turbulent, more chaotic and dynamically changing marketplace. Increasingly innovative strategies are required for organisations to rise above competition (Pryor et al, 2010). Organisational creativity theory posits that organisational leaders should interfere with the natural development of an organisation by creatively destroying the existing, making the organisation permeable for new ideas; breaking their own rules that keep them from being innovative; organising an adaptive environment that allows creative people to work creatively; and reflecting about the purpose of innovation in a macroscopic sense (Oetinger, 2005: 36; Pryor et al, 2010: 28).

Organisational creativity theory approaches organisational creativity and innovation from an open systems perspective. Organisational leaders must approach the issue of nurturing creative talent (intellectual capital) from a strategic, structural, cultural (social) and accountability viewpoint (Bethel, 2009; Pryor et al, 2010). Factors important to the fostering of creativity within an organisation include employees' motivation, group influence, organisational policies and structure, leadership and values, and environmental stimulus and challenge (Pryor et al, 2010).

The 4Rs creativity model of Pryor et al (2010) can be used as a diagnostic model for assessing change levers for stimulating innovation and creativity in an organisation. The 4Rs denote four organisational system components: right strategies, right structure, right culture and values, and right accountabilities for performance:

1. **System component—right strategy:** Managers must make strategic choices regarding the speed of the change effort, the amount of

preplanning, the involvement of others, and the relative emphasis they will give to different change approaches. Decisions must be made based on the amount and kind of anticipated resistance, the power of potential resisters, and the people who have the relevant data for designing the initiative and implementing it. Decisions about a strategy for creativity and innovation drive the decisions about structure (Pryor et al, 2010).

2. **System component—right structure:** The structure of the organisation and the messages that organisational leaders communicate have a major effect on creativity and innovation. The organisational structure must therefore be adapted to support the organisational strategy for innovation and creativity. A highly bureaucratic structure with many levels of hierarchy will, for example, impede attempts to propose new ideas. The communication process between top management and employees is vital to the strategy for creativity and may be impeded by a bureaucratic structure that tends to filter ideas out as they pass through the long vertical chain of command. Creative people tend to work best in a flexible organisation; in other words, a structure with positive leadership that encourages risk taking and shows enthusiasm for new ideas (Pryor et al, 2010). While some degree of freedom and flexibility is essential for productive innovative teams, management also faces the challenge of implementing an innovation control system which simultaneously supports resource efficiency and creativity (Pryor et al, 2010).

3. **System component—right culture and values:** Organisational leaders need to establish a psychologically and intellectually stimulating culture for people's natural creativity to emerge. People are more creative when they work in an environment that is favourable toward innovation. The organisational culture and leadership must have the capability to tolerate people who do not 'fit' into the organisation, as they may be the ones that generate the best ideas. To attract and retain creative people, leaders need to establish a culture that accepts diversity and offers a high degree of freedom, where creative people can thrive. Interactions between employees should be encouraged and leaders should strive toward building a cohesive working environment to stimulate employees to generate more ideas. Failures must be embraced as opportunities for learning (Pryor et al, 2010).

4. **System component — right accountabilities for performance:** Companies need to adopt a more proactive and creative stance toward management and leadership to survive in a more turbulent business environment. Organisational leaders must be held accountable for establishing appropriate systems that support the nurturing of creative talent

and innovation. These include accountability for establishing appropriate and aligned strategies, structure, culture and values, and employee performance accountabilities. Creativity should be regarded as a core leadership competency that can increase an organisation's long-term viability and success (Pryor et al, 2010).

Activity

Review the case study on Etiket on pages 147–157. Identify the principles of creativity theory that were applied in the OD planned change process.

Resistance to change

Resistance to change is inevitable, and OD consultants therefore have a strong interest in studying this phenomenon in the action research (see Chapter 8) and planned change process. OD consultants and managers strive in their CM efforts to promote change-supportive behaviour that denotes a **readiness for change** (see Chapter 9). In order to facilitate readiness for change, one has to understand the potential sources of resistance, the forms of its manifestation, and tactics to deal with it (see Figure 6.5 on page 166).

Individual sources of resistance

As shown in Figure 6.5, individuals resist change for both rational (parochial self-interest) and psychological reasons (fear of the unknown, loss of the familiar, and fear of failure). Parochial self-interest relates to the need of individuals to maintain the status quo, which engenders a degree of resistance. People differ in their assessments of the personal costs and benefits of a change. They have something they value about their work, for instance income or its substitutes, power over others, prestige, status, security or convenience, which were acquired by personal expenditure of time, energy and commitment. Change may be perceived as a loss of these aspects which cannot be recovered, and hence the change is resisted (Rollinson, 2005).

People also vary in their capabilities to cope with change. A change with unknown consequences can be highly threatening for people who have a low tolerance for ambiguity (Rollinson, 2005). Change can be a negative experience for many employees, who may prefer to remain with existing organisational arrangements due to a fear of the unknown. Some organisational changes such as, for example, cutbacks and retrenchments, are not always in the best interest of the employees who are affected by the planned change programme. Change often comes as a shock, as it tends to reduce the predictability of individuals' working lives and destroys the level of familiarity and sense of security that employees felt with their previous routines. Individuals have a tendency to pay attention to and retain only information that supports their existing worldviews. Change can call into question the reality that individuals define for themselves based on their perception of the world as they experience and understand it. They may, as a consequence, reject or resist change that clashes with their existing frames of reference (Martin, 2005) and threatens their feelings of security. Changes in job tasks or established work routines can arouse economic fears if people are concerned that they will not be able to perform the new tasks or routines to their previous standards, especially when pay is closely tied to productivity (Robbins et al, 2008).

Group and organisational sources of resistance

At a group or organisational level, resistance to change is often a consequence of misinformation, structural and group inertia, a perceived breach of previous agreements, and the perceived threat associated with the change (see Figure 6.5). Control over information provides opportunities for a group to impart particular interpretations to information and so facilitate resistance, often fuelled by rumours and gossip. Negative rumours about changes to jobs and working conditions, poor CM, and the nature of the organisational change and its consequences on organisational performance tend to be more prevalent during change than positive ones (Martin, 2005). Individuals will resist change if they do not know or understand the reasons for it and its impact on them. Resistance is amplified where there is a lack of trust in the proposer of the change, because this tends to result in selective perceptions about what the proposer says (Rollinson, 2005).

Changes to bureaucratic organisational structures which were designed to deliver consistency and predictability are often met with resistance. The systems and procedures that such organisations create to provide control and stability can also restrict the ability to introduce change. Arrangements entered into with another group or organisation are designed to control events in the future, and restrict the ability to make changes in the interaction between these groups (Martin, 2005). Change can disrupt the unconscious and conscious bonds between people. These bonds are a consequence of the underlying assumptions, traditions and unwritten rules of behaviour that form part of the organisational culture and which empower teams in the organisation. Depending on the culture of affected employees, the disruption of cultural traditions and group norms may cause a serious negative reaction (Weiss, 2001).

Sources of resistance to change

Individual level
- Parochial self-interest
- Psychological reasons (fear of unknown, loss of the familiar, insecurity and fear of failure)
- Selective information processing and attention
- Lack of trust

Group/organisational level
- Misinformation
- Lack of trust
- Structural and group inertia
- Perceived breach of previous agreements
- Perceived threat to status and power
- Disruption of cultural traditions and norms
- Limited focus
- Innovation

Forms of resistance to change

Overt   Implicit   Immediate   Deferred

Tactics to deal with resistance to change

Education & communication   Participation   Building support & commitment   Negotiation

Motivation & co-optation   Selecting people who accept change   Coercion

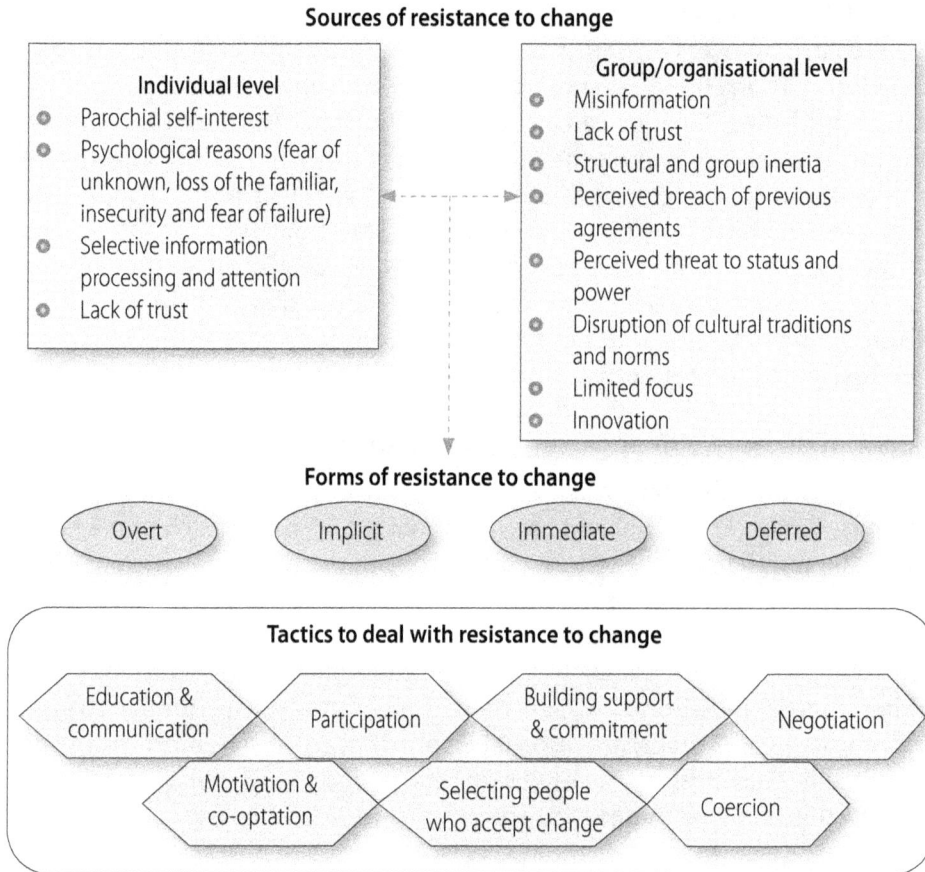

Figure 6.5 Sources and forms of, and tactics for dealing with, resistance to change (Author)

Change in organisations often takes on a limited focus, thus making it possible for situations to arise in which groups not immediately affected by changes can resist involvement, which eventually limits the benefits they could ultimately have gained from the change. Supervisors not involved in a planned change effort to address production problems in one department may, for example, see the introduction of team working (which involves the replacement of supervisors with team leaders) as an attempt to erode their status and job security (Martin, 2005). Any redistribution of decision-making authority can threaten long-established power relationships within the organisation. Groups in the organisation that control sizeable resources often see change as a threat, as they tend to be content with the way things are. Power struggles within the organisation will determine, to a large degree, the speed and quantity

166

of change. Managers who have spent their entire careers with a single organisation and eventually achieve senior position in the hierarchy are also often major impediments to change, as they view it as a very real threat to their status and position (Robbins et al, 2008). Research also shows that people higher up in the organisation tend to cling to the status quo, which implies that resistance can be more of an organisational-level phenomenon than one that exists in lower-level employees (Rollinson, 2005).

Innovation as a source of resistance

Innovation as a force of change is a drive toward continual revolution in order to be able to stay ahead in an increasingly competitive globalised world. In many organisations, innovation is an issue that finds resistance for a number of reasons: changing anything can create uncertainty, unfamiliarity and resistance because of a significant degree of inertia built into most organisations and concerns about the risk, costs and timescales involved in adopting a new invention. Innovation carries with it a measure of risk because it involves doing things differently. The invention of something radically new is generally met with greater resistance than is incremental change, as it carries a greater measure of risk, high costs and a longer timescale for development. The adaptation of existing technologies is often met with less resistance, as the change is more incremental and involves the fine tuning of that which already exists. However, the possible returns from the radical level of innovation are much higher than those at the incremental level. This dilemma makes innovation in planned change efforts a problematic issue (Martin, 2005).

Forms of resistance

As shown in Figure 6.5 on page 166, resistance to change can be overt, implicit, immediate or deferred. Overt and immediate negative responses to change such as, for example, employee complaints, threats to strike or work slowdowns are easier to deal with than resistance that is implicit and deferred. Implicit resistance behaviour is more subtle and difficult to recognise (eg loss of loyalty to the organisation, loss of motivation to work, increased errors or mistakes, or increased absenteeism). Deferred actions cloud the link between the source of the resistance and the reaction to it. A change may produce what appears to be only a minimal reaction at the time, but then resistance may surface weeks, months or even years later. Resistance to change can build up and then explode in some response that seems totally out of proportion to the change action it follows. Power struggles within the organisation will determine, to a large degree, the speed and quantity of change (Robbins et al, 2008).

Activity

Think about a major change that you experienced in your life. Identify the sources of your resistance to the change situation or event. In what form did your resistance manifest? What did you do to overcome your resistance and accept the change?

Tactics for dealing with resistance

Tactics for dealing with resistance need to centre on the reason for resistance and must be appropriate to the circumstances to be effective (Rollinson, 2005). OD consultants generally use seven tactics (shown in Figure 6.5 on page 166) to overcome resistance to change. These tactics can be used singly or in combination (Robbins et al, 2008; Rollinson, 2005):

- **Education and communication:** Helping organisation members affected by the change see the logic of a change through communication efforts can reduce resistance to change. Communication can minimise the effects of misinformation and poor communication, and sell the need for change. This tactic is most appropriately used where resistance is based on a lack of information, or inaccurate information and analysis. Once persuaded, people will often help to implement the change. However, this tactic can be very time consuming if large numbers of people are involved.

- **Participation:** This tactic is most appropriately used where the initiators of the change do not have all the information needed to design the change and where others have considerable power to resist. People who feel involved in a change effort and believe that their expertise will help make a meaningful difference to the change often feel more committed toward the change. Participation may also help to increase the quality of the change decision. However, participation may also be time consuming and result in poor solutions.

- **Building support and commitment:** This tactic is most appropriately used where people resist because of adjustment problems that are involved. Organisational support in the form of employee wellness services, counselling and trauma therapy, training in new skills or a short paid leave of absence may facilitate adjustment to the change. Inspiring employees toward the change can help to build emotional commitment in both employees and managers. However, this tactic can be very expensive and time consuming, and may still fail.

- **Negotiation:** This tactic is most appropriately used where some individual or group will clearly lose out in a change and where they have considerable power to resist. Exchanging something of value (eg a specific reward package) that meets affected individuals' needs for a lessening of the resistance can be negotiated. Negotiation as a tactic may be necessary when resistance comes from a powerful source such as, for example, trade unions. However, negotiation can be costly and open up the possibility of blackmailing by other individuals in positions of power.

- **Manipulation and co-optation:** These tactics are most appropriately used where other tactics will not work or are too expensive. Manipulation and co-optation are relatively inexpensive and easy ways to gain the support of adversaries. However, once discovered, the OD consultant's credibility may be negatively affected. Manipulation is a covert influence attempt to distort and twist facts to make them appear more attractive. Undesirable information may be withheld and false rumours may be created to get employees to accept change. Co-optation – a form of both manipulation and participation – seeks to buy off the leaders of a resistance group by giving them a role in the change decision.

- **Selecting people who accept change:** This tactic is most appropriately used where sponsors for a change are required. Change can be positively facilitated by selecting people who score high on characteristics such as openness to experience, positive attitude toward change, optimism, willingness to take risks and behavioural adaptability.

- **Coercion:** This tactic is most appropriately used where speed is essential and change initiators possess considerable power. Coercion as a tactic to reduce resistance to change is the application of direct threats to or force on the resisters. Threats of transfer, loss of promotions, negative performance evaluations and poor letters of recommendation are examples of some forms of coercion.

Conditions for success in planned change efforts

OD planned change programmes are focused on developing learning organisations that thrive in stable and turbulent times. A learning organisation is one that proactively creates, acquires and transfers knowledge, and that changes its behaviour on the basis of new knowledge and insights (Kinicki & Fugate, 2012: 439). Successful planned change programmes are opportunities for organisational members (leaders and employees) to learn what the organisation did right in terms of accomplishing a goal or implementing a project. Constant readiness for change, adaptation and growth, tapping into the best knowledge available to implement change, collaboration and a commitment to learning exist across the learning organisation. Continuous planning and the creation of flexible plans, improvised implementation and action learning by means of constant re-evaluation of the change are typical characteristics of learning organisations (Brown, 2011).

Planned change approaches are generally successful when the following conditions exist (Rothwell, Sullivan & McLean, 1995; Weiss, 2001):

- The organisation is externally focused, customer-centred and market-driven.
- The business is focused on creating value in products and services in an ethically responsible manner.
- At least one key decision maker in the organisation perceives a need for change, and executive/senior management supports it. They are also willing to commit to long-term improvement and provide the resources necessary to support OD expertise, either inside or outside the organisation.
- Some trust and cooperation exist within the organisational system and its decision makers.
- The perceived need for change is caused by conditions in the work environment, such as new technology or relations between and among individuals and groups.
- The organisational system and its members are mobilised toward a shared vision and value system, and are committed to positive continuous learning, innovation and continual change. They are also committed to measuring progress against world-class standards of excellence.
- The organisation takes ownership for the changes.

Managing change ethically

Organisational change puts individuals' rights, dignity and privileges at risk, as it involves the redistribution of power, information, resources, status, authority and influence. To manage change ethically is a key concern for OD consultants. They therefore consider certain ethics-related issues while planning a change programme by evaluating whether the change plan, policies and procedures, implementation process and planned outcomes consider the rights of individuals affected by the change (eg the right to know, the right to privacy, the right not to be terminated without just cause, and the right to due process). They consider whether justice to the individuals affected by the change is taken into account (eg how fairly the benefits and burdens of the process and outcomes have been distributed, how clear and fair the procedures for distributing the costs and benefits of the change were explained, and how those who were treated unfairly will be compensated). The fairness of plans, implementation and methods used in the change is also an important concern (eg whether the needs, welfare and dignity of those affected by the change were respected; OD consultants assess whether manipulation, force, deceit or coercion was used and whether these harmed those involved emotionally, physically or in any material way) (Weiss, 2001: 421). Finally, it is evident that the interventions stemming from OD change programmes present ethical challenges to OD consultants and managers leading the change effort.

OD consultants should take care that the chosen intervention, theory and model or diagnostic tools to manage change programmes appropriately represent their level of competency and are relevant to the goals of the OD change programme and unique client context. Ethical dilemmas that may arise include misrepresentation of the chosen OD intervention to organisational members and of one's skills and professional competency, and collusion with the client in choosing an inappropriate intervention (Anderson, 2013).

Conclusion

This chapter discussed selected theories and models relevant to planned change approaches. Sources and forms of resistance to change were explored, and tactics to overcome resistance were discussed. Finally, the chapter reviewed a number of conditions for successful planned change efforts. In conclusion, the application of OD technology is growing rapidly. New theories, models, techniques and approaches to planned change are constantly being developed to assist organisations with their adaptation to a more complex and challenging business environment. OD consultants will continue to play a critical role in helping organisations embrace and adjust to the changing forces and trends that affect them. Knowledge of and insight into the psychological underpinning of planned change and the dynamics of complex adaptive systems have become essential for OD consultants. The course of change anticipated for OD will predominantly surround issues of a changing workplace and workforce, global competence, organisational renewal and adaptation, and technological awareness. Only a few selected theories and models of planned change were discussed in this chapter. It is imperative for OD consultants to keep up to date with the latest theories, models and techniques relevant to planned change. OD consultants must be competent and capable of all the necessary tasks and processes involved in a successful planned change effort. It is important to recognise that resistance to change is a natural occurrence, and organisational members can be made part of the implementation to reduce their resistance.

Reflection questions

1. Explain the concept of planned change in OD. Elaborate on the success factors (conditions) for planned change efforts.
2. Why is it important to manage change ethically?
3. Why are organisations forced to plan organisational change initiatives? Consider the role of the forces for change (see Chapter 1) and open systems theory in the formulation of your answer.

4. Differentiate between Lewin's three-step model of planned change and Kotter's eight-step plan for leading organisational change. Explain how these models can benefit planned change efforts in the organisation.
5. Explain why the Burke–Litwin model, the organisational efficiency model and the organisational effectiveness measurement framework can be regarded as examples of open systems models of planned change.
6. Explain the concept of organisational diagnostics. Would you regard the Burke–Litwin model, the organisational efficiency model and the organisational effectiveness measurement framework as examples of diagnostic frameworks for planned change in OD initiatives? Give a reason for your answer.
7. Explain the concept of complex adaptive systems.
8. How can the principles of creativity theory help to inform planned change efforts in today's more turbulent, continuously changing marketplace?
9. Why do people resist change and in which forms does employees' resistance manifest? Differentiate between individual, group and organisational sources of resistance. Also, reflect on how resistance to change influences readiness for change (see Chapter 9).
10. Suggest some tactics that organisations can apply to help overcome employees' resistance to change.

Multiple-choice questions

1. The South African perspective on OD emphasises:
   a. continual organisational improvement processes through diagnostic data and measurable appropriate solutions that optimise the purpose and strategy of the organisation
   b. continual organisational improvement processes through measurable planned change and the application of behavioural science principles to optimise organisational effectiveness
   c. continual organisational improvement processes through the application and transfer of behavioural science knowledge and practice to optimise organisational adaptation to change and effectiveness
   d. All of the above

2. OD consultants use a certain set of criteria to determine the effectiveness, appropriateness and usefulness of an organisational change model. Which of the following statements relate to such criteria?
   a. The model focuses on three levels of analysis: individual, group and organisational.

    b. The model clearly defines the organisational components and relationships between the components.

    c. The model has a sound theoretical base and there is empirical evidence of its reliability, face validity and generalisability.

    d. All of the above

    e. b and c

3. Planned change approaches are generally successful if the organisation is internally focused on building trust, is customer-centred and market-driven, and focuses on short-term gains.

    a. True

    b. False

4. Lewin's model of planned change is an example of a planned change model that helps organisational members:

    a. manage and lead change

    b. plan and measure organisational change

    c. adapt to change

5. The Burke–Litwin model of organisational performance and change is an example of a planned change model that helps organisational members:

    a. manage and lead change

    b. plan and measure organisational change

    c. adapt to change

6. Veldsman's organisational efficiency model is an example of a planned change model that helps organisational members:

    a. manage and lead change

    b. plan and measure organisational change

    c. adapt to change

7. Which of the following OD models is highly relevant to assist organisations and their members to adapt to today's increasingly turbulent, more chaotic and dynamically changing marketplace?

    a. Organisational creativity theory

    b. Lewin's three-step model of organisational change

    c. The Burke–Litwin model of organisational change and performance

    d. Chaos and complexity theory

    e. a and d

    f. All of the above

8. Which one of the following tactics to deal with resistance to change is most appropriate when used where people resist because of adjustment problems that are involved?
   a. Education and communication
   b. Negotiation
   c. Building support and commitment
   d. Coercion
   e. b and d
   f. All of the above

References

Anderson, DL. 2013. *Organization development: the process of leading organizational change.* London: SAGE (Kindle edition).

Bethel, SM. 2009. 'New breed of leader'. *Leadership Excellence* 26(12): 3–4.

Britten, N, Campbell, R & Pope, C. 2002. 'Using meta-ethnography to synthesise qualitative research: a worked example'. *Health Services Research Policy* 7: 209–215.

Brooks, I. 2009. *Organisational behaviour: individuals, groups and organisation.* London: Pearson.

Brown, DR. 2011. *An experiential approach to organizational development.* Upper Saddle River, NJ: Pearson.

Burke, WW & Litwin, GH. 1992. 'A causal model of organisational performance and change'. *Journal of Management* 8(3): 523–546.

Chawane, T, Van Vuuren, LJ & Roodt, G. 2003. 'Personal change as a key determinant of the outcomes of organisational transformation interventions'. *South African Journal of Human Resource Management* 1(3): 62–76.

Cooperrider, DL & Whitney, D. 1999. *Appreciative inquiry.* San Francisco, CA: Berrett-Koehler.

Cummings, TG & Worley, CG. 2005. *Organisation development and change.* 8th ed. Mason, OH: Thomson, South Western.

French, WL & Bell, CH. 1999. *Organizational development, behavioural science interventions for organisational improvement.* 6th ed. Upper Saddle River, NJ: Prentice Hall.

Holt, L & Brockett, RG. 2012. 'Self-direction and factors influencing technology use: examining the relationships for the 21st century workplace'. *Computers in Human Behavior* 28: 2075–2082.

Hout, TM. 1999. 'Books in review: are managers obsolete?' *Harvard Business Review* 77(2): 161–168.

Jones, BB & Brazzel, M. 2006. *The NTL handbook of organizational development and change. Principles, practices and perspectives.* San Francisco, CA: Pfeiffer.

Kinicki, A & Fugate, M. 2012. *Organizational behavior: key concepts, skills and best practices.* New York: McGraw-Hill.

Kotter, JP. 1995. 'Leading change: why transformation efforts fail'. *Harvard Business Review* 73(2): 59–67.

Kraut, AI. 1996. *Organizational surveys: tools for assessment and change.* San Francisco, CA: Jossey Bass.

Lewin, K. 1951. *Field theory in social science.* New York: Harper & Row.

Martin, J. 2005. *Organizational behavior and management.* London: Thomson.

Martins, N & Coetzee, M. 2009. 'Applying the Burke-Litwin model as a diagnostic framework for assessing organisational effectiveness'. *South African Journal of Human Resource Management* 7(1): 144–156.

Oetinger, BV. 2005. 'Nurturing the new: patterns of innovation'. *The Journal of Business Strategy* 6(2): 29–36.

Okes, D. 2003. 'Complexity theory simplifies choices'. *Quality Progress* 36(7): 35–38.

Oldham, GR & Da Silva, N. 2015. 'The impact of digital technology on the generation and implementation of creative ideas in the workplace'. *Computers in Human Behavior* 42: 5–11.

Olivier, BH. 2011. *Programme in applied organizational development: study guide – Module 3.* Pretoria: University of South Africa.

Olivier, BH. 2015. The development and validation of an assessment framework for measuring organisational effectiveness of a metropolitan municipality in South Africa. Unpublished doctoral thesis. Pretoria: University of South Africa.

Olsen, EE, Eoyang, GH, Beckhard, R & Vaill, P. 2001. *Facilitating organization change: lessons from complexity science.* San Francisco, CA: Pfeiffer.

Oxman, JA & Smith, BD. 2003. 'The limits of structural change'. *MIT Sloan Management Review* Fall: 77–82.

Pryor, MG, Singleton, LP, Taneja, S & Toombs, LA. 2010. 'The 4Rs model for nurturing creative talent'. *International Journal of Business and Public Administration* 7(1): 27–39.

Riley, T & Hawe, P. 2009. 'A typology of practice narratives within a preventive community intervention trial'. *Implementation Science* 4: 80.

Robbins, SP & Judge, TA. 2011. *Organizational behavior.* London: Pearson.

Robbins, SP, Judge, TA, Millett, B & Waters-Marsh, T. 2008. *Organisational behaviour.* French Forest, NSW: Pearson.

Rollinson, D. 2005. *Organisational behaviour and analysis: an integrated approach.* London: Prentice Hall.

Rothwell, WJ, Sullivan, R & McLean, GN. 1995. *Practicing organization development: a guide for consultants.* Johannesburg: Pfeiffer.

SABPP (South African Board for People Practices). 2014. *HR management standards for South Africa*. Johannesburg: SABPP.

Sherman, HJ & Schultz, R. 1998. *Open boundaries: creating business innovation through complexity*. Reading, MA: Perseus Books.

Sinding, K & Waldstrom, C. 2014. *Organisational behaviour*. 5th ed. London: McGraw-Hill.

Smit, H & Carstens, L. 2003. 'The influence of leadership role competencies on organisation change outcome in the manufacturing industry in South Africa'. *SA Journal of Human Resource Management* 1(2): 45–52.

Veldsman, D. 2013. 'The Organisational Efficiency Model'. Personal documentation received directly from author with permission to use.

Waldrop, MM. 1992. *Complexity: the emerging science at the edge of order and chaos*. New York: Simon & Schuster.

Walonick, DS. 1993. Organizational theory and behavior. http://ww.statpac. org/walonick/organizational-theory.htm (Accessed 19 December 2012).

Weiss, JW. 2001. *Organizational behavior and change: managing diversity, cross-cultural dynamics and ethics*. Cincinnati, OH: Thomson.

Wheatley, MJ. 2006. *Leadership and the new science*. San Francisco, CA: Berrett-Koehler.

Chapter 7

The organisation development process

Frances de Klerk

Learning outcomes

After reading this chapter, you should be able to:

- understand the various phases of the organisation development (OD) process
- apply basic marketing principles
- know how to prepare when meeting a prospective client for the first time
- prepare a written proposal for the consultation
- prepare a written contract for a consultation
- develop a solid working relationship with a client
- understand how to diagnose problems in a company
- choose the correct interventions
- know when and how to terminate a relationship with a client.

Introduction

> *If I —*
>
> *know my area of expertise (a given),*
>
> *behave authentically with the client,*
>
> *tend to and complete the business of each consulting phase, and act to build capacity for the client to solve the next problem on their own —*
>
> *I can legitimately say I have consulted flawlessly.*
>
> (Block, P. 2011. Flawless Consulting. A guide to getting your expertise used, 3rd edition. John Wiley & Sons, Inc.)

To 'consult flawlessly' (Block, 2011: 48) should be the aim of any person working in the organisation development (OD) field. There are too many horror stories, especially in the South African economy, of consultants who have left companies in disarray after their so-called interventions. In this chapter, the OD process will be discussed with the aim of giving the novice consultant a broad overview and guidance regarding what to expect.

The OD consultant usually enters an organisation when it is at its most vulnerable. One or more key managers realise there might be a problem or room for improvement. Consultants are brought in to attend to three common business ailments: organisational crises, personnel problems or personal dilemmas. Each problem can be resolved through simple problem solving, or regarded as a vehicle for the organisation to learn how to better manage its organisational life and decision making (Waddell, Cummings & Worley, 2011).

In this chapter, the various phases of the OD cycle will be discussed, from the initial contact between the OD consultant and client until the OD intervention(s) is institutionalised, making the changes a permanent part of the everyday functioning of the organisation.

Overview of the organisation development process

Any OD process follows roughly the same process, which can be combined into four major phases that consultants and the client jointly need to carry out during the process, namely:
1. entry and contracting
2. diagnosis
3. action planning and implementing of interventions
4. evaluation and institutionalising.

It is important to keep in mind that the length and depth of each phase may vary for each situation and that the OD process is a cycle that includes a feedback loop (Burke, Lake & Paine, 2009).

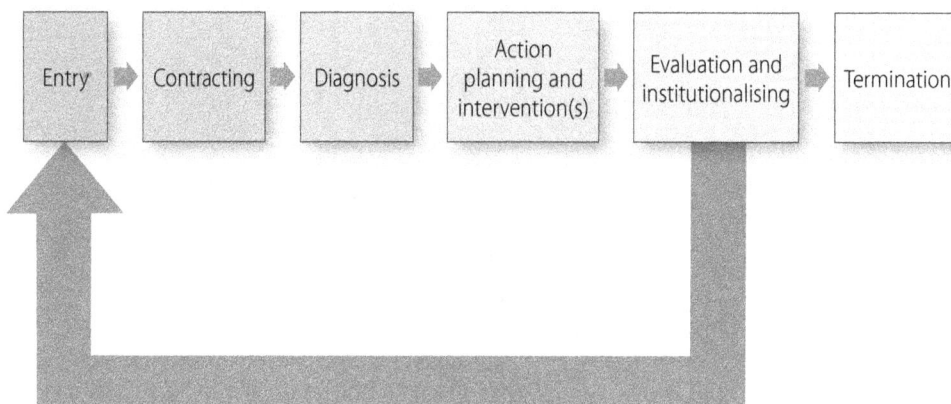

Figure 7.1 The organisation development process (Author)

Table 7.1 describes the various phases and activities during the OD process the consultant usually follows.

Table 7.1 The various phases and activities during the organisation development process (adapted from Burke et al, 2009; Carbery & Cross, 2015; Cummings & Worley, 2015)

Steps	Activity
Entering and contracting	1. **Entry (initiation):** A problem within the organisation is discovered. Someone or a group of people in the organisation looks for a person who can assist, and invite consultants to tender for the project. This is usually the first client–consultant encounter. If they realise they are compatible for collaboration, a relationship built on trust and mutual respect must be developed between all parties.
	2. **Contracting:** Once the relationship is established, the expectations of the client regarding the project outcome(s), deliverables and the schedule need to be clarified. Parties need to sign a written agreement in which their claims, contributions and responsibilities regarding the necessary resources, deadlines of execution and expected effects are included.
Diagnosis	3. **Data collection and diagnosis:** The consultant needs to collect valid and reliable data in order to make the correct diagnosis. Without a proper understanding of the situation and issues involved, any planned intervention is unlikely to succeed. Because employees will react in different ways when they know they are being observed, carrying out the diagnosis can in itself be an intervention. This reaction can change the client system.
	4. **Assessment feedback:** Once the consultant has collected all the relevant data, he/she needs to provide feedback regarding the analysis, findings and any preliminary recommendations to the decision makers and those having a stake in the process. The OD consultant should be prepared to encounter and address any resistance before proceeding.
Action planning and implementing of interventions	5. **Planning change/action planning:** The OD consultant works with decision makers and stakeholders to identify specific courses of action that address the situation and to develop action plans for implementation. The OD consultant should take a facilitative role at this stage and help the client to identify the steps that can be taken to achieve the goal.
	6. **Interventions:** Before implementing any intervention it is necessary to consider the potential results of the technique, the potential implementation of the technique (including costs versus benefit) and the potential political acceptance of the technique. Implementing the specific intervention in the organisation is where the application of high-quality change management (CM) practices is important. ➔

Evaluation and institutionalising	7.	**Evaluation:** During the evaluation, the OD consultant and client need to assess the results of the intervention and determine any future courses of action. It is vital that the method of evaluation is decided upon during the entry and contracting phase. If future courses of action are needed, the process restarts at the contracting phase.
	8.	**Adoption/institutionalising:** Members of the organisation accept ownership of the change, and the change is implemented throughout the organisation.
	9.	**Termination/separation:** The OD consultant prepares to leave the organisation. As part of the process, the OD consultant works to disengage while ensuring that improvement will continue after his/her departure. This step is only possible after the knowledge and skills from the OD consultant have been transferred to the organisation.

Marketing

Before any OD consultants (both internal and external) can gain entry into the client system, they will have to market themselves and their services. The marketing of a service is more complex than the marketing of goods. Products are usually concrete, and customers can therefore use all their senses to make a decision. However, in the case of a service, customers need to rely on the intangible and as a result they sometimes need to use intuition to come to a final conclusion.

Irrespective of the product or service, there are five key ingredients for successful marketing, namely (Kennett & Tomkins, 2001):
1. the right product(s)/service(s)
2. the right target audience(s)
3. the right promotional channel(s)
4. the right price(s) and proposition(s), which are available only through appropriate research
5. the right timing(s).

The marketing of OD services usually occurs on two levels simultaneously. The first is institutional marketing and the second is client-specific marketing.

During institutional marketing, consultants develop marketplace awareness of their name and expertise as well as OD processes, purposes and values. It is critical for OD consultants to link education about OD and its benefits with an awareness of them and their expertise. Public speaking, seminars, social media and special-interest groups (SIGs) can all play a very important role in this regard.

During client-specific marketing, consultants will approach an individual client to sell their services. Consultants may gain access to a client as a result of network referrals or contacts they initiate. Regardless of how this occurs, it is always important to do in-depth research about the organisation's history, current market position, stage of organisation/product/service life cycle and leaders before the first meeting.

The OD consultant will need to take the following elements into consideration during the marketing of the service (Kennett & Tomkins, 2001):

- **Intangibility:** Services are intangible. There are no physical products the customer can hear, see or touch. The customer does not always see the efforts that go into the OD process as a whole, and as a result it is more difficult for the marketer to leave an impression than it is with, for example, new office furniture. In essence, the OD consultant is asking the client to buy a promise.

- **Inseparability:** Clients' perception of the OD consultant becomes their perception of the service itself. It is important to remember that an OD service starts with the first contact, before the client's needs are even known, continuing when the diagnosis is done and while the interventions are implemented, and remaining long after the process is evaluated and the relationship terminated. The relationship between the client and the OD consultant is of utmost importance, because the client becomes a factor in the nature of the service. The name of the OD consultancy becomes synonymous with the service it will provide.

- **Perishability:** Unlike products, services cannot be inventoried, which makes it difficult to match supply with demand. An OD consultant will be available even when there are no clients, and will need to pay the office rent even when it is empty, which can increase the costs and therefore the price of the services.

- **Non-standardisation:** The experience a client has with a service varies from one company to another. When marketing his/her service, the OD consultant needs to ensure that the client knows exactly what to expect, and should provide a detailed outline of the process. It is further advisable for the consultant to provide examples of the services that can be standardised, for example the type of reports the client can expect. In this way, customers will be confident that the consumption experience will be what they expect.

- **Regulation:** Service products tend to be more rigidly regulated than goods are, because they are so difficult for the consumer to assess. Moreover, purchasing services, such as an OD intervention or a psychological service, is particularly risky for the client. Currently, in South Africa, regulation for OD consultants does not exist. Industrial psychologists operating in the OD field are regulated by the Health Professions Council of South Africa (HPCSA) under the Health Professions Act 56 of 1974. The South African Board for People Practices (SABPP) is continuously working towards better regulation of the human resources field in general and has implemented a set of standards which include OD as part of the functional and cross-functional HR value chain. The OD standard will contribute to HR good governance and ethical practices (Meyer & Abbott, 2019). There is also the South African Organisation Development Network (SAODN), a not-for-profit company which actively promotes the practice and sets the standards of OD in South Africa. This network works in partnership with the SABPP and is busy establishing career and competency frameworks and standards for OD consultants. Not only will better regulation of the field offer better protection for consumers, it will also protect well-established OD consultants from opportunistic fly-by-night operators.

Word of mouth

Word of mouth is much more influential in a service purchase than it is in a goods purchase. This client-to-client promotion includes internet communications and marketing, such as a website. The wise OD consultant will establish a web presence and a social media presence, and encourage participation in peer-to-peer web interaction.

Tendering

One way in which the public or private sectors invite individuals or businesses to provide services on a contractual basis is by putting them out to tender. Bidding for tenders should therefore be seen as part of the marketing process. National and provincial government departments, municipalities, parastatals (such as Eskom, Spoornet, the SABC, etc) and big companies in the private sector issue tenders for various services, including OD.

Major national and provincial tenders are advertised in the *Government Tender Bulletin*, which is published on a weekly basis. This bulletin is obtainable from the Government Printer or it can be downloaded from the internet at http://www.gov.za/documents/tender. Most government tenders are also advertised in the major national newspapers and local ones, as well as on notice boards at government departments, post offices, police stations and elsewhere.

Subscriptions to commercial services such as Tenderscan and Tradeworld are also good sources for possible tenders.

The awarding of tenders in South Africa is based on the following three principles (Van Rooyen, 2015):

1. **Functionality:** All tenders are first evaluated on their functionality. It is therefore important for OD consultants to ensure they understand the scope of the tender, and respond to all the requirements.
2. **Price:** Price is usually the determining factor during the awarding of a tender. The best products or services need to be procured at the best price. Government bodies usually adjudicate 80% of the tender on price and 20%

on the previously disadvantaged individual (PDI) status or gender of the business owner for tenders under R500 000. For tenders above R500 000, 90% is adjudicated on price and 10% on the PDI status or gender of the business owner.

3. **Broad-based Black Economic Empowerment (B-BBEE):** All public or private sector tenders must be evaluated on their B-BBEE levels. This practice is in line with the Preferential Procurement Policy Framework Act 5 of 2000 and the Amended Codes of Good Practice that came into effect on 1 May 2015.

A tender is therefore a way of inviting businesses to provide goods and services on a contractual basis. Once the business completes and submits the tender document, it becomes an offer. As soon as the offer is accepted, it becomes part of the contract.

Ethical marketing

Although the OD field is currently not regulated in South Africa, the SAODN is busy developing a Code of Ethics for the practice of OD. The Professional Board of Psychology has established certain rules of conduct when it comes to the advertising or marketing of services for industrial psychologists (HPCSA, 2004). It is a good idea for all OD professionals to abide by these rules in order to ensure more professionalism in the field.

Guidelines with regard to advertising and other public statement activities (adapted from HPCSA, 2004)

1. Never misrepresent in any manner your professional qualification with regard to education, experience or areas of competence.
2. Never make false, deceptive or fraudulent statements concerning your:
   - education and training, experience or competence
   - academic and/or professional qualifications
   - credentials
   - institutional, association or professional society affiliations
   - services
   - the clinical or scientific basis for or the results or degree of success of your consultancy
   - fees
   - publication(s) or research finding(s).
3. Only claim a qualification as a credential for your services if you earned such qualification from a nationally accredited institution.
4. Never compensate employees of the press, radio, television or other communication media in return for publicity in a news item.

5. If a paid advertisement pertaining to the consultancy services rendered is published, such services must be identified or clearly recognisable as such, unless this is already apparent from the context of the advertisement.

6. A consultant who provides advice or comment by means of a public lecture, demonstration, radio or television programme, pre-recorded tape, printed article, mailed material, internet or other electronic transmission, or via other media, shall take reasonable precautions to ensure that:

    - such advice or comment is based on appropriate OD literature and practice, and is consistent with these rules
    - the recipients of such advice or comment are not encouraged to infer that a relationship has been established with them personally
    - immediate steps are taken to correct any misrepresentation of him-/herself that may be made by others in any media.

Entry and contracting

The first contact between the client and the consultant is of crucial importance. Whilst it is important for consultants to display that they have the necessary expertise from the outset, too many consultants overpromise and underdeliver.

It is a mistake to assume that clients make decisions to use consultants based on purely rational reasons. In most cases their primary question is: 'Is this consultant someone I can trust? Is he/she someone I can trust not to hurt me, not to con me? Someone who can both help solve the organisational or technical problems I have and, at the same time, be considerate of my position and person?' (Block, 2006: 371).

To get the attention of the client, the consultant will have to prepare well for the first meeting and build a lasting relationship with the client during the entry phase. This relationship will lay an important foundation for the future working relationship after the client has accepted the consultant's proposal and the contract between the parties has been signed.

According to Anderson (2015: 114), a central question to be answered during the initial phases of the engagement is: Who is the client? In any helping relationship, the helper deals with more than one part of the client system. Because some parts may not have the same needs or expectations as others, these multiple relationships can lead to ethical dilemmas (Schein, 1997).

Schein (1997: 1–2) created a simplifying model to help consultants understand types of clients and client relationships. He divided the client system into six broad 'client types', namely:

1. **contact clients:** the individual(s) who first contacts the consultant with a request, question or issue

2. **intermediate clients:** the individuals or groups that get involved in various interviews, meetings and other activities as the project evolves
3. **primary clients:** the individual(s) who ultimately 'owns' the problem or issue being worked on, typically also the ones who pay the consulting bills or whose budget covers the consultation project
4. **unwitting clients:** members of the organisation or client system above, below and in lateral relationships to the primary clients, who will be affected by interventions but who are not aware that they will be impacted
5. **indirect clients:** members of the organisation who are aware that they will be affected by the interventions but who are unknown to the consultant and who may feel either positively or negatively about these effects
6. **ultimate clients:** the community, the total organisation, an occupational group or any other group that the consultant cares about and whose welfare must be considered in any intervention that the consultant makes.

As the project proceeds, the consultant must be careful to distinguish between the client types. The impact of social systems, networks, lines of influence, power relations and other socio-psychological concepts must always be taken into consideration and will have a direct impact on the relationship.

It is also important to remember to discuss the termination during this phase (Livingston, 2006). Therefore, success criteria of the OD process should be established as part of the entry and contracting phase in order for both parties to recognise when to terminate the relationship.

Entry

The importance of the first meeting between client and consultant cannot be emphasised enough. During this crucial meeting, both the consultant and the client need to determine the state of and possibilities for the partnership, the strength of the client's commitments to achieving the sought-after objectives, and how successes in the intervention initiative will be determined and ultimately resolved (Weisbord, 2006). Consultants should not underestimate the symbolic significance and complexity of the entry phase (Anderson, 2015). During this phase the consultant has the first opportunity to become connected to the social environment of the organisation and to start building valuable relationships and trust with organisational members.

It is useful to provide the organisation with as much information as possible about the consultant before the first meeting. This will minimise doubts, and ensure undivided attention during the first meeting on the issues that require attention. For similar reasons it is the duty of the consultant to know as much as possible about the client before the first meeting (Jackson, 2006). Typical questions the OD consultant needs to find answers to are the following (Rothwell, Sullivan & McLean, 1995):

- What is the organisation's size?
- What is the organisation's general reputation in the industry?
- What is the organisation's business?
- What are its product lines?
- Who are the key decision makers? What biographical information about them is available? What are their values? What are their visions for the organisation? What are their shared beliefs?
- What is reported in industry publications about the organisation's history, missions and goals, strategies in the marketplace or industry and structure?

During the first meeting, the following issues should be kept in mind (Burke, 1987; Weisbord, 2006):

- **Background of the consultant:** The client needs to know enough about the potential consultant to feel that he/she will be able to help.
- **Problems in the client system:** Are the real problems being discussed or are they only symptomatic of other hidden issues? Asking for examples in terms of observable behaviour can help to solve this problem.
- **Changes the client would like to see:** What things would the client observe happening that would be an indication of desired outcomes?
- **The first event:** What first event would be appropriate to move the system in the desired direction?
- **Readiness of the client to change:** What is the extent of resources the client is willing to commit towards supporting a change effort? This will include costs, timelines and availability of contact persons on all levels within the organisation.

Building the relationship

During the start of a relationship between the OD consultant and the client, the OD consultant might play more a therapeutic role. Similar to a therapist, the OD consultant needs to be prepared to deal with problems which are often hidden in the subconscious of the organisation (Young & Litterer, 1991). The real problem might be such a mutually concealed phenomenon that all the managers within the same organisation are relatively unaware of its presence. Owing to the hidden nature of the real problem, it will be impossible to address or solve it. During such an occurrence, the OD consultant will have to act as 'therapist' and assist the managers to raise their consciousness. To achieve this, the consultant must adopt an essentially neutral and relatively objective position. The essential skill of the consultant will be an interpretative one. He/she will have to be able to understand the content and structure of the map guiding organisational behaviour and be able to ascertain where and why it is deficient or misguided. Bringing concealed problems to the surface can be very threatening; they are usually concealed because individuals or groups do not want to deal with them. Feedback on these issues need to be beneficial and any stress needs to be kept to a minimum.

In typical therapeutic style, it can thus be recommended that the OD consultant follows a person-centred approach from the start of the relationship. This will lead to a relationship conducive to healing, growing and development.

Rogers (1961) identified three characteristics, or attributes, of the therapist which will form the core part of the therapeutic relationship—congruence, unconditional positive regard (UPR) and accurate empathic understanding.

1. **Congruence:** Congruence implies that therapists are real and/or genuine, open, integrated and authentic during their interactions with the client. They do not have a façade; that is, their internal and external experiences are one and the same. In short, they are authentic. This authenticity functions as a model of a human being struggling toward greater realness. In the case of the OD consultant, authentic behaviour is perhaps the secret ingredient that will ensure client commitment and the establishment of an everlasting relationship between the consultant and the client. According to Block (2006), authentic behaviour means you put into words what you are experiencing with the client as you work.

2. **Unconditional positive regard (UPR):** This refers to the therapist's deep and genuine caring for the client. The therapist may not approve of some of the client's actions but does approve of the client. In short, the therapist needs to have an attitude of 'I'll accept you as you are'. Research indicates that the greater the degree of caring, appreciating, accepting and valuing the client in a non-possessive way, the greater the chance that an intervention will be successful.

3. **Accurate empathic understanding:** This refers to the ability to understand the client's experience and feelings in the here-and-now, sensitively and accurately. Empathic understanding implies that the client's feelings are understood as if they were one's own; it means to stand in the other person's shoes and see the world from his/her perspective without wanting or trying to analyse or judge it.

Writing a winning proposal

Whether a consultant is applying for a government tender or has received a personal request by the CEO of a company to deliver an OD service, he/she will always have to write and submit a proposal.

Once the consultant has done a preliminary investigation, he/she needs to suggest a possible action plan to the client. An OD intervention proposal typically summarises a problem and recommends a solution. The proposal will play a significant role to get the buy-in the consultant will need for the intervention to ultimately be a success.

Table 7.2 Basic layout of an effective organisation development proposal (adapted from Cummings & Worley, 2015; Freedman & Zackrison, 2001)

Element	Description and action steps
Background/overview	The proposal document should start with an overview that summarises the methods used to gather data from key stakeholders, identifies the main symptoms of the current situation and describes the risk of not taking action to rectify the problem.
Objectives/outcomes of proposed project	Define the issue and explain how you intend to fix it. The proposal should list the goals and outcomes in clear and concise terms, and also state assumptions and constraints. Goals should be specific, measurable, attainable, realistic and time-constrained.
Proposed process or action plan	Provide an overview of the process to be used. This usually includes a diagnosis (including how data will be collected), the feedback process, an action planning or implementation process as well as evaluating the project. (Action planning is discussed in detail in Chapter 8.)
Roles and responsibilities	List the key stakeholders in the process and the specific responsibilities for which they will be held accountable. Remember to include all recognised unions as key stakeholders to the process. Without buy-in and support from unions, any intervention will be unlikely to succeed.
Recommended interventions (project work plan)	Describe the proposed change strategies, including training, off-site meetings, systems or processes to be redesigned, and other activities.
Fees, terms and conditions	The proposal should identify how much the intervention will cost and what sponsorship is required to make it a success. It should include a table that lists each item and the estimated cost. You can also indicate potential sources of funding. Payment terms and any other conditions which might impact on the project must be listed. By clearly defining all the resources required to conduct the intervention, you can ensure that you get everything you need right from the start.
Qualifications of consultant and team members	In this section, you can insert information such as your résumé, information about your company and a list of references of former clients. It is also important to include the B-BBEE status of your company.

Contracting

All activities during the entry phase are a prelude to developing an OD contract between the consultant and the client. Once the client is satisfied with the proposal, they will continue with the drafting of a contract, based on the proposal. The main purpose of the contract is to clarify how the OD process will proceed. It typically establishes the expectations of the parties, the time and resources that will be expended, and the ground rules under which the parties will operate (Cummings & Worley, 2015).

Anderson (2015: 119–122) identified the following purposes contracting might serve during an OD process:

- **To further explore the problem:** The consultant should view the contracting phase as an early stage of data gathering and diagnosis. During this phase it is important for the consultant to understand what the real problem is, what the root of the problem is, how it impacts on the organisation and how solving (or failing to solve) it will affect the business.
- **To clarify the client's goals and objectives for the request:** It is important to understand from the onset what results the client expects to see when the relationship is finished. All goals and objectives must be discussed as concretely as possible. Goals and objectives will determine how the impact of interventions will be evaluated, and will provide guidance on when to terminate the relationship.
- To allow the client to **get to know** the consultant and the consultant to get to know the client and the organisation, and for both parties to validate that the consultant has the knowledge and the skills to accept the project.
- To understand the organisation's **commitment to change**.
- **To create an environment** in which consultation can succeed by agreeing on mutual roles and needs.
- **To clarify time pressures and expectations:** Time expectations should be explored for all stages along the way, for example data gathering and feedback, implementing interventions, measuring outcomes, etc.
- **To clarify how the client and consultant will interact:** This will involve practicalities such as the number and schedule of meetings as well as expectations for an equal relationship of authenticity and honesty.
- **To clarify confidentiality needs:** It is important to remember that confidentiality is the client's decision. The client will decide who is entitled to know about the existence of the consultation, who will have access to data or receive copies of reports of other documents, etc. The consultant needs to clarify any doubts immediately with the client.
- **To plan the next steps:** At the end of the contracting process, both consultant and client need to know exactly what is expected of them.

Contracting is equally important for external as well as internal consultants. Where external consultants will rely on written documents to ensure that the client's expectations are met and to protect themselves, internal consultants will have to rely more on verbal and informal contracts. Without a proper contract in place, internal consultants are especially vulnerable. While external consultants might only risk losing a client, internal consultants risk compromising their future working conditions and even their careers if proper boundaries and expectations are not negotiated clearly during the contracting phase (Jackson, 2006).

The keys to drafting lucid, manageable contracts are: (1) properly articulating the issues at hand; (2) clearly laying out the ground rules that will guide the process and expectations for the client–consultant relationship; (3) establishing and nurturing mutual trust and disclosure; and (4) articulating the changes and developmental initiatives that the client would like to see enacted (Weisbord, 2006).

Unlike most other contracts, the OD contract focuses more on the process than on the content. According to Weisbord (2006), the OD contract refers to the explicit exchange of expectations that has to clarify critical areas for both the consultant and the client, namely:

- what each expects to get from the relationship (mutual expectations)
- how much time each will invest, when and at what cost (allocation of time and resources)
- the ground rules under which the parties will operate (ground rules).

Mutual expectations

The expectations of both parties must be addressed. The client must state the outcomes to be provided by the OD consultant and should also describe what the organisation expects from the process and the consultant. In the same way, the OD consultant should also state what he/she expects to gain from the OD process. This can include, but is not limited to, trying new interventions, publishing an article or receiving appropriate compensation (Cummings & Worley, 2015).

Time and resources

Both the OD consultant and the organisation need to commit time and resources to the process. It is important that they be clear about how much energy and resources they will dedicate to the process.

Resources can be divided into (Block, 2006; Cummings & Worley, 2015):

- **essential requirements:** things that are absolutely necessary if the change process is to be successful
- **desirable requirements:** those things that would be nice to have, but are not absolutely necessary.

Ground rules

Specify how the client and the OD consultant will work together. Parameters might include such issues as confidentiality, how the OD consultant will become involved in personal or interpersonal issues, how to terminate the relationship, whether the OD consultant is supposed to make expert recommendations or help the manager to make decisions (Cummings & Worley, 2015).

Agree from the start how and when the relationship will end. All contracts have a natural life, and are usually outgrown or rendered obsolete by changing organisational climates. It is important for both client and consultant to have a clear picture of when their relationship should come to an agreed-upon end (Weisbord, 2006).

However, keep in mind that the OD contract should allow for flexibility. It is good practice for the OD consultant and client to renew or renegotiate the contract periodically during their working relationship (Burke, 1987).

The organisational diagnosis phase

The diagnostic process is one of the most important activities in OD and will be discussed in detail in Chapter 8. During this phase, the OD consultant needs to gather all relevant information needed in order to design the correct intervention. Unlike the medical model, the OD consultant needs to make a diagnosis without the advantage of a highly developed diagnostic taxonomy. As a result, the OD consultant and the client need to jointly determine which organisational issues to focus on, how to collect and analyse data to understand it, and how to work together to develop action steps from the diagnosis (Cummings & Worley, 2015). Although the consultant might know a lot of organisation theory, most theories are either too narrow to include everything the consultant might wish to understand or too broadly abstract to give much guidance (Weisbord, 2006).

OD consultants treat the diagnostic process in itself as an intervention. They realise that, more likely than not, the act of searching for and gathering information sends a message and triggers a 'ripple effect' throughout the client system's interdependent levels and subsystems. They anticipate that diagnostic interventions evoke a wide range of reactions from subsystem members.

They also know that imposed diagnoses and derivative recommendations are usually resented, rejected and resisted. It is therefore important to involve intact work units and key individuals who will be affected by the execution of any implementation plans from the start. OD consultants know that buy-in or a sense of ownership of the diagnosis and conclusions is critical to assure that people will support plans to change the organisation. This will also take the mystery out of the diagnostic process by making it as transparent as possible by describing the entire process and explaining why they do what they do at each step (Freedman & Zackrison, 2001).

During the diagnostic process there are about five key tasks the consultant needs to complete, as shown in Table 7.3.

Table 7.3 Tasks and actions associated with the diagnosis (adapted from Noolan, 2006)

Tasks	Actions
1. Determine approach to be used	Decide if a diagnostic or dialogic approach will be followed. If a diagnostic approach will be followed, determine the preferred diagnostic model. Be clear about the purpose of the diagnosis and determine data-collection methods in collaboration with the client. It is important to establish confidentiality-of-data agreements from the start. Involve the union or union representatives from the start.
2. Announce project	Draft, and have management (with the support of the union) distribute, an announcement alerting staff to the organisational diagnosis, time frames and process that will be used. Meet with employees, to answer questions or address concerns and to ensure buy-in.
3. Prepare for data collection	Maintain rapport with the client system and restate confidentiality-of-data agreements. Ensure that top management understand what they can expect from the results. Identify or develop interview guides, questionnaires, or other data-gathering methods and request relevant internal records. Establish time frames for the project.
4. Collect data	Carry out data collection using agreed-upon approaches and ensuring confidentiality.
5. Analysing, interpreting and presentation of the data	The goal is to make the data easy for the client to absorb, not to show how much data has been collected. Analysis of the data can be done by using qualitative tools like content analysis or hermeneutics of quantitative tools like SPSS. During the presentation it is important to group information according to themes or according to the diagnostic model you have used. Always prepare a written report with your presentation.

Diagnostic models

During the diagnostic phase, the consultant needs to know what information to look for as well as how to analyse and interpret it (Burke, 2009); therefore, when an OD consultant conducts an organisational diagnosis it is essential to have some implicit model or theoretical framework in mind. (Refer to Chapter 6 for a detailed discussion of the core theories and models.) This can be quite difficult because OD is a continuously developing field that draws on a mixture of theories. Furthermore, it was built on different contributing disciplines such as sociology and psychology, management and leadership, and engineering management and industrial engineering (Al-Haddad & Kotnour, 2015). As a result, the perfect OD diagnostic model simply does not exist. How consultants diagnose will differ with each individual as well as from situation to situation. It will depend on the consultant's background and experience as well as the theoretical framework the OD consultant feels most comfortable with.

What is important is for the consultant to ensure that all relevant information is analysed. The consultant needs to look at more than just social processes that occur mainly among individuals and within groups, and also investigate the strategies and design components for the total organisation.

The OD consultant should look for a model which will minimise bias in what is collected, constitute a mechanism for data analysis, and provide a common vocabulary for people to use (Galant & Rios, 2006). Without a framework, any data the OD consultant collects from the client will be a mass of confusion (Burke, 1987). For data to become understandable and workable they must be viewed in terms of a conceptual framework or model. This framework will point out what areas to examine and what questions to ask in assessing how the organisation is functioning (Cummings & Worley, 2015).

When selecting a model, the OD consultant should use the following criteria (Burke, 1987; Noolan, 2006):

- The OD consultant should thoroughly understand the model and feel comfortable with it.
- It should fit the client organisation as closely as possible.
- It should be sufficiently comprehensive to enable data to be gathered about the organisation according to the model's parameters but without missing key bits of information.

Some popular conceptual frameworks or diagnostic models in OD include:

- Blake and Mouton's Grid Method of Organisation Development
- Bolman and Deal's Four Frames Model
- the Burke–Litwin model of individual and organisation performance
- the Freedman Swamp Model of Sociotechnical Systems
- Galbraith's Star Model

- Hornstein and Tichy's Emergent Pragmatic Model
- Lawrence and Lorsch's Contingency Theory
- Levinson's Clinical-Historical Approach
- the McKinsey Seven-S Model
- the Nadler–Tusman Congruence Model
- the systems model (open systems model)
- Tichy's Technical Political Cultural (TPC) Framework
- Weisbord's Six-Box Model.

In a South African study by Martins and Coetzee (2009), the utilisation of the Burke–Litwin model as a diagnostic framework for categorising and analysing collected data contributed to an increase in the validity and reliability of the organisational diagnosis process and outcomes concerned. The use of the model further increased the involvement of employees and management, and helped to create a very strong platform for future organisational improvement actions. The study also found that one of the most valuable outcomes of the use of the diagnostic approach was the expanded conceptual map or picture that the client organisation developed of itself as a result of using the model in reporting and presenting the recorded data.

Consultants should guard against using models blindly. When using a model, keep in mind that they all represent simplifications of reality. Each model will emphasise certain organisational features as critical while ignoring other features. If OD consultants focus their attention only on particular features to the exclusion of others, this can lead to a biased diagnosis; therefore, they need to choose the diagnostic model and process very carefully and ensure it addresses the organisation's presenting problem (Cummings & Worley, 2015).

Regardless of the choice of theoretical framework or diagnostic model, a diagnosis should, as a minimum, provide a valid, accurate, reliable and adequate response to the following questions (Van Tonder & Dietrichsen, 2008):

- How does the organisation define or describe performance/effectiveness?
- What is the specific primary problem, challenge or change need that the organisation experiences?
- How does this problem, challenge or change need impact on or alter the organisation's performance/effectiveness in the past, now and in future?
- How does the problem, challenge or change need relate to its surroundings (ie the micro- meso-, macro- and internal–external organisational environments)?
- What are the multiple causes that contribute to this problem, challenge or change need, and how are they interrelated?
- What is required in order to deal effectively with the problem, challenge or change need?
- What is the organisation's capability and capacity relative to that required for dealing effectively with the problem, challenge or change need?

Data collection

The collection methods, techniques and instruments used with a view to setting a diagnosis are the same as in the case of any other kind of research. The four major techniques for gathering diagnostic data are questionnaires, interviews, observations and consulting secondary sources, for example the organisation's documents. Each method has its own strengths and weaknesses under different circumstances. The OD consultant would typically rely on a combination of data-gathering instruments in order to ensure the validity and reliability of the information he/she would use to formulate a diagnosis.

Franklin (1995) identified six key criteria an OD consultant can use to decide which data-collection method will be best to use:

1. **Efficiency:** This includes such factors as the financial cost involved and the time required for collecting and analysing information from a specific number of sources.
2. **Objectivity:** This reflects to what degree the method is subject to consultant or respondent bias.
3. **Comparability:** This indicates how easy it is to compare results across time to determine progress.
4. **Completeness:** This indicates how well the method can cover a broad range of issues and levels of measurement.
5. **Accuracy/validity:** This includes criteria 2, 3 and 4, and also the perception that the information reflects what actually exists in the organisation.
6. **Flexibility:** This indicates how well the method can be modified, based on information gathered during the initial stages of the process.

Feedback to the client

During the feedback session it is not only necessary for the client and the OD consultant to achieve a common understanding of the organisation's current condition, but also to arouse organisational action and to direct energy toward problem solving (Cummings & Worley, 2015). It will therefore be crucial to facilitate ownership of the feedback data. The content and the process of data communication will both be critical factors during the feedback process.

The content needs to meet the following criteria in order to ensure maximum impact (Cummings & Worley, 2015: 143–144):

- **It must be relevant.** This can be achieved only by including managers and representative employees of the organisation in the activity of information and data collection.
- **It must be understandable.** This can best be achieved through the use of graphs and outlines as frequently as possible.

- **It must be descriptive.** This attribute refers to the fact that the data communicated must be related to actual behaviours; in this respect, the use of examples and illustrations is recommended.
- **It must be verifiable.** Information must always be accurate and valid.
- **It must be limited (restricted).** This is important in order to guard against overloading employees with information which will have a negative effect on any subsequent actions.
- **It must have impact.** It is best to restrict data and to focus only on problems that people can handle and change.
- **It must be comparative.** This can best be achieved by using benchmarks wherever possible in order to locate the target group in a wider context.
- **It must not be finalised.** Keep in mind that the data communicated are not a purpose in themselves, but rather an action stimulus, a starting point for discussions, supplementary diagnoses (if necessary) and problem solving.

The most important objective of the feedback process is to ensure that the organisation members take ownership of the data. Ownership refers to people's willingness to take responsibility for the data, their meaning and the consequences of using them to devise a change strategy.

The following features of successful feedback processes will generally accelerate ownership of the feedback data (Anderson, 2015; Cummings & Worley, 2015):

- **Motivation to work with the data:** Members of the organisation need to feel that working with the data will have beneficial outcomes. It is important that people feel free to raise issues and to identify concerns during the feedback session.
- **Structure for the meetings:** Feedback meetings need definite structure or there will be a real danger that it may degenerate into chaos or aimless discussions. An agenda or outline for the meeting and the presence of a discussion leader are needed to provide the necessary direction.
- **Appropriate attendance:** All employees who have a common problem and can benefit from working together should be included in the feedback meeting. Adequate composition will ensure better ownership.
- **Ensuring adequate strength (of the group members):** This entails identifying and clarifying the distinction between issues they can change, issues they can recommend ideas for, and issues that are out of their control.
- **Process help:** People in feedback meetings require assistance in working together as a group. When the data are negative, there is a natural tendency to resist the implications, and deflect the conversation onto safer subjects. The OD consultant needs to ensure that members stay focused on the subject and improve feedback discussion, problem solving and ownership.

- **Ensuring assistance in using the data:** Members of the organisation need to feel safe and know that the OD consultant will be with them for the duration of the project.
- **Always beginning with the positive data:** Encourage the client to accept and appreciate the organisation's strengths and to use them to compensate for or to address weaknesses.
- **Choice of language:** This is important during the presentation. The use of non-evaluative, descriptive language will ensure that feedback is accepted and acted upon.
- **Not projecting personal feelings, but focusing on the facts:** Consultants should not project their own feelings onto the client and assume, for example, that the client will be angry. Focus objectively on the facts and report them to the client.
- **Not avoiding tough issues:** The consultant should guard against minimising feedback in order to create a harmonious relationship or to avoid upsetting the client. The client needs to know exactly what the findings are and take them seriously.

The process of feedback is usually achieved within a meeting or a series of meetings. Although consultants usually develop their own preference on how to structure the feedback process, the suggested structure in Table 7.4 for feedback of an employee survey (ES) will provide a valuable guideline.

The biggest challenge for the consultant will be to keep control of the feedback meeting in order to cover the agenda of the meeting. Keep in mind the presentation of the data to the client is only a small part of the agenda. Unfortunately this is where most clients get stuck, especially if the facts seem like criticism directed at the management team. The main goal of the meeting is to work on the decision about what to do. The more the feedback meeting can address what to do, the better the chance of implementation (Block, 2006).

Table 7.4 Feedback structure (Borg & Mastrangelo, 2008: 324)

Introduction	The goal of the introduction is to set the stage for the presentation. Include the following:
	● Overall goals of the process
	● Overview of phases, steps and milestones
	● Participation rates
	● Data quality
	● Reminder of questionnaire items: format, answer scale
	● Statistics: which were used, why, how to interpret

Results	1. Results by facets/dimensions of the organisation climate:
	<ul><li>Organisation as a whole</li><li>External benchmarking</li><li>Results from previous surveys</li><li>Results vs prognoses</li><li>Differences among major organisation functions, regions, etc</li><li>Differences among managers and non-managers</li></ul>
	2. Results within a framework, eg the performance-satisfaction (PS) motor. <ul><li>Explain core of PS motor</li><li>Link various items to boxes and/or connectives in the PS motor</li><li>Introduce extended PS motor</li><li>Report results on commitment, trust, contextual performance drivers</li></ul>
	3. Empirical/statistical structure of items, eg multidimensional scaling (MDS) <ul><li>Explain MDS structure of items</li><li>Show position of variables of particular interest within MDS plot</li><li>Discuss influences, what drives what</li></ul>
	4. Special topics <ul><li>Items that show progress and decline since the last survey</li><li>Hot topics given current business context</li><li>Items for managers only</li></ul>
	5. Business perspectives onto the ES data <ul><li>ES data in the balanced scorecard, SWOT (strengths, weaknesses, opportunities, threats) analysis, etc</li><li>Linkage analysis</li></ul>
	6. Some Monday morning platforms for actions: Identify some platforms that offer the individual manager a chance to make use of the results without much additional planning, complex coordination or deep thinking
Ending	<ul><li>Summary of all the results</li><li>Recommendations for global areas of focus</li><li>Recommendations on next steps, time line</li></ul>

The intervention phase

The purpose of an intervention is to move the organisation and its members from the present state to a new, healthier one. Choosing the correct intervention can be very difficult. In the words of Weisbord (2006: 397): 'OD is like playing the market. Every intervention is a calculated risk. There are no guarantees.' However, there are certain conditions that will enhance or inhibit the impact of any intervention.

When deciding on an intervention, the OD consultant must consider important variables such as (Farquhar, 2006):

- the purpose(s) of the intervention
- the environment in which the organisation functions
- the organisation's culture, including its core technology, leadership and professional identity/ies
- the circumstances in which the strategy will be used
- the appropriate depth of the intervention (going only as deep as necessary to address the goal)
- the likelihood and consequences of the collateral effects of the intervention
- the fit of the strategy within the available time frame and its flow inside the sequence of the intervention
- the client's response to the proposal.

Argyris (1970) established the following criteria which must be present in order for any intervention activity to succeed:

- **Valid information:** The consultant and client should base all decisions on information that is relevant to the situation and which is as full and correct as possible. Any omissions and limitations must be understood and taken into account. If plans are based on invalid information, then everything else will be invalid, including decisions, communications and actions.
- **Free informed choice on the client's part:** When the client makes decisions, it should be without explicit or implicit pressure from others. The decision should be based on valid information available rather than social reasons such as avoiding criticism or avoiding harm to others. In practice, this can be very difficult, as organisations are social institutions staffed with people who have their own desires and agendas that may not align well with higher strategies and decisions of the organisation.
- **Internal commitment by the client to learning and change:** Only when people are truly committed to decisions will they act on them with passion and energy. If they are not, all efforts will be half-hearted and can easily fail. This is especially the case when group decisions are made or where a leader makes a decision that requires others to act. It is always important to be able to prove that any decisions were based on valid information. If decisions appear to be self-serving or based on weak data, the chance of gaining commitment from others will be unlikely.

These basic rules will ensure that the power dynamic stays within the client system. If any one of these criteria is not met and the OD consultant fails to provide constant monitoring, there is a good chance that the intervention will fail.

Overview of interventions

In Chapters 9, 10 and 11, various interventions will be discussed in detail. According to Cummings and Worley (2015), all interventions can be roughly grouped into four major types, as discussed in the following sections.

Human process interventions

Human process interventions focus on people within the organisation and the processes they use to accomplish organisational goals, for example problem solving, communication, leadership, etc. These interventions focus on helping members of the organisation to grow and develop, and to enhance the way in which they work together to the benefit of the overall organisation. Human process interventions might be particularly appropriate during any change project, especially when different cultures are starting to work together, there is a lot of conflict, there are signs of low morale (eg high absenteeism), teams are not performing optimally, new work teams are established, etc. These interventions mainly derive from psychology and social psychology, and can be either interventions that deal with interpersonal relationships and group dynamics or those that are more system-wide.

- **Interventions that deal with interpersonal relationships and group dynamics:** Examples include T-groups (training groups), process consultation, third-party interventions, coaching, mentoring, teambuilding, diversity awareness, conflict management, virtual teams, etc.
- **Interventions that deal with human processes that are more system-wide:** These focus on the total organisation or an entire department as well as the relationships between groups. Examples include organisation confrontation meetings, intergroup relations, large-group interventions (LGIs), force field analysis, appreciative inquiry (AI), etc.

Techno-structural interventions which will modify an organisation's structure and technology

These interventions focus on improving the performance of the organisation by primarily modifying technology (eg its task methods and job design) and structure (eg division of labour and hierarchy). Techno-structural interventions might be particularly helpful when the organisation experiences rapid growth but has few internal systems to sustain that growth; there is a lot of confusion about roles; a new major technology or process has been introduced; the company is experiencing many complaints from customers; or the organisation is new, and internal operational systems must be developed and implemented, etc. The interventions are mainly rooted in the disciplines of engineering, sociology and psychology, and in the applied fields of socio-technical systems and organisation design. Consultants place emphasis both on productivity and human fulfilment. Interventions can be divided into techno-structural interventions concerned with restructuring organisations, those concerned with methods for involving employees in decision making and those concerned with individuals and interactive groups.

- Interventions concerned with **restructuring organisations** are, for example, structural design, downsizing and re-engineering.
- Interventions concerned with methods for **involving employees in decision making** all attempt to move knowledge, power, information and rewards downward in the organisation. Examples of interventions include parallel structures, high-involvement organisations (HIOs), total quality management (TQM) and work design.
- Interventions concerned with **designing work for individual jobs and interactive groups** are, for example, job enrichment and self-managed work teams.

Human resource management interventions that seek to improve member performance and wellness

These interventions aim to enhance overall organisational performance by improving the performance of individuals and groups within organisations. They are rooted in labour relations and the applied practices of compensation and benefits, employee selection and placement, performance appraisal, career development, and employee diversity and wellness. There is a strong focus on the people in organisations, and the underlying belief is that organisational effectiveness results from improved practices for integrating employees into organisations. Interventions can be divided according to three broad aims: those concerned with performance management, those which focus on human resource development and those intended to support individual members.

- Interventions concerned with **performance management** are, for example, goal setting, performance appraisal, reward systems, establishing performance goals, performance plans, observation and feedback, evaluating performance, rewarding performance, recognising performance problems ('performance gaps') and personal development plans.
- Interventions concerned with **managing, developing and retaining organisational talent** are, for example, coaching and mentoring, management and leadership development, career planning and development, instrumented feedback, guided study, personal development plans, etc.
- General interventions which will **support individual organisational members** are, for example, managing workforce diversity, employee wellness, stress management, employee assistance programmes, HIV/AIDS in the workplace, counselling, coaching, etc.

Strategic interventions that involve managing the organisation's relationship to its external environment, and the internal structure and process necessary to support a business strategy

These interventions link the internal functioning of the organisation to the larger environment, and transform the organisation to keep pace with changing conditions. Interventions are usually implemented organisation-wide, and may include employees, groups, technologies, products and services, etc, with the aim of bringing about a fit between business strategy, organisation design and the larger environment. These interventions may be particularly helpful during the following situations: rapid changes in the external environment, rapid or stagnant sales, significantly increased competition, rapid market expansion, mergers and acquisitions, the need for quick and comprehensive change throughout the organisation, etc. These interventions are rooted in the disciplines of strategic management, organisation theory, economics and anthropology:

- Interventions that **transform the way the organisation relates to its environment or operates internally** are, for example, integrated strategic change, organisation design and culture change.
- Interventions that are designed to **support continuous organisational change** are, for example, dynamic strategy making, self-designing organisations, learning organisations and built-to-change organisations.
- Strategic interventions which **shape how organisations collaborate with each other** are, for example, mergers and acquisitions, alliances, networks, trans-organisation development, etc.

Designing and prioritising interventions

The intervention phase builds on the knowledge an OD consultant has on all the various levels within an organisation. A common hazard during the design phase is for the OD consultant to jump too quickly to a specific design. The role of the OD consultant during the design phase will be to guide the organisation in making choices for intervention actions (Farquhar, 2006). This can require several meetings to consider all alternative interventions before coming up with a work plan.

The intervention phase usually consists of (Farquhar, 2006):
- defining the present state and a desired future
- planning and designing a programme to bring about change
- implementing actions to bring about change
- following up the actions.

When deciding on the appropriate intervention to use, the OD consultant needs to consider the following three aspects (Gallos & Schein, 2006):

1. **The potential results of the intervention:**
   - Will the intervention solve the basic problem(s)?
   - Does it have any additional positive outcomes?

2. **The potential implementation of the intervention:**
   - Can the intervention actually work in a practical application?
   - How much will implementation cost?
   - How does the estimated cost compare with the expected results?
   - Does the OD consultant have the required abilities, knowledge and skills to implement the intervention?
   - Is there enough time to implement the intervention?

3. **The potential acceptance of the intervention:**
   - Is the intervention acceptable to the client?
   - Does the intervention match the culture of the organisation?
   - Has the intervention been adequately developed and tested?
   - Has the intervention been explained and communicated to members of the organisation?

It is difficult to establish the real cost of a failed intervention. Apart from the tangible cost, such as wasted time and resources, there will also be huge intangible costs for both the consultant and client, such as an increase in self-doubt (Anderson, 2015).

Anderson (2015: 192–194) identified 10 reasons why interventions fail:
1. The intervention tried to solve the wrong problem.
2. The wrong intervention was selected.
3. Goals were ambiguous, unclear or too lofty.
4. The intervention was undertaken as an event rather than a programme of activities with multiple targets for change.
5. Not enough time was devoted to change.
6. The intervention was poorly designed to reach the specified goals.
7. The change agent was not skilled at implementing the intervention.
8. Responsibility for change was not transferred to the client.
9. Organisational members resisted or were not committed to the intervention.
10. The organisation was not ready for change.

Once the consultant and client mutually agree on which interventions to implement, the consultant can continue to draw up a project work plan.

Table 7.5   Example of a project work plan (Author)

Goals (expected results)	Intervention	Means of verification	Presenters/ resource person	Logistical information	Supporting material	Timetable (dates and time)
Objective 1:						
Objective 2:						

The evaluation and termination phase

The consultant and client must work closely together to design the content of the evaluation plan. Not only will this build the capacity of the client, it will also ensure that the client receives first-hand knowledge of the impact of the intervention in various parts of the organisation. The plan should include evaluation questions, information needed to answer each question, and methods to gather and analyse that information. Burke (1987) emphasised the importance of evaluating effectiveness. Proper evaluation will prevent the implementation of programmes because they 'feel good' instead of using programmes with measured effectiveness. Other reasons why evaluation is such an important step include the following (Anderson, 2015):

- **It will provide focus:** If both the client and consultant are serious to include an evaluation plan, this will prompt them to return to the original objectives of the engagement, to be specific about what outcomes were desired, and to document whether those objectives were achieved.
- **Evaluation results may facilitate support:** Evaluation results will provide the necessary proof to clients that the OD effort was worthwhile, and these clients will be more likely to support such efforts in the future. With the necessary permission, the OD consultant will be able to retain the evaluation results and use them as part of a professional portfolio.
- **Results provide feedback for change:** An evaluation can uncover barriers to change and the results can point to future possibilities for improvement.
- **Client and consultant growth:** Evaluation will help the consultant to understand the aspects of the intervention strategy that did or did not work as anticipated. The consultant will be able to learn from this experience and correct it the next time.

Unfortunately there sometimes seems to be a resistance to the evaluation of interventions. As a result, published cases of OD evaluation are difficult to find (Anderson, 2015). Some of the most significant barriers to evaluation seem to be the following (Martineau & Preskill in Anderson, 2015: 350–351):

- **Additional resources:** Many consultants and clients are unwilling to commit even more resources to evaluation after an already lengthy cycle.
- **Fear of results:** The client might fear that although resources were spent, there is no change or there may even be deterioration in the situation. In the same way, the consultant might fear negative feedback or the possibility of developing a reputation for managing interventions which do not obtain the desired results.
- **Energy required:** Unfortunately many clients and consultants would rather commit energy to producing change and not to evaluating it.
- **Acceptance of proof:** The clients or consultants may accept, from past experience or reports from others, that the intervention worked. As a result they do not see the need to evaluate it themselves.
- **Uncertainty of what to evaluate:** If clear goals were not established in the contracting phase, both clients and consultants might be unsure about what to evaluate.
- **Seen as optional:** In most cases, evaluation is seen as a 'nice to have' step and not a requirement.
- **Training of the consultant:** Many consultants are not formally trained in evaluation methods.
- **Complexity of interventions:** Owing to the complex nature of organisational intervention, it may not always be possible to establish conclusively whether the results are due directly to the specific activities of the OD programme.

Evaluating interventions

Table 7.6 contains an evaluation checklist that can be used to evaluate the effectiveness of an intervention.

Table 7.6 Evaluation checklist (adapted from Livingston, 2006)

Use of resources	To what extent were adequate resources available to ensure successful implementation of the change? Were there enough time, money and resources to accomplish the goals and objectives of the OD process?
Participation	Did all the right people in all the right parts of the organisation participate fully in the change process? In particular, did those who are most directly affected by the change have an opportunity to make their voices heard, and were they listened to? ➔

Access and support	To what extent was access to and support from the key decision makers in the client system available? What was the impact of their involvement in the outcome of the OD process?
Communication	How were communications handled throughout the change process? What was the influence of verbal and non-verbal communications? What was the impact of the words, tone and metaphors used to draw people into the process? What about cultural differences? (This is especially important when working across geographic cultures, both domestically and internationally.)
Hard outcome measures	What was the impact on quantifiable and other measures that were agreed to in the entry and contracting stage of the OD process?
Role integrity	How well did the client and consultant work together? What role clarification problems developed, if any, and how were they handled?
Perspective	What differences were there, if any, in how the outcomes are perceived—the client's versus the OD consultant's perspective?
Confidentiality	Where important and appropriate, how was confidentiality handled throughout the OD process?
Conflict and decision making	How were conflict and decision making handled throughout the OD process?
Speak truth to power	Both the OD consultant and the client operate with a certain amount of power, and it is important that both parties recognise each other's power position. The client holds the chequebook; the OD consultant holds the knowledge of the process. It is important to be willing to look at oneself and management objectively and recognise when one's style or philosophy may be part of the problem.

Institutionalising organisational changes

One of the most important stages in the process is to manage the institutionalisation of the successful OD programme so it persists. It is also unfortunately a stage which is mostly neglected. Real commitment from both the consultant and the client is needed to ensure the sustainability of the change process (Livingston, 2006).

Cummings and Worley (2015) have identified five processes that can directly affect the degree to which OD interventions are institutionalised:

1. **Socialisation:** This aspect concerns the transmission of information about beliefs, preferences, norms and values with respect to the intervention.
2. **Commitment:** This aspect includes initial commitment to the programme, as well as recommitment over time. In order to promote high commitment and stability, it is important that people select the necessary behaviour freely, explicitly and publicly. Commitment should also be derived from

several organisational levels, including the employees directly involved as well as the middle and upper managers who can support the interventions.

3. **Reward allocation:** This aspect involves linking rewards to the new behaviour required by an intervention. It is important to use a combination of both intrinsic and extrinsic rewards to reinforce new behaviour. It is equally important that employees see the reward allocations as equitable.

4. **Diffusion:** This aspect refers to the process of transferring changes from one system to another. Many interventions fail because they run counter to the values, purpose or identity of the larger organisation.

5. **Sensing and calibration:** This aspect involves detecting deviations from the desired intervention behaviour and taking corrective actions.

There are five indicators which can be used to assess the level in change persistence (Cummings & Worley, 2015), namely:

1. knowledge of the behaviours associated with an intervention
2. the degree to which intervention behaviours are actually performed
3. the degree to which members of the organisation privately accept the organisational change
4. the extent to which people agree about the appropriateness of the organisational changes
5. the social consensus on values relevant to the organisational changes.

The more of the above indicators are present in a situation, the higher will be the degree of institutionalisation.

Terminating the relationship

Termination is the final stage of the OD process. It is important for any consultant to know when it is time to leave and not overstay his/her welcome.

The following signs might indicate that it is time to terminate the relationship (Livingston, 2006):

- if either the client or the consultant makes and then forgets agreements
- if the consultant feels he/she is more heavily invested than the client
- if the client is truly doing better and no longer needs outside help.

When both parties agree it is time to terminate the relationship, there are some tasks the OD consultant needs to perform (Livingston, 2006):

- The consultant needs to determine how to end the OD process (this can take, for example, the form of a closing meeting).
- The consultant needs to give and receive feedback from the client, which will assist with any future services.
- Finally, the consultant needs to contract with the client for any future relationship they both wish to have.

Conclusion

This chapter presented an overview of the OD process. It is important to realise that a time limit cannot be attached to any of the phases. One of the most important phases in the cycle is the establishment of a relationship between the consultant and client. If this is healthy, a significant change in the functioning of the organisation is likely. This relationship needs to be clarified in the contract between the parties to reduce any misunderstanding.

Without valid and reliable data, the OD consultant will be unable to make the correct diagnosis. Only after all the data have been thoroughly analysed can the consultant, in consultation with the client, start making a diagnosis and recommend possible interventions.

It is, furthermore, important to evaluate the impact continuously. After all parties are satisfied that the correct outcome has been achieved, the change needs to become part of the organisation's normal functioning. Once the change is institutionalised and all the outcomes have been met, it is time to terminate the relationship.

Reflection questions

1. How would you describe the OD process to a potential client?
2. Why is it important to know who the client is? Explain your answer by referring to the different client types in the consultant–client relationship.
3. Why is it important to draft a contract between the consultant and the client?
4. Discuss the important factors which must be included in an OD contract.
5. Explain why the diagnostic process can also be seen as an intervention.
6. Why is it important to have an implicit model or theoretical framework in mind when conducting a diagnosis?
7. What criteria will you use to select a diagnostic model?
8. Explain how you would ensure ownership of the feedback data.
9. How will you know your change interventions have been institutionalised by the company?
10. Design a checklist you can use to evaluate the effectiveness of your interventions.

Multiple-choice questions

1. Before implementing an intervention, it is necessary to:
   a. consider the potential results of the technique
   b. consider the potential implementation of the technique
   c. consider the potential political acceptance of the technique

d. consider the cost of the technique

e. All of the above

2. Members of the organisation who are aware that they will be affected by the interventions, but who are unknown to the consultant, are known as:

a. unwitting clients

b. ultimate clients

c. indirect clients

d. intermediate clients

e. contact clients

3. AI is an example of a:

a. human process intervention

b. techno-structural intervention

c. human resource management intervention

d. strategic intervention

4. The most important objective of the feedback process is to:

a. keep the client informed of progress

b. ensure that the organisation members take ownership of the data

c. achieve a common understanding of the organisation's current condition

d. provide direction to the organisation members

e. All of the above

5. The aspect concerned with the transmission of information about beliefs, preferences, norms and values with respect to the intervention is known as:

a. socialisation

b. commitment

c. diffusion

d. sensing

e. calibration

Useful websites

Association for Talent Development (ATD): https://www.td.org/

Chartered Institute of Personnel and Development (CIPD): http://cipd.co.uk/

Coaches and Mentors of South Africa (COMENSA): http://www.comensa.org.za/

International Society for Performance Improvement (ISPI): http://www.ispi.org/

MarvinWeisbord.com, The Productive Workplaces Archives: http://www.marvinweisbord.com/

Productivity SA: http://www.productivitysa.co.za/

South African Organisation Development Network (SAODN): http://www.saodn.net/

The Organization Development Network (ODN): http://www.odnetwork.org/

The following websites are good sources for possible tenders:

South African government tenders: http://www.gov.za/documents/tender

Online tenders: https://www.onlinetenders.co.za/

SA tenders: http://www.sa-tenders.co.za/

Case study

Prestige Interiors is a medium-sized shop-fitting and furniture manufacturing contractor based in Cape Town. The company was established in 1979 and has been providing a first-class interior fitting-out service for retail and commercial companies to an impressive range of clients across the African continent. Contracts have also been undertaken in Bahrain, Dubai and Mauritius.

The company was started by Phillip de Castro, a hardworking Portuguese immigrant, who has worked as a qualified carpenter for the past 15 years. After his retirement in 2010, his son, Christopher, took over the business.

Christopher's management style was quite different from his father's, and it was not long before some of the older-generation employees started to resign. According to most staff members, Mr de Castro senior was a 'very gentle boss' to work for and always tried to help the workers. They described Christopher as a tyrant who was only interested in making money.

Christopher knew what the workers were saying behind his back. He also knew that the company had not made any profit in the five years before his father retired at the age of 70. During these last few years his father was no longer as actively involved in the business as before. Currently the company is providing jobs to 90 full-time and 40 part-time employees (refer to the organogram on page 211).

I was called into the business by the newly appointed financial director, Mia Hosking. According to her, the company needed to improve morale among all the workers, and she asked me to design a teambuilding intervention.

During the first meeting, the whole management team was present. The management team consisted of the managing director (Christopher de Castro), the financial director (Mia Hosking), the contracts director, the sales director, four contract managers, the production manager, the dispatch supervisor, the human resources administrator and three workshop supervisors. ➡

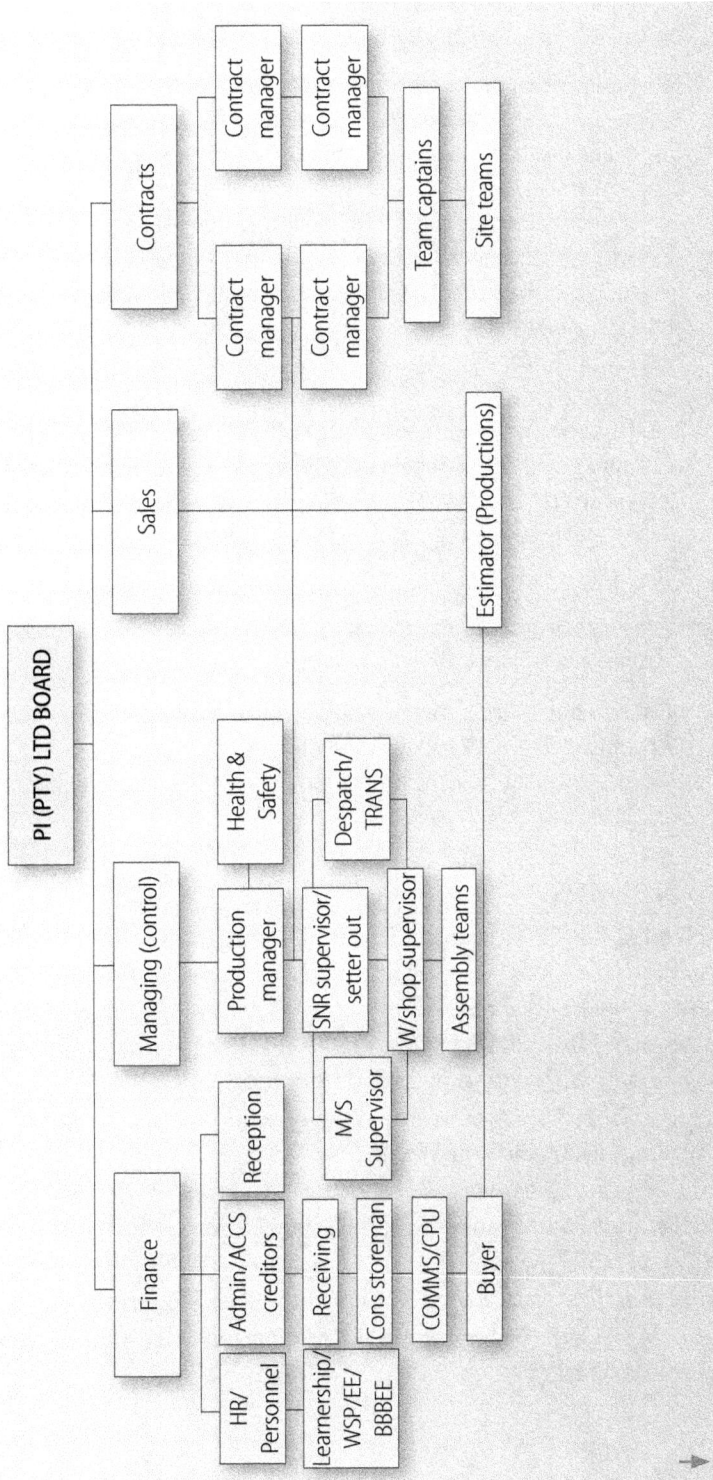

PI (PTY) LTD BOARD

- Finance
  - HR/Personnel
  - Learnership/WSP/EE/BBBEE
  - Admin/ACCS creditors
  - Receiving
  - Cons storeman
  - COMMS/CPU
  - Buyer
  - Reception

- Managing (control)
  - Production manager
    - M/S Supervisor
    - Health & Safety
    - SNR supervisor/setter out
    - W/shop supervisor
    - Assembly teams
    - Despatch/TRANS

- Sales
  - Estimator (Productions)

- Contracts
  - Contract manager
  - Contract manager
  - Contract manager
  - Contract manager
  - Team captains
  - Site teams

As I spoke to the team, the complexity of the problem became more apparent:

- The human resources administrator told me that morale among all workers was at an all-time low. She mentioned the workers felt that the company was trying to change its culture and had become more customer- and profit-centric, not worrying about the needs of the employees.
- The sales manager was concerned about the poor relationships between the production team and the contracts team, which had started to impact on product delivery. According to the production manager, the team leaders bypassed the workshop supervisors and shouted at the assembly teams.
- The workshop managers blamed the arrogance of the contracts managers for the poor morale in the company.
- The managing director was concerned that the clients' needs were not being met on time. The company's brand as a provider who delivered excellent service on time had been affected. He was also tired of being the only leader in the organisation, and wished that the managers would begin to take responsibility and act like leaders.

After the meeting I agreed to present a proposal to the team within two weeks. I knew that I had to provide much more than they had asked for in their workshop objective, and even far more than the problems on which they had briefed me.

1. What would your next steps be before writing the proposal?
2. Prepare a proposal outline for Prestige Interiors.
3. How would you structure the agenda for the proposal presentation meeting?

References

Al-Haddad, S & Kotnour, T. 2015. 'Integrating the organizational change literature: a model for successful change'. *Journal of Organizational Change Management* 28: 234–262.

Anderson, DL. 2015. *Organization development: the process of leading organizational change*. 3rd ed. Thousand Oaks, CA: SAGE.

Argyris, C. 1970. *Intervention theory and method: a behavioral science view*. Reading, MA: Addison-Wesley.

Block, P. 2011. *Flawless Consulting. A guide to getting your expertise used*, 3rd edition. San Fransisco: John Wiley & Sons, Inc.

Borg, I & Mastrangelo, IP. 2008. *Employee surveys in management. Theories, tools, and practical applications*. Cambridge, MA: Hogrefe.

Burke, WW. 1987. *Organization development: a normative view*. Reading, MA: Addison-Wesley.

Burke, WW. 2009. 'Understanding organizations: the process of diagnosis', in *Organization change: a comprehensive reader*, edited by WW Burke, DG Lake & JW Paine. San Francisco, CA: Jossey-Bass: 259–272.

Burke, WW, Lake, DG & Paine, JW. 2009. *Organization change: a comprehensive reader*. San Francisco, CA: Jossey-Bass.

Carbery, R & Cross, C (eds). 2015. *Human resource development: a concise introduction*. London: Palgrave Macmillan.

Cummings, TG & Worley, CG. 2015. *Organization development and change*. 10th ed. Stamford, CT: Cengage Learning.

Farquhar, K. 2006. 'Intervention phase', in *The NTL handbook of organization development and change: principles, practices, and perspectives*, edited by BB Jones & M Brazzel. San Francisco, CA: Pfeiffer: 212–230.

Franklin, J. 1995. 'Assessment and feedback', in *Practicing organization development: a guide for the consultant*, edited by WJ Rothwell, R Sullivan & GN McLean. Amsterdam: Pfeiffer: 139–170.

Freedman, A & Zackrison, R. 2001. *Finding your way in the consulting jungle*. San Francisco, CA: Jossey-Bass/Pfeiffer.

Galant, SM & Rios, D. 2006. 'Entry and contracting phase', in *The NTL handbook of organization development and change: principles, practices, and perspectives*, edited by BB Jones & M Brazzel. San Francisco, CA: Pfeiffer: 177–191.

Gallos, JV & Schein EH. 2006. *Organization development: a Jossey-Bass reader (The Jossey-Bass Business and Management Reader Series)*. San Francisco, CA: Jossey-Bass.

HPCSA (Health Professions Council of South Africa). 2004. 'Guidelines for good practice in the health care professions'. Ethical and professional rules of the health Professions council of South Africa as Promulgated in *Government Gazette* R717/2006. Booklet 2. https://www.hpcsa.co.za/Uploads/Professional_Practice/Ethics_Booklet.pdf.

Jackson, L. 2006. 'Client systems: entry, contracting, action planning and termination', in *The NTL handbook of organization development and change: principles, practices, and perspectives*, edited by M Brazzel & BB Jones. San Francisco, CA: Jossey-Bass: 123–132.

Kennett, S & Tomkins, P. 2001. 'Marketing', in *How to be your own management consultant: consultancy tools and techniques to improve your business*, edited by C Markham. London: Kogan: 45–60.

Livingston, RE. 2006. 'Evaluation and termination phase', in *The NTL handbook of organization development and change: principles, practices, and perspectives*, edited by BB Jones & M Brazzel. San Francisco, CA: Pfeiffer: 231–245.

Martins, N & Coetzee, M. 2009. 'Applying the Burke–Litwin model as a diagnostic framework for assessing organisational effectiveness'. *SA Journal of Human Resource Management/SA Tydskrif vir Menslikehulpbronbestuur* 7(1), Art. #177, 13 pages. https://doi.org/10.4102/sajhrm.v7i1.177.

Meyer, M & Abbott, P. 2019 *National HRM Standards for South Africa: Setting professional standards for practice*. Roodepoort: SA Board for People Practices.

Noolan, JAC. 2006. 'Organization diagnosis phase', in *The NTL handbook of organization development and change: principles, practices, and perspectives*, edited by BB Jones & M Brazzel. San Francisco, CA: Pfeiffer: 192–211.

Rogers, CR. 1961. *On becoming a person: a therapist's view of psychotherapy*. Boston, MA: Houghton Mifflin.

Rothwell, WJ, Sullivan, R & McLean, GN. 1995. *Practicing organization development: a guide for consultants*. Amsterdam: Pfeiffer.

SEDA (Small Business Development Agency). 2015. Factsheets: How do I tender?

Schein, EH. 1997. *The concept of client from a process consultation perspective: a guide for change agents*. http://dspace.mit.edu/bitstream/handle/1721.1/2647/SWP-3946-36987393.pdf (Accessed 28 September 2015).

Van Rooyen, W. 2015. The 3 principles of tenders in South Africa.

Van Tonder, C & Dietrichsen, P. 2008. 'The art of diagnosis', in *Organisation development: theory and practice*, edited by G Roodt & CL van Tonder. Pretoria: Van Schaik: 133–166.

Waddell, D, Cummings, TG & Worley, CG. 2011. *Organisational change: development and transformation*. 4th ed. South Melbourne, Vic: Cengage Learning.

Weisbord, TM. 2006. 'The organization development contract', in *The NTL handbook of organization development and change: principles, practices, and perspectives*, edited by BB Jones & M Brazzel. San Francisco, CA: Pfeiffer: 397–408.

Young, S & Litterer, J. 1991. 'Organisational development diagnostic categories: a clinical approach'. *Journal of Organizational Change Management* 4: 58–71.

Chapter 8

Organisational diagnosis

Nico Martins

Learning outcomes

After reading this chapter, you should be able to:

○ justify the conducting of an organisational diagnosis

○ prepare all stakeholders for – and involve them in – an organisational diagnosis

○ explain how to develop a world-class diagnosis

○ prepare and develop a survey instrument

○ explain the survey administration process

○ analyse and interpret organisational diagnosis

○ explain the various feedback processes

○ explain the steps available to evaluate the effectiveness of an organisational diagnosis.

Introduction

Organisational diagnosis – whether by means of a quantitative process (typically a survey) or a qualitative process (typically interviews or focus groups) – is gaining popularity worldwide and in South Africa. In their research, Borg and Mastrangelo (2008) reported that 80 % of the 820 largest industrial companies in German-speaking countries had conducted employee surveys. According to Brown (2014), survey research and feedback is a widely used process in which organisation development (OD) practitioners and members of the organisation can collaboratively collect data and then use it as a basis for changing organisational relationships. Organisations decide to conduct organisational diagnosis for a variety of reasons, some better than others. The organisational diagnosis process can be used to determine employee satisfaction and is often conducted by human resource practitioners and industrial psychologists in collaboration with the organisation as part of an action research process (French & Bell, 1999). A diagnosis is the process of understanding how the organisation is currently functioning, and it provides the information necessary to design change interventions (Cummings & Worley, 2015) if these are needed. Very often the initial motivation is little more than a senior manager's whim arrived at after reading an interesting article about a survey or after a discussion with a colleague in another company. Read the case study below.

Case study

Why do we need to survey our employees anyway?

A colleague was once asked by the regional personnel manager of a well-known company to conduct a survey of its employees. 'Fine,' she said. 'Only too happy to oblige. Now, why do you want the survey exactly?'

Embarrassed, the personnel manager shuffled his papers. 'Oh, well, you know—we think it's a good idea. Lots of people are doing them, aren't they? Participative management and all that.'

'Yes, indeed,' said my colleague. 'But why do you want to conduct one now particularly?'

'Well, you know,' said the personnel manager, shuffling his papers some more. 'Always a good idea to find out what everyone thinks. Get everyone's views. That kind of thing.'

'Yes, indeed,' replied my colleague, patiently, sensing a potentially lucrative assignment evaporating before her eyes. She decided to try another tack. 'So, what do you want to find out? What kind of subjects do you want the survey to cover?'

'Subjects?' asked the personnel manager, looking slightly startled. 'Well, I don't know, exactly. I thought we'd leave that up to you. I mean, you're the experts. What do surveys normally cover?'

'Well, it depends,' said my colleague, deciding that patience is definitely a virtue, if not necessarily an easy one. 'Some look at the employees' overall levels of satisfaction with the employer or with their work. Some look at management style or corporate culture. Some look at specifics, like the payment system or working methods. Some get right back down to basics, looking at things like the working environment or even the staff restaurant.'

'Yes, yes,' interrupted the personnel manager. 'That sounds about right. It could cover all those things.'

At this point, my colleague's patience finally began to wear a little thin, and she asked the personnel manager exactly where the idea of a survey had come from. He hesitated and blushed slightly. Then he admitted that the idea had not been his, but had come from his boss, the personnel director. 'Perhaps,' my colleague suggested, 'we should talk to him and see what he had in mind?'

After some further hesitation the personnel manager agreed, and a meeting with the personnel director was arranged. To my colleague's dismay, the personnel director's response to her questions was identical to that of his subordinate. So finally, as before, she asked the personnel director where the idea had come from. 'Well, actually,' he admitted, 'it wasn't my idea. It was the MD's. He put it in my annual objectives. I think he'd read an article about employee surveys in *The Economist*.'

Source: Walters (1999)

This is not typically the reason someone would like to conduct an organisational diagnosis. In many instances, organisational diagnoses are more than simply a waste of time—they are also expensive and cause more aggravation than they are worth. Does this mean, though, that all organisational diagnosis should be dumped?

Organisational diagnoses that aggravate rather than serve as a means to remedy a situation are usually flawed for the following reasons:

- There was no prior planning, because the diagnosis was conducted on the spur of the moment.
- The questionnaire was compiled without any real understanding of what was to be measured.
- No real effort was made to understand the environment to be measured.
- There was little professional involvement in planning the diagnosis and compiling the questionnaire or interview guides.
- Employees were not prepared for the organisational diagnosis.
- There was little understanding of the current company climate or culture.
- Confidentiality was not sensitively handled right from the start.
- Not all the stakeholders who were affected were included in the change process (in other words union representatives, employees, managers and non-unionised staff).
- Feedback was incomplete or non-existent.
- No clear action plan was implemented and, where action could not be taken, this was not communicated to all participants.
- The action plan did not include due dates for the completion of specific actions, nor did it **identify** those responsible for these actions.
- Management wants the results changed so that it reflects more positively on themselves.
- No specific and reliable organisational diagnostic model was used.

Increasing the rate of success

To increase the chances of an organisational diagnosis being a success, it is important to:

- allow time for thorough planning
- use a researched theoretical model
- ensure that confidentiality is respected at all times
- provide full and honest feedback as soon as it is available
- involve all those affected in the change process
- incorporate a second diagnosis into the action plan to evaluate the success of the change plan.

Allow time for thorough planning

Before undertaking any organisational diagnosis (quantitative or qualitative), it is important to spend some time carefully planning the process as, very often, mistakes made early in the process cannot be rectified at a later stage. If biographical or demographical data are omitted from the questionnaire, or if inappropriate questions are asked or questions are incorrectly phrased, these mistakes will affect the quality of the end results. It is important to be familiar with the target population and to understand how the diagnosis may affect their responses. The following questions are relevant here:

- Will the target population fully understand the questionnaire?
- Will they find it threatening and, if so, how will this affect their responses?
- Could they possibly have a vested interest in a particular result?
- Should multiple-choice or open-ended questions be used?

Use a researched theoretical model

Any organisational diagnosis should be regarded as a phase in the total OD process. OD is planned change in an organisational context, and in conducting an organisational diagnosis, it is important to use some of the proven models and theories in OD as a base. As opposed to the traditional, structured and rigid approaches, modern theories have adopted an open systems approach, which allow a greater degree of flexibility in analysing organisations. See Chapter 4 for some of the models that can be used.

Ensure that confidentiality is respected at all times

Employees who are not sure that their confidentiality will be respected are unlikely to provide information of a sensitive nature. This, in turn, will impact negatively on the quality of the end results. A breach of confidentiality will also have negative effects on any future diagnosis undertaken. The difficulty is to balance the matter of confidentiality against obtaining as much information as possible. Age, length of service, position occupied, department and gender are important biographical information that adds meaning to the analysis yet increases the possibility of identifying respondents. It is important to explain the need for this biographical information to respondents and to treat it with the utmost confidentiality. A further problem is that of race. In an employment equity survey in particular, it is important to be able to distinguish between the different race groups for any meaningful analysis to be made, yet it is this biographical question that raises the most objections, such as the following recent audit responses: 'We are all South Africans now, why ask about race?'; 'We are colour blind—you are not!'; 'None of the above—South African'. Explaining the need for this kind of information reduces this type of response.

Activity

Compile an action plan for the first five steps in a diagnostic survey: the project setup, schedule planning, strategic positioning, conducting personal interviews and the facilitation of focus groups.

See Exhibit 8.2 on pages 245–248 at the end of the chapter.

Provide full and honest feedback

If an organisation goes to the expense and trouble of conducting an organisational diagnosis among its employees, then it needs to communicate the results of that diagnosis to those employees. After all, they deserve the respect of a response after having made the effort to complete and return the questionnaire. This feedback needs to be honest as well. Employees will soon see through any attempts at hiding negative findings or distorting the truth.

There is an element of truth in the often-asked question: **Does a diagnosis serve only to confirm what management and staff already know?** A diagnosis does tend to confirm what is already known in general terms, but it also serves to provide depth and structure to this body of knowledge, highlighting sensitive issues. A typical response from a manager was: 'We all knew that we had a problem and had a good idea of what it was. What we did not realise was the extent of the problem and exactly where it lay. This now makes it clear and it really is no surprise.' If handled correctly, an organisational diagnosis can provide a safe and objective basis from which to deal with sensitive issues, and also offer an ideal opportunity to focus on the problem and remain objective rather than focus on a personal and subjective level.

Where surveys are used merely as a means of rating individuals, teams, departments or companies, and do not include any meaningful action plans, the chances are good that they will prove to be more harmful than beneficial.

In situations where more emphasis is placed on action plans with tangible results, it is more likely that the diagnosis will become a useful tool in creating positive company climates. However, the important thing in these action plans is that all those involved need to participate in the process of change. Change cannot be imposed; it is more successful when proposed. Refer to Chapter 6 where we discussed various models of change.

Incorporate a second organisational diagnosis in the action plan to evaluate the success of the change plan

In many instances, a company will conduct only one organisational diagnosis without an indication of a second, follow-up survey. The purpose of a follow-up organisational diagnosis is specifically to determine if the recommended actions have been implemented and if they have been successful or not.

As mentioned previously, many organisational diagnoses originate from a manager's whim. On the other hand, many organisations decide to embark on a diagnosis only when a problem arises. Typical indicators for – and reasons to embark on – an organisational diagnosis are:

- high employee turnover
- high absenteeism rates
- low performance and low productivity
- too many disciplinary actions—or too few
- changing conditions
- management not receiving the correct information
- management needing a realistic baseline or benchmark
- management needing information for strategic planning
- a need to separate facts from opinion—there might be too much gossip or complaining in the organisation
- a need to identify areas of opportunity
- a need to obtain unbiased management information—top management often receives information via the organisational structure but such information is not always trustworthy
- to obtain a bottom-up view of the organisation in order to understand employee perceptions.

The above are typical indicators of a retrospective diagnosis—and all or some of them might prompt an organisation to embark on an organisational diagnosis. Another option is to conduct a prospective diagnosis, which will help to inform subsequent actions or decisions or provide a baseline for future evaluation (Walters, 1999). Table 8.1 provides an overview of prospective and retrospective organisational diagnoses.

Table 8.1 Prospective and retrospective organisational diagnoses (adapted from Walters, 1999)

	General	Specific
Prospective diagnosis	<ul><li>Informs overall OD or change initiatives, eg culture change, total quality management (TQM), business process re-engineering, organisational restructuring, performance improvement initiatives, and acquisitions or mergers</li><li>Provides baseline data to help evaluate subsequent progress</li></ul>	<ul><li>Informs specific human resource or operational initiatives, eg new pay or reward strategies, performance management, relocation or new working or operational practices</li><li>Provides baseline data on attitudes to such initiatives, eg current attitudes to pay</li></ul>

➝

Retrospective diagnosis	<ul><li>Evaluates OD initiatives, both during and after implementation</li><li>Assesses progress or achievements against original baseline data</li></ul>	<ul><li>Evaluates specific human resource or operational initiatives following implementation, such as a change management (CM) programme or leadership training</li><li>Assesses progress against original baseline data</li></ul>

A number of researchers use either steps or phases to conduct their organisational diagnoses, which they then use as checklists to ensure all steps are adhered to. The next section deals with the 10 phases and steps in the diagnostic process. This process is illustrated in Figure 8.1 and in Exhibit 8.2 on pages 245–248.

The diagnostic process

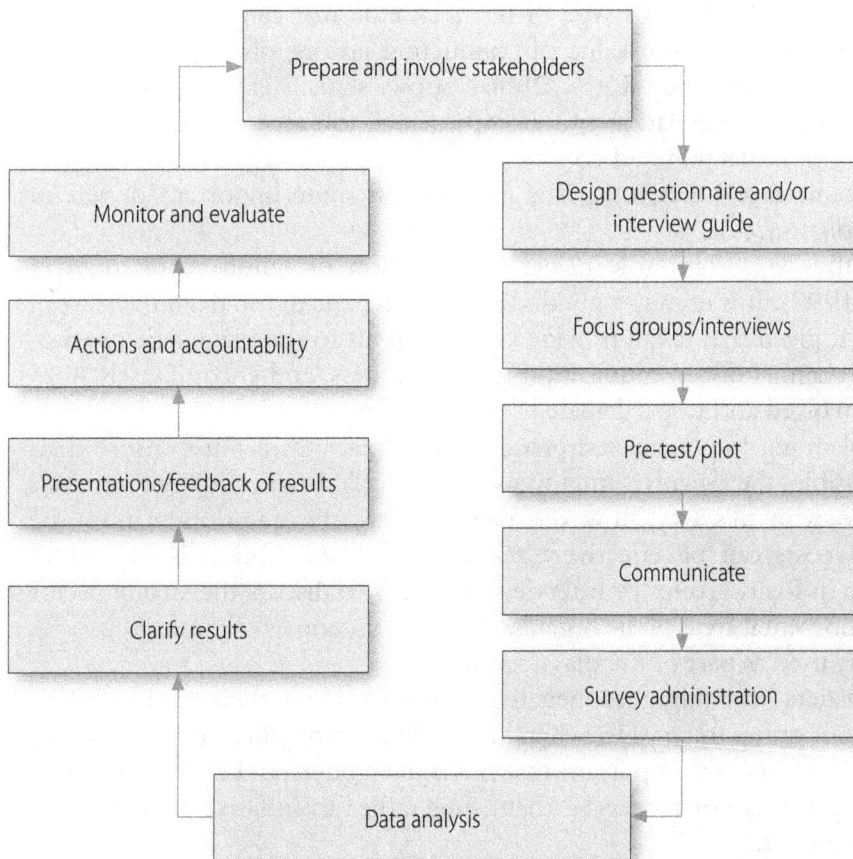

Figure 8.1 Phases of an organisational diagnosis (Author)

Involving all stakeholders in the organisational diagnosis and the project plan

One of the main tasks of an OD consultant is to position the organisational diagnosis. The consultant needs to consider what will be necessary in order for the survey to have real impact and to ensure commitment from top management. Top management should not only support the diagnosis emotionally, but should also understand what they can expect from the survey and what not (Borg & Mastrangelo, 2008). One of the tasks of the OD consultant is to present the theory behind the diagnosis, diagnostic models, illustrative examples, cases, anecdotes, and so on. Top management are, in many instances, not aware of the value or impact of an organisational diagnosis. A typical argument that can be used is to show the impact that a satisfied workforce can have on revenue growth, as illustrated in Figure 8.2 on page 223. The results indicate that, in this example, a five-unit increase in employee attitude will result in a 0.5 % increase in revenue growth (Rucci, Kirn & Quinn, 1998). This type of financial indicator can usually convince top management as to the value of conducting an organisational diagnosis. Harrison, Newman and Roth (2006) show statistically that individual effectiveness has a correlation of 0.5 with overall job attitude, an index that combines job satisfaction and commitment. Thus, if an organisation embarks on an organisational diagnosis, it is focusing on some important drivers of organisational success.

Another important role player is the union or union representatives (Walters, 1999). It is usually a good idea to involve the union from the start of the project, given that it can provide valuable input to the diagnostic process, serve as a channel of communication to its members, and encourage them to become involved and to participate.

In planning the diagnostic process, the project team must ensure that, where possible, they involve employees on all levels. Involving large numbers of employees in this way, however, usually raises the question of how the associated costs can be effectively managed. A good option is to involve employees in focus groups or interviews in order to discuss the strong points and developmental areas of the organisation. The outcomes of these discussions can also be used as part of the diagnosis report.

Managers (who might fear negative assessments from their employees) are an important group to consider when undertaking an organisational diagnosis. To allay such fears, it is important that managers understand that the purpose of the diagnosis is not to expose them, but rather to indicate possible areas for improvement.

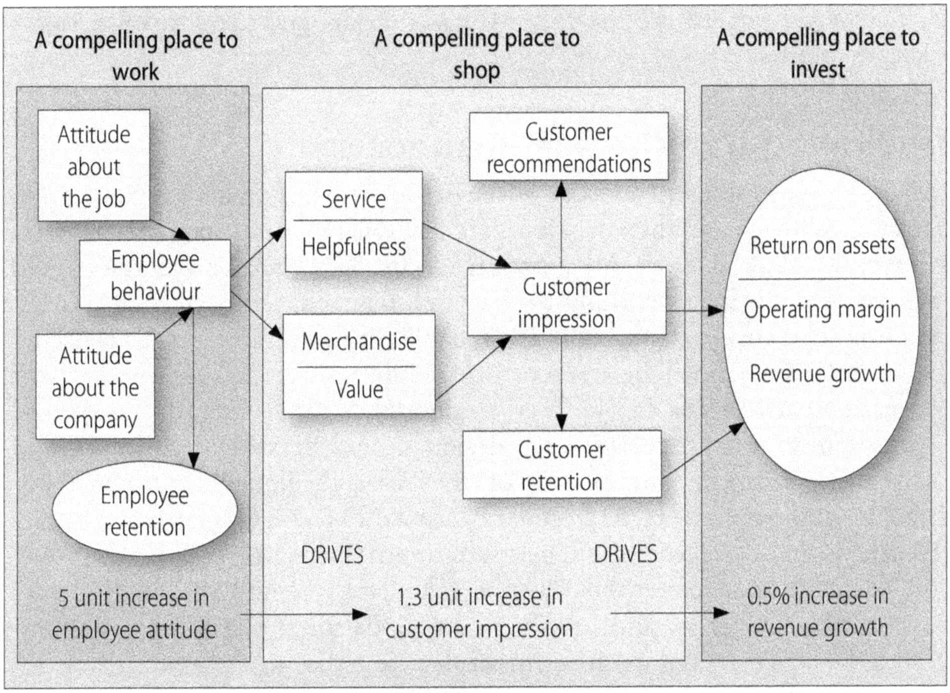

Figure 8.2 Employee–customer profit chain (adapted from Rucci et al, 1998)

Planning the project

As with any project, it is important to plan an organisational diagnosis carefully, and certain matters should be considered. For instance, what resources does the organisation need? How long will the diagnosis take? Who will be responsible for what? Will it be a qualitative or quantitative diagnosis, or a combination of the two? Will the organisation use internal or outside OD consultants? Will feedback be given to the employees, and so on? (The list reflected here is not exhaustive.)

Exhibit 8.2 on pages 245–248 provides an overview of a typical detailed action plan for a combined quantitative and qualitative diagnosis, using paper and electronic questionnaires. While it certainly does not include all the steps necessary, it can provide a useful guideline for an organisation intending to embark on a diagnosis.

Deciding on a diagnostic model

A number of diagnostic models were discussed in Chapter 6. It is important that the OD consultant guide the organisation to use or adapt an applicable diagnostic model for the diagnosis to be carried out. Two typical models that can be considered are the Burke–Litwin model and the Organisational Efficiency Model.

Developing a world-class diagnosis

Organisations use different approaches when they conduct diagnoses. Some will contact consultants and then decide to use an available measuring instrument. Others will follow a more organisation-specific approach and develop the diagnostic instruments according to their unique needs. In both instances, it is important to ensure that a valid and reliable measuring instrument is used. The second approach will be further discussed in this chapter.

A number of steps can be used to develop a world-class diagnosis for an organisation. Firstly, the research design should be structured in such a way that it enhances the validity of the research findings (Mouton & Marais, 1996; Sekaran, 1992: 92). An approach followed by many researchers in the OD field is the so-called mixed methods approach. According to Creswell (2003: 1), quantitative methods have been available to the social and human sciences for many years, and qualitative methods for the last three or four decades; however, to put both forms of data together as a distinct research design or methodology is new. The emergence of mixed methods as a third methodological movement in the social and behavioural sciences began during the phase of mixed methods as a 'movement' during the 1980s (Tashakkori & Teddlie, 2003). Creswell and Creswell (2005: 317) defined mixed methods research as a research design or methodology for collecting, analysing, and mixing both quantitative and qualitative data in a single study or series of studies in order to better understand the research problems'. Creswell (2009: 4) noted that 'a mixed method is more than simply collecting and analysing both kinds of data; it also involves the use of both approaches in tandem so that the overall strength of a study is greater than either qualitative or quantitative".

While both quantitative and qualitative research approaches (survey and focus groups) have benefits and limitations, they can be highly effective when combined (Madrigal & McClain, 2012).

One of the main benefits of using a multi-method approach in social research is that it gives the researcher greater confidence that the data are valid. The quantitative data of employees' survey results can be enhanced with the qualitative information gathered in the focus groups. If, for instance, a challenge is exposed by the quantitative data, it can be verified and discussed in the focus groups. A single observation provides only a limited view of the complexity of human behaviour and interaction in different situations, with the risk of bias and distortion creeping into the researcher's findings (Cohen, Manion & Morrison, 2007). In their research, Martins and Martins (2014) concluded that 'the methods used in tandem in this research produced informative results based on a combination of the two models discussed. The methodology applied ensured that the researchers could report with confidence the survey findings and the recommendations'.

Creswell and Creswell (2005: 320) have identified three basic research designs, illustrated in Figure 8.3.

Exploratory mixed methods design

| QUALITATIVE Data and results | Building → | QUANTITATIVE Data and results |

Triangulation mixed methods design

| QUANTITATIVE Data and results | + Interpretation → | QUALITATIVE Data and results |

Nested mixed methods design

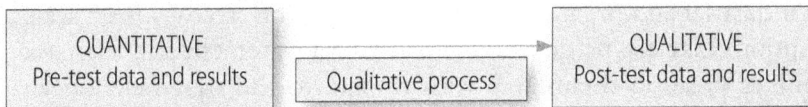

| QUANTITATIVE Pre-test data and results | Qualitative process → | QUALITATIVE Post-test data and results |

Figure 8.3 Basic mixed methods designs (Creswell & Creswell, 2005: 320)

In organisational diagnosis, the OD consultant needs to decide which of these approaches will fit his/her research the best. The methods can be used in tandem to produce full and informative results based on a combination of the two models of Stekler et al (1992, cited in Nicholls, 2011) and are represented in Figure 8.4 on page 226.

Having conducted the focus groups and/or interviews, the next step will be to analyse the results and to determine specific themes or topics from it. In Chapter 5 the facilitation skills of the OD consultant are discussed in detail. The next step will be to compile items or questions. It is now important to consider your chosen diagnostic model. The model can provide good guidance to develop your items. The next section will firstly discuss questionnaires as one of the techniques to gather diagnostic data, and then interviews or focus groups will be discussed.

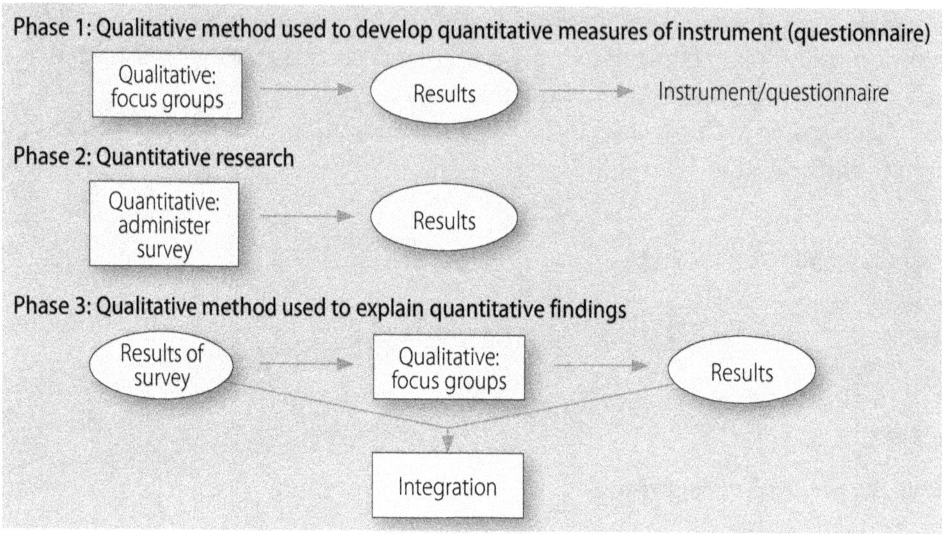

Figure 8.4 Using qualitative and quantitative measures (Nicholls, 2011)

Developing the survey instrument

Once the themes or topics have been decided upon, the next step is to formulate questions. In industrial and organisational psychology, the typical Likert scale is a popular option. Likert-type questions first make a statement and then ask the respondent to position themselves with respect to the statement on an 'agree-to-disagree' scale (Borg & Mastrangelo, 2008). Some researchers and consultants prefer 7- or 9-point scales, while others use a 3-point answer scale. For a more comprehensive discussion on the development of questions, consult Borg and Mastrangelo (2008) or Church and Waclawski (1998).

Activity

Think about the various scales you have come across in organisational diagnoses. Which scale do you prefer or do you think is the most effective?

The following are examples of scales. Each has advantages and disadvantages and should be adapted to an individual company's needs:

1. Likert scale

Differ strongly	Differ	Uncertain	Agree	Agree strongly
1	2	3	4	5

2. Semantic differential

Unhelpful clerks	1	2	3	4	5	6	7	Helpful clerks
Terrible displays	1	2	3	4	5	6	7	Great displays
Slow checkout	1	2	3	4	5	6	7	Fast checkout
Inconvenient location	1	2	3	4	5	6	7	Convenient location

3. Forced ranking

Team T-shirt

The following colours have been reduced from a larger list. Please rank in order of your preference, starting with the number 1:

Blue ☐
Green ☐
Red ☐
Grey ☐

4. Multiple choice

Who did you come with today?
(Mark all that apply.)

☐ Family ☐ Friends
☐ Spouse ☐ Date
☐ Colleague ☐ Alone

5. Multiple scales

	Importance					Our rating				
	Little			Extreme			Poor			Excellent	
Product quality	1	2	3	4	5		1	2	3	4	5
Product variety	1	2	3	4	5		1	2	3	4	5
Product price	1	2	3	4	5		1	2	3	4	5
Professionalism	1	2	3	4	5		1	2	3	4	5
Knowledge of staff	1	2	3	4	5		1	2	3	4	5
Customer service	1	2	3	4	5		1	2	3	4	5
Service quality	1	2	3	4	5		1	2	3	4	5

According to Borg and Mastrangelo (2008), the most common scale used in surveys today is the 5-point scale, as most benchmarks are based on it.

An important consideration in the development of questions is the number of questions. Based on 20 years of experience, the golden rule seems to be that a questionnaire should not be too long (a maximum of ± 60 scale-based questions), but also not too short. A questionnaire consisting of only 10 questions might portray a lack of commitment on the part of the researchers to conducting proper research. Another important rule is to ensure that each theme or topic is covered by at least five items.

Once the survey questions have been developed, the next step is to compile the biographical questions and to decide on the layout of the questionnaire. In this regard, it is important to consider the following aspects:

- **A cover page and introduction:** These will include items such as the name of the survey, the date and the company logo. A second page will explain the purpose of the survey, how anonymity is guaranteed, ethical issues, how to complete the survey, how long it should take and the survey process (for instance how feedback will be given and clarification of any words or concepts).
- **Demographical questions:** Important demographical questions referring to aspects such as gender, age, business unit, department, and so on, are usually added. It is, however, important to ensure that the questions do not jeopardise anonymity.
- The scale-based questions – properly laid out – now follow. A typical example of scale-based questions appears in Table 8.2.
- It is also a good practice to end the questionnaire by thanking the participant for his/her time. See Exhibit 8.3 on page 249–250, illustrating the first page of an electronic survey.

Activity

Bearing in mind the aspects of questionnaire design and layout discussed above, compile a draft questionnaire.

See Table 8.2 for a draft example of a survey questionnaire.

Table 8.2 Example of scale-based survey questions (Author)

Organisational trust					
	Never	Seldom	Often	Usually	Always
I trust top management.	☐ 1	☐ 2	☐ 3	☐ 4	☐ 5
I trust my immediate manager.	☐ 1	☐ 2	☐ 3	☐ 4	☐ 5
I trust my colleagues (team members).	☐ 1	☐ 2	☐ 3	☐ 4	☐ 5

	Never	Seldom	Often	Usually	Always
My immediate manager trusts me.	☐ 1	☐ 2	☐ 3	☐ 4	☐ 5
Top management trusts employees.	☐ 1	☐ 2	☐ 3	☐ 4	☐ 5
My colleagues trust me.	☐ 1	☐ 2	☐ 3	☐ 4	☐ 5
The organisation responds quickly to changes in its external environment.	☐ 1	☐ 2	☐ 3	☐ 4	☐ 5

After developing the questionnaire, it is good practice to pre-test it. Pre-testing can be done by inviting employees from different levels to a session during which they complete the questionnaire. The purpose is to determine if respondents understand the questions and that the terminology has been correctly applied. The instructions for such a session would typically:

- state the purpose of the survey and of the pre-test session
- note that participants will be working with the real questionnaire to be used
- note that the purpose is not to test the participants' opinions but to test the questionnaire and to fine-tune it
- contain a request that participants should read each question carefully and that they should note anything they do not understand
- inform the participants that all their inputs will be discussed with them after the session
- request feedback about the layout and ease of completing the questionnaire.

Such a session is also an opportunity to ask the group if they have any suggestions regarding the distribution of the questionnaire. Ask questions such as: 'Will all levels understand the questions? Are you comfortable with the demographical questions? When is the best time to distribute a paper questionnaire? Would employees understand the instructions if the questionnaire were to be distributed electronically? Are you comfortable with the layout?'

Once this process is complete, the OD consultant can finalise the questionnaire and have it signed off by the responsible manager.

Survey administration

Once the questionnaire has been finalised, the next step will be either printing (if it is to be a paper-based questionnaire) or programming (if it is to be distributed electronically). See below for a discussion of the various options available for data collection. During this phase, the survey team must also decide if it will be a convenience survey in which all employees will be invited to participate, or a sample survey. The decision will depend on the purpose of the survey and the costs involved. Many organisations conduct annual surveys in which they invite all their employees to participate. Various sample selections are available and many survey software packages have built-in sample selections which the OD consultant can use (see Figure 8.5).

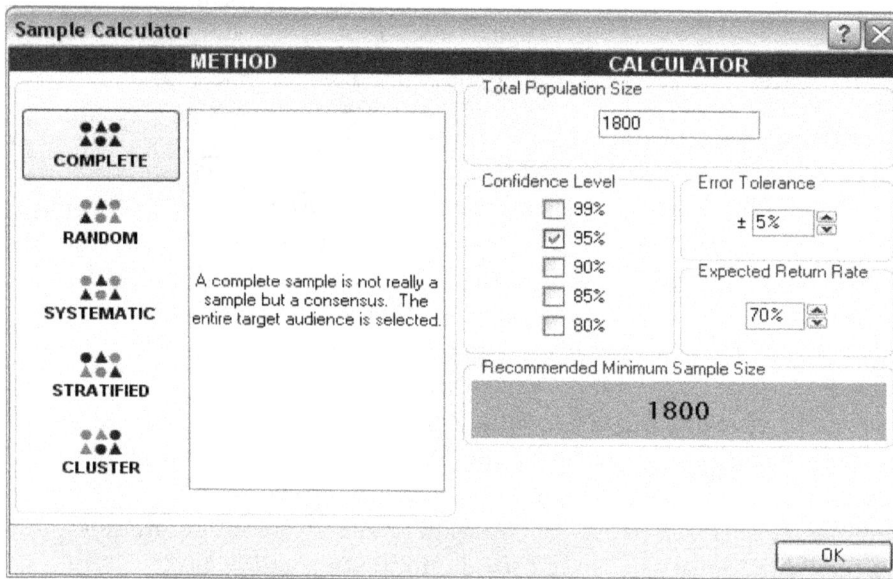

Figure 8.5 Sample selections (SurveyTracker software package, www.surveytracker.com)

Adequate sampling is critical in order to gather valid diagnostic data. According to Cummings and Worley (2015), OD literature has paid little attention to this issue. OD practitioners should ensure that they obtain fundamental knowledge in this area, or use the professional help of a statistician.

Collecting data using technology

Companies can use more than one method to collect data using technology. There are three options available, which can be used alone or as a combination. These are a computer with an internet connection, the so-called electronic survey option, a smartphone or a scanned questionnaire/paper questionnaire. In many instances companies might decide to use a combination of technology- and paper-based questionnaire methods. This decision is usually based on the population of the sample. If the company has a very sophisticated workforce, all with access to computers, an electronic survey and possibly the smartphone will be the options. If some employees do not have access to a computer and do not have a smartphones, a paper-based and electronic survey option might be the best. Any combination can, however, be used depending on the organisational needs.

Electronic surveys

Online or electronic surveys is a popular survey method in South Africa. The characteristics and advantages of online questionnaires are listed below in Table 8.3.

Table 8.3 Characteristics of online questionnaires (adapted from Du Plessis, 2018)

Characteristic	Description
Population for which questionnaire is suitable	Computer-literate individuals who have access to the internet and e-mail.
Confidence that right person has responded	High if e-mail is used.
Likelihood of result contamination or distortion	Low. Researchers, however, are concerned about hackers or competitors that might access the website. The solution is to use an encrypted method of data collection. Secure Sockets Layer (SSL) is a standard security technology for establishing an encrypted link between a server and a client—typically a web server (website) and a browser.
Sample size	Large; can be geographically dispersed.
Response rate approximation	10 % or lower.
Feasible length of questionnaire	Approximately six to eight A4 pages.
Time allocation	Allow respondents two to six weeks to complete the questionnaire. Approximately two reminders should be sent.
Financial resource implications	An online survey tool can imply an expensive capital layout.
Data input	Automated, accurate, real time.
Anonymity of respondents	Respondents can be anonymous or known.
Special features	Streaming media software allows use of graphics and animation. Some software packages include a web survey design that is more usable for people who are visually impaired.

In her research Du Plessis (2018) summarised the disadvantages of and some solutions for electronic questionnaires.

Possible disadvantages of electronic questionnaires include, firstly, low response rates and problems with non-response bias. Secondly, the OD consultant is not present to explain the instructions and/or purpose of the questionnaire to the respondents. The OD consultant is also not present to clarify items and answer questions to reduce uncertainty. The OD consultant therefore has no control over the quality of the responses. Thirdly, it might be difficult to obtain a sample that is representative of the population. Generalisability is therefore compromised. Lastly, respondents might not appreciate the colours, fonts, graphics and other formatting options of an electronic questionnaire.

In order to overcome the disadvantages associated with using online questionnaires, the OD consultant can ensure that the items and instrument were designed according to the guidelines offered in the first phase of the instrument development process–a newly developed questionnaire or purchased one. Secondly, the OD consultant can engage with the survey administrator expert to ensure that the questionnaire is visually stimulating and do not cause response fatigue or non-response bias. Thirdly, the OD consultant can ensure that the instructions included in the e-mail and in the introductory letter are clear and concise to reduce/eliminate uncertainty. Fourthly, the instrument should be subjected to an expert review and cognitive interviewing to ensure that items are clear, concise and readable. Lastly, owing to the possibility of obtaining a low response rate, reminders can be sent to the target population to encourage their participation.

For the smartphone option all the above apply. Usually survey software includes an app version, which supplies a link to the smartphone application.

Paper distribution

The most efficient method for administering questionnaires is to assemble a group of participants and allow them to complete the questionnaire at the same time (Schoeman, 2020). According to Martins and Ledimo (2017) the **group administration** of a survey affords the OD consultant the opportunity to collect data immediately from participants. While it is applicable for participants who can competently read and write, this method is also ideal for participants with a low literacy level. In a diverse sample population, participants can be grouped based on their respective home languages for facilitators to read and explain statements in the questionnaire to them.

The advantage of paper-based completion is that it allows participants who do not have access to computers and the internet the opportunity to participate in the survey. The limitation of group administration using facilitators may be that some may feel embarrassed to indicate that they need assistance to complete the surveys and decline to participate. Another limitation is the cost involved in using facilitators. Despite the method of paper administration the OD consultant may choose, OD consultants need to be cognisant that securing a high response rate to the survey is difficult to control.

As mentioned, paper-based questionnaires can either be set up on a scannable form or be a copied paper questionnaire. If it is a scannable form, arrangements need to be made for scanning of the questionnaires. If it is a printed paper questionnaire, the responses need to be manually captured. Both these options need to be well planned and coordinated, with experts for scanning the questionnaires or with data capturers for the data capturing. In both instances quality control is very important to ensure the data are correctly captured. The author has in a number of instances observed how poor quality control and poor management of this phase of a survey project can delay the project for weeks as the captured data need to be checked and re-checked for correctness. Unfortunately in many instances the mistakes are only noticed when the results are available. It is then that the client starts asking questions about the validity of the data.

Depending on the needs of the organisation, any combination of survey methods can be used. A combination of survey methods, however, needs to be well planned and executed. For instance, when using two different methods of distribution it is crucial that the questionnaires are aligned, with a similar layout and item sequence. If not, it will not be possible to import the data into one data base for further analysis.

Collecting data via interviews or focus groups

A second important measurement technique is the individual interview or focus group. The value of the two techniques is that they allow the OD consultant to clarify and probe the statistical results. Many OD consultants use questionnaires and interviews or focus groups in tandem. The purpose of using such a nested approach, as discussed earlier, is to obtain richer information. The number of interviews or focus groups will be determined by the saturation of the data, meaning if no new data emerges, the interviews or focus groups can be stopped.

Analysing and interpreting the data

We have already proposed that an OD consultant can use either qualitative or quantitative techniques – or a combination – to gather data. As discussed earlier, if both techniques are used we refer to a mixed methods approach.

Qualitative tools

Two of the popular techniques used to analyse qualitative data will be briefly discussed in the following sections.

Content analysis

Content analysis is a technique used by researchers to acquire a richer understanding of data supplied by knowledge informants. It involves identifying the major concepts or issues discussed in an interview or focus group, for example, and then counting the number of occurrences (Remenyi, 2014). According to Cummings and Worley (2015), a well-performed content analysis can reduce hundreds of comments into a few themes that effectively summarise the issues or attitudes of a group of respondents. Qualitative data analysis looks for meaning from any sort of data – even from what appears to be quantitative data – but it does not use inferential techniques in doing so.

Hermeneutics

Hermeneutics is a holistic approach to interpreting and understanding the meaning of data. This approach analyses data without the detailed fracturing that occurs in content analysis. The context in which a concept and theme is mentioned, as well as its relationship to other concepts and themes, may be given more importance than the number of times it is mentioned. In a hermeneutics approach, whole sentences, or even a paragraph, may be understood as one concept. According to Remenyi (2014), hermeneutics can include both verbal and non-verbal responses (communication). See http:// plato.stanford.edu/entries/hermeneutics/#Beginnings for more information.

Quantitative tools

Various quantitative tools are available to analyse data, such as SurveyTracker or SPSS, which is used for more sophisticated statistical analysis, for example multivariate analysis. Most such analysis is routinely produced by statistical packages, and mathematical calculations are therefore not discussed here. The most economical and straightforward way to summarise quantitative results is by means of descriptive statistics. These are summaries of numerical data that make them more easily interpretable and include the mean, variance, standard deviation, range standard error of the mean, kurtosis and skewness in particular (Colman, 2006). See Figure 8.6 on page 235 for an example.

A question that is often asked is what cut-off point between positive and developmental items and based on a mean score a company should use. Some companies use a mean of 3.20 as their cut-off point, based on work done by the Human Sciences Research Council (HSRC) of South Africa. As alternatives, the Best Companies to Work For survey uses a mean of 3.70 to distinguish between favourable and excellent results, while some IT companies use a mean of 4.00 for information security assessments. All of these cut-off points are based on a Likert scale of 5 (Castro & Martins, 2010; Da Veiga & Martins, 2015).

Questions	Count	Mean	Std. dev.	Category percentages 0 20 40 60 80 100	Favourable	Neutral	Unfavourable
Trust							
61. I trust my immediate manager	36	3.86	1.313		77.8%	0.0%	22.2%
62. I believe what my immediate manager says	36	3.86	1.150		77.8%	5.6%	16.7%
63. My immediate manager trusts me	36	3.72	1.210		69.4%	13.9%	16.7%
64. Management delivers what they promise	36	3.44	1.252		69.4%	2.8%	27.8%
65. Management is transparent	36	3.08	1.381		47.2%	13.9%	38.9%
Overall averages	36.0	3.59	1.2612		68.3%	7.2%	24.5%

Count = Number of respondents

Mean = The total of the scores divided by the number of responses

Category percentages/scales

▪ (Favourable %) = 5 – Strongly agree, 4 – Agree

▪ (Neutral %) = 3 – Unsure

░ (Unfavourable %) = 2 – Disagree, 1 – Strongly disagree

Figure 8.6 Descriptive statistics (Author)

If we look at the results reflected in Figure 8.6, it is clear that one item or statement falls below the 3.20 cut-off point while all the others are above it. If the Best Companies to Work For cut-off point is used here, two items are above. It is proposed that the cut-off point to be used should be discussed with the project team in each instance. If a cut-off is too strict for the organisation, it might discourage the implementation of interventions. Some companies also develop their in-house benchmarks based on their own previous surveys, or use national or international benchmarks.

The next phase of analysis is inferential statistics. The primary purpose of this is to draw conclusions and make predictions about the broader population, based on the numerical data collected for a specific sample. Inferential statistics assists in drawing conclusions beyond our immediate samples and data (Marczyk, DeMatteo & Festinger, 2005). Typical inferential statistics will be

T-tests, ANOVA, regression and correlation analysis. A number of researchers and OD consultants also use structural equation modelling (SEM) to explain the relationships among multiple variables and to develop or test theoretical models. Hair et al (2010) describe SEM as follows: 'Multivariate technique combining aspects of multiple regression (examining dependence relationships) and factor analysis (representing unmeasured concepts – factors – with multiple variables) to establish a series of interrelated dependence relationships simultaneously.' SEM is an excellent approach if an OD consultant intends to develop and test if a theoretical model is valid. Some of these models are discussed in Chapter 6. It is, however, very important that, before an OD consultant continues with any analysis, he/she must first determine the validity and reliability of the measuring instrument. (Various statistical techniques are used for this, such as factor analysis and item analysis. However, discussion of these statistical steps and analyses does not form part of this chapter.) The concepts of validity and reliability are defined as follows (also see Figure 8.7):

- **Validity** is the extent to which a measure or set of measures correctly represents the concept of study, such as organisational culture or climate.
- **Reliability** is the extent to which a variable (dimension) or set of variables (dimensions) is consistent in what it intends to measure. If multiple measurements are taken, reliable measures will be consistent in their values. (Hair et al, 2010).

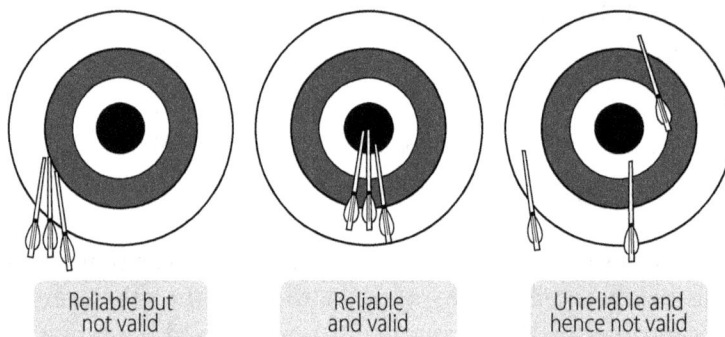

| Reliable but not valid | Reliable and valid | Unreliable and hence not valid |

Figure 8.7 Reliability and validity

After the first round of analysis, the OD consultant can decide if further information is needed or if some of the results need further clarification. The initial analysis can then be followed up by focus groups or interviews, or both. The purpose of these will be to clarify results which do not make sense, to check contradictory results, or simply to confirm specific results.

The next step in the process will be finalising the report and giving feedback to the organisation.

Report writing

A survey project usually concludes with a written report or a PowerPoint presentation detailing its purposes, findings and methods. A good report summarises the entire project and makes the data available to others who might benefit from the conclusion or conclusions reached.

There are three levels of reports that people in business are generally called upon to produce—and the distinctions between them apply equally to reporting on a survey project. The highest level is the executive report, and the mid-level reports fit in at lower levels. Each report is designed to provide a different level of detail and to achieve a different purpose.

Activity

List the topics you would include in an executive report.

Each of these reports will now be discussed briefly.

The executive report

This is the type of report that is usually prepared for the upper management of an organisation. The purpose is to provide a condensed summary of the main findings, themes, relationships, positive results and developmental issues identified as well as the most important recommendations. This report includes the elements that are of most interest to those who must make decisions for the organisation as a whole, such as:

- the purpose of the survey
- the planning that went into the project
- the projected and the actual budgets (Were you on or over your budget?)
- an overview of the methodology used
- a summary of the geographical groups who participated in the survey
- a summary of the overall results of the survey, the statistical analysis, focus groups, interviews or any other analysis done
- multi-analysis results (comparative results of geographical groups)
- detailed analysis of any strength or weakness revealed
- comparisons with previous and benchmark surveys
- key levers for change
- conclusions drawn from the survey
- suggestions for actions to be taken.

The mid-level report

This is designed for supervisors and other middle management who need the survey data to better oversee the day-to-day functions and activities of the organisation. This report will go into more detail than the executive report and will include items such as:

- the purpose of the survey
- the planning that went into the project
- the schedule that the project followed
- a copy of the survey instrument
- the methodology used to analyse the results
- a summary of the geographical groups who participated in the survey
- a summary table of the overall results
- a comparison of the results of specific groups or departments with the overall results
- a detailed analysis of any strengths or weaknesses revealed
- any pertinent responses to open-ended questions or opportunities to make comments
- a comparison of the results of previous surveys or benchmark data
- conclusions drawn from the survey data
- suggestions for actions to be taken in specific departments or areas.

Feedback and action planning

The next step in any organisational diagnosis will be the provision of feedback. It is usually good practice to provide feedback to the project team first so as to ensure that any uncertainties can be clarified and that the report and presentations to follow will be according to the client's expectations. In most instances, the first feedback session will be to senior management, followed by presentations to middle management, supervisors and employees. The presentation to senior management will focus on overall results, specific trends, benchmark results, key relationships, main recommendations and aspects to highlight in the follow-up presentations.

In many organisations, the feedback process stops at this point, after the presentation to senior management. This is a major disadvantage and usually has a negative impact on responses to future surveys. It is considered best practice not only to present the results to the various groups, but also to involve them in action planning, as discussed in Chapter 9.

Evaluation

Activity

The evaluation of the impact of any change activity is crucial. How will you evaluate the impact of an organisational diagnosis and the follow-up action planning?

See Exhibit 8.2 on pages 245–248 for some specific steps.

Despite the numbers of surveys companies are involved in, it appears as if they do not always put enough effort or time in planning the change (Church & Waclawski, 1998). Borg and Mastrangelo (2008: 389) add to the importance of action after a diagnosis. In their words: 'The ES [employee satisfaction] literature usually strongly recommends conducting an ES only if it leads to actions.' The planning component of action planning is thus a crucial step in bringing about desired change. Part of the process of action planning needs to be an evaluation of the actions planned. This can be done either by means of a follow-up survey or by using feedback from an appointed task team.

Ethical considerations

The field of OD has always shown concern for the ethical conduct of its practitioners. Professional bodies in South Africa, such as the South African Board for People Practices (SABPP: http://www.sabpp.co.za) and the Health Professions Council of South Africa (HPCSA: http://www.hpcsa.co.za) – with which OD consultants are usually registered – have their own ethical codes.

The general ethical guidelines of the HPCSA – which are certainly applicable to OD consultants – are provided below by way of an example. These guidelines provide a very good basis for the OD practitioner.

GENERAL ETHICAL GUIDELINES FOR THE HEALTH CARE PROFESSIONS EDITED BY THE HUMAN RIGHTS, ETHICS AND PROFESSIONAL PRACTICE
CORE ETHICAL VALUES AND STANDARDS FOR GOOD PRACTICE

Everything ethically required of a professional to maintain good professional practice is grounded in core ethical values and standards—the latter are the directives that follow the core values. These core values and standards are presented as a linear list for the sake of simplicity.

In concrete cases, the demands of these core values and standards may clash, thus making competing demands on health care practitioners. The only way to address such clashes is through ethical reasoning.   ➔

The core ethical values and standards required of health care practitioners include the following:

1. **Respect for persons:** Health care practitioners should respect patients as persons, and acknowledge their intrinsic worth, dignity, and sense of value.
2. **Best interests or well-being:** Non-maleficence: Health care practitioners should not harm or act against the best interests of patients, even when the interests of the latter conflict with their own self-interest.
3. **Best interests or well-being:** Beneficence: Health care practitioners should act in the best interests of patients even when the interests of the latter conflict with their own personal self-interest.
4. **Human rights:** Health care practitioners should recognise the human rights of all individuals.
5. **Autonomy:** Health care practitioners should honour the right of patients to self-determination or to make their own informed choices, and to live their lives by their own beliefs, values and preferences.
6. **Integrity:** Health care practitioners should incorporate these core ethical values and standards as the foundation for their character and practice as responsible health care professionals.
7. **Truthfulness:** Health care practitioners should regard the truth and truthfulness as the basis of trust in their professional relationships with patients.
8. **Confidentiality:** Health care practitioners should treat personal or private information as confidential in professional relationships with patients—unless overriding reasons confer a moral or legal right to disclosure.
9. **Compassion:** Health care practitioners should be sensitive to, and empathise with, the individual and social needs of their patients and seek to create mechanisms for providing comfort and support where appropriate and possible.
10. **Tolerance:** Health care practitioners should respect the rights of people to have different ethical beliefs as these may arise from deeply held personal, religious or cultural convictions.
11. **Justice:** Health care practitioners should treat all individuals and groups in an impartial, fair and just manner.
12. **Professional competence and self-improvement:** Health care practitioners should continually endeavour to attain the highest level of knowledge and skills required within their area of practice.
13. **Community:** Health care practitioners should strive to contribute to the betterment of society in accordance with their professional abilities and standing in the community.

Source: http://www.hpcsa.co.za/downloads/conduct_ethics/rules/generic_ethical_rules/booklet_1_guidelines_good_prac.pdf.

If we think about an organisational diagnosis, some additional ethical guidelines will apply, which should take the following into consideration:

- **Misinterpretation:** This can occur when an OD consultant claims that an intervention will produce results which are unreasonable for the change programme and the situation.

- **Misuse of data:** Misuse of data can occur when data are used as a punitive tool to pinpoint specific good or bad managers. It is important to include the use of data at the initial contract phase.
- **Coercion:** This can happen when employees are forced to participate in an organisational diagnosis or change process.
- **Value or goal conflict:** This ethical conflict can occur when the purpose of the change effort is not clear or when the client and the OD consultant disagree on how to achieve the goals. It might, in some instances, be best not to deliver a specific service if values and goals are in conflict.
- **Technical ineptness:** This is an ethical dilemma that can arise when an OD consultant implements interventions in respect of which he/she is not skilled.

In some instances an OD consultant is limited to proposing only interventions in which he/she is skilled. This may mean that the most appropriate intervention cannot be used (Cummings & Worley, 2015).

Activity

Would you conduct a quantitative diagnosis for an organisation if you are skilled only in qualitative analysis?

Conclusion

In this chapter we have described and explained the role of organisational diagnoses in organisations, which appear to be becoming increasingly important. Some organisations, in fact, have annual diagnoses from which they calculate various indexes, such as a morale or customer-satisfaction index. These figures are taken very seriously by senior management and some companies even include them in their annual performance appraisals for managers and departments. Although some employees resent the time taken to complete a questionnaire or participate in an interview, many are happy to do so if they believe management will take the results seriously and act upon them.

Lastly, one of the important functions of organisational diagnoses is that they provide essential data upon which management can base important decisions. Given their usefulness and comparatively low costs, it is no surprise that human resource professionals are increasingly conducting organisational diagnoses in their organisations.

Reflection questions

1. What is the difference between qualitative and quantitative diagnoses? How can you use these methods to support each other?
2. How can you increase the chances of an organisational diagnosis being a success?
3. What are important aspects to consider in the design and layout of a questionnaire?
4. What are typical indicators for and reasons to embark on an organisational diagnosis?
5. What will you include in a report prepared for the senior management of an organisation?

Multiple-choice questions

1. Why are organisational diagnoses so often flawed?
   a. No real effort is made to understand the environment being measured.
   b. Feedback is incomplete or non-existent.
   c. The OD consultant is not qualified.
   d. The company reduces the original budget.
   e. All of the above

2. Typical reasons for embarking on a diagnosis are:
   a. when the CEO requires a diagnosis
   b. that conditions are changing/have changed
   c. to identify areas of opportunity
   d. that confidentiality is not being correctly handled in the organisation
   e. All of the above

3. Which of these is a typical example of an answer scale?
   a. Likert scale
   b. Semantic differential
   c. Forced ranking
   d. Open-ended questions
   e. Multiple scales

4. Which of the following is NOT a sample selection method?
   a. Population
   b. Random
   c. Stratified
   d. Cluster
   e. Complete

5. Which of the following is NOT seen as an ethical value for OD consultants?
   a. Respect for persons
   b. Integrity
   c. Tolerance
   d. Autonomy
   e. Planning

Case study

Study Exhibit 8.1 on the next page. Apply the Burke–Litwin model as a diagnostic tool and work through the following activities:

1. Review the results of the diagnostic survey by Martins and Coetzee (2009) summarised on the adapted version of the Burke–Litwin model.
2. What cut-off point was used to distinguish between positive and developmental dimensions?
3. What relationships can you distinguish between the various dimensions?
4. What recommendations can you formulate for the organisation based on these results?

Exhibit 8.1 Applying the Burke–Litwin model as a diagnostic tool in OD (Martins & Coetzee, 2009: 153)

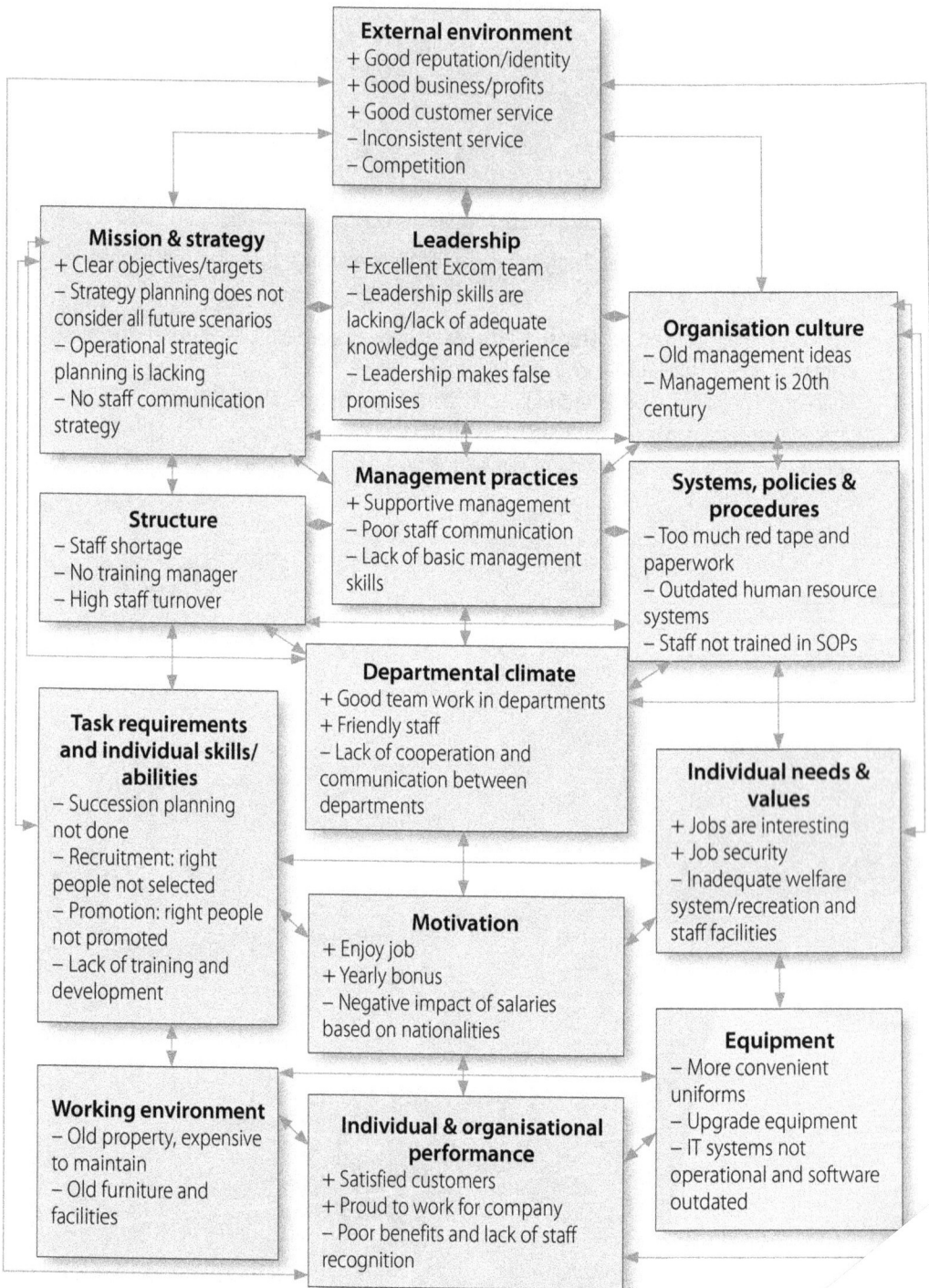

External environment
+ Good reputation/identity
+ Good business/profits
+ Good customer service
− Inconsistent service
− Competition

Mission & strategy
+ Clear objectives/targets
− Strategy planning does not consider all future scenarios
− Operational strategic planning is lacking
− No staff communication strategy

Leadership
+ Excellent Excom team
− Leadership skills are lacking/lack of adequate knowledge and experience
− Leadership makes false promises

Organisation culture
− Old management ideas
− Management is 20th century

Structure
− Staff shortage
− No training manager
− High staff turnover

Management practices
+ Supportive management
− Poor staff communication
− Lack of basic management skills

Systems, policies & procedures
− Too much red tape and paperwork
− Outdated human resource systems
− Staff not trained in SOPs

Departmental climate
+ Good team work in departments
+ Friendly staff
− Lack of cooperation and communication between departments

Task requirements and individual skills/ abilities
− Succession planning not done
− Recruitment: right people not selected
− Promotion: right people not promoted
− Lack of training and development

Individual needs & values
+ Jobs are interesting
+ Job security
− Inadequate welfare system/recreation and staff facilities

Motivation
+ Enjoy job
+ Yearly bonus
− Negative impact of salaries based on nationalities

Working environment
− Old property, expensive to maintain
− Old furniture and facilities

Individual & organisational performance
+ Satisfied customers
+ Proud to work for company
− Poor benefits and lack of staff recognition

Equipment
− More convenient uniforms
− Upgrade equipment
− IT systems not operational and software outdated

Exhibit 8.2 Detailed organisational diagnosis action plan

Activity	Activities	Start date	End date	Responsibility	Comments
1. Project setup	● Sign contracts ● Schedule initial dates ● Establish project team ● Clarify roles ● Confirm project deliverables, timeframes and responsibilities			Procurement and ESC Organisation CT and ESC CT and ESC CT and ESC	ESC Include union.
2. Schedule planning	● Plan communication/ marketing around the survey ● Identify role players to be interviewed ● Schedule interviews and focus groups ● Identify documents for review ● Collect documents and hand to consultant ● Review documents ● Develop interview schedules			CT and ESC CT and ESC CT CT CT ESC ESC	Include employees on all levels.
3. Strategic positioning	● Design workshop on strategic positioning of the survey ● Decide who should attend the workshop and invite role players ● Conduct workshop ● Develop broad OD model to be used as framework for survey results and integration			ESC ESC and CT ESC ESC	Include union. Use a model that is applicable to the organisation.
4. Conduct personal interviews	● Conduct interviews ● Collate information ● Identify themes			ESC ESC ESC	→

Legend for roles

CT = Coordinating team

ESC = Employee satisfaction consultant

Activity	Activities	Start date	End date	Responsibility	Comments
5. Facilitate focus groups	● Conduct focus groups ● Collate information ● Identify themes			ESC ESC ESC	Ensure facilitators are allocated according to the language groups.
6. Develop and compile organisa-tional assessment question-naire	● Present themes to project team ● Develop draft questionnaire (dimensions and statements) and align to vocabulary of XYZ ● Test questionnaire for face validity ● Present questionnaire to project team for face validity ● Conduct pilot study ● Finalise questionnaire ● Submit questionnaire to executive team for sign-off ● Set up software for programming the questionnaire			ESC ESC ESC ESC ESC ESC ESC ESC	Include ±20 employees on all levels. Project team needs to approve draft questionnaire.
7. Distribute question-naire: Electro-nically	● Communicate importance and process of survey ● Draft invitation ● Distribute questionnaires electronically ● Track response rate ● Encourage participation (managers) ● Data cleaning			CT ESC ESC ESC ESC ESC	Top management to approve. ESC team needs to ensure validity of data.
Paper-based	● Arrange sessions to facilitate questionnaire completion ● Conduct session ● Capture questionnaire data			CT ESC ESC	➝

Activity	Activities	Start date	End date	Responsibility	Comments
8. Integrate the information	◉ Analyse data ◉ Conduct statistical analysis			ESC ESC	Conduct validity and reliability analysis as the first step.
9. Conduct preliminary analysis	◉ Interpret the results, compile graphs and tables, compile first draft ◉ Discuss the results with project team and other specialists to identify areas that need to be further explored ◉ Draft initial high-level report			ESC ESC and CT ESC	
10. Conduct additional focus group discussion to explore certain issues in greater depth	◉ Conduct further focus groups/discussions ◉ Integrate focus group findings into initial report ◉ Discuss findings with multidisciplinary team, prepare recommendations and finalise report ◉ Prepare PowerPoint presentation on the findings ◉ Submit report to XYZ			ESC ESC ESC ESC ESC and CT	Only if needed to clarify results
11. Discuss and digest report with strategic role players	◉ Distribute report electronically to strategic role players ◉ Schedule workshop/meeting to discuss report ◉ Identify next steps			CT ESC CT	Include all levels and union.
12. Feedback to employees	◉ Provide feedback to employees ◉ Review and identify learning insights (project team)			ESC and CT CT	All departments to be included. ➔

Activity	Activities	Start date	End date	Responsibility	Comments
13. Actions	Action planning ● Plan actions: company-wide and global ● Plan actions: in functions, areas, subsidiaries ● Plan actions: locally, in work groups			CT CT CT	Conduct action planning workshops.
	Implementing actions ● Monitor and control actions and implementation ● Conduct reporting within management lines			CT CT	
14. Evaluation	● Position the evaluation (goals, timing, criteria) ● Decide on mix of methods ● Decide on and construct measurement instruments ● Collect and analyse data ● Present results ● Conduct follow-up evaluation processes			CT CT CT CT CT CT	

Exhibit 8.3 Example of a draft electronic questionnaire

Company ABC
Climate Survey—April 2015

Company ABC
Climate Survey — April 2015

Scroll to the bottom of the screen and click on NEXT

Company ABC
Climate Survey—April 2015

Instructions

Thank you for participating in the survey. The questionnaire consists of 92 questions. It takes approximately 20 to 30 minutes on average to complete it. Your answers will remain completely confidential. In cases where a sub-group is smaller than five people, the demographic data will not be revealed, to protect the confidentiality of the respondents.

Please complete the survey in one session (cannot be book marked or saved and returned to later).

Explanation of terms:

Management refers to the heads of departments.
Immediate manager refers to the person you report to.

Thank you for your cooperation!

Technical difficulties
For any technical difficulties please contact:
Ellen/Anthea at +27 11 432 2006

Company ABC
Climate Survey—April 2015

Section 2: Statements

In Section 2, decide whether you agree or disagree with each statement and click in the white circle below the scale (eg strongly disagree, disagree, unsure, agree, strongly agree).

Make sure that a bullet appears in the circle that you select.

Please avoid answering the column marked 'unsure' (neither positive nor negative) too often, as this might skew the results.

Trust

	Strongly disagree	Disagree	Unsure	Agree	Strongly agree
1. I trust my immediate manager.	○	○	○	○	○
2. My immediate manager trusts me.	○	○	○	○	○
3. I believe what my immediate manager says.	○	○	○	○	○

References

Borg, I & Mastrangelo, PM. 2008. *Employee surveys in management. Theories, tools and practical applications.* Toronto: Hogrefe.

Brown, D. 2014. *Experiential approach to organization development.* 8th ed. Harlow: Pearson.

Castro, M & Martins, N. 2010. 'The relationship between organisational climate and employee satisfaction in a South African information and technology organisation'. *SA Journal of Industrial Psychology/SA Tydskrif vir Bedryfsielkunde* 36(1), Art #800, 10 pages, https://doi.org/10.4102/sajip.v36i1.800.

Church, AH & Waclawski, J. 1998. *Designing and using organizational surveys. A seven-step process.* San Francisco, CA: Jossey-Bass.

Cohen, L, Manion, L & Morrison, K. 2007. *Research methods in education*. 6th ed. London: Routledge.

Colman, AM. 2006. *Oxford dictionary of psychology*. New York: Oxford University Press.

Creswell, JW. 2003. *Research design: qualitative, quantitative and mixed methods approaches*. 2nd ed. Thousand Oaks, CA: SAGE.

Creswell, 2009. *Research design: qualitative, quantitative and mixed methods approaches*. 3rd ed. Thousand Oaks, CA: SAGE Inc.

Creswell, JW & Creswell, JD. 2005. 'Mixed methods research: developments, debates, and dilemmas', in *Research in organizations: foundations and methods of inquiry*, edited by RA Swanson & EF Holton. San Francisco, CA: Berrett-Koehler: 315–326.

Cummings, TC & Worley, CG. 2015. *Organizational development and change*. 10th ed. Stanford, CT: Cengage Learning.

Da Veiga, A & Martins, N. 2015. 'Information security culture and information protection culture: a validated assessment instrument'. *Computer Law and Security Review* 31: 243–256.

Du Plessis, 2018. Constructing and validating a measurement instrument for coping with occupational stress. Unpublished doctoral thesis. University of South Africa, Pretoria.

French, WL & Bell, CH. 1999. *Organization development: behavioral science interventions for organization improvement*. 6th ed. Upper Saddle River, NJ: Prentice Hall.

Hair, JF, Black, WC, Babin, BJ & Anderson, RE. 2010. *Multivariate data analysis*. 7th ed. Englewood Cliffs, NJ: Prentice Hall.

Harrison, DA, Newman, DA & Roth, PL. 2006. 'How important are job attitudes? Meta-analytic comparisons of integrative behavioural outcomes and time sequences'. *Academy of Management Journal* 49: 305–325.

Madrigal, D & McClain, B. 2012. Strengths and weaknesses of quantitative and qualitative research. http://www.uxmatters.com/mt/archives/2012/09/strengths-and-weaknesses-of-quantitative-and-qualitative-research.php (Accessed 25 March 2016).

Marczyk, G, DeMatteo, D & Festinger, D. 2005. *Essentials of research design and methodology*. Hoboken, NJ: John Wiley & Sons.

Martins, N & Coetzee, M. 2009. 'Applying the Burke-Litwin Model as a diagnostic framework for assessing organisational effectiveness'. *SA Journal for Human Resource Management* 17(1): 144–156.

Martins, EC & Ledimo, O. 2017. 'Survey administration process', in *Organisational diagnoses. Tools and applications for practitioners and researchers*, edited by N Martins, EC Martins & R Viljoen. Midrand: KR Publishing.

Martins, EC & Martins, N. 2014. 'Combining focus groups and quantitative research in organisational diagnosis'. Proceedings of the 12th European Conference on Research Methodology for Business and Management Studies. University of Minho, Guimaraes, Portugal, (July).

Mouton, J & Marais, HC. 1996. *Basic concepts in the methodology of the social sciences.* 5th ed. Pretoria: HSRC.

Nicholls, C. 2011. The advantages of using qualitative research methods. http://www.alexander-technique-college.com/files/2011/10/books_articles_qualitative.pdf (Accessed 28 December 2013).

Remenyi, D. 2014. *A dictionary of concepts and issues.* Reading, UK: Academic Conferences and Publishing International.

Rucci, AJ, Kirn, SP & Quinn, RT. 1998. 'The employee–customer–profit chain at Sears'. *Harvard Business Review* January–February: 83–92.

Schoeman, PG. 2020. Developing a measuring for coping in high stress security occupations: A stress management model approach. Unpublished doctoral thesis. University of South Africa, Pretoria.

Sekaran, U. 1992. *Research methods for business: a skill-building approach.* 2nd ed. New York: Wiley.

Tashakkori, A & Teddlie, C. 2003. 'The past and future of mixed methods research: from data triangulation to mixed model designs', in *Handbook of mixed methods in social and behavioural research*, edited by A Tashakkori & C Teddlie. Thousand Oaks, CA: SAGE.

Walters, M. 1999. *Employee opinion attitude & opinion surveys.* Institute of Personnel and Development. London: IPD House.

Chapter 9

Designing interventions

Dirk Geldenhuys

Learning outcomes

After reading this chapter, you should be able to:

- explain intervention as a phase in the organisation development (OD) process
- distinguish between interventions and motivate a personal approach
- apply the different principles of intervening in a case study
- identify an appropriate intervention in a case study
- differentiate between joint action plans and explain the different steps to follow in conducting them
- set up a monitoring plan.

Introduction

We dealt with organisational diagnosis in Chapter 8. From now on we will be discussing the action thrust of organisation development (OD). This chapter is about designing interventions. The focus is on the approaches to interventions, the principles of intervening, the structuring of interventions, the joint action planning (JAP) meeting, and the evaluation and monitoring of interventions. Individual and team interventions are discussed in Chapter 10 and large-scale interventions in Chapter 11.

Designing interventions, or JAP, is the next phase after an organisational diagnosis has been done and accurate feedback on the functioning of the organisation has been provided to the client. More specifically, the purpose of this chapter is to consider the design of interventions. The outcome of the process is a comprehensive intervention plan or strategy and a monitoring process. The term 'joint' refers to the joint nature or collaboration between the consultant and the client. The power of engagement and dialogues is just as valid during the designing phase as during the feedback phase of the OD process.

An OD intervention is a sequence of planned activities with the purpose of enabling the client to function more efficiently and effectively. Interventions constitute the action thrust of OD—they make things happen (French & Bell, 1999). In practice, however, it should always be remembered that even by entering a client system, an intervention has already been made. The first encounter with the client implies an influence on the behaviour of the system.

According to Argyris (2005: 115), 'to intervene is to enter into an ongoing system of relationship, to come between or among persons, groups, or objects for the purpose of helping them'. There are important implicit assumptions in this definition that should be explicated.

First, the definition refers to an **'ongoing system'**. An intervention is made into the ongoing life of an existing organisational system consisting of a number of subsystems, such as organisational units, organisational structure, culture and relationships, to name a few. Organisations also form part of a broader system or societal context. This is especially evident in the trade union movements that have interests in different sectors of the industry, and also in companies with cross-border operations in countries with different national cultures. The client should always remember that intervening in one part of the system has implications for all the other parts as well. Intervening in a system cannot happen in isolation.

Second, the definition refers to **'coming between'** persons, groups or objects, implying an interruption of the current system or subsystems, which is often met by resistance. Intervening therefore implies not only the implementation of a rational process but also a shift in the emotional life of people. Aspects such as creating a readiness for change should therefore always form part of the planning process.

Third, the definition refers to **'helping'** the system as the purpose of interventions. In order to determine if interventions are effective, the following criteria have been identified (Cummings & Worley, 2015):

- Information on which the interventions are based should be valid, and based on an accurate diagnosis of the organisation. It should therefore fulfil the identified needs of the organisation. Effective interventions provide the members with opportunities to make free and informed choices about the interventions, thereby also gaining the commitment of the employees to the planned changes.

- The interventions should have a scientific basis, meaning that there should be valid knowledge that the chosen interventions will lead to the undertaken outcomes. This emphasises the importance of setting up a monitoring plan.

- Effective interventions should enhance the organisation's capacity to manage change. After an intervention, the members involved should be empowered to better implement change activities themselves. The involvement and engagement of the affected members throughout the OD process are thus of paramount importance.

Approaches to interventions

Today it is acknowledged that OD is a value-based discipline and that the values subscribed to are meant to influence the behaviour of the client system. OD interventions can be contemplated from different paradigm perspectives. These perspectives not only influence consultants' views on organisational behaviour, but also the manner in which they plan and effect change interventions. The different paradigm perspectives lead not only to debates on the appropriateness of the perspectives, but even to splits between advocates of different perspectives. It is therefore important that OD consultants consider the different approaches and openly communicate their approach or approaches to their clients, including the strengths and possible risks involved.

The humanistic approach

OD is traditionally based on humanistic principles, and humanism also still serves, to a large extent, as an underlying approach to most OD interventions. According to the humanistic approach, individuals have an inherent inclination toward their own growth and the actualising of their own potential. They have freedom of choice and also take responsibility for themselves. Hence, they are actively involved in the design of their own behaviour, strive toward the actualisation of their own potential and possess creative capabilities. The human being is regarded as inherently good or at least neutral (Meyer, Moore & Viljoen, 1992; 2002). Humanism emphasises the:

> subjective experiencing person in a process of emerging, the subjective world perceived by the experiencing human being; self-reflection and self-transcendence—rising above the limitations of the self by setting goals and ideals, and rising above circumstances by choosing specific attitudes towards them. (Meyer et al, 2002: 327)

Founded on the humanistic approach to human behaviour, the human relations schools were the first to recognise that organisations cannot be understood properly if behaviour that is motivated by more than economic forces is not taken into account (Durlabhji, 1985). People's primary needs have shifted toward freedom, self-esteem, personal development and self-actualisation, according to the theories of Maslow and Hertzberg (Basadur, 1997).

Two focus areas have developed within the human relations school, namely a focus on the total person, in an attempt to satisfy his/her needs, and a focus on the interaction between people in an organisational context (Durlabhji, 1985). The human element in organisational life is described in terms of participation, trust, openness, confrontation involvement, commitment, motivation and satisfaction.

The following normative values are emphasised by the application of the humanistic approach to interventions (Burke, 1997):

- **Human development:** People in organisations must be provided with opportunities for learning and personal growth in order to realise their full potential.
- **Fairness:** People in organisations must be treated with dignity and without discrimination.
- **Openness:** Communication in organisations should be open, honest and done with integrity.
- **Choice:** People in organisations should be free from force and the arbitrary use of power.
- **A balance between autonomy and boundaries:** People in organisations should have the freedom and autonomy to do their jobs as they see fit, but within reasonable boundaries.

Humanistic interventions are based on psychotherapeutic models that are mostly non-directive methods whereby a group is assisted by a consultant to investigate its own behaviour and the relationship among the members of the group (Greiner, 1977). This approach forms the basis of process consultation.

The systems-psychodynamic approach

The systems-psychodynamic role of the OD consultant was discussed in Chapter 4. In this section, we are exploring OD interventions from a systems-psychodynamic approach. There seems to be a new surge in researching and applying psychoanalytic constructs in South African organisations (Rothmann & Cilliers, 2007). This occurs on the basis of a systems-psychodynamic approach, which has its roots in the Tavistock or object relations movement. The system-psychodynamic approach is based on an integration of a systemic and psychodynamic view of organisational behaviour. From this perspective, it is argued that traditional interventions are not suitable for contemporary complex organisations, especially during the unstable phase of change, as behaviour during change is characterised by an inherent unpredictability, unknown patterns, permanent fluidity, surfacing of an implicit order, and an implicit self-organising system (Critchley, 1997). Interventions based on a humanistic approach are also considered to be too rigid as they do not take into consideration the anxiety experienced by employees during change and, hence, the unconscious functioning of people, especially as members of groups. Guerin (1997: 2) stated that:

> teamwork models predominant in the workplace assume conscious dynamics and are not comprehensive enough to describe the complexity of group behaviour. Insights from theory, research, and case studies drawing on psychodynamic constructs have not entered the workplace vernacular.

The purpose of interventions from a systems-psychodynamic perspective is in most cases to provide insight into those covert dynamics influencing the functioning of the group (Huffington et al, 2004). By studying an intervention that was done from this perspective (Geldenhuys, 2012), it was found that an awareness of these dynamics enabled group members to develop more maturity in understanding and managing the boundary between their own inner world and external realities, to manage themselves in their roles and to become less absorbed by group and organisational dynamics. Only after becoming aware of their role in the group did the option to change behaviour become available. Based on the findings, it was argued that these interventions can be regarded as group diagnostic interventions with the following advantages:

- The participants are actively involved in the diagnostic process, allowing for ownership of problems and solutions. The consultants will, for instance, offer working hypotheses during a team development intervention on how they experience the influence of group dynamics on the behaviour of the members, while the members themselves will decide to accept or reject the hypotheses as valid or not. Consultant and client thus work collaboratively on an interpretive diagnosis of what is happening during the team development session. The diagnosis is thus not made before, but in the here-and-now of the actual event.

- Growth and change take place during the intervention as opportunities are provided to own projections. The participants in the experiential event will not only study the behaviour of the group; opportunities are also provided during the intervention to experiment with alternative forms of behaviour. The systems-psychodynamic group diagnostic intervention is discussed in Chapter 10 as an example of an intervention that is based on this approach.

However, using the systems-psychodynamic approach differs from other group diagnostic interventions in the sense that, instead of identifying and analysing 'the problem', the consultant will rather ask questions about the functional role of 'the problem' in the systemic context of the **group-as-a-whole**. The consultant, together with the target group, will thus, for instance, attempt to understand how and why they put certain members in certain roles in certain circumstances (Geldenhuys, 2012). This approach to interventions is in line with the view of change as conceptualised by Diamond (2008) and Van Tonder (2008). Diamond (2008: 357), for instance, stated that '[g]enuine organizational change (ie, change that affects culture and identity, not simply strategies and structure) is rooted in the character of self and other relations in the context of the organization'.

The systems-psychodynamic approach may be regarded as interventions that are similar to the traditional T-group (training group) interventions.

Although the focus of T-group training is primarily on interpersonal relations, leadership and group dynamics are also incorporated in the learning. The use of T-groups became known as teambuilding and is seen as one of the first OD interventions.

Social constructionism as an approach

Frances, Holbeche and Reddington (2012) are congruent with new developments in OD by stating that, although OD was primarily based on psychological concepts derived from psychoanalysis and humanistic values, the field has moved away from its original roots of behavioural dynamics, action research and the application of systems thinking. These new developments have a major impact on the planning and execution of interventions, and can be grouped under the umbrella of postmodern approaches.

Social constructionism is regarded as a postmodern paradigm, representing a number of theoretical frameworks such as relational constructionism, conversational construction or relational practices (Hosking & Bouwen, 2000; Van der Haar & Hosking, 2004). It also serves as foundation for dialogic interventions (Anderson, 2015) and appreciative inquiry (AI).

Berger and Luckmann (1966) laid the foundation for social constructionism in the social sciences in their seminal work entitled *The social construction of reality: a treatise in the sociology of knowledge*. This is deemed a postmodern reaction to modernism, and challenges the assumptions that are taken for granted by the positivistic scientific approach of modernism. As a paradigm, it primarily relies on the philosophical perspectives of phenomenology, structural linguistics, modern hermeneutics and existentialism (Hosking & Morley, 2004; Mattila & Aaltio, 2006).

Hosking and McNamee (2006) define social constructionism as a way of engaging with the world with the focus on relational practices and the social realities these practices create, maintain and transform. The focus is on the relational processes or activities *between* individuals and the meanings that are constructed during conversation between them. Social construction is thus about 'relating' and relatedness; that is, the interactive processes, the conditions of being in relation and the products of this interaction (Anderson, 2007).

Social constructionism argues that there is no objective independent reality outside the observer that has to be discovered through scientific research. Realities are thus socially constructed, and so are viewed as interdependent constructions that exist and are known only in relation to one another (Hosking & Bouwen, 2000).

Language plays a major role in social construction—not in the sense of being a tool to describe our world or representing an objective entity or idea, but as a vehicle through which people construct, make sense of and transform their world (Anderson, 2012; Gergen & Gergen, 2003). Social construction thus emphasises the generative or transformative power of dialoguing (Anderson & Gehart, 2007; Gergen, 1985).

The power of words does not only assist in constructing a current reality when people engage in conversation, it also offers the possibility of creating future worlds (Anderson & Gehart, 2007). In this sense, it is argued that language opens up the possibility of transformation. It provides the opportunity for collaboratively transforming our current realities into new future ones (Anderson, 2012).

Building relationships entails an inquiry in an effort to bring to the surface, legitimise and/or learn from the variety of perspectives, cultures and/or narratives that coexist in the system, which may help to establish a new context with more effective patterns of organising these different perspectives (Marshak & Grant, 2008). This approach asserts that change happens when people become aware of the variety of stories they have about themselves and each other and understand their own part in creating unproductive patterns of interaction (Bushe & Marshak, 2009). The change process thus emphasises changing the conversations, including the language used, that normally take place in the system. The assumption is that this process will result in new images, narratives, texts and socially constructed realities that affect the way people think and act. Complexity thus allows for the creation of new possibilities.

In applying social constructionism as a framework for AI, the emphasis is also on dialoguing as a means through which the stories of the other party is appreciated. Appreciated ways of relating provide participants with resources for connecting with each other and the possibility of constructing a future reality (Watkins & Mohr, 2001). By the words people use, they co-construct the preferred reality into which they might collaboratively engage. Transformation can commence with the very first question that is asked.

In applying social constructionism as a framework for dialoguing interventions (Anderson, 2015), the design will engage the people who will ultimately embody and carry out the change, along with leaders and other stakeholders, in discussions regarding what changes ought to occur. Members will also identify the changes they want to take responsibility for themselves (Bushe, 2013). Narrative mediation and AI are examples of interventions that are primarily based on social constructionism as an approach to interventions (see Chapter 10). This approach is also in line with the more recent approach to use storytelling or narratives as a qualitative method for organisational diagnosis and change.

Activity

Reflect on the different approaches to interventions, and identify your own preference. How would you approach a client whose preference differs from yours?

This could certainly become an ethical dilemma! If you find it difficult to answer this question, it is recommended that you again consult the section on the role of ethics in consulting in Chapter 4.

Principles of intervening

Determining an intervention strategy is based on a number of important principles that have to be considered in order to intervene effectively. These principles include the congruency of the intervention with the diagnosis, the readiness and capability of the client for change, decisions regarding the starting point of intervening, the depth of the intervention and the sequence of activities (Anderson, 2015).

The congruency of the intervention

As was already alluded to in the introduction of this chapter, one of the most important principles is that the interventions should be congruent with the data gathered during the diagnostic phase of the OD process as well as the context of the client system. The primary needs of the client that were identified during the diagnostic phase should be addressed. The consultant's expertise or preference for a specific intervention should not be the criterion for choosing an intervention.

Readiness for change

Readiness for change refers to the organisation's motivation, willingness and commitment to change. If the recipients of the intervention are not ready for change, they will not take responsibility and accountability for the success of the intervention. The process then belongs to the consultant and/or management, who often try to impose control measures or rewards in attempting to 'make it work'. Intervening then becomes a superficial process of going through the motions without real sustainable change.

Readiness for change can be assessed by means of qualitative methods such as interviews and observation, as well as quantitative instruments such as surveys. It is important, though, that the instruments used should adhere to reliability and validity requirements. The development of survey instruments was discussed in Chapter 8.

Certain indicators have been identified and instruments have been developed to measure readiness for change. For example, one set of criteria includes the organisation's sensitivity to pressures for change, its dissatisfaction with the status quo, the availability of support mechanisms, and the commitment of significant management time (Cummings & Worley, 2015). Anderson (2015) refers to a recent scale that assesses whether the members of the organisation view the change programme as appropriate, whether they believe there is management support, whether they believe the organisation is capable of being successful with the change effort, and whether they believe that the change will be of personal benefit.

When readiness for change is low, interventions should first focus on increasing motivation, willingness and commitment to change. This can be done through persuasive communication, participation in change-related meetings and conversations, and through sharing external information to back up the internal communication (Anderson, 2015). It is also important not to overemphasise resistance to change, but rather to identify and employ available resources and energy for change initiatives.

Capability to change

Closely related to an organisation's readiness to change is its capability to change. Capability refers to the change-related knowledge and skills available in the organisation, systems and resources devoted to change and the organisation's experience with change (Cummings & Worley, 2009). If change management (CM) competencies and infrastructure are not in place, training interventions might be needed before meaningful designing can be done.

Depth of interventions

The depth of an intervention refers to the scope and intensity of the OD efforts. The idea is depicted using a metaphor of an iceberg (see Figure 9.1 on page 262), which draws attention to two important components: the formal and informal aspects of organisations. The formal components of an organisation are analogous to the part of an iceberg above the water; the informal components refer to the part which lies below water, unseen but there nevertheless. The formal components are usually observable, rational and oriented to structural factors. In contrast, the informal components are usually affective, oriented to process and behavioural factors, and not observable to all people.

Generally speaking, the greater the scope and intensity of the problem, the more likely it is that these components lie in the informal components. Depth of intended change thus refers to how deep the consultant must go into the organisational iceberg to solve the problem. At one extreme, or above the water, are problems with the work content, and overt group issues such as communication and conflict. The solution can probably involve the changing of job definitions, departmentalisation bases, spans of control and delegated authority. At the other extreme are problems below the surface, such as hidden group dynamics, values and beliefs, and the unconscious (Reddy, 1994). While these behaviours can certainly be affected by changes in structure, they are ordinarily deep-seated.

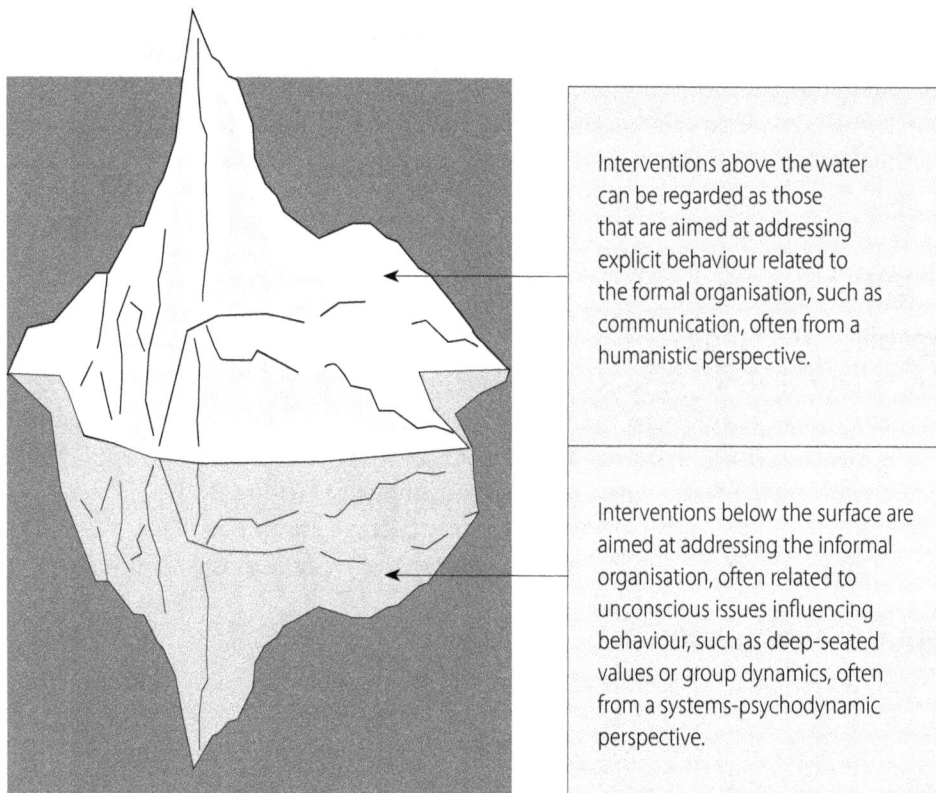

Interventions above the water can be regarded as those that are aimed at addressing explicit behaviour related to the formal organisation, such as communication, often from a humanistic perspective.

Interventions below the surface are aimed at addressing the informal organisation, often related to unconscious issues influencing behaviour, such as deep-seated values or group dynamics, often from a systems-psychodynamic perspective.

Figure 9.1 The iceberg model (adapted from Brown, 2014: 152)

Harrison (1970) observes that organisational change interventions vary substantially in the amounts of emotional involvement they require of members of the organisation. According to Harrison (1970: 181), change strategies differ in accordance with 'how deep, value laden, emotionally charged, and central to the individual's sense of self are the issues and processes about which a consultant attempts to obtain information and which he seeks to influence.

In other words, a structural intervention based on facts and research would be much less threatening, evocative of deep feelings and emotionally disruptive than would be a three-day T-group that delved into people's innermost feelings.

According to Harrison (1970), different strategies accomplish different things; they are not different ways of doing the same thing. However, a practical guideline is never to go more deeply than necessary into solving an immediate problem, and secondly, not to go to a level beyond the limit of the available energy and resources.

Starting point and sequence of activities

An intervention plan will, in most cases, consist of more than one activity. Decisions should then be made on where to start and what sequence to follow with the different intervention activities.

There is general agreement among consultants that it is more appropriate to start with task-related interventions, followed by personal or relational interventions. If, for example, teambuilding activities are planned as part of an intervention strategy to address conflict, it will most probably be more appropriate to start with role clarification before intervening on an interpersonal level, as the conflict may to a large extent be addressed by means of the role clarification exercise. Some consultants, however, are of the opinion that addressing the task-related issues does not lead to solving the soft issues; they therefore opt for an integrated approach (Anderson, 2015).

Beer (1980) has identified the following six criteria to assist in sequencing intervention activities:

1. **Maximise diagnostic data.** Interventions with a diagnostic nature should be conducted first, as this will provide more data about the organisation and assist in customising the interventions that follow.
2. **Maximise effectiveness.** If initial interventions can build enthusiasm for change or confidence in success, interventions that follow will probably be more successful.
3. **Maximise efficiency.** Initial interventions should conserve energy, time and money as far as possible.
4. **Maximise speed.** Initial interventions should not negatively impact on the client's need for the pace of change.
5. **Maximise relevance.** An intervention strategy should be set up in such a manner that the primary problem is addressed first.
6. **Minimise psychological and organisational strain.** (Harrison, 1970: 181). The first interventions should be safer and produce low anxiety.

As these guidelines may contradict each other in specific situations, the best practice is to engage the client in determining the most appropriate criterion or criteria that will assist in sequencing the interventions to address the change agenda. Care should be taken not to approach the client with pre-set plans of what has to be implemented and how this should be done. Clients should be engaged to choose accountability for the designing of the interventions. This is most often not a linear, straightforward step-by-step process (Block, 2000).

Activity

Reflect on the type of preparation needed for a meeting with the client after feedback was provided on the functioning of their organisation. What are the most important aspects you would consider?

Did you include considering how, and to what extent, you would make provision for including the client's wishes?

Classification of interventions

Although there are different ways in which OD interventions can be clustered, two dimensions are included as contingencies that impact on the success of interventions, namely the issue that the intervention is intended to resolve, and the level of the organisational system at which the intervention is expected to have a primary impact (Cummings & Worley, 2015). Regarding the issues to be addressed, a distinction can be made between interventions that are intended to address behaviour, also known as human process interventions, and those that are addressing techno-structural issues. Two well-known examples of human process interventions are process consultation and teambuilding, while structural and work design are examples of techno-structural interventions.

The second dimension refers to the organisational level or focus of attention at which the intervention is primarily targeted. A distinction is made between individual, group and large-scale interventions that are aimed at the organisation as a whole. However, from a systemic perspective, it should be remembered that one intervention can address more than one issue, while a secondary target is always involved and affected by an intervention. Interventions must therefore be designed in such a manner that they apply to specific organisational levels, address the possibility of cross-effects, and possibly integrate interventions affecting different levels (Cummings & Worley, 2015). A classification of the different interventions into categories is presented in Table 9.1. Examples of interventions that are mostly used will be discussed in Chapters 10 and 11, supplemented with more recent developments.

Table 9.1 Four categories of OD intervention used in organisation change (adapted from Cummings & Worley, 2015; Kormanik, 2005; McNamara, 2009)

Category	Focus	Application
Human process interventions	Interventions focusing on individual, interpersonal and group behaviour within organisations, and how individuals meet their objectives and accomplish the tasks assigned to them	Interventions related to the individual: ● Diagnostic instruments such as the Myers-Briggs Type Indicator (MBTI) and assessment centres ● Executive coaching ● Career management and development. Interventions related to interpersonal relations and group dynamics: ● **Process consultation**: The aim is to help members to develop skills and to understand and be able to identify group and interpersonal problems themselves. ● **Third-party intervention**: The third-party intervener helps to resolve conflict that may develop from substantive or interpersonal issues by using methods such as problem solving, conciliation and bargaining. ● **Teambuilding**: The OD practitioner helps work groups to become more effective in the accomplishment of tasks. Interventions related to system-wide process: ● **Organisation confrontation meeting**: This is used when management needs to organise resources for immediate problem solving. They identify problems, set targets and work on problems. ● **Intergroup relations**: This refers to interaction between departments and groups in the organisation. OD practitioners use the intergroup conflict model so that the two groups become aware of and understand the cause of conflict. The groups then use an appropriate method to solve the problem. →

Category	Focus	Application
Techno-structural interventions	Interventions focusing on the structure (division of labour and hierarchy) and technology (task methods and job design)	Techno-structural interventions concerned with restructuring the organisation: ○ **Structural design**: This refers to division of labour away from the traditional organisational overall work process to a more integrative and flexible one. ○ **Downsizing**: This refers to decreasing the size of the organisation through redesign, outsourcing and employee layoffs. ○ **Re-engineering**: This refers to a radical redesign of the organisation's core work process. Techno-structural interventions that involve employees in decision making: ○ **Parallel structure**: These structures ('union and management') operate together with formal organisation and offer members alternative settings to address problems and come to solutions. ○ **Total quality management (TQM)**: Organisational members want to improve the quality of management as part of their normal operation at work. ○ **High-involvement organisations**: A high level of employee involvement is promoted when changes take place in structure, human resource management practices and work design. Techno-structural interventions that involve engineering, motivational and sociotechnical approaches to work design: ○ **Job enrichment**: This creates jobs where employees will experience high levels of autonomy and performance feedback. ○ **Self-management teams**: Self-management work teams are set up to solve problems, implement solutions and take responsibility for the outcomes. Kormanik (2005) also includes the following as methods of techno-structural intervention: organisational structure and systems, space and physical settings, organisational process redesign, CM, job enrichment and design, knowledge management, organisational learning and competency-based management. →

Category	Focus	Application
Human resource interventions	Interventions with a focus on the integration and incorporation of employees in the organisation. The notion here is to integrate employees in the organisation in an acceptable manner and develop the potential and talent of employees.	Human resource management interventions concerning performance: ● **Goal setting:** Periodically, meetings take place between managers and subordinates to plan work, review and achieve goals. They make use of management by objectives. ● **Performance appraisal:** This provides feedback with regard to goal setting and reward systems. ● **Reward system:** This is a process to improve employee satisfaction and performance by using innovative pay, promotion and benefits approaches. Human resource management interventions concerning talent management and development: ● **Coaching and mentoring:** This intervention involves a one-on-one process that focuses on personal learning between the OD practitioner and the client. ● **Management and leadership development:** This focuses on competencies needed to lead the organisation into the future by using action learning, simulations and case studies. ● **Career planning and development:** This focuses on the retention of valuable staff and the improvement of their quality of work life. Human resource management interventions concerning supporting members in the organisation: ● **Management of workforce diversity:** This implies making organisations more accommodating of diversity regarding lifestyle preferences, cultural values and other differences. ● **Employee stress and wellness:** This intervention makes use of employee assistance programmes (EAP) and stress management programmes. →

Category	Focus	Application
Strategic change interventions	Interventions with a focus on the internal functioning of the organisation, and a link to the larger environment that changes and transforms at a rapid pace	Strategic change interventions that relate to the organisation's internal operations and environment: ○ **Organisational redesign:** This addresses elements such as structure, work design and human resource management practices to align them to the organisation's strategy. ○ **Integrated strategic change:** This intervention helps with how planned change can add value to the organisation's strategy. ○ **Culture change:** This intervention helps members pull in the same direction to form a strong organisation culture. Strategic change interventions that relate to continuous organisational change: ○ **Dynamic strategising:** This intervention helps with the building of a strategic system that can adapt to the changing process. ○ **Self-designing organisations:** This intervention helps with how to solve existing problems. ○ **Learning organisations:** This intervention focuses on the capability of the organisation and the development of new knowledge to increase the performance of the organisation. ○ **Built-to-change organisations:** This intervention helps with the continuous change process to make it more efficient for the organisation. Strategic change interventions that relate to how organisations collaborate with one another: ○ **Mergers:** The intervention helps two or more organisations form a new identity when they merge. ○ **Alliances:** The intervention helps two or more organisations form a joint ground for sharing resources. ○ **Networks:** The intervention helps two or more organisations to solve problems together, performing the task by addressing current network problems.

The joint action planning meeting

Now that the fundamental aspects regarding the design of interventions have been addressed, the actual meeting with the client will be discussed.

The consultant should attempt to contract a four-hour JAP session with the client at the conclusion of the feedback session. These sessions should be attended by the same people. Once again, the JAP session is a group session which must be handled as a **facilitation session**. The meeting should aim at engaging the participants in the form of a dialogue and thereby building support for the intervention plan (Block, 2000). All the consultant's micro-skills will be necessary in order to ensure that the JAP session is a success. An important difference regarding the JAP session is that while consultants adopted a process-consultation role during the previous phases of the action-research process, they will now need to play more of an expert role during the JAP session. This means that they will have to prepare themselves thoroughly before the session takes place, especially regarding possible interventions to address the identified problems, but still allowing for the engagement of the client throughout the process. The main outcomes of a JAP session are comprehensive intervention and monitoring plans.

Structure of a joint action planning meeting

Taking the above-mentioned into account, the following structure can be followed during a JAP session:

Step 1: Confirm the main problem area, as determined in the feedback session. The feedback session should have been concluded by a summary of all the main problem areas identified that have to be addressed. The action planning session can be opened by a summary of these areas. This will ensure that you refresh the memory of the planning session members so that all can start from a common understanding of what needs to be done.

Step 2: Define the change problem. The group considers the main problem areas and defines the underlying change problem. Care must be taken at this stage **not to confuse symptoms with causes**. The model used to interpret and explain the data can now also be used to understand the underlying change problem. The questions to be asked here are: 'What do the problem areas tell us? What is the actual underlying problem facing this organisation?'

Step 3: Determine appropriate change objectives. In this step, change objectives are **clearly and specifically defined**, in both behavioural and quantitative terms, so that they are appropriate to and consistent with the particular organisation. Too often, a practitioner initiates standard interventions without having identified what needs to be accomplished or changed. Spending time in determining objectives increases the **probability for success** and enhances the practitioner's image as a contributor to the organisation.

Step 4: Develop an appropriate intervention plan. In planning the individual steps for implementation, the consultant and client must be jointly concerned with **which** interventions to use, **where** in the organisation to start, **who** is to be involved in the effort, **how much time** is required, **which** resources are needed and **how** the effort will be monitored. In view of the fact that organisational change is a process and that the consultant must remain flexible and responsive to new developments, it is helpful to establish a flow diagram that accounts for each step. This practice enables the consultant and client to analyse the progress of the effort and whether it is leading where they intended. In addition, it enables managers to become intimately involved in the process and convinces them that the consultant is indeed committed to reaching specific objectives that will benefit the organisation.

Step 5: Develop a monitoring plan. Here it is necessary to determine **how** the progress of the total change effort will be monitored, **who** will monitor **what**, and **when** the monitoring will take place. **To whom** will it be reported?

Step 6: Conclusion. The session can be concluded by summarising all decisions and by doing follow-up contracting for what must now follow, and by whom.

The intervention plan

As mentioned previously, one of the main outcomes of a JAP session is an intervention plan. This stipulates **how** the identified problems will be addressed. More specifically, this plan sets out: (1) the identified problems; (2) the proposed intervention(s); (3) the target group for the intervention; (4) who will be involved in the intervention; (5) the duration of the intervention; (6) when it will be implemented; and (7) who will be responsible for coordinating its implementation.

It is important that the plan is approved by top management, that it is cost-effective, and that it is flexible to make provision for the possibility of new information that might influence the plan (Cummings & Worley, 2015). In this regard, it may be necessary to supplement desired future objectives with midpoint goals as part of the plan. The intervention plan is the client's and consultant's project plan for the implementation phase of the OD project, and it is essential to be able to monitor the progress of the project as well. An example of an intervention plan is presented in Table 9.2.

Table 9.2 Example of an intervention plan (Author)

Problem	Proposed intervention	Target groups	Who is involved	Duration	When	Responsible person to coordinate
1. Organisational structure not supporting strategy	Restructuring of marketing and public relations	Marketing and public relations departments	Heads of departments Human resources	10 days	July 20…	Head of human resources (James)
2. Lack of succession planning	Assessment centres Career planning	All supervisors in the finance department All sales personnel from the designated groups on job level 8	Human resources External consultants All identified personnel and their line managers	1 day × 5 sessions	Aug 20…	Training section head (Peter)
3. Conflict between managers	Team-building	Management team	All members of the Exco	1 day session	Sep 20…	OD section head (Sarah)

Activity

Reflect on the possible advantages of not combining the feedback session with the JAP session.

Evaluation and monitoring interventions

While the consultant (and/or client) is/are busy with the interventions, it is important to continuously determine whether intervening is making a positive difference; that is, the change process must be continually monitored. However, it remains a difficult task to determine if the intervention does what it is supposed to do. **A monitoring plan assists in determining to what extent we have achieved our change objectives**. The following questions can assist the consultant and client in this process:

- Are our interventions relevant?
- Is our timing correct?

- Are our activities producing the effects we intended and wanted? If not, why not? If so, why?
- Is there continued 'ownership' (involvement, commitment, investment) in the programme by the client?
- What are the total system ramifications of our efforts? Did we anticipate these ramifications? Are any of the ramifications undesirable? If yes, what do we do about them?
- What about the behaviour of our own OD group? Must it be changed in any way? Are we solving problems effectively, managing against clearly understood goals, and modelling the kind of interpersonal climate we think is desirable in the organisation?

Consider other planned monitoring activities (ie follow-up interviews, organisational members completing the same questionnaire at regular intervals, and so forth).

The easiest way to monitor the implementation of interventions is to compile a monitoring plan. This can be done jointly with the client group during the JAP session. This plan sets out: (1) the change objective being monitored; (2) the monitor action; (3) who will do the monitoring; (4) what technique will be used to carry out the monitoring; (5) when the monitoring action will be carried out; and (6) what format the reporting will entail and to whom the reporting will be done. An example of a monitoring plan is presented in Table 9.3.

Table 9.3 A monitoring plan (Author)

Change objective no	Monitoring action	Who	What	When	Reporting
1. To align structure of the marketing and public relations departments with the company's strategy	Check for alignment	Heads of marketing and public relations departments	Compare the newly designed structure with the strategy of the company	31 July 20…	Present a report to Exco by 5 Aug 20…

Change objective no	Monitoring action	Who	What	When	Reporting
2. To do succession planning	Determine if all identified staff attended assessment centre and career-planning workshops	Heads of departments	Scrutinise the succession plans	1–20 Aug 20…	Present succession plans to Exco by 31 Aug 20…
3. To improve teamwork in the organisation	Determine the degree of teamwork among all work teams	OD section	Conduct focus groups with team members of all work teams	15–31 Aug 20…	Present results to the management team by 15 Sep 20…

Conclusion

In this chapter you have learnt that to intervene is to enter into an ongoing system of relationships, to come between or among persons, groups or objects for the purpose of helping them. You have also learnt that there are different approaches underlying interventions, namely the humanistic approach, the systems-psychodynamic approach and the social constructionist approach. Furthermore, the different principles of intervening were discussed and you were provided with guidelines in conducting a JAP and setting up a monitoring plan for an intervention. Examples of the different interventions will be discussed in the chapters to follow.

Reflection questions

1. Provide a detailed description of organisational interventions as the action thrust of the OD process.
2. Critically compare the different approaches to OD interventions.
3. Discuss five important principles that have to be considered in order to intervene effectively and indicate the possible consequences if these principles are ignored.
4. Provide a classification of the different OD interventions.
5. Differentiate between an intervention and a monitoring plan.

Multiple-choice questions

1. Which of the following statements regarding the design of interventions is not correct?
   a. By entering a system, you are already making an intervention.
   b. An intervention implies an interruption in an existing system.
   c. Interventions should be based on a sound diagnosis.
   d. In order to make scientific interventions, care should be taken not to be influenced by the client.
   e. Intervening in one part of the system has implications for all the other parts as well.

2. The humanistic approach emphasises:
   a. a balance between boundaries and autonomy
   b. the unconscious experience of people
   c. dialoguing as a means through which the stories of the other party are appreciated
   d. relational processes or activities **between** individuals
   e. None of the above

3. Which of the following is a not a criterion to assist in sequencing intervention activities?
   a. Maximise effectiveness.
   b. Maximise efficiency.
   c. Maximise speed.
   d. Maximise psychological strain.
   e. Maximise relevance.

4. Which of the following statements regarding human process interventions is not correct?
   a. Human process interventions focus on individual, interpersonal and group behaviour.
   b. Human process interventions include the use of diagnostic instruments.
   c. Human process interventions include the implementation of self-management teams.
   d. Human process interventions include process consultation.
   e. Human process interventions include conflict resolution.

5. Which of the following statements is/are correct?
   During joint action planning it is important:
   a. to ensure flexibility
   b. to obtain approval from top management
   c. to set midpoint goals as part of the plan
   d. to ensure the cost effectiveness of the plan
   e. All of the above

Read the case study and answer the questions that follow.

Case study

A negative climate in one of the departments of a beverage company was identified by means of a climate survey. One important dimension of concern was a lack of open communication within the department. As a follow-up, you attended a management meeting of the department to gain information on the team's functioning through observing the members' behaviour. During the meeting you realised that there were a number of 'undiscussables', also referred to by one member during the tea break when talking to her friend as the 'elephant in the room'. You have realised that there could be more than a communication problem; rather, it is a case of an underlying tension and subgroup forming, especially among the male managers and some of the female ones, more specifically those who are younger than the rest. The younger managers could not find their voice during the meeting, even when their opinion was asked for. It also seemed that the head of the department, who was chairing the meeting, was aware of the tension during the meeting, but did not know how to deal with the issue. After the meeting, he also requested that you assist him with an intervention in his department as a matter of urgency.

1. Provide a critical discussion on the relevancy of the principles of intervention for the above scenario.
2. Propose and motivate two possible interventions that would probably be appropriate for addressing the issue in the case study. Also motivate the underlying approach to your intervention.

References

Anderson, DL. 2015. *Organization development: the process of leading organizational change.* 3rd ed. Thousand Oaks, CA: SAGE.

Anderson, H. 2007. 'A postmodern umbrella: language and knowledge as relational and generative, and inherently transforming', in *Collaborative therapy*, edited by H Anderson & D Gehart. New York: Routledge: 7–19.

Anderson, H. 2012. 'Collaborative relationships and dialogic conversations: ideas for a relationally responsive practice'. *Family Process* 51: 18–24. https://doi.org/10.1111/j.1545-5300.2012.01385.x.

Anderson, H & Gehart, D (eds). 2007. *Collaborative therapy.* New York Routledge.

Argyris, C. 2005. 'Intervention theory and method', in *Organization development and transformation: managing effective change*, edited by WL French, CH Bell & RA Zawacki. 6th ed. New York: McGraw-Hill: 115–118.

Basadur, M. 1997. 'Organizational development interventions for enhancing creativity in the workplace'. *The Journal of Creative Behavior* 31(1): 59–72.

Beer, M. 1980. *Organization change and development: a systems view*. Santa Monica, CA: Goodyear.

Berger, P & Luckmann, T. 1966. *The social construction of reality: a treatise in the sociology of knowledge*. New York: Penguin.

Block, P. 2000. *Flawless consulting: a guide to getting your expertise used*. 2nd ed. New York: Pfeiffer.

Brown, D. 2014. *Experiential approach to organization development*. 8th ed. Harlow: Pearson.

Burke, WW. 1997. 'The new agenda for organization development'. *Organizational Dynamics* Summer: 7–20.

Bushe, GR. 2013. 'Dialogic OD: a theory of practice'. *OD Practitioner* 45(1): 11–17.

Bushe, GR & Marshak, RJ. 2009. 'Revisioning organization development: diagnostic and dialogic premises and patterns of practice'. *The Journal of Applied Behavioral Science* 45(3): 348–368.

Critchley, B. 1997. 'A Gestalt approach to consulting', in *Developing organisational consultancy*, edited by JE Neumann, K Kellner & A Dawson-Shepherd. London: Routledge: 127–139.

Cummings, T & Worley, CG. 2009. *Organization development and change*. 9th ed. Mason, OH: South-Western Cengage Learning.

Cummings, T & Worley, CG. 2015. *Organization development and change*. 10th ed. Mason, OH: South-Western Cengage Learning.

Diamond, MA. 2008. 'Telling them what they know: organizational change, defensive resistance, and the unthought known'. *Journal of Applied Behavioral Science* 44(3): 348–364.

Durlabhji, S. 1985. 'Freud in the organization: the unconscious in American and Japanese management'. *Management and Labour Studies* 10(3): 105–117.

Frances, H, Holbeche, L & Reddington, M. 2012. *People and organizational development: a new agenda for organizational effectiveness*. London: Chartered Institute of Personnel and Development.

French, WL & Bell, CH. 1999. *Organization development: behavioral science interventions for organization improvement*. 5th ed. Englewood Cliffs, NJ: Prentice Hall.

Geldenhuys, D. 2012. 'Group-as-a-whole as a context for studying individual behaviour: a group diagnostic intervention'. *SA Journal of Industrial Psychology/SA Tydskrif vir Bedryfsielkunde* 38(2), Art #1011, 12 pages. https://doi.org/10.4102/sajip.v38i2.1011.

Gergen, KJ. 1985. 'The social constructionist movement in modern psychology'. *American Psychologist* 40(3): 266–275. https://doi.org/10.1037/0003-066X.40.3.266.

Gergen, M & Gergen, KJ (eds). 2003. *Social construction: a reader*. London: SAGE.

Greiner, LE. 1977. 'Reflections on OD American style', in *Organizational development in the UK and USA: a joint evaluation*, edited by CL Cooper. London: Billing & Sons: 65–82.

Guerin, ML. 1997. 'Teamwork at Barton Company: a psychodynamic perspective'. Paper presented at the 1997 symposium of the International Society for the Psychoanalytic Study of Organizations.

Harrison, R. 1970. 'Choosing the depth of organizational intervention'. *The Journal of Applied Behavioral Science* 6 (2): 181–202.

Hosking, DM & Bouwen, R. 2000. 'Organizational learning: relational-constructionist approaches: an overview'. *European Journal of Work and Organizational Psychology* 9(2): 129–132.

Hosking, DM & McNamee, S (eds). 2006. *The social construction of organisation.* Herndon, VA: Copenhagen Business School Press.

Hosking, D & Morley, IE. 2004. 'Social constructionism in community and applied social psychology'. *Journal of Community and Applied Social Psychology* 14(5): 318–331. https://doi.org/10.1002/casp.801.

Huffington, C, Armstrong, D, Halton, W, Hoyle, L & Polley, J. 2004. *Working below the surface: the emotional life of contemporary organizations.* London: Karnac Books.

Kormanik, MB. 2005. White males in transition: developing the experiences of a stalled career. Unpublished doctoral dissertation, The George Washington University, Washington, DC.

Marshak, RJ & Grant, D. 2008. 'Organizational discourse and new organization development practices'. *British Journal of Management* 19(7): 8–19.

Mattila, M & Aaltio, I. 2006. 'From tools to social construction of organizational reality: studying value dissemination in three case companies'. *Electronic Journal of Business Ethics and Organization Studies* 11(2). http://ejbo.jyu.fi (Accessed 30 May 2016).

McNamara, C. 2009. Organisational change and development: managing change and change management. http://www.authenticityconsulting.com (Accessed 30 May 2016).

Meyer, WF, Moore, C & Viljoen, HG. 1992. *Persoonlikheidsteorieë: van Freud tot Frankl.* Johannesburg: Lexicon.

Meyer, WF, Moore, C & Viljoen, HG. 2002. *Personology: from individual to ecosystem.* Sandown: Heinemann.

Reddy, WB. 1994. *Intervention skills: process consultation for small groups and teams.* San Francisco, CA: Jossey-Bass.

Rothmann, S & Cilliers, FVN. 2007. 'Present challenges and some critical issues for research in industrial/organisational psychology'. *Journal of Industrial Psychology.* 33(1): 8–17.

Van der Haar, D & Hosking, D. 2004. 'Evaluating appreciative inquiry: a relational constructionist perspective'. *Human Relations* 57(8): 1017–1036. https://doi.org/10.1177/0018726704045839.

Van Tonder, CL. 2008. 'Stacking the dominoes ... courting catastrophe at the "edgeof-chaos"'. Paper presented at the 9th IFSAM World Management Conference, Shanghai, People's Republic of China, 26–28 July.

Watkins, JM & Mohr, BJ. 2001. *Appreciative inquiry: change at the speed of imagination.* San Francisco, CA: Jossey-Bass/Pfeiffer.

Chapter 10

Interventions: From the individual to the team

Dirk Geldenhuys

Learning outcomes

After reading this chapter, you should be able to:

- compare the use of the Myers–Briggs Type Indicator (MBTI) and assessment centres for diagnosing individual behaviour
- explain the executive coaching process from two different approaches
- develop a career development programme
- stipulate how using the Johari window can contribute to better interpersonal communication
- clearly differentiate between the phases of narrative mediation
- compare process consultation, teambuilding and a systems-psychodynamic group diagnostic intervention
- differentiate between using appreciative inquiry (AI) for teambuilding with existing teams, and the establishment of new teams.

Introduction

If a consultant has a hammer at his/her disposal, everything should not become a nail! Similarly, interventions should be fit for purpose. Appropriate interventions should always be based on a sound organisational diagnosis. Although this does not imply that one intervention cannot simultaneously address more than one change objective, it certainly means that care should be taken in the identification of the most appropriate one and to envisage the possible impact of the intervention, not only on the intended target, but also the possible unintentional impact on the rest of the system. The systemic perspective of interventions is especially evident when some interventions that are aimed at teambuilding create a silo mentality or conflictual relationships between one team and others. Empowering individual employees might also be experienced as counterproductive by their managers, as they might start challenging their managers on their decisions. Studying this chapter will assist you in identifying and executing appropriate interventions.

The classification of interventions was discussed in Chapter 9. With the focus on some of the most well-known and used interventions, all the different interventions that were dealt with in Chapter 9 will not be repeated. However, some of the more recent, cutting-edge interventions, such as AI and narrative mediation, will be included.

The discussion of the interventions in this chapter is based on the target of the intervention, namely individual, interpersonal and team interventions. The different interventions can also, to some extent, be classified according to their broad purpose: those that can be grouped under the umbrella of diagnostic interventions, such as the systems-psychodynamic diagnostic group intervention, and those that are developmental in nature, for example AI. There are, however, also interventions that endeavour to address both, such as the classical coaching process and narrative mediation. Taking this into account, examples of interventions according to the target of the intervention will now be discussed in more detail.

Individual interventions

Individual employees can be regarded as the first building block of organisations and therefore play an important role in any organisation development (OD) effort. Organisational change will not be sustainable if the individual members are not motivated to change. Interventions aimed at the individual, such as those intended for personal growth, management and career development, can be extremely helpful in supplementing group and organisational-level interventions, and should be considered as part of a comprehensive OD intervention strategy. Although individual-level interventions traditionally focused mainly on the development of managers and executives, as they are the most influential units in an organisation, the recent emphasis on talent management has led to the inclusion of interventions to assist individual members to progress through their work life (Cummings & Worley, 2015).

Individual interventions or instruments are often aimed at assessing and providing feedback on the current behaviour or personality of the individual. The use of diagnostic instruments and assessment centres will be discussed as two well-known examples of individual interventions.

Diagnostic instruments and assessment centres

It is argued that, in order to improve the performance of individual organisation members, assessments and feedback on them are needed to identify their potential, strengths and development areas regarding relevant areas such as leadership style, conflict style, work preferences and aptitudes. The main purpose of these interventions is to create self-awareness that can serve as a stimulus for change and development.

One of the most well-known instruments in OD, the Myers-Briggs Type Indicator (MBTI) and a more qualitative assessment technique, namely assessment centres, will be discussed as examples of diagnostic tools and approaches to individual assessment.

The Myers–Briggs Type Indicator

The MBTI is based on Jung's theories of personality types, and distinguishes between 16 of them, based on a combination of the following four preference categories (Myers et al, 1998):

1. **Extraversion versus introversion preference (E-I):** This dimension refers to the preference for what energises a person. An extroverted person is energised by people; introverted people are energised by being alone.

2. **Sensing versus intuition preference (S-N):** This dimension refers to a person's preference for collecting information. A sensing person will prefer using facts, and realistic and practical ideas, whereas those with a preference for using intuition will tend to trust gut feeling to generate possibilities.

3. **Thinking versus feeling preference (T-F):** This dimension refers to the preference for decision making. Thinking types prefer to use analysis and logical reasoning in decision making, while feeling types prefer to base decisions on subjective, interpersonal criteria and their effect on people.

4. **Judging versus perceiving preference (J-P):** This dimension refers to an orientation to the world in general. Judging types prefer their world to be structured and ordered, and prefer to be in control, whereas perceiving types are spontaneous and flexible.

According to Anderson (2015), the use of diagnostic tools has a number of advantages. For instance, they are individualised and pose a relatively low threat; they provide respondents with an understanding of their own behaviour as it is conceptualised; they can assist in exploring previously unknown areas; they can allow for understanding others and also for comparison with others; they promote involvement in self-discovery; and they can be administered at multiple times to compare changes before and after interventions.

However, care should be taken in the use of diagnostic tools. For instance, they should not be regarded as 'tests' to determine what is right and wrong; they should not be used for the wrong purpose; they should not be used to label people; they should not foster a dependency on the administrator of the instrument or the instrument per se; and they should not lead to an experience of being exposed. It is therefore important to consider the ethical implications of using these instruments and to ensure they are administered and interpreted by qualified practitioners. As the use of these instruments requires extensive training, registration by the Health Professions Council (HPCSA) is needed in South Africa.

Activity

The MBTI is presented as an intervention aimed at the individual. Reflect on the application of the MBTI for teambuilding purposes. How can this assist in enhancing decision making in a team? What does this teach us about the systemic character of OD?

Could you think of any possible shortcomings when using the MBTI for teambuilding purposes?

Assessment centres

Assessment centre interventions were originally designed for selecting people for managerial positions. They are regarded as a valid tool for the identification and assessment of managerial competencies that are difficult to discover through objective tests and traditional interviews. However, assessment centres are also used for the selection of people to fit new work designs such as self-management teams, for organisation change, and for career development purposes (Cummings & Worley, 2015; Lehman et al, 2011).

Conventionally, assessment centres were conducted over a period of two to three days with 12 to 15 people. The activities comprise a comprehensive interview, tests for the assessment of mental ability and knowledge, and between four and five simulation exercises intended to simulate managerial work, such as in-basket trays.

During an assessment centre, the behaviour and performance of each candidate are assessed by an assessment team, consisting of specialists and experienced managers. They provide an overall score for each participant, indicating his/her potential for the position he/she was assessed for.

More recently, assessment centres have been used not only for the identification of potential, but also for developmental purposes, such as career development (Cummings & Worley, 2015). The emphasis with these centres is on providing feedback to the participants on their strengths and developmental areas, based on the results of the assessments. Cummings and Worley (2015) point out that trained staff can also assist the participants with support and direction with career development, for instance by identifying training experiences and job assignments to promote career progress. According to these authors, this is especially relevant at the advancement stage of career development, when employees have to assess their talent in light of long-term career commitments. Although assessment centres are complex and very expensive to use, the predictive validity and cost-effectiveness of well-developed ones have been established (Lehman et al, 2011).

Executive coaching

Although the boundaries between coaching, mentoring and therapy are not always clear, especially in practice, it is necessary to distinguish between these different concepts. Coaching is defined by Anderson (2015: 216) as 'a one-on-one intervention in which an individual works to improve a specific personal, interpersonal, or skills area, or to take actions to reach a desired future goal, working with a facilitator on the process of personal change'. Whereas the coach uses question frameworks to help the client to work out solutions to specific issues, the mentor would use his/her own expertise to advise and direct the mentee (Stout-Rostron, 2012) with a focus on the content of the job. A mentor will therefore, in most instances, be someone within the organisation who can act as a teacher, expert and role model for the mentee.

The boundaries between coaching and counselling are more blurred than those between coaching and mentoring, as both deal with personal development. It is also difficult to manage the boundaries in practice, as some coaching sessions, especially in executive coaching, might tend to slip into therapy. However, coaching and therapy primarily differ in terms of the issues to be addressed and the goals of the helping relationship (Anderson, 2015). Regarding the issues, a coach will in most instances not deal with the inner psychological experiences of the client or with psychological pathology, and will therefore use a less diagnostic approach than the therapist. The goals are also different. Whereas the coach will more often deal with the potential of the client and ways of reaching this potential in future, the therapist will more often focus on the psychological states of the client or analysing problems that are based on psychological issues of the past. Furthermore, the coaching relationship does not allow time for the development of a therapeutic relationship between the coach and the client.

Coaching in organisations can vary from leadership coaching, performance coaching, career coaching and executive coaching, of which executive coaching can currently be regarded as the most popular type. Executive coaching is defined by Kilburg (2000: 65–66) as:

a helping relationship formed between a client who has managerial authority and responsibility in an organisation and a consultant who uses a variety of techniques and methods to assist the client to achieve a mutually identified set of goals to improve his or her professional performance and personal satisfaction and consequently to improve the effectiveness of the client's organisation within a formally defined coaching relationship.

More specifically, the goals of executive coaching are to help clients improve their capacity to manage an organisation, especially during times of transition; the ability to manage themselves and others, as well as their career; and the ability to improve the organisation's effectiveness (Anderson, 2015).

There are a number of coaching models that apply different approaches consisting of different processes. The typical coaching process is similar to the OD process, as discussed in Chapter 7. The consultant will firstly establish a relationship and contract with the client. After entering into an agreement, an assessment will typically be done. Thereafter, feedback will be provided and a plan of action will be developed. Possible obstacles for implementation will be addressed, and the action plan, consisting of short- and long-term goals, will then be executed and the results will be assessed (Anderson, 2015; Cummings & Worley, 2015).

Kilburg (2000) presents the process of a coaching session, consisting of six stages, as follows:

- **Stage 1** entails the establishment of a contract, the re-establishment of the interpersonal connection, and inviting the client to work together.
- **Stage 2** entails the client telling a story about his/her present situation.
- **Stage 3** allows for progressively exploring and reflecting on the situation.
- **Stage 4** entails a choice on the foci of the session.
- **Stage 5** encompasses a working dialogue in the form of cycles of disclosure and feedback loops. Different methods and skills are applied during this phase, such as active listening, client-centred methodology, interpretations and confrontations, goal setting, role modelling and behavioural rehearsals.
- **Stage 6** is the final stage, during which a closure is reached, often by a formal time limit set for the session.

More recent approaches to coaching can be grouped under the umbrella of postmodern or strength-based coaching. These approaches rely on social constructionist paradigms (see Chapter 9), positive psychology and the so-called strengths-based movement in management of Marcus Buckingham.

Appreciative coaching (Orem, Binkert & Clancy, 2007) can be regarded as one of the strengths-based approaches that is currently becoming very popular in the OD world. These coaching models are based on the AI approach to OD interventions that was developed by David Cooperrider. AI will be discussed in more detail as an approach to teambuilding.

The coaching process follows the typical stages of the appreciative inquiry (AI) process (Rock & Page, 2009):

- **Define phase:** The client and the coach identify the most important topics for the client to explore.

- **Discovery phase:** The client is asked to identify his/her energising and life-giving forces regarding the identified topic.
- **Dream phase:** The client's dream of a better future is explored.
- **Design phase:** By means of generative conversations, scenarios that are based on the dream are constructed and a beginning is made to identify those that capture the passion and commitment of the client.
- **Destiny:** Generative actions are planned during this phase that will leverage the client's energy for implementation.

The demand for coaching is increasing, even as a discipline or profession in its own right. This implies a need for measuring the impact of coaching. Although research regarding the effectiveness of executive coaching is still in an infancy stage, empirical research provides significant support for its effectiveness (Bozer, Sarros & Santora, 2014). These authors refer to a meta-analysis, indicating that executive coaching is positively related to job performance and skills, wellbeing, coping, work and career attitudes, as well as goal-directed self-regulation.

Activity

Reflect on the following: You were contracted by a company to coach one of its managers, assisting him with his interpersonal behaviour. However, after the third session, you realise that the coaching is not really helping, as his problem is probably due to trauma he experienced as a child. How would you deal with the client?

Remember, the same ethical principles apply as with the use of psychometric instruments. Consider the possible consequences for yourself, your client and the organisation in making a decision whether to continue working with this manager.

Career planning and development

Resulting from the talent war, talent management has become a major concern for South African companies. Companies are pressurised by skill shortages, especially on a managerial level, by social demands such as those from government, and also by the changing nature of the workforce, to put in more effort to develop and maintain a sustainable, skilful and knowledgeable workforce. Skilled workers, especially those from minority groups who are in demand, are prepared to leave their jobs for better career opportunities elsewhere. It is argued that, in the contemporary world of work, upward mobility within an organisation is not regarded as the only option for career development anymore; the obtaining of new skill sets in a variety of contexts is also significant (Cummings & Worley, 2015). Career planning and development interventions have therefore become an imperative tool for up-skilling and retaining a workforce that will enhance the competitiveness of organisations and render better services.

Cummings and Worley (2015) differentiate between career planning and career development, viewing career planning as a process whereby individual employees assess themselves and make choices about their own jobs, occupations and organisations through the different life stages of their careers, such as the establishment phase, the advancement stage, the maintenance stage and the withdrawal stage. Career development entails the organisation's interventions to assist individuals in achieving their career objectives. This can, for example, be done by the eight interventions proposed by Cummings and Worley (2015), namely the provision of realistic job previews, the use of assessment centres, the implementation of job rotation, mentoring, performance management, developmental training, work–life balance and phased retirement.

Although there are a number of career-planning interventions that can be implemented to assist employees with making appropriate career choices, they all apply goal setting and achievement as a means for employees to gain control over their careers (Brown, 2014). Brown (2014) presents the following career-planning programme, consisting of five steps, for assisting employees with achieving their career objectives:

Step 1: Each participant compiles a list of career goals, including career, professional, personal and interpersonal goals.

Step 2: The participant and the employee work through the list to identify realistic as well as conflicting goals, and to set priorities.

Step 3: Each participant compiles a second list with all his/her achievements, including peak experiences and satisfactions.

Step 4: The two lists are compared to identify incongruences between them. After pointing out the incongruences to the participant, they together prepare a new list of prioritised goals.

Step 5: Action plans are developed by the participants, indicating how they could reach the goals they have set.

Coetzee and Roythorne-Jacobs (2012) indicate that career development will in future be more tailor-made to suit the political, economic and demographical characteristics of a country. Currently, the high unemployment rate in South Africa leads to the experience of a permanent dislocation from jobs, occupational immobility and diminished feelings of self-worth and personal identity among its citizens. All these issues need to be addressed to provide not only new career possibilities, but also hope for employees that find themselves in rigid, self-defeating patterns.

Interpersonal interventions

It has already been pointed out that the same interventions often address more than one change agenda. Self-development on the individual level, for instance the development of self-awareness and self-insight, also influences interpersonal relations. If employees are aware of their own feelings, they will, for instance, be aware of the impact they have on other people, especially in group format. One of the earliest OD interventions, namely T-groups (training groups) – also called laboratory training or sensitivity training – was developed for this specific reason. Although T-groups are less often used nowadays as a training technique, some of the principles are still used as part of other interventions.

The focus of this section will be on the Johari window and narrative mediation as examples of interpersonal interventions. The Johari window serves as the base for a number of other techniques, while narrative mediation is still not well known in the OD literature.

The Johari window

The Johari window (developed by Joe Luft and Harry Ingram) is a technique for identifying and improving interpersonal communication, based on the interaction of two dimensions, namely self-disclosure and feedback from others. Self-disclosure refers to the extent to which an individual is aware of his/her own behaviour, thoughts and feelings, and openly communicates this to others, while behavioural feedback refers to how the person is experienced by others. On the basis of these two dimensions, a matrix is formed, consisting of four window frames, representing a specific area of knowledge regarding the person's behaviour, thoughts and feelings (Brown, 2014). These four areas — the open window, the blind area, the hidden area and the unknown area — are represented in Figure 10.1 on the next page.

- The **open window** represents behaviour and motivations that are known to the self and others. This area refers to those aspects where a person sees him-/herself in the same way that he/she is seen by others. It is the ideal area where free and open communication enables a productive relationship. The size of this area therefore influences the effectiveness of the relationship.
- The **hidden area**, or mask, represents the information known to the self but withheld or hidden from others. This serves to protect and defend the self in the sense that information regarded as potentially threatening to the relationship is kept private for reasons related to fear, desire or power.

		Known	Unknown
Others	Known	Open window	Blind area
	Unknown	Hidden area	Unknown area

Known   Unknown

Self

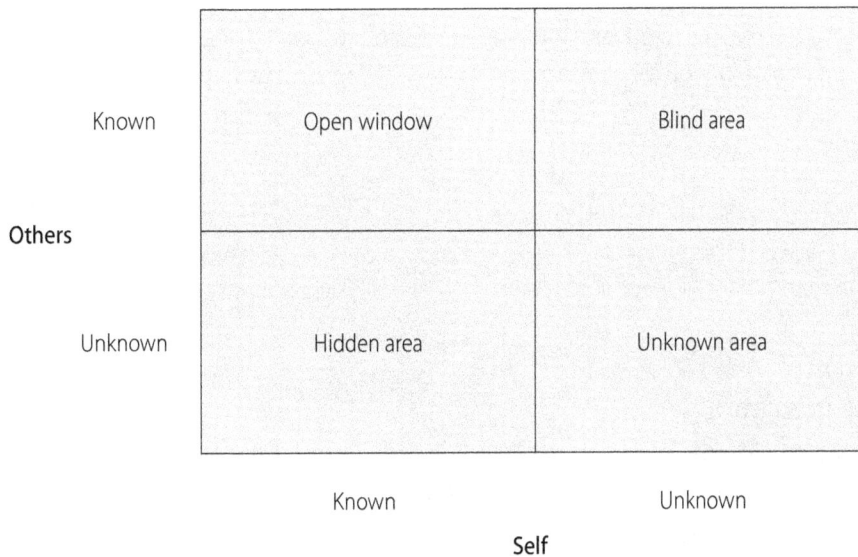

Figure 10.1 The Johari window (adapted from Brown, 2014: 201)

- The **blind area** represents behaviour that is unknown to the self but known to others, for example when a manager is under the impression that she treats her subordinates respectfully but her behaviour illustrates the opposite, for instance by belittling them. This area therefore represents an interpersonal handicap that reduces interpersonal effectiveness.
- The **unknown area** consists of those aspects of behaviour that are related to psychodynamic data, hidden potential, unconscious uniqueness and the database for creativity. This information is not known by the self or by others, but becomes known as interpersonal efficiency increases.

The Johari window represents a dynamic process. Through self-disclosure, the horizontal line moves downwards so that the open area is enlarged while the hidden area becomes smaller. This activity can be controlled directly by the person, and it can be used as a mechanism for building a relationship of trust.

By means of behavioural feedback, the vertical line will move to the right, which enlarges the open area at the expense of the blind area. Although this activity requires some initiative from the self, it largely depends on the willingness of others to provide information on their experience. A person therefore has less control over the outcome of behavioural feedback than over the process of self-disclosure. The blind area can become smaller only with the cooperation of others. This means that the size of the open area is a function of self-disclosure and the amount of feedback a person receives from others.

The processes of self-disclosure and behavioural feedback can be practised on an interpersonal as well as on a group level. Most of the methods and techniques for self-development are, however, based on these principles.

Activity

When comparing the four areas of the Johari window, in which of the four panes would you say it is the most difficult to communicate? Think of an experience when you have found yourself in such a pane. How did it influence your communication and/or relationship with the other party?

Narrative mediation

Narrative mediation is a third-party intervention, in the form of interpersonal conflict mediation, that was developed by Gerald Monk and John Winslade (2013) and is principally based on a social constructionist view (as discussed in Chapter 9), feminist politics, post-structuralism and narrative therapy. The following discussion is based on the work of Monk and Winslade (2013).

From a social constructionist perspective, the contextual nature of reality, and therefore human beings, is emphasised. We create social realities with different cultural contexts but we also form part of these realities that we have created. Dominant cultural narratives shape people's attitudes, beliefs and even identities. Understanding behaviour therefore implies an understanding of the cultural context of the person in relation to the cultural context of other people. People's responses in conflict situations are thus formed out of the forces at play between these different cultural contexts.

Being part of a social reality, people have privileged access to their own reality and its assumptions, and are able to understand their own cultural context in ways that others outside their culturally developed world cannot (Hosking & Morley, 2004). When differences are experienced, the different parties evaluate the facts of the other party and base their own arguments on the basis of the logical, coherent frameworks that they have developed for themselves, without acknowledging that the perspective or argument of the opposing party is in a similar manner based on what is coherent and logical for them, based on their cultural context.

Furthermore, the most powerful party may impose itself on the party with less power, thereby attempting to silence or influence the dominated party. This implies the establishment and maintenance of power structures between different socially constructed realities. In this sense it can also be argued that conflict per se is socially constructed, involving power relations. The focus of the intervention is on the abilities of the parties to differentiate themselves from the dominant cultural assumptions and to generate possibilities for future cooperation by gaining an understanding of the opposing party's cultural context or frame of reference.

The goals of narrative mediation are threefold, namely to create conditions for new narratives of cooperation in the face of conflict, to build a narrative of relationship that is incompatible with the current dominant conflict narrative, and to open a space for people to negotiate new understandings (Monk & Winslade, 2013).

The principles underlying narrative mediation can be summarised as follows (Monk & Winslade, 2013):

- Conflict is viewed as a product of internalised cultural forces, and people's responses in conflict situations are thus formed out of these forces.
- Conflict always involves a power relation.
- Narrative mediation is built on the assumption that the **problem** is the problem and not the **person**.
- The focus of narrative mediation is on building relational narratives of increased understanding, respect and cooperation.
- The goal is not to reach agreement but to help conflicting parties to determine a way forward.
- Complexity is welcomed, as it provides alternative pathways of response.
- As impartiality is not realistic, the mediator should practise in a reflexive manner, taking accountability for his/her biases.
- It is preferable for the mediator to meet conflicting parties separately before a joint mediation meeting.

Stages of narrative mediation

Stage 1: Separate meetings

Attempts are always made to meet separately with the parties in conflict. The purpose of these sessions is to build mutual trust and an understanding of the specific issues that are experienced by the parties. The separate meetings also provide the mediator with an opportunity to obtain information on the emotional effects of the issue. Furthermore, these meetings allow the parties to express feelings and to offer sensitive information that they would not be willing to share in front of the other party for fear of retaliation or escalation of the conflict.

In the separate meetings, an externalising and deconstructing conversation is conducted to name the issues and to define their effects. The mediator explores the emotional landscape and the concerns underlying these issues.

Toward the end of the separate meetings, the mediator would establish if the parties want to meet, and if so, what they would like to address and to achieve in these sessions. These meetings help the parties to connect with and clarify their desired outcomes, to determine if their expectations are realistic, to examine the cultural narratives that might impact on the outcomes, and to set the rules of conduct for the joint sessions, especially if the meetings get threatened by problem-saturated narratives (Monk & Winslade, 2013).

Stage 2: Joint meetings

If agreement was reached by the parties during the separate meetings, these meetings are then followed by meetings involving both parties. In the joint sessions, the ultimate goal is to generate the best possible mutual understandings of the narratives that brought about the conflict, and shared ideas about how to move forward (Monk & Winslade, 2013). In the first of the joint meetings, the facilitator's role is clarified as being non-judgemental and non-evaluative about who is right and who is wrong.

Only after a safe space for conversation, characterised by respect, is created, the mediator commences with exploring specific content items. This is done by using tools that are well known in narrative therapy, such as reframing, externalising and mapping the effects of a conflict, building narratives of cooperation, and generating understanding as a basis for cooperating in future.

The two interpersonal interventions that were discussed can be regarded as examples of quite a number of interventions in the OD literature. In most instances, these interventions incorporate aspects of the Johari window, such as self-disclosure and feedback, as a requirement for open and honest communication. Although narrative mediation is still relatively new in the OD field, the overall evaluation of postmodern approaches per se is gaining momentum, probably because results are often achieved in a relatively short time frame (Corey, 2009).

Teambuilding interventions

When using the word 'teambuilding', the immediate reaction of management is that of scepticism, even if this could be of crucial value to the organisation. Only those not footing the bill might at times be excited. The reason for this is often the association of teambuilding with fun, outdoor activities such as game drives, or even having a couple of drinks together, costing the company a lot of money without a return on investment.

However, teambuilding as defined in the literature and practised by competent consultants has a different connotation. Although the terms 'teambuilding' and 'team development' are used interchangeably in the literature, Anderson (2015) points out that team development programmes involve working with teams to help them through the different stages of group processes, namely forming, storming, norming, performing and adjourning. Opportunities are thus offered to develop in a more healthy way when teams are not dysfunctional or incompetent. In contrast, teambuilding can be seen as a more reactive intervention, designed to address problems that teams are currently experiencing. Teambuilding can therefore be defined as 'the activity of attempting to improve a work group's effectiveness at doing its work, maintaining the relationships of its members and the team's contributions to the wider organizational system' (Coghlan, 1994: 21).

Three of the four examples of teambuilding interventions discussed in this chapter, with the exception of AI, have a strong diagnostic orientation. Furthermore, both process consultation and the systems-psychodynamic group diagnostic interventions value the involvement of the participants in the diagnostic process, with the latter including unconscious group dynamics as a major dimension of the diagnosis. Although AI also focuses on the involvement of the participants, this intervention focuses on the building and expansion of the collective strengths of the system. Regarding the formal teambuilding intervention, the consultant, by using different techniques, plays a more active role and focuses on the task of the group. The different interventions will now be discussed in more detail.

Process consultation

Teambuilding and process consultation are often regarded as synonymous, as most teambuilding interventions include aspects of process consultation. Process consultation is based on a humanistic approach, mainly making use of non-directive client-centred techniques for interventions, as discussed in Chapter 9. Edgar Schein (1988: 11), who can be regarded as the originator of process consultation, defines it as 'a set of activities on the part of the consultant that help the client to perceive, understand, and act upon the process events that occur in the client's environment in order to improve the environment as defined by the client'. Furthermore, instead of focusing on the group task, process consultation focuses on the process, or how the group is functioning in executing its task. The difference between content and process interventions was discussed in Chapter 5.

The purpose of process interventions is to facilitate a process whereby the group learns to diagnose and solve their own problems regarding their functioning as a group. The consultant refrains from telling the group how to solve its problems; rather, he/she makes use of the different micro-skills as discussed in Chapter 5 as different techniques for intervening.

Process interventions focus on the following critical areas of effective functioning, as presented by Brown (2014):

- **Communication processes:** The consultant will observe, analyse and provide feedback to the group to better understand their own communication processes on aspects such as who talks the most, who are the best listeners, and who interrupts whom.
- **Taking up roles:** This refers to an awareness of the different roles that members prefer to take up. These roles can be categorised as group task roles (where participants focus on the task of the group), group building and maintenance roles (where participants focus on the relationships) and self-serving roles (where participants focus on their own interests).
- **Decision making and problem solving:** The focus is on the manner in which the group is making decisions and solving problems. For instance, does the group make use of a formal problem-solving process and do the members strive to reach consensus?
- **Group norms and growth:** The group is helped to understand its norms and to determine if they are dysfunctional regarding aspects such as allowing certain behaviour to occur, and the possible sanctions that are applied if behaviour is not acceptable.
- **Leadership and authority:** The group is helped to understand the impact of leadership styles and authority issues on its functioning, for instance which members are authorised as informal leaders and what impact they have on the functioning of the group.

Formal teambuilding

Some consultants prefer to use a well-known teambuilding intervention that is based on a thorough diagnosis of the functioning of a team in executing its task (Plovnick, Fry & Burke, 1982). This type of intervention usually follows a similar process as the OD process discussed in Chapter 7, but with the focus on the team.

The process starts with a diagnosis. The consultant will typically interview the individual team members on issues, analyse the data and provide feedback to the team. The feedback can be provided to a joint teambuilding meeting where individual members are given the opportunity to make contributions. Subgroups and pairs can also be used to discuss the data regarding the issues in detail and to exchange ideas. According to Beer (1980), the illumination of data about the dissatisfaction of the functioning of the group and its involvement in the process often leads to solutions that are acceptable to the members.

After feedback is provided, the consultant and the team jointly decide on an action plan. The interventions are implemented to address the specific issues that were identified during the diagnosis, with follow-up and evaluation.

The rationale for this approach is that consultants are often approached to help with addressing interpersonal problems. Those are the observable behaviours. However, by doing a diagnosis of the team's functioning, it is often found that interpersonal problems are only symptoms of issues that are task related. Bad feelings and conflict among team members often disappear when the root cause of the problem is successfully addressed (see Figure 10.2). French and Bell (1999) indicate that 'when a team engage in problem-solving activities directed toward task accomplishment, the team members build something together. It appears that the act of *building something together* builds a sense of camaraderie, cohesion, and *esprit de corps*'.

A typical model that is used as a diagnostic framework consists of the following functions that are identified as crucial for effective teamwork:

- **Goals** refer to the core mission, priorities and outcomes of the team.
- **Roles** refer to who is expected to do what.
- **Procedures** refer to the way the work is organised.
- **Interpersonal relationships** refer to how people feel about each other.

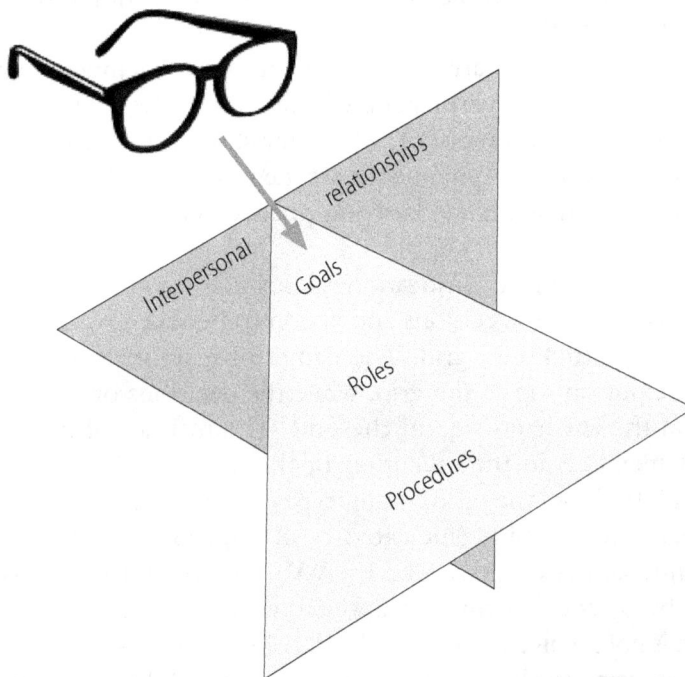

Figure 10.2 The inverted triangle: interpersonal problems (observed first) will become less as the task proceeds (Author)

The dimensions of the model will be applied in the same sequence, starting with clarification of the goals, followed by role clarification, then work procedures, and lastly interpersonal relationships.

There are at least three well-known techniques available to clarify and to adjust the roles of the different team members, namely role profiling, role negotiation and responsibility charting. The underlying assumption is that the behaviour of the team member is not only influenced by interpersonal relations but also by the individual's view of the other members' expectations. The techniques normally entail a group discussion or negotiations with the aim of adapting the roles to satisfy the needs of the group and its individual members (Geldenhuys, 2008).

With role profiling, every team member shares his/her perceptions of his/her own role with the rest of the team. The team members then individually share their expectations of the other members with the rest of the group. After discussion and review of all the different roles as the next step, the roles are offered for approval by the group. The analysis includes clarifying the rationale for the existence of each role, each role's place in the team and the achievement of the group's objectives, and the specific duties related to the role (French & Bell, 1999).

With role negotiation (Harrison, 1982), the team members negotiate each other's behaviour. Each participant will make a request of the others, detailing what they should do more of, what they should do less of and what they should keep on doing. Agreements are negotiated and contracted in writing. Role negotiation assists in clarifying goals without working through difficult interpersonal issues.

A third technique for role clarification is known as responsibility charting (Beckhard & Harris, 1977). Decisions and action to be taken by the different team members are plotted on a grid. The names of team members involved in the process are put on top of the grid, while the decisions or actions to be taken are put on the left-hand side of the grid. The manner of involvement of the different members in the execution of the different decisions is then discussed and plotted on the grid. Four types of involvement have been identified, namely responsibility (indicated by R), approval need or right to veto (the accountable person, indicated by A-V), support for the decision or task (indicated by S) and information about the decision or task (indicated by I). If a person is not involved in a particular decision, a dash (–) is allocated. An example of a responsibility chart is presented in Figure 10.3 on the next page.

Actions/ decisions	Tshepo (fin)	Linda (admin sup)	John (supervisor)	Betty (facilitator)
1. Prepare training material	–	S	A-V	R
2. Determine cost	R	–	A-V	I
3. Arrange all logistics	S	A-V, R	I	S
4. Conduct workshop	I	S	I	A-V, R

Figure 10.3 Responsibility chart (Author)

Systems-psychodynamic group diagnostic intervention

The systems-psychodynamic approach to interventions was discussed in Chapter 9. Systems-psychodynamic interventions are aimed at the collective behaviour within and between groups, organisations and communities, with the emphasis on group dynamics. Group dynamics refers to the unconscious functioning of groups or basic assumptions of group behaviour as identified by Bion (1961; 1982) and extended by Lawrence, Bain and Gould (1996), namely dependency, fight/flight, paring, oneness and me-ness.

The purpose of these interventions is to provide opportunities to change the key relationships among the group members. The assumption is that this can be accomplished by the group members gaining a unique insight into the dynamics that influence the group's functioning and the individual members' roles in these dynamics. In general terms, an awareness of these dynamics allows people to develop more maturity in understanding and managing the boundary between their inner worlds and the realities of their external worlds—in other words, maturity to authorise themselves in their roles and to become less captive to group dynamics (Miller, 1989).

Systems-psychodynamic interventions are based on experiential learning. The role of consultants during the intervention is to provide a safe environment for learning. They observe the behaviour of the group as it happens in the here-and-now and formulate working hypotheses for the group to work with, to accept or to reject. They work with the group to identify and examine the unconscious dynamics of the group itself by working through the dynamics. However, consultants will draw attention to the behaviour of the group-as-a-whole, and point out how it uses its members to express its own emotions, and how it exploits some members so that others can absolve themselves from responsibility (Rice, 1965). This type of consultation is also called working with the 'gut of organisations' (Long & Newton, 1997), 'the organisation in the mind' (Clarkson, 1997), 'struggling with the demon' (Kets de Vries, 2004) and 'working below the surface' (Huffington et al, 2004).

The systems-psychodynamic group diagnostic intervention has the following advantages (Geldenhuys, 2012):

- The participants' involvement allows them to participate in an experiential manner in the diagnostic process and to own problems and solutions.
- Growth and change occur during the intervention because participants experience and learn about the dynamics influencing their behaviour.
- Diagnosis and intervening happens simultaneously as part of the same process, and this makes it possible to reduce the unfulfilled expectations that participants often experience after diagnosis.

Appreciative inquiry

Instead of working with the influence of the group's unconscious dynamics on behaviour, AI, with its focus on what works, started as a revolutionary approach to OD in the 1980s. It is one of the more recent approaches that is primarily based on a social constructionism approach to interventions (see Chapter 9) and has now become a widely recognised and accepted approach to teambuilding. Together with positive psychology and strengths-based management, AI focuses on positive institutions, elevating wellbeing and human strengths (Stratton-Berkessel, 2010).

AI is defined as 'the cooperative co-evolutionary search for the best in people, their organisations, and the world around them. It involves the discovery of what gives "life" to a living system when it is most effective, alive and constructively capable in economic, ecological, and human terms' (Cooperrider, Whitney & Stavros, 2008: 3). 'Appreciate' refers to appreciating the best in people or the world around us, and also to increase in value, whilst 'inquire' refers to the act of exploration and discovery, asking questions and being open to new possibilities (Cooperrider & Whitney, 2005).

AI is based on a number of principles, of which the following five are identified by Stratton-Berkessel (2010):

1. **The constructionist principle:** Words create worlds. Congruent with social constructionism, the emphasis is placed on the use of language and the role of collaboration. Through our conversations we create realities, and our realities shape us. Through positive conversations, we sow the seed for change for the good and for positive actions.

2. **The simultaneity principle:** The very first question we ask starts the change. The questions we ask and the way we ask them already determine what we will find. AI therefore involves the art of crafting questions that are uplifting and inspiring, and elicit future possibilities.

3. **The poetic principle:** What we focus on grows. Congruent with the broaden-and-build theory of positive emotions in the positive psychology movement, a 'broadening' effect of opening up cognitively, emotionally and physiologically is experienced when positive emotions are aroused. Focus on positivity also accumulates over time. With AI, the focus is thus on our generative capacity, those life-giving forces that we want more of.

4. **The anticipatory principle:** Image inspires action. The images we hold of ourselves, others and our future play out in our daily behaviour. If we hold an image of an abundant world, our behaviour will be very different from that if we hold an image of scarcity and deprivation.

5. **The positive principle:** Positive affect leads to positive action. Positive emotions and close connections correlate with better health, resiliency and optimal functioning. The more positive our affect, the more capable we are to deal with the unknown and to accept change.

A typical AI process starts with an affirmative topic choice; this is the most strategic aspect of any AI process (Cooperrider & Whitney, 2005). The topic serves as an agenda for learning, sharing and action; sets the table for a strategic course of action; and determines the '4D phases' of the AI process.

The process then follows the following phases, also known as the 4D cycle (Cooperrider & Whitney, 2005; Stratton-Berkessel, 2010):

Phase 1: Discovery. This refers to identifying the best of what is–what gives life to the human system when it is functioning at its best. This is done by participants interviewing each other, using an interview protocol. Participants will share highpoint experiences and success stories that will identify the system's positive core.

Phase 2: Dream. The purpose of the dream phase is to co-create a desired future based on the past successes discovered and the future possibilities envisioned. Dream statements are crafted that serve as the foundation for the positive change agenda.

Phase 3: Design. During this phase, possibility propositions of the ideal organisation are created. Design elements, including the ideal structure, policies, processes, roles, technologies, leadership, relationships, brand and reputation, are chosen to assist in realising the identified dream.

Phase 4: Destiny. This entails enabling the system to build hope and sustain momentum for ongoing positive change and high performance.

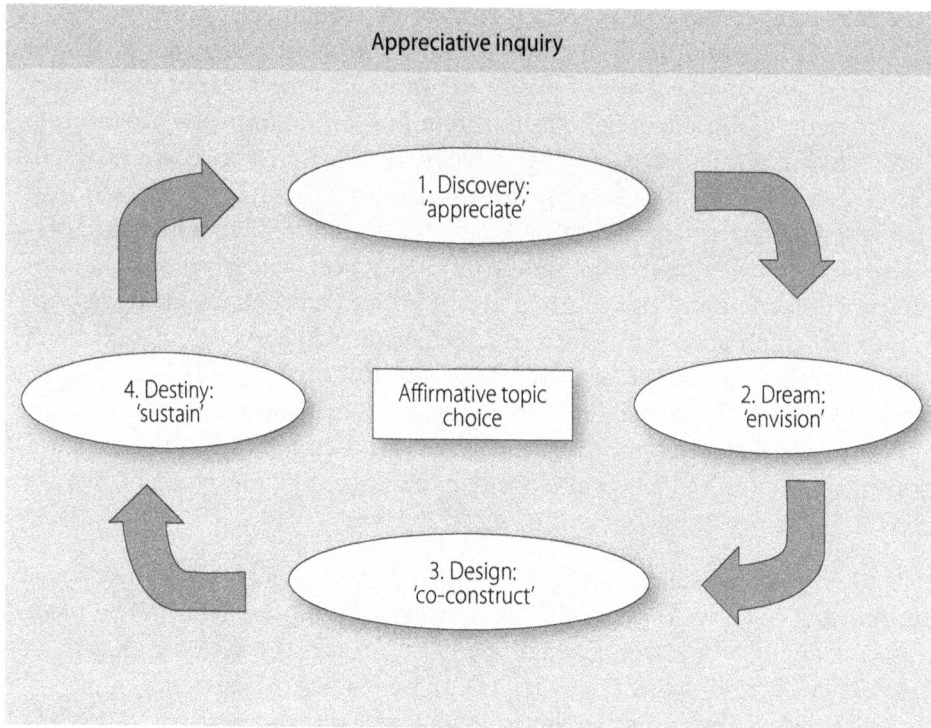

Figure 10.4 The appreciative inquiry process (adapted from Cooperrider & Whitney, 2005: 16)

Following a typical AI process as discussed above, AI can be applied for teambuilding with existing teams, and also for the establishment of new teams (Bushe, 1998). For existing teams, questions will be designed and included in the interview protocol around typical issues that are relevant for the particular team, such as leadership, conflict, decision making or relationship issues that will be framed in a positive manner.

Regarding newly formed teams, AI can be used to establish the team's identity by asking questions referring to the members' previous experiences of forming part of a high-performing team, the values and strengths they bring to the new team and their dreams and hopes for the team's future.

An assumption regarding the use of AI for new teams is that the process will help the team to work through the group processes without having to experience conflict during a storming phase, which is characteristic of traditional group processes (Bushe, 1998).

In concluding this section on teambuilding, it is clear that all interventions do have a specific place in a specific context, addressing a specific need. It should be emphasised, though, that the competency of the consultant is in most instances more important than the choice of a specific intervention.

Activity

Teambuilding is often seen as just having fun! In comparing the different approaches to teambuilding, you have realised that there is much more to teambuilding than this. Which of the different interventions would, according to you, elicit the most resistance to change when being implemented?

Do you think that there is a relationship between the depth of an intervention, as discussed in Chapter 9, and resistance to change during a teambuilding intervention? Could you relate your answer to the depth of an intervention as discussed in Chapter 9?

Conclusion

This chapter was the first of two specifically dealing with the action thrust, or heart, of OD, namely interventions. By studying this chapter, you have firstly learnt about interventions related to the individual as a building block of organisations. This included using the MBTI and assessment centres for diagnosing individual behaviour, executive coaching, and career planning and development. Although these interventions are aimed at the individual, they also impact on interpersonal behaviour. Two examples of interpersonal-level interventions were also discussed, namely the Johari window – which can contribute to better interpersonal communication – and narrative mediation, which was specifically developed to address interpersonal conflict by a third party. Following on interpersonal interventions, you were exposed to some of the different types of teambuilding interventions, namely process consultation, teambuilding and a systems-psychodynamic group diagnostic intervention. The chapter concluded with a discussion on the use of AI as an intervention for teambuilding with existing teams, and also for the establishment of new ones.

Up to now, you have learnt about individual, interpersonal and teambuilding interventions. In the next chapter you will be exposed to large-group and organisation-wide interventions.

Reflection questions

1. Provide a critical discussion on the use of the MBTI and assessment centres for diagnosing individual behaviour.
2. Compare career planning and career development.
3. Explain the executive coaching process from two different approaches.
4. Discuss narrative mediation as an example of an interpersonal intervention.
5. Compare process consultation, teambuilding and a systems-psychodynamic group diagnostic intervention.

Multiple-choice questions

1. Which of the following statements regarding the use of diagnostic tools is not correct?
   a. The use of these instruments poses a real threat to participants.
   b. They can foster a dependency on the test administrator.
   c. They can assist in exploring previously unknown areas.
   d. They should not be used to label people.
   e. They can allow for understanding others.

2. Executive coaching refers to:
   a. analysing problems that are based on psychological issues of the past
   b. a form of counselling
   c. working with a role model
   d. working with a facilitator to achieve a mutually identified set of goals to improve the client's professional performance
   e. therapy for executives

3. Which of the following statements regarding career planning and development is not correct?
   a. Upward mobility in organisations is not regarded as important.
   b. Career planning is a process whereby individual employees assess themselves and make choices about their jobs, occupations and organisations through the different life stages of their careers.
   c. Career development entails the organisation's interventions to assist individuals in achieving their career objectives.
   d. All career-planning interventions apply goal setting and achievement as a means to gain control over people's careers.
   e. Career development will in future be more tailor-made to suit the political characteristics of a country.

4. Interpersonal interventions:
   a. often address a number of change agendas
   b. include examples such as T-groups and the Johari window
   c. are also known as third-party interventions
   d. can be based on different approaches to interventions
   e. All of the above

5. Which of the following statements is/are not correct?
   a. Formal teambuilding starts with a diagnosis.
   b. Responsibility charting is a technique that is used to clarify roles.
   c. The role of consultants during a systems-psychodynamic group diagnostic intervention is to change the way in which group members relate to each other.
   d. AI is a widely recognised approach to teambuilding.
   e. All of the above

Read the case study and answer the questions that follow.

Case study

Mr Robinson, the MD of a small manufacturing company, called you after he was referred to you by a friend to assist him with conflict management. During your first meeting, Robinson provided you with the following information about the company.

He started the company as a family business about 10 years previously, but the business grew so fast that he had to appoint five more employees, including a manager for the paint shop, adding up to a total of 20 employees. Since the appointment of the manager, the morale of the employees has changed for the worse. There was major conflict between the manager and one of Robinson's friends who started the business with him. Robinson feels as if everyone is pulling in opposite directions, accusing each other of not doing what they are supposed to do. The manager was also accused of wasting paint, and he in turn blamed Robinson for interfering with his work. This conflict impacted negatively on the rest of the employees, especially those working in the paint shop. Although Robinson, with his training as an engineer, has excellent technical skills, he has not attended any managerial training and hence could not deal with the issue.

After interviews with the manager, Robinson's friend and two other supervisors, you had a feedback and joint action planning (JAP) sessions with Robinson on the way forward.

1. If you decide on teambuilding, which approach would you follow? How would you explain the approach and the reason for your proposal to Robinson?
2. Provide a critical view on the use of an interpersonal intervention.
3. Propose a recommendation for Robinson on enhancing leadership skills in the company.

References

Anderson, DL. 2015. *Organization development: the process of leading organizational change.* 3rd ed. Thousand Oaks, CA: SAGE.

Beckhard, R & Harris, R. 1977. *Organizational transitions: managing complex change.* Reading, MA: Addison-Wesley.

Beer, M. 1980. *Organizational change and development: a system view.* Santa Monica, CA: Goodyear.

Bion, WR. 1961. *Experiences in groups.* London: Tavistock Publications. https://doi.org/10.4324/9780203359075.

Bion, WR. 1982. 'Group dynamics: a review', in *Psychoanalytic group dynamics*, edited by S Scheidlinger. New York: International Universities Press: 77–107.

Bozer, G, Sarros, C & Santora, JC. 2014. 'Academic background and credibility in executive coaching effectiveness'. *Personnel Review* 43(6): 881–897. https://doi.org/10.1108/PR-10-2013-0171.

Brown, D. 2014. *Experiential approach to organization development.* 8th ed. Harlow, Pearson.

Bushe, GR. 1998. 'Appreciative inquiry in teams'. *The Organization Development Journal* 16(3): 41–50.

Clarkson, P. 1997. 'Consulting in rapidly changing conditions of uncertainty', in *Developing organisational consultancy*, edited by JE Neumann, K Kellner & A Dawson. London: Routledge: 159–179.

Coetzee, M & Roythorne-Jacobs, H. 2012. *Career counselling and guidance in the workplace.* 2nd ed. Cape Town: Juta.

Coghlan, D. 1994. 'Managing organizational change through teams and groups'. *Leadership & Organization Development Journal* 15(2): 18–23.

Cooperrider, DL & Whitney, D. 2005. *Appreciative inquiry: a positive revolution in change.* San Francisco, CA: Berrett-Koehler.

Cooperrider, DL, Whitney, D & Stavros, JM. 2008. *Appreciative inquiry handbook.* 2nd ed. Bedford Heights, OH: Lakeshore.

Corey, G. 2009. *The art of integrative counselling.* 2nd ed. Belmont, CA: Thomson.

Cummings, T & Worley, CG. 2015. *Organization development and change.* 10th ed. Mason, OH: South-Western Cengage Learning.

French, WL & Bell, CH. 1999. *Organization development: behavioral science interventions for organization improvement.* 5th ed. Englewood Cliffs, NJ: Prentice Hall.

Geldenhuys, D. 2008. 'Small-group interventions', in *Development: theory and practice*, edited by CL van Tonder & G Roodt. Pretoria: Van Schaik.

Geldenhuys, D. 2012. 'Group-as-a-whole as a context for studying individual behaviour: a group diagnostic intervention'. *SA Journal of Industrial Psychology/SA Tydskrif vir Bedryfsielkunde* 38(2), Art #1011, 12 pages. https://doi.org/10.4102/sajip.v38i2.1011.

Harrison, R. 1982. 'Role negotiation: a tough-minded approach to team development', in *Organization development: exercises, cases and readings*, edited by MS Plovnick, RE Fry & WW Burke. Boston, MA: Little, Brown & Company: 343–351.

Hosking, D & Morley, IE. 2004. 'Social constructionism in community and applied social psychology'. *Journal of Community and Applied Social Psychology* 14(5): 318–331. https://doi.org/10.1002/casp.801.

Huffington, C, Armstrong, D, Halton, W, Hoyle, L & Pooley, J. 2004. *Working below the surface: the emotional life of contemporary organizations*. London: Karnac Books.

Kets de Vries, MFR. 2004. *Struggling with the demon: perspectives on individual and organizational irrationality*. Madison, CT: Psychosocial Press.

Kilburg, RR. 2000. *Executive coaching: developing managerial wisdom in a world of chaos*. Washington, DC: American Psychological Association.

Lawrence, WG, Bain, A & Gould, L. 1996. 'The fifth basic assumption'. *Free Associations* 6/1(37): 28–55.

Lehman, MS, Hudson, JR Jr, Appley, GW, Sheehan, EJ Jr & Slevin, DP. 2011. 'Modified assessment center approach facilitates organizational change'. *Journal of Management Development* 30(9): 893–913.

Long, S & Newton, J. 1997. 'Educating the gut: socio-emotional aspects of the learning organization'. *Journal of Management Development* 16(4): 284–301.

Miller, EJ. 1989. *The Leicester model: experiential study of group and organizational processes*. Occasional paper no 10. London: Tavistock Institute of Human Relations.

Monk, G & Winslade, J. 2013. *When stories clash: addressing conflict with narrative mediation*. Chagrin Falls, OH: Taos.

Myers, IB, McCaulley, MH, Quenk, NL & Hammer, AL. 1998. *MBTI manual (a guide to the development and use of the Myers Briggs type indicator)*. 3rd ed. Palo Alto, CA: Consulting Psychologists Press.

Orem, SL, Binkert, J & Clancy, L. 2007. *Appreciative coaching: a positive process for change*. San Francisco, CA: Jossey-Bass.

Plovnick, MS, Fry, RE & Burke, WW (eds). 1982. *Organization development: exercises, cases and readings*. Boston, MA: Little, Brown & Company.

Rice, AK. 1965. *Learning for leadership*. London: Tavistock.

Rock, D & Page, LJ. 2009. *Coaching with the brain in mind: foundations for practice*. Hoboken, NJ: Wiley & Sons.

Schein, E. 1988. *Process consultation: its role in organization development* (vol 1). Reading, MA: Addison-Wesley.

Stout-Rostron, S. 2012. *Business coaching: wisdom and practice*. Randburg: Knowres.

Stratton-Berkessel, R. 2010. *Appreciative inquiry for collaborative solutions*. San Francisco, CA: Pfeiffer.

Chapter 11

Organisation–wide/large-scale intervention

Elsabé Keyser

Learning outcomes

After reading this chapter, you should be able to:

- discuss the concept and the effect of large-scale organisational intervention in general
- explain in detail the classification of large-scale organisational intervention
- explain the role of culture in organisational intervention
- know what tools and techniques of intervention will provide the best practices to fit South African organisations' outcomes requirements
- know what knowledge economy is and how it links to organisational intervention
- know who is involved in large-scale group interventions within an organisation.

Introduction

Large-group intervention (LGI) as a system-wide approach is one of the fastest-growing areas in organisation development (OD) and has received considerable attention in different countries such as South Africa, India, Pakistan, China, Australia, England and Mexico. From the 1960s, academics and researchers have worked on models for OD. Since the publication of Friedlander and Brown's 'Organization development' in 1974, facilitators and practitioners in this field have constantly attempted to classify intervention work into three intervention categories, namely individual, group or the entire organisation (French & Bell, 1999).

Organisations today are under a lot of pressure to reduce costs, speed up cycle times of products, increase productivity, increase participation, improve morale and clarify directions (Covin, 1992). Organisations make use of large-scale intervention (LSI) when the task is urgent and complex, and when multiple people are required to accomplish it (Bunker & Alban, 1992).

LSIs are characterised by the following (Bunker & Alban, 1992: 581):

- A wide variety of participants are involved in the process. LSIs include a greater variety of stakeholders than in the early 1990s. Today, LSIs involve sizeable groups, with hundreds or even thousands of participants.
- Greater timelines for the intervention exist, as the process often involves multiple activities over a longer period.
- There is a change in the consultant's role. The OD consultant or practitioner's role is 'that of a community organizer who structures, and helps focus the issues'.

As seen in the box below, Gallos (2006) mentions that there are multiple problems that OD consultants face with LSI.

The dilemma of LSI for OD consultants

There are multiple reasons why so few OD consultants do OD. For many, it is not having the comprehensive systems view that is necessary. For others, they are caught in a chicken-and-egg dilemma. Because they are not involved in systemwide change, they are not selected to help with the LSIs. Instead, they are only brought in perodically to use some OD techniques or to clean up an implementation mess (Gallos, 2006: 845).

Cummings and Worley (2015) explain that LGIs run with groups of between 50 to more than 2 000 participants, and the process lasts between one and five days. Large-group processes are usually planned and structured, but some are more informal.

This chapter describes LSI by focusing on culture change, knowledge economy, learning organisations, and different methods of use for it.

Culture change

Culture change within organisations is one of the important re-emerging topics within organisations. Today, management looks beyond the traditional sources such as products, technology and markets. Organisations in an ever-changing and demanding environment need to link business strategies with organisational culture to be successful (Jaeger, 1986).

The changing environment in which organisations are involved requires managers to re-evaluate and adapt their internal capacities. Managers can use organisational cultures as a tool to adjust to these new conditions (Anderson & Ovaice, 2006). As explained by Stephen Renecle & Associates (SRA) in South Africa (see the next page), assessment of culture and climate is important in the OD of groups, and this may lead to organisation failure or success.

When an organisation's current culture differs from the current business strategies, it needs culture change intervention. Change interventions fail because managers do not give sufficient attention to leadership or cultural change. In the UK, the culture change failure rate exceeds 80%. Culture failure may seriously damage the organisation and have unintended psychological consequences for manager and employees. A high turnover rate and training and retraining costs are some of the consequences if the cultural change fails within an organisation (Parumasur, 2012).

OD: assessment of organisational culture, climate and dynamics

Stephen Renecle & Associates specialises in the field of organisational diagnostics, whereby the culture, climate and dynamics impacting an organisation are assessed. It is often difficult to distinguish between the concepts of organisational climate and culture; however, SRA has a sound theoretical basis for doing so and this is reflected in the assessment procedures applied. In order to measure these concepts within an organisation, a combination of quantitative measurement through survey methodology and qualitative information-gathering through interviews and focus groups is undertaken. This provides a rich source of data from which SRA may construct a theoretical and visual model of the dynamics at play in the individual organisation.

Organisational culture and climate affect all areas of an organisation's functioning, thus determining change readiness and the capacity to innovate in times of competitive need. Hence, organisational culture and climate impact on any organisational initiative, often determining success or failure.

Accordingly, it is the understanding of the culture and climate dynamics operating within a company that indicates problem areas within the organisation and how these should be addressed to encourage change readiness, optimum effectiveness and competitiveness. The range of constructs measured within organisational culture and climate is extensive and diverse, and SRA consults closely with the client organisation prior to embarking on such an exercise to determine their specific needs.

(Source: SRA, 2015)

Different definitions exist with regard to an organisation's culture. Martins (1989: 15) gives a broad definition of organisational culture:

> *Organisational Culture is an integrated pattern of human behaviour, which is unique to a particular organisation and which originated as a result of [the organisation's] survival process and interaction with its environment. Culture directs the organisation to goal attainment.*

Martins' (1989) theoretical model of organisational culture includes different dimensions, as can be seen in Figure 11.1.

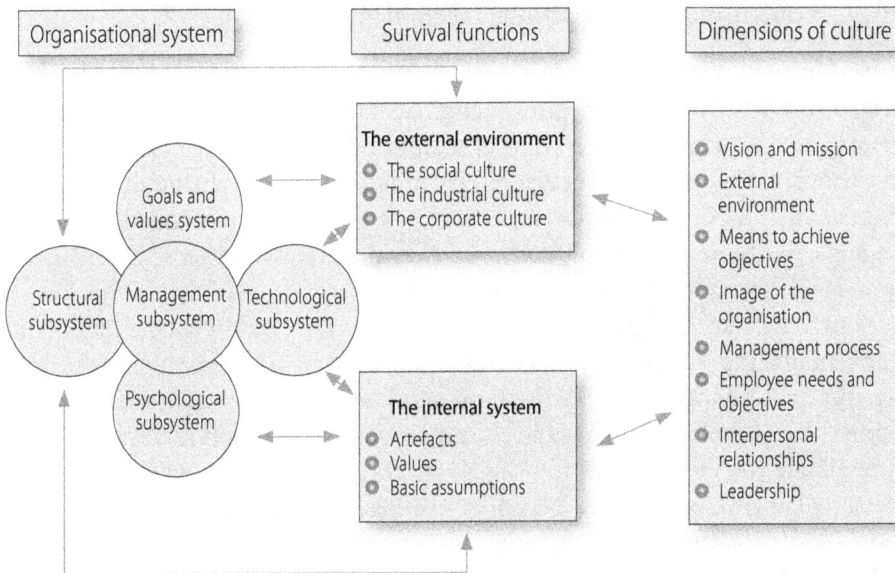

Figure 11.1 Interaction model between organisational subsystems, internal systems and the dimensions of culture (as adapted in 1997 from Martins, 1989)

The model in Figure 11.1 shows that any change in the organisational system, such as the goals and values, and structural, managerial, technological and psychosociological subsystems, directly and indirectly influences the survival functions of the organisation, namely the external (social, industrial and corporate culture) and internal (artefacts, values and basic assumptions) functions, and the dimensions of culture. The organisational system, survival functions and dimensions are interrelated and need to be integrated when dealing with OD intervention. Effective intervention is designed to fit the needs of the organisational system, is based on set goals and outcomes, and transfers competence to manage change to organisation members; thus it depends on the national culture and the stage of economic development of the country. Practitioners see organisations as human social systems, where individuals are actively influenced by organisational culture (Jaeger, 1986).

The national culture of a country influences the management practices of an organisation (Hoppe, 2004) and this, together with economic development, can have a powerful effect on the implementation and design of OD intervention (Jaeger, 1986). The national culture and economic development can determine whether change within an organisation:

- proceeds slowly or quickly
- involves a few or many members
- is directed by hierarchical authority or by consensus
- focuses on business, organisational or human process issues.

Cultures in Africa also have direct roles to plays in providing a people-centred approach. African countries recognise language pluralism and cultural diversity, but Africans believe that globalisation and colonial powers have been subordinating their local culture (Parumasur, 2012). Multicultural team management is a complex problem in Africa, and synergy depends largely on managers' ability and OD consultants to create a management system that integrates differences (Mutabazi & Derr, 2006).

South African companies such as SA Breweries claimed their place in *Fortune* magazine for placing psychometrics on the map in the USA, and flying out consultants to perform these services. These consultants need to recognise the global effects they have on their clients and themselves. National culture affects the implementation of OD intervention and the pace of change processes (Parumasur, 2012). National culture and economic development can reveal four different international settings, as explained by Cummings and Worley (2015):

1. **Low cultural fit, moderate industrialisation:** OD practice embraces industrialising economies with some cultural values that align poorly with traditional OD values. The Middle East, South America and the South Pacific depend highly on their natural resources and have a small manufacturing base. Executive managers see OD as a process that is too soft to meet business needs, and to reach technical rationality and efficiency they equate OD facilitators with human process interventions in the organisation such as training, conflict management and teambuilding. If organisational change is experienced, OD intervention in these countries usually contains settings that:
   - fit local customs
   - address business and economic problems
   - have senior management that supports the implementation
   - are centrally controlled

- take place slowly
- have an information flow through a flat hierarchy
- use a company-wide vote to make strategic decisions
- want to achieve technical rationality
- want to achieve efficiency.

2. **Low cultural fit, high industrialisation:** Planned change in countries such as Central America, Eastern Europe and Eastern Asia includes four types of interventions, namely human process intervention, techno-structural intervention, strategic change interventions and human management intervention. In high-context cultures, such as China, Japan, Korea, Mexico and Venezuela, autocratic and paternalistic decisions are normal practices. The intervention focuses on teamwork, employee involvement and work processes, and does not influence the autocratic and paternalistic decision making in organisations such as Nissan, Toyota, Hyundai and NEC. When OD intervention is taking place, OD practitioners need to understand:

   - the customs and rituals when communicated information
   - the power distance with regard to the hierarchal status (high-level titles) differences, roles and working conditions within the country
   - that the implementation of change in organisations takes place slowly and methodically
   - that the roles and behaviours are specified, as management controls the change process using problem-solving groups
   - that the lower-status groups are not included in diagnostic or implementation activities because inclusion is against cultural norms and the status quo of the country
   - that the OD process is less personal, as people need to act in a way that does not bring disgrace and embarrassment to the group
   - the OD focus on workflow.

3. **High cultural fit, high industrialisation:** This occurs where the culture of industrialised countries, such as Sweden, Norway, Finland and Denmark, fits well with the traditional practices in OD values. Strong economic development and a high standard of living are experienced in these countries. Saab and Volvo in the Scandinavian countries pioneered socio-technical intervention to improve the quality of work and productivity of the organisations. Democratic and highly participative practices between governments, managers, employees and unionists are involved in all the stages of change within the organisation. The OD intervention in the change process:

   - focuses on the needs of all the members in the organisations
   - gives unions the right to participate in technological innovations
   - improves productivity
   - increases the quality of products.

4. **High cultural fit, moderate industrialisation:** Countries such as India and South Africa focus on the use of techno-structural and strategic intervention. OD practice in South Africa was influenced by political and culture change in the country and as a result has forced South African organisations into new processes such as restructuring, organisation re-design and downsizing, to be able to compete in the global market (Denton & Vloeberghs, 2003). In the global world, national boundaries are no longer important (Goodman, 1995). The South African degree of cultural fit (poor versus good) and economic development (industrialising versus industrial) is described as one 'close to good fit, industrial setting' (Cummings & Worley, 2015: 169).

National and economic development plays an important role in the way OD interventions are designed and implemented in a country. Each country has its distinct differences in individual behaviour, values and organisations based on national culture. The most compelling tool for improvement is cultural change. OD interventions play a significant role in dealing with the dramatically changing world. Intervention helps the organisation to develop behaviour, beliefs, values and norms that lead to a culture within the organisation (Cummings & Worley, 2015). This view supports Hofstede's four dimensions to identify the impact of national culture on OD intervention (Fagenson-Eland, Ensher & Burke, 2004).

In 2004, Fagenson-Eland et al compared different OD interventions using Hofstede's (1980; 1998) groundbreaking work on the four dimensions of culture to study practices within seven countries (South Africa, Finland, Ireland, the Netherlands, New Zealand, the UK and the USA):

1. **Power distance** is the extent to which a society accepts that power is distributed unequally in an organisation (Hofstede, 1980). South Africa, as indicated by the study, has the highest degree of power distance. During the last two decades, the political and social environment in South Africa has undergone change because of the dissolution of apartheid. OD practitioners would use intervention to manage resistance to social, political and organisational change, using group problem solving as a technique to resolve issues between relevant parties (Fagenson-Eland et al, 2004). The UK and South Africa experience little difference with regard to power distance. South African managers are influenced strongly by British practices, as the majority of managers and decision makers in organisations were educated under British influence, which has affected OD practices in South Africa (Cummings & Worley, 2015).

2. **Uncertainty avoidance** is the extent to which members of organisations do not tolerate unpredictability and ambiguity (Hofstede, 1980).

Finnish OD practitioners use strategic planning in the process of intervention. By using this strategic planning, OD practitioners achieve certainty and avoid ambiguity in the high-uncertainty-avoidance score as experienced in Finland. OD practitioners in Finland, Ireland and the Netherlands will avoid culture change interventions such as organisational radical structure change and cultural shift. The UK and the USA are culturally diverse, as they have many laws and societal norms that guard against discrimination and they are more willing to follow teambuilding approach sessions more openly (Cummings & Worley, 2015: 169).

3. **Individualism** is the extent to which people believe that they should be primarily responsible for themselves as opposed to the collective (Hofstede, 1980). All seven countries involved in this study experienced relatively high individualism. They promote competitiveness, personal initiative, achievement and individual decision-making processes (Fagenson-Eland et al, 2004; Hofstede, 1996).

4. **Masculinity/femininity** of cultures affects OD practices. Feminine cultures tend to value the social aspect of work and have lower levels of stress and conflict. Masculinity is the extent to which organisational members value assertiveness, material goods, the acquisition of power and other resources. The USA, with high scores in masculinity is a world leader in technological intervention. OD practitioners in South Africa and the UK are more likely to use technology integration than those in Finland and the Netherlands, and they are more likely to use training and development and career development initiatives than practitioners in low-masculine countries such as the Netherlands and Finland.

OD interventions could be influenced by not only the interaction between national and organisational culture but also the dimensions of national culture (Lau & Ngo, 2001), and practitioners need to consider dimensions of national culture when recommending OD interventions for global clients.

Organisations need to adapt their OD intervention practice to fit the values of a particular country, and, as explained by Golembiewski (1993), OD intervention has to deal with the alignment between intervention and cultures. When practitioners deal with OD intervention, they need to be alert and sensitive to different contexts and they need to make situational adjustments to the culture in which they operate.

Taras, Steel and Kirkman (2011: 192) explain:

> *Like the weather, culture is harder to predict precisely at the local level and easier at the aggregate. For example, you might not know whether it will rain next month on your doorstep, but you can tell what months are rainy and whether there is more precipitation on the coast or on the plains.*

Activity

It is important that OD practitioners in Africa take culture into consideration when they want to apply Western ideas of changes, as these ideas generally do not succeed in Africa. Sulamoyo (2010) explains it thus: 'Ubuntu represents a powerful philosophy and cultural approach whereby Africans view their existence through others in society'.

This explains why practitioners in OD might benefit from understanding the African cultural concept of Ubuntu and can use it as an advantage in South Africa.

The knowledge economy

Changes in the nature of organisations, the shift to a knowledge economy and the new information age brought about new resources that organisations use in business approaches (Jelenic, 2011). OD intervention effectiveness depends on organisations' approaches to developing the core skills or abilities of people. Organisations need engaged and up-skilled employees. Building a knowledge economy is a difficult and complex task (Brinkley et al, 2010). Although 'knowledge economy' is a term widely used around the world, limited definitions exist. The concept is defined by the UK Economic and Social Research Council (ESRC) (2005) as follows:

> [E]conomic success is increasingly based on the effective utilisation of intangible assets such as knowledge, skills, and innovative potential as the key resource for competitive advantage. The term 'knowledge economy' is used to describe the emerging economic structure.

From this definition, it is clear that two important features of the knowledge economy exist (Brinkley et al, 2010):

1. All sectors are affected by a shift towards a knowledge-based economy.
2. The knowledge economy is part of a long-term process, is seen as a transition and is regarded as 'soft discontinuity'.

Knowledge economies face five new science and technology growth areas for the future, namely health, environment, electronic communications, biotechnology and nanotechnology (OECD, 2009). Knowledge economies do not respect national or industry boundaries. Companies within the UK, USA, France and South Africa have invested massively in knowledge-based intangibles (Neely, 2009).

Observers of business trends propose that the knowledge economy of the late 1990s and the beginning of the 2000s has been transformed into the creativity economy (Nussbaum, Berner & Brady, 2005). The BMW group, for example, when developing a new car, forms a project team (engineering, design production, purchasing, marketing and finance) that is relocated to the research innovation centre. The new-venture team is responsible for developing and initiating innovations. These venture teams are also known as skunkworks. Skunkworks is, for instance, where a company like Xerox uses small, informal, highly autonomous and often secret groups that focus on breakthrough ideas for the business.

The rise of the knowledge economy has placed emphasis on learning at organisational level by focusing on managing knowledge, and intellectual and human capital. In today's knowledge economy, organisational learning is important, and usually encompasses diverse ways of perceiving, thinking and behaving in organisations (Argyris & Schön, 1996). OD practitioners recognise the potential of employees who are motivated in an organisation, and this trend has become an increasingly important factor to consider in a knowledge economy, where employees represent talent and human and intellectual capital. The rise of the knowledge economy has placed more emphasis on organisational learning (Garrow, 2009).

OD practitioners in the knowledge economy need to develop processes, reward systems and frameworks that help organisations to sustain and build knowledge, as resources in the knowledge economy are scarce. Knowledge and skills have value in the labour market and help to develop marketable skills. OD practitioners need to incorporate organisational diagnoses and interventions aimed at increasing organisational effectiveness, and to support organisational transformations that require the development of new and enhanced knowledge-based capabilities (Mohrman, 2006).

Today, OD practitioners need to learn to work effectively in a global environment where they are proficient in tying together theory and practice in ways that correlate with competitive advantage and sustainability, and to apply new, more comprehensive OD methodologies in the knowledge economy (Rothwell & Sullivan, 2005).

The learning organisation

For decades, learning has been present within organisations and for employees, but most of the academic attention with regard to learning focuses on it as an adaptive change in behavioural response to a stimulus (Levitt & March, 1988); therefore the concept 'learning organisation' is an extension of organisational learning. Within a learning organisation, knowledge leads to behaviour change, new knowledge generations, growth and competitiveness. Learning includes the behaviour change based on the existing capacity of the organisation (Kondalkar, 2009).

Gravin (1993: 80) defines the learning organisation as 'an organisation skilled at creating, acquiring, and transferring knowledge and modifying its behaviour to reflect new knowledge and insights'.

He further mentions that the learning organisation needs to be skilled at five main activities:

1. **Systematic problem solving:** Business unit teams need to be supplied with tools in four areas—generating ideas and collecting information (brainstorming, interviews and surveys), reaching consensus (rating forms and weighted voting), analysing and reporting data (force field analysis, causes and effect diagrams) and planning action (flow charts).

2. **Experimentation with new approaches:** This involves a scientific method for the systematic testing of and searching for new knowledge. Problem solving and experimentation foster learning by upgrading knowledge.

3. **Learning from experience and history:** This involves the systematic assessment process, where organisations review their successes and failures.

4. **Learning from the experience and best practices of others:** This involves benchmarking practice by uncovering, analysing, adopting and implementing practices, where the organisation investigates and learns from the best industry practice after studying others' practices and performances.

5. **Transferring knowledge quickly and efficiently throughout the organisation:** Knowledge and ideas need to be shared by teaching the behaviour needed. This is done to set the opportunity for activity experimentation of the new ideas.

In the 1970s, learning was introduced in a positive way by Argyris and Schön (1978). For survival, and to succeed and to be leaders and remain so, organisations need to be effective, and this depends on their focus on learning and organisational intervention. Kolb, Rubin and McIntyre (1971) explain that for an organisation to become healthy and effective it needs to be a learning organisation. A learning organisation follows a learning cycle, which is the process whereby an organisation increases its potential, capabilities and capacity. This cycle encompasses:

- **training:** the increasing of capabilities
- **development:** the increase of the overall potential of the organisation.

The capability and capacity of an organisation consist of different levels, from routine and repair capabilities – for problem solving and maintenance, respectively – through anticipatory strategic capacities, to the highest-order capacity of self-renewal.

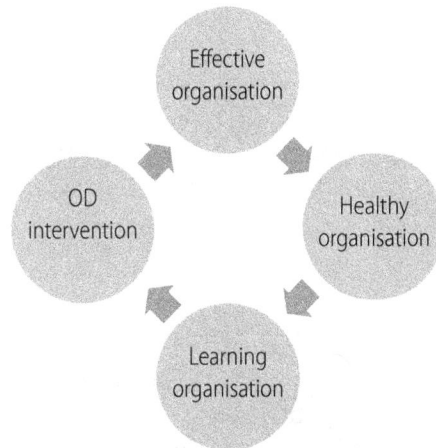

Figure 11.2 Effective organisation and healthy organisation (Author)

Senge (1990) explains that five different disciplines with regard to learning as a cornerstone exist:

1. **System thinking:** to understand through the learning process the integration and interdependence of the world
2. **Personal mastery:** lifelong learning and the personal clarification of visions and challenges that exist in the changing world of work; employees should commit themselves to the process
3. **Mental models:** to develop reflection and inquiry skills and awareness, and to test assumptions and generalisations we hold about the world
4. **Building shared visions:** to share visions of the future with one another and to develop guiding practices to reach this goal
5. **Team learning:** group interaction to maximise the team insights of individuals through dialogue and discussions to prevent patterns that undermine the learning process.

The Tax Shop

The Tax Shop Franchise (Pty) Ltd sold its first franchise licence in 2007. It has since grown to a national footprint of over 80 franchised operations in South Africa, one in the United Arab Emirates and one in Namibia. However, the organisation is not established as a well-known or 'household' brand. Inadequate brand positioning and marketing, insufficient internal branding and unsuccessful building of brand equity amplified by the virtual nature of the franchise system and operations may cause the lack of brand awareness.

The Board of Directors of the Tax Shop had spent several months creating a new long-term plan in order to better the position of the franchised operation for the future. A Real Time Strategic Change event was held with franchisees from across the association; attendance was voluntary.

$\rightarrow$

The Tax Shop identifies that organisations need to have clear structures and purposeful and goal-directed processes in place, and prevent past thinking. They further need to focus on the current and future challenges of the changing environment to market their 'brand'. As an effective, healthy organisation, the Tax Shop wants to set clear structured, purposeful and goal-directed processes, resources and relationships with the environment to market the organisation.

Source: The Tax Shop, 2014

Organisational effectiveness depends on production, quality, efficiency, flexibility, satisfaction, competitiveness, development and survival (Gravin, 1993). As mentioned by Gallos (2006: 24):

The increasing diversity of people, environments, goals, knowledge, and organizational practices and processes reinforces OD's core assumption that there is no one-size-fits-all definition or path to organizational health and effectiveness. Human contribution, creativity, and commitment are essential. But so are the organizational efficiencies and smart strategic choices that ensure organizational survival in an increasingly competitive work world. As OD's founders reminded us more than fifty years ago, individuals and organizations share a common goal, and when both meet their needs, both benefit. OD knows something important about the route to that shared destination. And OD practitioners rise best to the challenge when they expand their horizons and welcome new insights and possibilities, regardless of source, that help all do their work better.

OD, for example, has an increasingly important role to play in a world where individuals have morphed into human capital, where 'lean and mean' too often replaces an emphasis on quality of work life, where an unrelenting focus on bottom-line profits trumps loyalty and learning, and where ethical decision making across sectors seems akin to standing on shifting sands. No other field is better prepared or set to address these kinds of challenges or to understand their long-term impact on organizational innovation, productivity, and survival. To do that well, OD needs to keep its values straight, its resolve strong, and its eye on the prize: improved organizational health and effectiveness.

Large-scale change/interventions

Organisations can manage change effectively through OD intervention, as it plays an important role in dealing with a dramatically changing world. The success of OD intervention in organisations depends on the extent to which the values and assumptions match the level of economic development within a country (Parumasur, 2012). Intervention for organisational change implies interdisciplinary research, and needs to address a broad range of audiences (Mackenzie & Ling, 2009).

Since 1980, different methods and change approaches have been developed, known as participative change. LSI is part of the participative approaches used to involve people in change processes. These organisational changes include OD, restructuring, strategic planning, organisational redesign, visioning, values, global learning and development.

LSI is defined by Van der Zouwen (2011: 48) as a:

trajectory for change or learning in which stakeholders of the whole system (organisation or community and its context) are invited to contribute at all stages of the trajectory. One or more occasions, the entire system is invited into one room to address strategic issues.

The definition clearly indicates that intervention takes place with the whole system in the room, embedded in a change process of the LSI trajectory. The LSI process can be utilised as a catalyst for sustainable change (Van der Zouwen, 2011). Distinctions are made by different authors with regard to change with LSI and non-LSI. Table 11.1 gives an overview of the key distinctions between LSI and traditional top-down change approaches.

Table 11.1 Large-scale intervention and top-down approaches (adapted from Jacobs, 1997; Leith, 2004; Van der Zouwen, 2011)

Aspect	LSI	Top-down approach
View	Change is seen as an integral part of people's work.	Change is viewed as a process of the real work of people.
Focus	The focus is on future possibilities.	The focus is on identifying and solving current problems.

Aspect	LSI	Top-down approach
Vision	The whole system is involved.	Only an elite group of senior managers and experts is involved.
Involvement of stakeholders	The large group forms part of the involvement, and the stakeholder is extensively involved in the process.	Stakeholder involvement is limited. External stakeholders are often ignored.
Leadership and ownership	Whole groups are responsible for the organisation's effort. The need for change is a process of self-management and is self-determined.	Responsibility is on the individual for his/her part in the change process.
Change strategy communication	Two-way communication process takes place through conversations.	One-way communication takes place via messages.
Thinking process	Involves system thinking.	Involves linear thinking.
Change process	Takes place in the whole organisation at the same time.	Takes place in a sequential manner.

The different LSI methods are complex collections of concepts, tools, techniques and procedures. Facilitators that use LSI methods in practice change the method to fit the organisation's needs (Bryson & Anderson, 2000) or combine methods. Van der Zouwen (2011: 50) mentions that the roots of LSI consist of four phases, which are discussed in Table 11.2.

Table 11.2 The roots of large-scale intervention development (Author)

1950–1980 Development of theory and understanding organisational change	1980–1993 Early development of LGI methods	1993–1997 Growing acceptance and adoption of LGI methods	1997 to present Diffusion, experimentation and embedding
Three intellectual traditions are fundamental in this period, namely: ● social psychology (Kurt Lewin)	In the 1980s, consultants focused on process to improvement by using strategies such as survey feedback, teambuilding and other strategies.	The LGI methods have been developed through testing, experimenting and modifying methods working with the whole system.	Large-group methods are part of present OD practice. OD and change consultants also focus on community building and participation.　→

⦿ psychoanalytic theory (Alfred Bion) ⦿ system theory (Ludwig van Bertalanffy).	These types of implementation strategies were too fragmented and slow for the fast-changing world. Transformational change was a new change strategy for changing the whole organisation at once. The whole system involves: ⦿ getting employees, supervisors and managers involved to redesign the organisation (Axelrod, 1992) ⦿ charting the way organisations change (Dannemiller & Jacobs, 1992) ⦿ designing the architecture of participation in large groups to effect organisational change (Gilmore & Barnett, 1992).	Bunker and Alban group LGI methods into three categories: ⦿ **Creating the future together:** Search conference, Future Search, real-time strategic change (RTSC), Institute of Cultural Affairs (ICA) strategic planning ⦿ **Work design:** Conference model, fast-cycle full-participation work design, real-time work design, participative design ⦿ **Whole-system participative work:** Semi-real, work-out, open space technology (OST), large-scale interactive events.	Since 1997, methods have been developed, and practitioners have mixed designs (hybrid designs). A tendency exists to modify methods or re-label them for a consultant's or practitioners' own purpose in order to address the needs of their clients. Examples of a few of these hybrid methods are: ⦿ Preferred futuring—future and RTSC combined (Lippitt, 1980) ⦿ Technology of Participation™ ⦿ Collaboration in community development method (Holman & Devane, 1999) ⦿ Appreciative Future Search—Appreciative inquiry (AI) and Future Search combined (Fuller, Griffin & Ludema, 2000) ⦿ Swedish study circles (Brown, 2001) ⦿ Multi-stakeholder collaboration roundtable—world café (Turcotte & Pasquero, 2001) ⦿ Knowledge e Kopitiam—world cafés in Singapore (Tan & Brown, 2005).

Large-scale meetings can lead to better change proposals if a combination of small-group meetings is used in this process. A shortcoming of this method is that it can become a communication play regarding the change proposal between members of the small group instead of leading to effective organisational change.

Large-group intervention

The LGI is a system-wide approach. It is one of the fastest-growing areas in OD and has received considerable attention. LGI occurs where organisations put systems thinking into practice as part of a larger, more holistic strategy for change (Van der Zouwen, 2011). LGI is defined in different ways. Bunker and Alban (1997: xv–xvi) define it as:

> *methods for involving the whole system, internal and external, in the change process. These methods may go by different names, but the key similarity is that these methods deliberately involve a critical mass of the people affected by the change, both inside the organisation (employees and management) and outside it (suppliers and customers). This whole-system change process allows a critical mass of people to participate in: (i) understanding the need for change; (ii) analysing the current reality and deciding what needs to change; (iii) generating ideas how to change existing processes, and implementing and supporting change and making it work.*

LGI focuses on whole-system change and involves all the parties affected by the change. The intervention can include hundreds and even thousands of participants working together at the same time and in the same space, and the emphasis during this intervention is on mutual understanding and dialogue among organisational members (Manning & Binzagr, 1996).

The terms 'LGI', 'Future Search conference', 'search conference', 'principle-based meeting design', 'open-system planning', the 'AI summit', 'decision acceleration' and 'world cafés' are often used interchangeably in the context of OD (Cummings & Worley, 2015). These terms have somewhat different geographical and theoretical foundations (Weisbord & Janoff, 2003). Future searches are used worldwide in countries such as Australia, South Africa, the Americas, the Scandinavian countries, Northern Europe, India, Bangladesh, Indonesia, Thailand, Singapore, Kenya, Ethiopia and Algeria. The Ford motor company, Boeing, Marriott Hotels and Shell are just a few organisations that are using LGI methods for the planning of meetings and conferences. Leith (2001) explains that with LSI, organisations want to change from traditional thinking to new thinking, as in Table 11.3 on the next page.

Table 11.3 Conventional thinking and new thinking (Author)

Conventional thinking	New thinking
○ Dependence on authority and realising oucomes; much blaming	○ Individual and collective responsibility taken for setting and realising outcomes
○ Criticism of 'their' plans	○ Ownership of 'our' plans
○ Low level of cooperation	○ High level of cooperation
○ Response to change: half-hearted agreement, resigned acceptance, resistance, work-arounds, sabotage	○ Response to change: wholehearted commitment
○ Slow results or no results	○ Fast results
○ Small pockets of improvement	○ Across-the-board improvement
○ Little or no increase in organisation's capacity to initiate/respond to change	○ Big increase in organisation's capacity to initiate/respond to change

LSI is a highly structured process that is utilised as a tool for creating awareness of organisational opportunities and problems. Action research forms the primary conceptual basis for OD, and starts by searching for problems to be addressed. Lippitt (1980) explains that beginning with issues within the organisation may lead to members experiencing a loss of energy and feeling tired. He believes that members would be more motivated if the organisation focused more on the future than on the past.

When dealing with LSI, there are two main emphases. Firstly, anticipate the needs of future organisation members. Secondly, focus on gathering 'the whole system', or, if the whole system is not possible, at least 10% of it (Austin & Bartunek, 2012). The whole system might be (French & Bell, 1999: 190):

- the representatives of top management
- employees from all levels
- managers in all functional areas in an organisation
- representatives of all the social services in a community
- suppliers' and customers' representatives.

Each activity in this structured process is planned beforehand for the meeting with the whole system. This is essential, because the entire system of stakeholders participates simultaneously in a meeting for the definition of the future state. This process assists with the future directions for action.

Cummings and Worley (2015) explain that processes involved in any LSI include three steps, namely:

1. preparing for the whole-group meeting (large-group meeting)
2. conducting the meeting
3. following up on the meeting outcomes.

There are at least 20 different LSI methods. LSI can be divided into the methods illustrated in Figure 11.3.

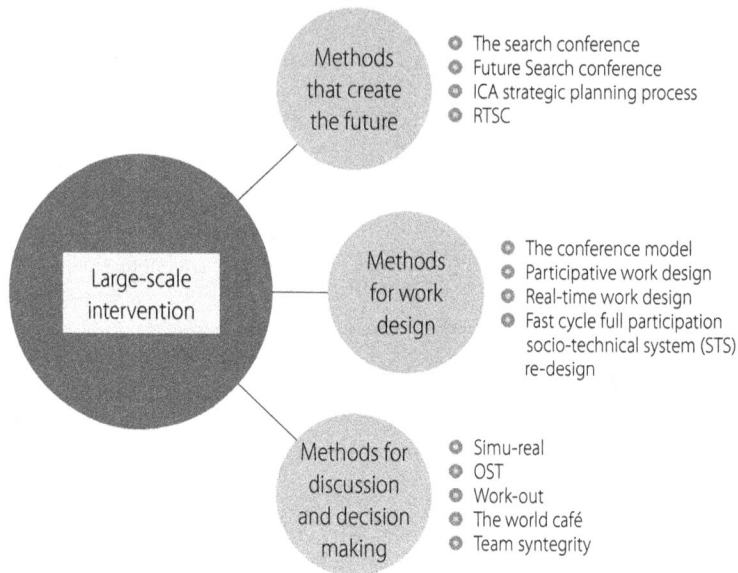

Figure 11.3 Methods of large-scale intervention (Author)

Practitioners can use any of a number of different methods in their journey towards LSI. In this chapter we focus only on a few of the methods available. OD practitioners should be familiar with different methods and tools. We look first at methods that create the future, methods for work design and methods for discussion and decision making.

A variety of LGI methods exist to assist organisations in addressing the challenges of change. For the methods to be successful, the active involvement and support of senior management are required. A few of the methods are discussed below.

Methods that create the future

The search conference

The search conference is a popular intervention process in continental Europe, England and Australia. Search conference is an off-site, retreat-like event that lasts for two and a half days. Search conference's basic design has three phases, according to Emery and Purser (1996: 40), which are illustrated in Figure 11.4 on the next page.

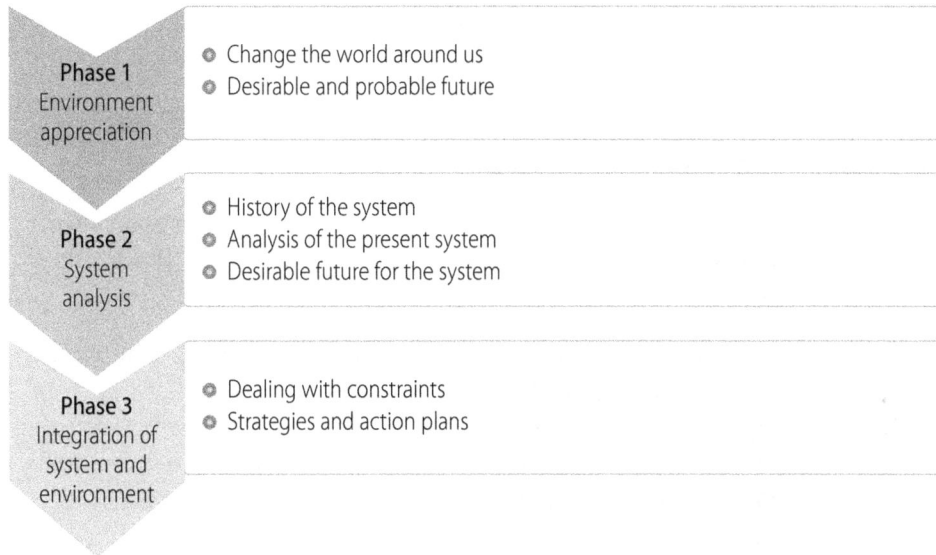

Figure 11.4 Search conference's three phases (Emery and Purser, 1996: 40)

Weisbord (1987: 295) explains:

> *The search conference links values and action in real time. It promotes a productive workplace by using more of each person's reality. It joins people who need one another, yet rarely interact, in a new kind of relationship. It stimulates creativity and innovation thinking. It offers a unique third wave springboard for planning and goal setting.*

Future Search conferences

This method is popular with American consultants, and shares similarities with the European search conference. The Future Search conference is an extension of the work of Kurt Lewin, who has influenced organisational consultation for 50 years with his work on field theory and action research. His work has also influenced the work of Emery and Trist (1964; 1973) on search conferences for strategic planning. His work also influenced that of Schindler-Rainman and Lippitt (1980) on the practice of future-orientated planning in community groups of 200–300 people in the 1970s (Weisbord & Janoff, 2003).

Weisbord and Janoff (2003) explain that future searches focus on three different ways of practising future-orientated planning, namely principle-based meeting design, a philosophy and theory for facilitating, and a global change strategy.

In *principle-based meeting design*, organisations and communities are enabled to transform their capability for action. The goal of this meeting is always an action plan for the future. The meeting requires two and a half days, and consists of five phases. It includes one or more diverse groups of people (between 50 and 70) who look at the past, present and future. They search for common ground and make action plans.

Different versions exist with regard to Weisbord's (1987: 285–292) Future Search model, but it consists mainly of the following steps:

Step 1: A voluntary committee consisting of four to six members meets with conference managers or consultants. They plan by focusing on dates, time, locations, who should attend, groups tasks, meals, etc.

Step 2: Representatives/participants are invited (50–70 people). The whole system is represented at the conference. It consists of representatives from the different levels and functional areas of the organisation, who may include customers, suppliers, trade union representatives, and persons of different race groups, gender and age. It is expected of the representatives to bring magazine and newspaper clippings that describe events they believe are shaping and influencing the organisation's future.

Step 3: Participants sit at tables of six to eight, depending on the focus and the tasks assigned to them, or based on self-selection. This group output is recorded on an easel paper. The participants do not need to agree with ideas, as all of them are seen as valid—the conference is there to generate awareness, mutual support and understanding. The participants do not solve problems; rather, at the end of the conference they make action recommendations.

Step 4: The conference focuses on four to five segments, which last for half a day. Each requires that the participants:
- build a database
- look at the database together
- interpret the findings
- draw conclusion for actions.

Step 5: Focus is given to past significant activity (see Figure 11.5 on the next page). It is expected of each participant to make notes about significant events and milestones they can recall from each of the past three decades and from three perspectives (self, company, society). These notes are then organised and transferred onto a sheet of paper on the wall according to each decade and topic. Each group analyses and reports to the total group on one theme by focusing on the three past decades with regard to self, company or society, and extracts patterns and meanings. The total group then interprets good and bad trends, and the direction of movement of each.

Step 6: The focus is on present internal and external factors that are shaping the future of the organisation (see Figure 11.6 below). The participants at each table look at the magazine and newspaper clippings, and identify and indicate why they think each is important as an external environmental influence. The group then makes a priority list according to importance, as identified from the clippings. Next, the internal factors, events and trends are analysed by looking at a list of 'sorries' and 'proud' relative to what is currently being experienced within the organisation, and the results are displayed and discussed. The participants vote for the 'proudest proud' and 'sorriest sorry', and these findings are displayed on flipcharts, where the conference manager summarises key statements.

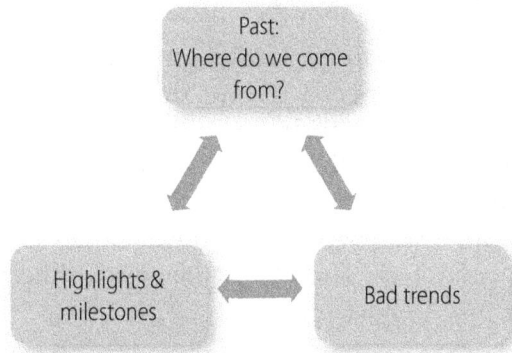

Figure 11.5 Good and bad trends (Author)

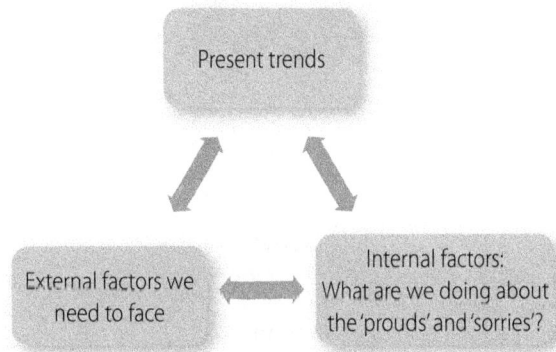

Figure 11.6 Present trends (Author)

Step 7: Focus is given to the future (see Figure 11.7 on the next page), and new groups are formed. The new groups need to develop a draft of a preferred future scenario within two hours. During this time, they make use of a variety of media (coloured paper, scissors, crayons) to discuss the most desirable, attainable future five years. The group then reports to the total conference.

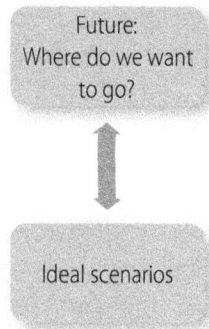

Figure 11.7 Future scenario (Author)

Step 8: The next-action steps are to ask the group to reflect on the relevant information discussed and surfaced during the process. The action steps depend on the group's nature, their function and the total organisation. Members of top management or the steering groups discuss proposals for the total organisation. They develop action plans, whereas members from the same department, as a group, will now set up action proposals for functional areas and decide on next-action steps. The groups then discuss the action plans with the total conference.

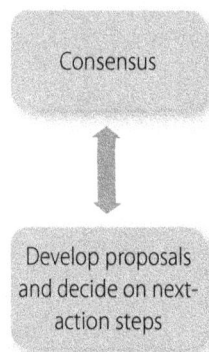

Figure 11.8 Consensus and action plan (Author)

Step 9: Information with regard to the conference is documented by volunteers, communicated to others and then carried forward to the next-action steps.

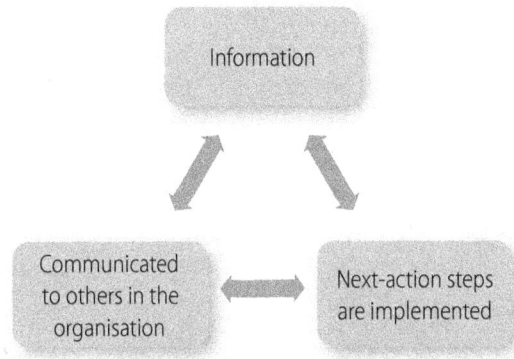

Figure 11.9 Communication process (Author)

Clippendale (2001) mentions that Future Search conferences have three linking threads:

- A large cross-section of stakeholders is invited. The members of this diverse group would normally not meet.
- The self-management tasks of the participants during the process are discovery, dialogue, learning and planning.
- The participants explore the whole system, looking at its history, global trends, ideas and constraints.

In terms of a *philosophy and theory for facilitating*, Weisbord and Janoff (2003) called the philosophy for managing and facilitating Future Search 'doing more by doing less'. They believe that people need to take responsibility for their work and that it is essential that the facilitators resist doing for a group what its members are capable of doing for themselves.

Future Search is a structural intervention process. In this process, people's behaviour cannot be changed, but people can be enabled to modify the structures under which they interact. During this process, it is important that:

- conditions are created where people can get the whole picture
- people within the groups understand one another and cross boundaries
- the groups are able to form new relationships and cooperate.

The job of the facilitator is to:

- ensure that the task is compelling so that it is worth people's time and energy
- help assure that the room includes people with resources, expertise and authority
- start and end on time
- manage group conversations so that everybody has a chance to speak.

In terms of a *global change strategy*, Weisbord and Janoff (2003: 3) raised the question: 'How can a separate meeting lasting a few days become a global change strategy?' The answer is by the collective accomplishment of Future Search Network (FSN). At any time, at least 350 dedicated practitioners applied and agreed to do the fundamental principles of Future Search in their work and carried out future searches as a form of public service. The FSN members agreed to share with others their learning, collaborate on projects and mutually reinforce each other's efforts.

In an interview with Marsha Pendergrass, an experienced Future Search facilitator, during a learning exchange of the FSN in South Africa in November 2007, Van der Zouwen (2011: 73) asked her where LSI starts, and she answered:

> *No, it does not start with a proposal for a sponsor, it starts when somebody says: We have to get our arms around this. Then someone says the magic words: I know a process that will help you. That is when it starts: let's talk about Future Search. How much does it cost? What do we need? Then call someone, or the Future Search network. The Future Search network will say: 'We will figure it out together'.*

Future research as a method is not without pitfalls. The success and pitfalls conditions for Future Search are given in the box below.

FUTURE SEARCH 👥 NETWORK

Future Search Methodology
(Usually four or five sessions each lasting 1/2 day)

Day 1, Afternoon

Focus on the past
People make time lines of key events in the world, their own lives and the history of the Future Search topic. Small groups tell stories about each time line and the implications of their stories for the work they have come to do.

→

	Focus on present, external trends The whole group makes a 'mind map' of trends affecting them now and identifies those trends most important to their topic.
Day 2, Morning	
	Focus on present, external trends Stakeholder groups describe what they are doing now about key trends and what they want to do in the future.
	Focus on present Stakeholder groups report what they are proud of and sorry about in the way they are dealing with the Future Search topic.
	Ideal future scenarios Diverse groups put themselves into the future and describe their preferred future as if it has already been accomplished. **Identify common ground** Diverse groups post themes they believe are common ground for everyone.
	Confirm common ground Whole-group dialogues are conducted to agree on common ground. **Action planning** Volunteers sign up to implement action plans.

FUTURE SEARCH 🏃🏃🏃 NETWORK

Conditions for success

- Get the 'whole system' in the room. Invite a significant cross-section of all parties with a stake in the outcome.
- Explore the 'whole elephant' before seeking to fix any part. Get everyone talking about the same world. Think globally, act locally.
- Put common ground and future focus front and center while treating problems and conflicts as information, not action items.
- Encourage self-management and responsibility for action by participants before, during and after the Future Search.

FUTURE SEARCH PRINCIPLES

- "Whole System" in the room
- Whole "elephant" as context for local action
- Focus on future and common ground – not past problems and conflicts
- Self-management and responsibility for action

And conditions for success ...

- Urge full attendance: Keep part-time participants to a minimum.
- Meet under healthy conditions: This means airy rooms with windows, healthy snacks and meals and adequate breaks.
- Work across three days (sleep twice): People need 'soak time' to take in everything that happens.
- Ask for voluntary public commitments to specific next steps before people leave.

(Source: adapted from http://www.futuresearch.net, with permission from Sandra Janoff)

Institute for Cultural Affairs' strategic planning process

The ICA strategic planning process is characterised as participative, fast, action-orientated creative and synergistic. This model is built on Spencer's Dialogue, which is used in community building, participation and empowerment of the community. In this process, the environment is scanned and then a shared vision is developed. The parties look at what is blocking them in attaining their vision and they then institute an action plan with a 90-day calendar for implementation.

This approach is people-centred, and puts the emphasis on the environment and on the personal involvement of the participants. This method is the closest of all to a spiritual and humanistic component of OD (Bunker & Alban, 1992; Smith & Smith, 1994).

Real-time strategic change

Robert Jacobs' RTSC intervention is a process similar to search conference. The term 'real-time' refers to 'the simultaneous planning and implementing of individual, group and wide organisational changes' (Jacobs, 1994: 21). Some of the organisations that have used this process are Boeing, Kaiser Electronics and Marriott Hotels. Ford's assembly plant in Dearborn, Michigan, has used this intervention, with 13 consultants supporting a 2 200-person event. This design at Ford Motor Company was developed by Kathleen Dannemiller together with Chuck Tyson, Al Davenpoort and Bruce Gibb.

In this change intervention process, hundreds of members sometimes gather for a three-day meeting to discuss organisation-wide issues. This process requires planning and the assistance of a facilitator. The assumptions fundamental to this event are the following (French & Bell, 1999):

- A leadership team has identified that the organisation **needs a new strategic direction** because of a change in the internal or external environment.
- The leadership team develops a **draft strategy** for the first meeting set up with members.
- The **members give feedback** to leadership and the leaders.
- In this event, a critical mass of people from the larger organisation come together to **participate**.

This intervention process has no fixed framework for the activities of the individuals, or small or large groups. The event design is customised around specific issues and is based on Dannemiller's (Dannemiller, 2000; Dannemiller & Jacobs, 1992; Dannemiller, James & Tolchinsky, 1999) revised formula of Beckhard and Harris's change. The formula is shown below:

$$Change = D \times V \times F > R$$

D (dissatisfaction with the current state of affairs), V (vision of how things could be) and F (first steps towards realising that vision) must be greater than R (resistance to change). If one or more of the elements is missing, change will not occur.

Jacobs (1994) explains that significant to this process is that every perspective and skill set, from the executive stockholders and suppliers to customers and front-line workers, are involved, and as soon as they share information with one another, the action begins to happen. He describes this as a point at which the stakeholders start to understand how the whole organisation fits within the total system. Dannemiller (Dannemiller, 2000; Dannemiller & Jacobs, 1992; Dannemiller, James & Tolchinsky, 1999) sees this process as a sense of alignment. The common-ground view is the 'one brain, one heart' effect, where a diverse group of individuals have a common purpose.

Methods for work design

The conference model

In early 1992, the conference model was pioneered by Dick and Emily Axelrod (The Axelrod Group, USA) and it is one of the most structured of all LGIs. This model is a combination of the socio-technical system, Future Search and the work of Robert Fritz. The primary purpose of this model is the accelerated redesign of an organisation into self-managed, high-performance work teams.

The model consists of a series of four consecutive large-scale conferences with a steering committee of around 20 people coming from all parts of the organisation, assisted by one or two consultants. The four consecutive conferences include the following, according to Leith (2001):

1. **Visioning conference:** Participants develop an understanding of the organisation's history and current situation. They form a vision of how they want the organisation to be in the future. This process is similar to Future Search.
2. **Customer–supplier conference:** Participants gain an understanding of the external and internal relationship between the customers and suppliers about how they work, and what is required and desired for the future.
3. **Technical conference:** The participants gain an understanding of the process of doing business, and determine the variations that occur and the current situation of the organisation.
4. **Organisational design conference:** During the organisational design conference, the vision of the organisation is clearly set. It is essential that participants meet the most important customers' and suppliers' needs and obtain variances as close to zero as possible.

Each of these conferences has a detailed agenda, scheduled presentations, group exercises and round-the-table discussions. There can be a fifth implementation conference in some cases. The periods between the successive conferences are used to communicate results and to get more input.

Participative work design

Participative design was developed in 1971 by Fred and Merrelyn Emery, and was modified by Bob Rehm. This design is an organisation-wide process where people who do the work know the most about it and therefore will make the most effective and efficient decisions. The design starts at the lowest level and proceeds to the top of the organisation, and starts by addressing 'what is their work now' (Bunker & Alban, 1997). This method was created in a way that tends to be flawed because of its incomplete assessment of reality.

The participative design, as set by Emery and Emery (1993), can be seen as psychological requirements that include the following:

- Individuals must manage themselves.
- On-the-job-training should take place.
- Multiple skills must be incorporated in work.
- Mutual support and respect must exist.
- It must be a meaningful design.
- There should be a career path.

Real-time work design

The process of work design takes months, with many small meetings. Real-time strategy, also known as whole-scale change, was developed by Dannemiller, and is a method that is flexible. The method includes hundreds and even thousands at an event, and the process is designed to include a particular client situation at each event. The process is based on future planning that includes suppliers, customers and experts (Bunker & Alban, 2006).

Fast-cycle full-participation socio-technical system redesign

Fast-cycle full participation aims to create change through the optimal design of an organisation's technical and social system. This method focuses on creating organisational design throughout the whole system, and on enabling key stakeholders to assess trends, development and events; analyse the technical and social environment; identify the needs of customers; and plan and create for the ideal system (Scott, 2009).

Methods for discussion and decision making

Simu-real

Simu-real was developed by Donald Klein and is a one-day session with a group of up to 50 participants. It entails both informal and formal participation in simulated activities and conversations. Within this simulation, the participants have the opportunity to experiment with future scenarios in an attempt to test assumptions, ideas and alternative ways of organising. The value of Simu-real is organisational harmony that is reached by heightened system awareness and open-minded action planning (Scott, 2009).

Open space technology

OST was invented by Harris Owen (1992; 1995; 2000). Large groups of people gather in a room and sit in a circle. OST is an unstructured process with no upfront planning, no defined agenda, no tables, few rules and no specific exercises. During the open space, the following happens:

- Structures emerge simultaneously as the event proceeds.

○ It arises from the adaptive self-organisation and relational process when the right type of space is created.

Owen's view is that organisations are, firstly, too rigid and, secondly, too controlling. There are two guiding rules with regard to OST. The first is the **law of mobility** (law of two feet), namely that during the course of gathering, any person who does not contribute to or learn from the process needs to use his/her two feet and go to a more productive place. Secondly, the guiding rules is based on OST methodology (Owen, 2000). There are five principles (Franco, Both & Harris, 2015):

1. Whoever comes are the right people.
2. Whenever it starts is the right time.
3. Wherever it happens is the right place.
4. Whatever happens is the only thing that could have.
5. When it's over, it's over.

Work-out

The work-out is a process developed by General Electrical (GE). Groups of employees, within a meeting, brainstorm ways to solve an organisational problem. The aim of this process is to help employees to solve and address problems without going through different hierarchical levels in the organisation. The process forces an organisational culture of rapid analysis of problems and work processes and of taking action immediately. In Figure 11.10, the seven steps of work-out are given.

The work-out processes of GE are widely copied and adapted to other organisations because of their effective contribution to the success of organisations (Draft & Marcic, 2011).

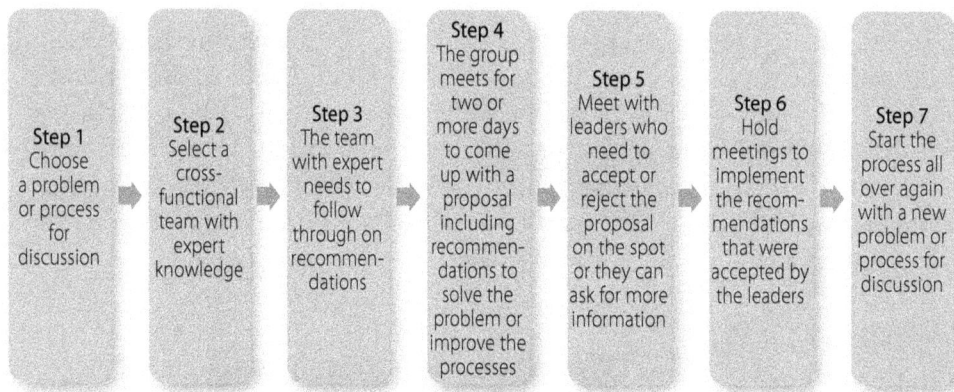

Figure 11.10   Seven steps for work-out (compiled by the author from the work of Bunker & Alban, 1996; Draft & Marcic, 2011)

The world café

The world café is a simple and flexible process for hosting large-group dialogue. 'Café' is a metaphor for an informal web conversation. The world café explores burning questions and accesses collective intelligence by creating a living, sharing knowledge where possibilities for actions are created (Van der Zouwen, 2011).

The world café's basic model consists of five components (The world café, 2016):

1. **Setting:** A special environment is created, with four chairs at a table, most often modelled after a café with a tablecloth, a vase of flowers, a block of paper and coloured pens.

2. **Welcoming and introduction:** The participants are welcomed warmly by the host, and the process and café etiquette are explained.

3. **Small-group rounds:** Conversations start among the members of small, seated groups in the first of three or more 20-minute processes. After 20 minutes, participants move to a new table and select a person as the table host for the next round. The host informs the new group about what happened at the previous round.

4. **Questions:** Each round is introduced with questions that are designed for the specific context and chosen for the purpose of the session. These questions can be used at more than one round, or they can follow upon each other to guide the participants.

5. **Harvest:** Individuals are invited to share their results and insights with the large group, which is often recorded in a graphic way (also referred to as reflective graphics or graphic listening) in the front of the room.

Dynamics and dilemmas in large-group intervention

The practitioner, when dealing with LGI, needs to give, according to Bunker and Alban (1997), special attention to the following four dynamics:

1. **The dilemma of voice:** Individuals who did not have an opportunity to speak or be heard in large groups may feel marginalised and will then withdraw from the process. Bunker and Alban (1997) mention that this will lead to the diffusion of responsibility by individuals as the group size increases and impacts their behaviour.

2. **The dilemma of structure:** If no structure or too much structure is present, anxiety occurs and people may act out. The dilemma is in not knowing how much anxiety is in a group and how to manage this.

3. **The egocentric dilemma:** Individuals see the world only from their own viewpoints or by their experiences. This may lead to a failure to view differences as potentially productive, which influences a healthy outcome.
4. **Affective contagion:** There is often a transfer of mood among individuals who work together, and in a large-group setting, positive or negative affect always has the possibility of spreading.

LGI managers need to take the following into consideration when dealing with the dynamics of dilemmas:

- Consider the right amount of structure to prevent anxiety.
- Use small-group processes to stimulate and encourage involvement.
- Use democratic methods and self-management principles so that the participants can take responsibility for their task outcomes.
- Encourage holistic thinking and group collaboration when selecting the group.
- Use individual voting and individual selection methods to maximise opportunities.

Conclusion

LGI is important in OD, and its implications are powerful during the change process, offering organisations a solution to facilitate radical changes. Traditional OD models do not embrace the complexity and dynamics necessary to effectively manage change in today's environment. LGI helps organisations to move from chaos to order by involving relevant parties in solving problems during the change. LGI is a practical process that can engage the whole system at a single point in time, a process based on information sharing, system integration and collaboration by the relevant parties.

Case study

A model for re-designing product lines at Ikea

By Marv Weisbord, co-director, Future Search Network

Perhaps my most eye-opening experience with Future Search came in 2003 when Janoff and I joined with Tomas Oxelman, an internal consultant with the furniture company IKEA, to do a feat of systems redesign I had thought impossible until now. The company had decided to overhaul its 'pipeline,' the flow of products from the drawing boards in Almhult, Sweden to its far-flung factories, thence to assembly and distribution points, stores, and ultimately customers in dozens of countries.

→

With 11 major product lines, 140 stores, manufacturing facilities around the world, and thousands of staff involved in tracking and managing the system, this would be a daunting task.

Oxelman and several executives had attended Future Search workshops. They persuaded us that extreme action was needed, and observed that Future Search principles supported their corporate values, reason enough to work this way. They would guarantee the right people in the room for whatever time was needed. Together we adapted the Future Search method to a single product, the 'Ektorp' sofa, to re-imagine its journey from design center to customer. This would be the prototype for all product lines. Catarina Bengtsson, the business group manager, set ambitious goals for Ektorp: double sales, improve quality and cut the price 30 % without cutting profit, make sofa shopping easier for customers, and cut delivery times.

In March 2003, 52 stakeholders including suppliers from Poland, Mexico and China, executives starting with the company president and top staff and line people from Sweden, Canada, the US and other countries, and several Ektorp customers from Hamburg, Germany (site of the meeting), came together for three days. Many had never met before. Nonetheless, they described the existing system, documented required changes, proposed a variety of new systems, agreed on common specs for a new design, created an implementation plan and got buy-in from all relevant levels and functions—design, production, distribution, information technology, retailing, and customers. In my nearly 35 years of consulting, I have typically seen such processes taking at least six months. Here the plan was made, validated at the top, and launched with multi-level task forces in 18 hours of work.

The most astonishing outcome for me was the common ground specs for a new system. They included greatly flattening the hierarchy, involving customers and suppliers in design from the very start, providing direct contact with suppliers and stores, changing the roles of central staff, and modifying information systems to give everyone greater influence on the system's coordination and control. What made this remarkable is that people made this up on their own, with no prompting from consultants on how to think about systems design. They muddled their way from a traditional, centralized system, breaking down the silos, by taking seriously customer concerns and matching a variety of designs against the proposed goals. There was one more thing, leadership. Throughout, top executives joined the dialogue without saying what form a new system should take. Rather, the president continually reiterated the importance of the prototype to the company's future. Ektorp—that sofa sitting in a corner of the meeting room with a coffee table in front of it—was a means to a larger goal, not an end in itself.

Within a month, seven task forces were at work around the world, redoing every aspect of the system. The main coordination and control mechanism? A regular conference call buttressed by emails. Having all in touch with one another enabled a degree of self-organizing not previously seen. 'I learned a lot and also got many insights into how we in IKEA cooperate amidst the complexity, and in how to run a workshop like this one', said Catti Bengtsson, who has no formal line authority over most of the players. 'We have complete documentation at our intranet site, which is updated continuously. The regular telephone conferences are helping us keep the focus and speed!'

→

Questions:

1. Why do you think this process was implemented within one month and not within six months?
2. Why do you think the president continually reiterated the importance of the prototype to the company's future?

Source: Weisbord, 2004 (for Future Search Network).

Reflection questions

1. How would you describe Future Search?
2. Why was Future Search implemented successfully within 18 hours in IKEA?
3. What are the pros and cons of Future Search? How can it be implemented successfully in an organisation?
4. Explain large-group methods for creating the future.
5. What is the future of large-group methods in South Africa?
6. Are you able to explain the following?
    a. The variety of LGI methods that can assist organisations in addressing challenges
    b. Why the active involvement and support of management are important in implementing LGI
    c. What the current trends in large-scale intervention worldwide and in South Africa are

Multiple-choice questions

1. LGIs run with groups of between:
    a. one to more than 100 participants
    b. 10 to more than 1 000 participants
    c. 20 to more than 1 500 participants
    d. 50 to more than 2 000 participants
    e. None of the above

2. In Africa, multicultural team management is a complex problem and synergy depends largely on:
    a. managers' ability
    b. workers' ability
    c. OD consultants to create a management system that integrates differences

    d. a and b

    e. a, b and c

3. OD practitioners in the knowledge economy need to:

    a. develop processes, reward systems and frameworks that help organisations to sustain and build knowledge

    b. place little emphasis on learning at the organisational level

    c. develop a structured process with clearly defined objectives

    d. recognise the global effects they have on their clients and on local customs

    e. All of the above

4. Which statement is true?

    a. LSI takes place in the whole organisation at the same time.

    b. LSI takes place in a sequential manner and requires linear thinking.

    c. LSI focuses on identifying and solving problems.

    d. LSI is a highly unstructured process used as a tool for opportunities and problem solving.

    e. All of the above

5. RTSC is best described as:

    a. the accelerated redesign of an organisation into self-managed, high-performance work teams

    b. an unstructured strategic change process with no upfront planning and no defined agendas

    c. the simultaneous planning and implementation of individual, group and organisation-wide changes

    d. a people-centred approach, putting the emphasis on the environment and on the personal involvement of the participants

    e. All of the above

References

Anderson, PT & Ovaice, G. 2006. 'Strategic organization development: a seat at the table'. *Organisational development Journal* 24(4): 29–37.

Argyris, C & Schön, DA. 1978. *Organizational learning: a theory of action perspective*. Reading, MA: Addison-Wesley.

Argyris, C & Schön, DA. 1996. *Organizational learning II: Theory and practice*. Reading, MA: Addison-Wesley.

Austin, JR & Bartunek, JM. 2012. 'Organization change and development: in practice and in theory', in *Handbook of psychology*, edited by N Schmitt &

S Highhouse. Volume 12: *Industrial and Organizational Psychology*. New York: Wiley: 390–410.

Axelrod, R. 1992. 'Getting everyone involved: how one organization involved its employees, supervisors, and managers in redesigning the organization'. *Journal of Applied Behavioral Science* 28: 499–509.

Brinkley, I, Hutton, W, Schneider, P & Coates-Ulrichsen, K. 2010. *Kuwait and the knowledge economy: a report prepared for KFAS*. The Work Foundation and the Kuwait Programme of Development, Governance and Globalisation in Gulf States.

Brown, J. 2001. *The world café: living knowledge through conversations that matter*. Fielding Institute.

Bryson, JM & Anderson, SR. 2000. 'Applying large-group interaction methods in the planning and implementation of major change efforts'. *Public Administration Review* 60(2): 143–162.

Bunker, BB & Alban, BT (eds). 1992. 'Conclusion: What makes large group intervention effective'. *Journal of Applied Behavioural Sciences* 28(4): 579–591.

Bunker, BB & Alban, BT. 1997. *Large group interventions: engaging the whole system for rapid change*. San Francisco, CA: Jossey-Bass.

Bunker, BB & Alban, BT. 2006. *The handbook of large group methods: creating systematic change in organizations and communities*. San Francisco, CA: Jossey-Bass.

Clippendale, P. 2001. Future Search conference—an introduction. http://www.minessence.net/articles/future_search_conferences.htm (Accessed 30 May 2016).

Covin, TJ. 1992. 'Common intervention strategies for large-scale change'. *Leadership & Organizational Development Journal* 14(4): 27–32.

Cummings, TG & Worley, CG. 2015. *Organisational development and change*. 10th ed. Stamford, CT: Cengage Learning.

Dannemiller, K. 2000. *Whole-scale change toolkit: tools for unleashing the magic in organizations*. San Francisco, CA: Berrett-Koehler.

Dannemiller, K & Jacobs, R. 1992. 'Changing the way organizations change: A revolution of common sense'. *The Journal of Applied Behavioral Science* 28: 480–498.

Dannemiller, K, James, S & Tolchinsky, P. 1999. *Whole-scale change*. San Francisco, CA: Berrett-Koehler.

Denton, M & Vloeberghs, D. 2003. 'Leadership challenges for organisations in the new South Africa'. *Leadership & Organizational Development Journal* 24(2): 84–89.

Draft, R & Marcic, D. 2011. *Understanding management*. Stamford, CT: South-Western Cengage Learning.

Emery, F & Emery, M. 1993. 'The participative design workshop', in *The social engagement of social science: a Tavistock anthology*, edited by E Trist & H Murray. Philadelphia: University of Pennsylvania Press: 599–613.

Emery, M & Purser, RE. 1996. *The search conference*. San Francisco, CA: Jossey-Bass.

Emery, FE & Trist, EL. 1964. 'The causal texture of organizational environments'. *Human Relations* 18(2): 21–32.

Emery, FE & Trist, EL. 1973. *Towards a social ecology*. New York: Plenum.

ESRC (Economic and Social Research Council). 2005. Knowledge economy in the UK. http://www.esrc society today.ac.uk/ESRC Info Centre/facts/UK/indes4.aspx?component=6978&Sourpageld=14971#0 (Accessed 11 May 2015).

Fagenson-Eland, E, Ensher, EA & Burke, WW. 2004. 'Organisation development and change intervention'. *The Journal of Applied Behavioral Sciences* 40(4): 432–464.

Franco, P, Both, M & Harris, J. 2015. *Guide to open space technology*. European Commission. Lifelong Learning Programme.

French, WL & Bell, CH. 1999. *Organization development*. 6th ed. Englewood Cliffs, NJ: Prentice Hall.

Friedlander, F & Brown, LD. 1974. Organization development. *Annual Review of Psychology* 25: 313–341.

Fuller, CS, Griffin, TJ & Ludema, JD. 2000. 'Appreciative Future Search: involving the whole system in positive organization change'. *Organisation Development Journal* 18(2): 29–41.

Gallos, JV (ed). 2006. *Organization development*. San Francisco, CA: Jossey-Bass Reader.

Garrow, V. 2009. *OD: Past, present and future*. Institute for Employment Studies Working Paper WP22. Brighton: IES.

Gilmore, T & Barnett, C. 1992. 'Designing the social archtecture of participation in large groups to effect organizational change'. *Journal of Applied Behavioral Science* 28: 534–548.

Golembiewski, RT. 1993. 'Organizational development in the third world: values, closeness of fit and culture-boundedness'. *Journal of Public Administration* 16(11): 1667–1691.

Goodman, M. 1995. *Creative management*. London: Prentice-Hall.

Gravin, DA. 1993. 'Building a learning organization'. *Harvard Business Review* 71(4): 78–91.

Hofstede, G. 1980. 'Motivation, leadership and organization: do American theories apply abroad?' *Organizational Dynamics* 9(1): 42–63.

Hofstede, G. 1996. *Cultures and organisations. Software of the mind: intercultural cooperation and its importance for survival*. New York: McGraw-Hill.

Hofstede, G. 1998. 'A case for comparing apples with oranges: international differences in values'. *International Journal of Comparative Sociology* 39: 16–31. https://doi.org/10.1177/002071529803900103.

Holman, P & Devane, T. 1999. *The change handbook: group methods for shaping the future.* San Francisco, CA: Berrett-Koehler.

Hoppe, G. 2004. 'An interview with Geert Hofstede'. *Academy of Management Executive* 18: 75–79.

Jacobs, RW. 1994. *Real-time strategic change.* San Francisco, CA: Berrett-Koehler.

Jacobs, RW. 1997. *Key distinctions between LSI and top-down approaches for change.* San Francisco, CA: Berrett-Koehler.

Jaeger, AM. 1986. 'Organisational development and national culture: where's the fit?' *The Academy of Management Review* 11(1): 178–190.

Jelenic, D. 2011. 'The importance of knowledge management in organisations—with emphasis on the balanced scorecard learning and growth perspective.' Knowledge as Business Opportunity: Proceedings of the Management, Knowledge and Learning International Conference 2011, International School for Social and Business Studies, Celje, Slovenia.

Kolb, DA, Rubin, IM & McIntyre, J (eds). 1971. *Organizational psychology: an experiential approach.* Englewood Cliffs, NJ: Prentice Hall.

Kondalkar, VG. 2009. *Organization development.* New Delhi: New Age International.

Lau, C & Ngo, H. 2001. 'Organizational development and firm performance: a comparison of multinational and local firms'. *Journal of International Business Studies* 32: 95–114.

Leith, M. 2001. *Leith guide to large group intervention methods: How to use large group intervention methods and collaborative gatherings to address complex strategic issues.* Brighton: Martin Leith.

Leith, M. 2004. Leith's guide to LG methods. http://www.martinleith.com (Accessed 29 June 2015).

Levitt, B & March, JG. 1988. 'Organizational learning'. *Annual Review of Sociology* 14: 319–338.

Lippitt, GL. 1980. 'Effective team building develops individuality'. *Journal of European Industrial Training* 4(1): 13–16.

Mackenzie, NM & Ling, LM. 2009. 'The research journey: a lonely planet approach'. *Issues in Education Research* 19(1): 46–60.

Manning, MR & Binzagr, GF. 1996. 'Methods, values, and assumptions underlying large group interventions intended to change whole systems'. *Journal of Organizational Analysis* 4: 268–284.

Martins, N. 1989. Organisational culture in a financial institution. DPhil thesis, University of South Africa, Pretoria.

Mohrman, SA. 2006. 'Designing organizations to lead with knowledge', in *The handbook of organisational development*, edited by T Cummings. Thousand Oaks, CA: SAGE.

Mutabazi, E & Derr, CB. 2006. 'The management of multicultural teams: the experience of Afto-Occidental teams'. Cahiers de Recherche, Lyon: École de management Lyon.

Neely, A. 2009. *The financial consequences of servitization of manufacturing.* AIM Research Paper. https://papers.ssrn.com/sol3/papers.cfm?abstract_id=1339189 (Accessed 27 July 2021).

Nussbaum, B, Berner, R & Brady, D. 2005. 'Get creative'. *Business Week* (August 1): 60–68.

OECD (Organisation for Economic Cooperation and Development). 2009. OECD Science, Technology and Industry Scoreboard 2009. http://www.oecd.org/sti/scoreboard.htm (Accessed 30 May 2016).

Owen, H. 1992. *Open space technology: a user's guide.* Potomac, MD: Abbott.

Owen, H. 1995. *Tales from open space.* Potomac, MD: Abbott.

Owen, H. 2000. *Constructionism.* Norwood, NJ: Albex.

Parumasur, SB. 2012. 'The effect of organisational context on organisational development (OD) interventions'. *SA Journal of Industrial Psychology* 38(1): 1–12.

Rothwell, WJ & Sullivan, RL. 2005. *Practicing organization development: a guide for consultants.* San Francisco, CA: John Wiley & Sons.

Schindler-Rainman, E & Lippitt, R. 1980. *Building the collaborative community: mobilizing citizens for action.* Riverside, CA: University of California, Extension.

Scott, BB. 2009. *Organization development primer: a review of large group interventions.* IRC Article Series, June 2009: 1–5.

Senge, PM. 1990. *The fifth discipline: the art & practice of the learning organization.* New York: Doubleday.

Smith, J & Smith, J. 1994. Notes from ASTD Future Search Conference, Apple Valley, MN: Southern Minnesota Section, American Society for Training and Development.

SRA (Stephen Renecle and Associates). 2015. Organisational development: assessment of organisational culture, climate and dynamics. http://www.stephenrecleandassociates.co.za/organisational-development.asp (Accessed 29 June 2015).

Sulamoyo, DS. 2010. '"I am because we are": *Ubuntu* as a cultural strategy for OD and change in sub-Saharan Africa', in *OD in Africa*, edited by TF Yaeger & PF Sorensen. Illinois: Benedictine University. *OD Practitioner* 43(3): 50–54.

Tan, S & Brown, J. 2005. 'The world café in Singapore: creating a learning culture through dialogue'. *Journal of Applied Behavioral Science* 41(1): 83–90.

Taras, V, Steel, P & Kirkman, BL. 2011. 'Three decades of research on national culture in the workplace: do the differences still make a difference?' *Organizational Dynamics* 40(3): 189–198.

Tax Shop. 2014. Newsletter. http://www.taxshop.co.za/storage/files/2014_Q3.pdf (Accessed 13 November 2014).

Turcotte, MF & Pasquero, J. 2001. 'The paradox of multi-stakeholder collaborative roundtables'. *Journal of Applied Behavioral Sciences* 37(4): 447–464.

Van der Zouwen, A. 2011. *Building an evidence-based practical guide to large scale interventions: towards sustainable organisational change with the whole system.* Delft: Eburon.

Viljoen, ME. 2015. *A strategy to strengthen the Taxshop brand.* Working paper. Business School, Netherlands.

Weisbord, M. 1987. *Productive workplaces.* San Francisco, CA: Jossey-Bass.

Weisbord, M. 2004. A model for redesigning product lines at Ikea. http://www.futuresearch.net/method/applications/uploads/business/ikea.pdf (Accessed 30 May 2016).

Weisbord, M & Janoff, S. 2003. *Three perspectives on Future Search: meeting design, theory of facilitating, global change strategy.* Draft 3. Future Search Network.

The world cafe. 2016. The world cafe methods. http://www.theworldcafe.com/key-concepts-resource/world-cafe-method/ (Accessed 30 May 2016).

Chapter 12

Major developments in organisation development

Nico Martins

Learning outcomes

After reading this chapter, you should be able to:

- explain the differences between the old and the new organisation development (OD)
- assess the effects of OD
- explain the impact of technology on OD and how to practise it in the virtual world
- explain the role of OD in an international context.

Introduction

Companies are realising that today's workforce has changed. There is a perception that employees from different generational cohorts have varying expectations of the workplace (Lester et al, 2012). Understanding the similarities and differences in what employees value, what contributes to their engagement and in which organisational culture they will flourish has become a critical strategic business objective (Lundby, Lee & Macey, 2012) and one of the principal challenges facing managers today (Lester et al, 2012). The 21st-century millennial workforce represents new challenges, more flexibility and higher demands coupled with a lack of specialists and highly skilled workers. This means that trends in OD are changing to align with the challenges of the 21st-century millennial workforce, and today's and tomorrow's business needs.

In South Africa and worldwide, the workforce now consists of four generational groups. The three well-known generations classified by Reynolds, Bush and Geist (2008) are Baby Boomers (those born between 1946 and 1964), Generation X (those born between 1965 and 1981) and Generation Y (those born in the 1980s and 1990s). The newest and upcoming generation is Generation 2020, born after 1998 (Anderson, 2015).

Recent studies in South Africa have confirmed that the three generations do view most of the dimensions of organisational culture differently (Moss & Martins, 2014). The 21st-century millennial workforce is comprised of tech-savvy, flexibility-demanding, highly collaborative and engaged talent. Passion and purpose drive the 21st-century millennials; they are not comfortable with the status quo. Millennials are a major force—but so are older workers, who remain engaged and valuable contributors. Companies are now faced with adding new and innovative OD capabilities to share knowledge, improve corporate learning and education capabilities, and connect with talent. The different generations have different characteristics and needs, and a different set of values that impact on the workplace. Lancaster and Stillman (2002) state that different generations shaped by different values, standards and policies are not necessarily compatible with the next generation. They believe that organisations that can understand and bridge generation gaps have a real competitive edge in the retention game. A better understanding of what drives the different generations and keeps them satisfied might assist managers to retain the best talent. Management's challenges are summarised by Anderson (2015), who believes that most organisational policies and management practices have been created to manage, develop, attract and retain workers in ways that no longer fit the needs, expectations and desires of the new generations.

Research by Martins and Martins (2014) indicates that organisations need to focus more on change management (CM), and especially on aspects such as consulting with employees regarding change, participation in change and preparing employees of all generations for change. These results confirm recent OD surveys conducted in early 2014 by WGA Consulting (2014) with human resource, OD and business leaders around the world identifying a number of common themes and initiative trends. The research identified critical trends organised into three broad areas that were helping to drive the human capital agenda for the following year and are transforming OD, namely develop and engage, leadership and succession, attract and retain.

According to Worley and Feyerherm (2003), the subject of change, CM and leadership – important and focal areas of OD – is at the top of CEO's agendas. It is the central subject in the business press and bestselling books, and at the core of an increasing number of academic programmes. The focus of this chapter will be on specific future trends for OD.

From the old to the new organisation development

During the 1980s, constructionist and postmodern approaches began to heavily influence the social sciences with ideas about multiple realities and the inherent subjectivity of experience. Many of these ideas have also influenced and/or been incorporated into aspects of OD thought and practice in recent years, although perhaps without the specific conscious intent to create a 'new OD'. The development of appreciative inquiry (AI), based in part on social constructionist premises where reality is at least partially, if not completely, a result of one's mindset, is a prominent example. This is reflected in the discussions about the impacts of 'deficit-focused thinking', alleged to be part of traditional action research, versus the 'positive-focused thinking' that forms the core of AI (Marshak, 2009). Marshak (2009) contrasts the more classical OD and the new OD, which is summarised in Table 12.1.

The question is: Why this different approach to OD? A number of authors and researchers have indicated that the organisation of the future will be different from today's. According to Brown (2015), OD, the newest discipline in planned change techniques, has emerged from the need for long-range strategies to improve organisational decision making and work relationships. According to him, OD is viewed by industry, government and health care as a field of expertise that can provide a viable option for planned change. This continuous state of change is also highlighted in Table 12.1.

Table 12.1 Classical organisation development and the new organisation development (adapted from Bushe & Marshak, 2008; Marshak, 2009)

	Classical OD	Postmodern OD
Differences	Influenced by classical science and modernist thoughts and philosophy	Influenced by the new sciences and postmodern thought and philosophy. Technology and social media will play an increasing role
	Organisation as a living system	Organisation as a meaning-making system
	Reality is an objective fact	Reality is socially constructed
	There is a single reality	There are multiple realities
	Truth is transcendent and discoverable	Truth is imminent, and emerges from the situation
	Reality can be discovered using rational and analytic processes	Reality is socially negotiated
	Collecting and applying valid data using objective problem-solving methods leads to change	Raising collective awareness and generating new possibilities and social agreements lead to change
	Emphasis on changing behaviour and what people do	Emphasis on changing mindsets and what people think
Similarities	Strong humanistic and democratic values	
	Consultants stay out of content and focus on process	
	A concern for capacity building and development of the system	

Assessing the effects of organisation development

There is always the need to develop better research designs and methods. For OD to be relevant, research will play a crucial role in evaluating change and other OD interventions. According to Brown (2015), many OD practitioners feel that the evaluation method should be designed into the change process itself.

Brown (2015) indicates that, in future, OD evaluations will be important to three groups, namely:

1. **decision makers** of organisations, who would want to see that the expenditures are providing the desired results
2. **participants** in an OD programme, who will need feedback about their change efforts
3. **OD practitioners**, who need evaluation so that they can develop their expertise.

An example of such an OD project was the research by Ledimo and Martins (2014) in a water utility organisation in South Africa. This longitudinal study detected positive changes and differences in employee satisfaction during organisational transformation. In a longitudinal study that was conducted over a period of three years, it emerged that the employees in Year 1 were less satisfied with their organisation prior to organisational transformation. In Year 2, after the implementation of change interventions, the employees' satisfaction levels increased, although they were still below 3.2, the cut-off point for the mean score. These results also suggested that employees who participated in the Year 3 sample appeared to be more satisfied, having the most employee satisfaction dimensions compared to those who participated in Year 1 and Year 2 samples. The researchers concluded that the longitudinal study provides a foundation for continuous improvement during the organisation's process of transformation, as the results indicated significant positive changes and differences in employee satisfaction during the three years of study. Typical changes implemented were the refocus of the organisational strategy and human resources strategy, restructuring, policy development, system change, policy amendments and implementation, and training programmes.

The evaluation of an OD programme involves an assessment of whether the OD interventions have been successfully implemented. The above case study provides an example of a data-based research project in the field of classical OD, but also portrays elements of new OD such as the fact that change is inherent and that change is continuous or cyclical, or both (see Table 12.1 on the previous page).

The question thus is: If OD is emerging, can we distinguish between different types of OD? According to Marshak (2009), and as shown in Table 12.2, three types of OD are emerging which OD practitioners and academics can pursue in the future, namely:

1. **classical OD**, based on the original humanistic values, principles and premises developed in the 1950s, 1960s and 1970s, combined with objectivist, action research methodologies (eg data-based interventions focused predominantly on behavioural processes such as data feedback team development)

2. **neoclassical OD**, which maintains a primary action research orientation but augments or amends the original humanistic values with both more emphasis on business values as well as on contemporary business issues and processes (eg system redesign or transformation efforts that might include 'right sizing' to help configure an organisation for competitive success)

3. **social interaction OD or new OD**, which presently ranges from humanistic to both humanistic and business values, but has been heavily influenced by postmodern constructionist and new sciences orientations (eg AI, which is based on a constructionist worldview).

Table 12.2 Three types of organisation development (Marshak, 2009)

Orientations	Modern, objectivist	Postmodern, constructionist
Dominantly humanistic with some business values	Classical OD	New OD
Humanistic with more business values	Neoclassical OD	New OD

Organisation development and information technology: Practising organisation development in the virtual world

Our discussion in the introduction referred to the changing work environment and the millennials as the new emerging generation who are more tech-savvy. Advances in the social media and communication technologies will impact and influence future OD interventions and methodologies. Cummings and Worley (2015) predict that the definition of OD in the future will depend on the forces within OD as well as economic, workforce, technology and organisational trends such as structures, systems, innovation, the removing of barriers to learning and the facilitation of how employees acquire, disseminate and organise knowledge assets. The OD consultant of tomorrow thus needs to be not only skilled in traditional OD skills and knowledge but also able to use and apply social media and new communication technologies (see Table 12.1). The new world of IT uses new technologies such as open-access technologies, social networking sites, blogs, video games, micro-blogging platforms, internet chat groups and rooms, internet brainstorming, web-based transactions, video conferences, e-banking and many more. Marshak (2009) states that the emphases would not necessarily negate other OD practices, but would ultimately require them to be practised in ways consistent with the philosophical premises of the new OD. Distinguishing and legitimating a new OD based on philosophical assumptions different to those of classical OD might also encourage academics and practitioners to more consciously pursue new approaches, and thereby encourage the discovery of new innovations and social technologies for addressing change in human systems. Cummings and Worley (2015) are of the opinion that innovation will be more synchronous (anytime and anywhere) as well as more virtual and less face to face. Innovations such as teambuilding, employee involvement and organisational learning will thus need to be planned and implemented in such a way that they encourage contributions across countries at times which are convenient to them. This use of technology to exchange ideas, implement change initiatives and collaborate will produce different types of outputs from those found in face-to-face meetings or discussions. OD practitioners will need to be comfortable with the new technologies and develop a different type of facilitation skill that can manage and deal with these new challenges. In a country such as South Africa, with its First and Third World economy, the OD practitioner will need to know when to use which—classical or new OD? It thus appears as if the mixed methods approach, as discussed in Chapter 6, will be used more and more with whichever type of OD. The complexity of the OD consultant's world of work is recapitulated by Anderson (2015), who sees the OD consultant as somebody who must remain attuned to the ways in which people collaborate and connect—they need to be sensitive to the implications of their technology choices in engagements.

Organisation development in an international context

The international environment of today asks of OD practitioners to work not only in their host country, but also across international borders and cultures. Traditionally, OD has mostly been practised in organisations within specific countries by OD consultants trained in those countries (Cummings & Worley, 2015). Changes in the international environment caused by mergers, acquisitions and organisations working in multiple countries brought about the need to work across countries and in different cultures. Think about organisations such as

SA Breweries and Investec, which operate worldwide, and MTN, Vodacom and a number of South African banks that are opening branches in Africa. At the same time, other countries such as China are investing in South Africa and bringing with them Eastern concepts of OD and change. This is creating new opportunities for OD practitioners, but it also brings new challenges.

Activity

1. Make a list of interventions you think might be applicable to use across different cultures.

2. List interventions you think might not be applicable to use across different cultures.

The OD practitioner thus needs to be open-minded to being trained in international OD practices. Many OD consultants regularly attend international conferences, workshops and training programmes to sharpen their skills and knowledge of the international field.

Our Western views on change and OD can be enriched by other cultures and traditions. Table 12.3 the next page provides an overview of some Eastern and Western concepts of change.

OD practitioners thus need to be open-minded about the fact that a shift in theories and mindsets will be a continuous process. South African researchers and academics have already invested time and money in developing culture-unbiased OD interventions, models and products. Some of these are:

- factorial invariance of the organisational culture assessment instrument (Martins, 2014)
- factorial invariance of the information security assessment instrument, which was tested in the UK and South Africa (Da Veiga & Martins, 2015)
- factorial invariance of the Adult State Hope Scale (Nel & Boshoff, 2014)
- a diagnostic model for assessing employee satisfaction (Ledimo, 2012)
- a model of knowledge retention (Martins & Martins, 2012)
- a change agent identification framework for South African change agents (Van der Linde-de Klerk, Martins & De Beer, 2014)
- an assessment framework for determining the organisational effectiveness of local government in South Africa (Olivier, 2015)
- a unified model of trust based on international research (Von der Ohe, 2015).

Table 12.3 Summary analysis of some East–West concepts of change (Marshak, 2009)

Traditional Western European worldview	Chinese Taoist and Confucian worldview
The universe is composed of separate independent entities normally in static or equilibrium states. Movement occurs when things act on each other. The universe had a beginning and will have an end. Progress or evolution is expected over time.	The universe is composed of constantly changing, interdependent manifestations of one entity. The universe is. Change is both spontaneous and cyclical.
Assumptions that change are: ● linear ● progressive ● destination-orientated ● based on creating disequilibrium ● planned and managed by people who are separate from and act on things to achieve their goals ● unusual, because everything is normally in a quasi-stationary or static state.	Assumptions that change are: ● cyclical ● processional ● journey-orientated ● based on maintaining equilibrium ● followed by people who are one with all and must act correctly to maintain harmony in the universe ● usual, because everything is normally in a continually changing, dynamic state.
Resulting change orientation: ● Focus on the future ● Assume satisfied people hold on ● Overcome resistance ● Think in terms of either/or ● Plan and manage change ● Think analytically ● Use reason and logic ● Measure progress	Resulting change orientation: ● Attend to the past-present-future ● Wise people let go and realign ● Maintain balance and harmony ● Think in terms of both/and ● Cultivate a system of self-renewal ● Think holistically ● Use artistry and composition ● Be values-centred

Conclusion

A number of researchers express positive views of the future of OD, for example:

● The future is bright, with a number of challenges (Jones & Brazzel, 2006).
● OD will develop interventions that drive effectiveness in a broader range of organisations (Cummings & Worley, 2015).
● Although new ideas are constantly being offered and improved, fundamental processes will remain and should not be lost sight of (Moerdyk & Van Aardt, 2003).
● OD is an expanding and vital technology.
● Managers need to understand that OD interventions have the potential to make the biggest difference in human development and bottom-line performance (Brown, 2015).

Reflection questions

1. Explain the differences between the three main generations and how they might influence the work of the OD practitioner.
2. Contrast classical and postmodern OD.
3. Explain the paths forward for OD.
4. Explain and contrast the differences between the traditional Western worldview of OD and the Chinese Taoist and Confucian worldview.
5. Summarise the three types of OD as seen by Marshak (2009).

Multiple-choice questions

1. Which South African organisation has maintained the longest OD effort to date?
   a. Sasol
   b. Old Mutual
   c. SANDF
   d. Armscor
   e. Liberty Life

2. From an OD perspective, which of the following academic institutions is presently playing a particularly prominent role in OD?
   a. Unisa
   b. North-West University
   c. University of Johannesburg
   d. Wits University
   e. University of Pretoria

3. Using as a criterion a person's membership in an OD 'professional' organisation, approximately how many people in South Africa would categorise themselves as OD practitioners?
   a. 500
   b. 1 000
   c. 1 500
   d. 2 500
   e. 4 500

4. Which of the following periodicals is the least relevant to OD?
   a. *Organisational Dynamics*
   b. *Harvard Business Review*
   c. *Journal of Applied Behavioural Science*

    d. *Psychology Today*
    e. *South African Journal of Human Resource Management*

5. The concept which best describes the OD consultant's 'approach' or model:
    a. Systems analysis
    b. Laboratory method of learning
    c. Social intervention
    d. Socio-technical
    e. Action research

Case study

Change management at General Motors (GM)

General Motors was established in 1908. At that time, the company was the sole car maker/dealer in the region (ie Michigan). It was a Buick holding company till 1920, when it became the world's largest motor manufacturing company. The company achieved tremendous success in the time of Alfred Salon due to his leadership, and was producing new styles and designs of cars every year. The brands of the company were Chevrolet, Pontiac, Buick and Cadillac, and this ensured that there were no other competitors. However, with the emergence of the Japanese automakers, the company felt threatened, especially by Toyota Japan, which to a great extent affected the profitability of GM, especially in the North American market. In 2001 the sales graph of GM was in decline, because Toyota had captured the market. GM received a loan from the US and Canadian governments to support the company during that crisis period. During 2009, the company filed bankruptcy and had to close several brands and sell out to a China-based company. Now the company has regained its position in the market by restructuring and making changes, and is continuing business in its core brands in the USA, such as Chevrolet, GMC, Buick and Cadillac.

Forces for change

The main forces which affected GM included the following:

- **External forces**: GM was greatly affected by the Japanese-based company, Toyota, which was the emerging competitor at the time, although North America was still GM's biggest marketplace. However, competitors did affect the total profitability of GM. The second external force which the company faced was the financial crisis, which caused a collapse in the cash flow of the company.
- **Internal forces**: Another force for change in GM was the high wage cost of employees, as the company was paying $74 per hour as compared to Toyota at $44 per hour. This was because GM was in an agreement with a trade union. GM also had to run the plant at a minimum of 80 % capacity. These factors played an important role in the bankruptcy of the company.

Questions

1. What types of changes and steps would you propose to GM?
2. What challenges/problems do you think GM will encounter?
3. What were the results of the implemented changes?

Recommendations

It has been shown how GM has made changes for the smooth running of the company, increasing sales volumes and maintaining market share around the world; however, these changes are not enough. The company needs to adopt several other changes to cope with the situation, to maintain the position of the business and to compete in the international market. The following sections outline some suggested recommendations for GM to reach its turnaround goals and increase its sales and market share.

Production of fuel-efficient automobiles

One criticism of the GM brand was that its cars were not fuel-efficient. The company was at the peak of sales in 1990 when oil was at a low price, but when the price rose in the international market, the company brand's reputation suffered. The company needs to produce fuel-efficient automobiles and must also focus on electric cars and hybrids so it can maintain increasing sales as well as customer loyalty and market share.

Improvement in public perception

GM must improve its product quality and customer service. Because public perception is all-important, if the public believes that it is getting value for money, the company's reputation will greatly improve.

Even after facing intense competition and bankruptcy, after making changes GM is still the world's largest car manufacturing company. The recent changes have also improved working conditions for employees, but the company must continually be aware of any weaknesses and focus on public perception to increase its sales and market share.

Source: Adapted from Journal of Business Administration and Management Sciences Research 3(1): 001-005

References

Anderson, L. 2015. *Organizational development; the process of leading change.* 3rd ed. Los Angeles, CA: SAGE.

Brown, D. 2015. *Experimental approach to organizational development.* Harlow: Pearson Education.

Bushe, G & Marshak, RJ. 2008. 'The postmodern turn in OD'. *OD Practitioner* 40(4): 9–11.

Cummings, TC & Worley, CG. 2015. *Organizational development and change.* 10th ed. Stamford, CT: Cengage Learning.

Da Veiga, A & Martins, N. 2015. 'Factorial invariance of an information security culture assessment (ISCA) instrument for multinational organisations with operations across data protection jurisdictions'. *Journal of Governance and Regulation* 4(4): 47–58.

Jones, BB & Brazzel, M. 2006. *The NTL handbook of organizational development and change.* San Francisco, CA: Pfeiffer.

Journal of Business Administration and Management Sciences Research Vol. 3(1): 1–5, January, 2014. Available online at http://www.apexjournal.org.

Lancaster, LC & Stillman, D. 2002. *When generations collide. Who they are. Why they clash. How to solve the generational puzzle at work.* HarperCollins e-books.

Ledimo, O. 2012. A longitudinal study of changes in employee satisfaction during organisational transformation: developing a diagnostic model. Unpublished thesis, University of South Africa, Pretoria.

Ledimo, O & Martins, N. 2014. 'A longitudinal study of employee satisfaction during the process of transformation in a water utility organization'. *Problems and Perspectives in Management* (Special Issue: South Africa) 12(4): 172–180.

Lester, SW, Standifer, RL, Schultz, NJ & Windsor, JM. 2012. 'Actual versus perceived generational differences at work: an empirical examination'. *Journal of Leadership and Organizational Studies* 19(3): 341–354.

Lundby, K, Lee, W & Macey, W. 2012. 'Leadership essentials to attract, engage and retain global human talent', in *Advances in global leadership* 7, edited by W Mobley, Y Want & M Li. London: Emerald Group: 251–270.

Marshak, RJ. 2009. *Organizational change: view from the top.* Bethel, ME: The Lewin Center.

Martins, N. 2014. 'Testing for measurement invariance for employee engagement across sectors in South Africa'. *Journal of Contemporary Management* 12: 757–774.

Martins, EC & Martins, N. 2012. 'A model development strategy to determine factors that influence knowledge retention in organisations'. Proceedings of the 11th European Conference on Research Methods in Business and Management. University of Bolton, UK (28–29 June).

Martins, N & Martins, EC. 2014. 'Perceptions of age generations regarding employee satisfaction in a South African organisation'. *Mediterranean Journal of Social Sciences.* Special Issue—Generation Y: 5(21): 129–140.

Moerdyk, A & Van Aardt, C. 2003. *Organisational development: new methods and models for Southern Africa.* Glosderry. Cape Town: New Africa Books.

Moss, M & Martins, N. 2014. 'Generational sub-cultures: Generation Y a sub-culture?' *Mediterranean Journal of Social Sciences,* Special Issue—Generation Y: 5(21): 147–160.

Nel, P & Boshoff, A. 2014. 'Factorial invariance of the Adult State Hope Scale'. *SA Journal of Industrial Psychology/SA Tydskrif vir Bedryfsielkunde* 40(1), Art #1177, 8 pages. https://doi.org/10.4102/sajip.v40i1.1177.

Olivier, B. 2015. The development of an assessment framework for determining organisational effectiveness of local government in South Africa. Unpublished thesis, University of South Africa, Pretoria.

Reynolds, L, Bush, EC & Geist, R. 2008. 'The Gen Y imperative'. *Communication World* 25(2): 19–22.

Van der Linde-de Klerk, M, Martins, N & De Beer, M. 2014. 'The development of a change agent identification framework for South African change agents'. *South African Journal of Labour Relations* 38(1): 93–115.

Von der Ohe, H. 2015. An explorative study on organisational trust relationships. Unpublished thesis, University of South Africa, Pretoria.

WGA Consulting, LLC. April 2014. Organizational development trends. http://www.wgaconsulting.com/new/2014/04/08/organizational-development-trends-2014/ (Accessed 30 May 2016).

Worley, CG & Feyerherm, AE. 2003. 'Reflections on the future of organization development'. *The Journal of Applied Behavioral Science* 39(1): 97–115.

Index

Note: Numbers in *italics* refer to pages with tables or figures.